NO
FOREIGN
GAME

In memory of Joe Quinn (1936–2021)
and Eric Cunningham (1934–2023) –
lovers of all games

James Quinn is a historian who has written widely on eighteenth- and nineteenth-century Ireland. He was formerly managing editor of the Royal Irish Academy's *Dictionary of Irish Biography*, for which he wrote over 250 entries, mostly on politics, sport and popular culture.

NO FOREIGN GAME

Association Football and the Making of Irish Identities

JAMES QUINN

MERRION
PRESS

First published in 2023 by
Merrion Press
10 George's Street
Newbridge
Co. Kildare
Ireland
www.merrionpress.ie

978 1 78537 473 9 (Paper)
978 1 78537 474 6 (Ebook)

A CIP catalogue record for this book is
available from the British Library.

Typeset in Calluna 11/15 pt

Cover design by riverdesignbooks.com

Front cover image: Northern Ireland manager Danny Blanchflower (right)
greets Ireland's John Giles as Northern Ireland's Martin O'Neill walks off with
him. © PA images/Alamy Stock Photo
Back cover image: The Shamrock Rovers All-Ireland XI for a friendly v Brazil
at Lansdowne Road on 3 July 1973. © Connolly Collection/SPORTSFILE

Merrion Press is a member of Publishing Ireland.

CONTENTS

Introduction

Throughout history, people have formed distinct groups to provide them with a sense of purpose, belonging and security in an uncertain world. In Ireland and Britain in the later nineteenth century, this tendency was often expressed by founding sports teams. These were usually based around existing entities, such as places of work, worship, residence or education, and helped to affirm local loyalties and allegiances. Many were formed to play the newly codified sport of association football, the recurrent competitions of which soon took root and helped create a more regulated and connected society. Association football began to express not just local but also national allegiances in regular international matches played by the four countries of the United Kingdom. The nation state's demand for commitment and sacrifice from its individual members was applied with particular rigour to sportspeople. International football matches became contests not just between teams, but between peoples, as the 'imagined community' of the nation took visible shape in the form of 'a team of eleven named people'.[1]

The Irish national team was among the first to participate in international competition, in the early 1880s, but at a time of political and cultural ferment some questioned who and what this team actually represented. Since association football was initially most popular in Belfast, the city that most closely resembled the industrial centres of Britain, international matches were played there rather than in the capital city of Dublin. They were arranged by an ostensibly non-political but predominantly unionist Irish Football Association (IFA) based in Belfast; the team, most of whom came from Belfast and its environs, played in shirts of St Patrick's blue under the Union flag and sang 'God Save the Queen' as its national anthem. Many nationalists recoiled from such symbols, and for some time there was little support for the team outside the north-east, a tendency compounded by regular hammerings by England and Scotland that did little to inspire national pride.

Long-standing tensions between North and South combined with the political turmoil of the 1919–21 period to drive the two sides further apart and prompt the founding of the Dublin-based Football Association of Ireland (FAI) in 1921. For the next century, the existence of two separate football associations on the island was a starkly visible sign of partition and helped create different soccer communities on both sides of the border. The tensions between them often mirrored the fraught political relations between the two parts of the island and the contrasting relations between the two Irish jurisdictions and the UK. The game found a comfortable place in a Northern Ireland state that was resolutely British in its orientation, with the IFA's focus centring on a 'Home' championship that featured the four national UK teams and allowed supporters to express a national allegiance that complemented a wider British identity.

The situation of the Dublin-based FAI was rather different. Frozen out of the British Championship and accorded only a grudging form of semi-recognition by the UK associations, the FAI looked to the European continent for international competition. Although matches were often hard to arrange, the Irish Free State was keen to join the European football community and, unlike the UK associations, took part in the FIFA World Cup from 1934 onwards. This helped secure greater official recognition for a sport regarded by some in government as incompatible with the Gaelic ethos of an independent Ireland. Some of the official distaste or indifference towards soccer eased when the FAI demonstrated that its national team could fly the flag for the new state and alert the rest of Europe to the fact that it was a genuinely independent polity, separate from the UK. The exploits of the national football team were also important to its supporters, drawn mostly from the urban working class, providing them with a means of expressing national identity on their own terms. Matches were often framed in a historical context as part of the national struggle for recognition and respect, with notable victories or defeats having more than just sporting significance.

The work that follows examines not just abstract themes of identity, but also particular personalities and teams, matches and tournaments: when identities are being forged, it matters who won and who lost, and how they won and lost. This is particularly so in the case of major international tournaments, which provide a world stage on which the fortunes of a football team can make or break national reputation. Although Northern Ireland was a latecomer to global competition, the team reached the quarter-final of the 1958 FIFA World Cup in Sweden and gained considerable international recognition in doing so. This was repeated with qualification for the 1982 and 1986 World Cups, which showed Northern Ireland in a positive light after years of bloody civil strife. The Republic of Ireland took rather longer, with several dispiriting near-misses, before its team qualified for the European Championships of 1988. Its exploits in West Germany marked the beginning of the team's most successful period, during which it secured qualification for the next two World Cups and achieved some memorable victories against powerful footballing nations. The team itself, managed by an Englishman and with half of its players born in Britain, stretched and redefined concepts of Irishness, drawing on a diaspora that had in the past often been ignored. Its success generated unprecedented nationwide support and gave rise to some of the most joyously exuberant celebrations that the state had seen since independence.

As one of the first countries to play the game, Ireland's influence on soccer was wide-ranging, with Irishmen contributing to the development of top European clubs such as Ajax Amsterdam, Real Madrid and Barcelona FC. This added to the country's sporting reputation, but the Irish influence was most strongly felt nearer home, in Scotland, where emigrants founded important clubs such as Hibernian FC in Edinburgh and Celtic FC in Glasgow. Celtic in particular provided a means for the Irish in Scotland to relate to wider society while also cultivating an identity that set themselves apart from it. The club's conspicuous Irish symbolism made it a focus for the loyalties, not just of Irish Catholics in Scotland, but for many throughout Ireland and the wider Irish and Scottish diasporas, forming an important and enduring link with their heritage. There has also been considerable Irish identification with leading English football clubs, such as Manchester United, Liverpool and Arsenal, home to some of Ireland's most talented footballers, who have often challenged national stereotypes and had an important and underrated influence on improving Anglo-Irish relations.

The popularity of British clubs in Ireland today stands as one of the most visible manifestations of a shared culture between these islands. Since the 1960s they have generally attracted far larger followings in Ireland than clubs in both domestic leagues, which have often struggled. Domestic clubs have, though, shown considerable resilience and retain strong cores of dedicated supporters for whom they represent important expressions of local, civic or regional identity, often beyond the game's original heartlands in Belfast and Dublin. However, for many years there were parts of Ireland in which very little soccer was played. For much of the twentieth century the Gaelic Athletic Association (GAA), the most popular sports organisation in the country, banned its members from playing and even watching soccer, which was routinely condemned as an alien and anti-national activity. In Ireland's long-running culture wars, sport was disputed ground to a far greater extent than in most other countries – even the term 'football' itself was a contested one. Soccer followers often found themselves on the defensive, but most regarded the game's foreign origins as irrelevant and found no contradiction between their sporting and national loyalties. The game managed to find an important niche in Irish life, supported by nationalists as diverse as Michael Davitt, Joe Devlin, James Connolly, Brendan Behan, John Hume and Martin McGuinness, who valued it as an expression of communal identity as well as a sport.

Since books about sport are often at their most interesting when they are about more than just sport, I have tried to weave the story of Irish soccer into a broader historical narrative, drawing on a wide range of primary sources, academic research and assorted histories, memoirs and journalism to explore the way in which the game has helped shape various forms of identity. Some of the main themes explored include soccer's relationship to class, religion, region and nation; its interaction with other sports, particularly rugby and Gaelic football; and its relationship to gender, outlining the hard struggle of the women's game for recognition and acceptance. Soccer could bring people from different backgrounds together in a spirit of amity and sportsmanship, but could also stir up and reinforce bitter rivalries, particularly as leading clubs developed distinct identities affirmed by their own colours, emblems and anthems. When political, ethnic or religious differences were thrown into the mix, these rivalries tended to become even more intense and could at times escalate into bigotry and violence.

For many who play and support it, football is no small matter. It can inspire an almost religious devotion, with communal singing, seasonal rituals and a strong sense of fellowship among followers. When the game clashed directly with entrenched religious beliefs in both Irish jurisdictions in the 1950s, in the South over the visit to Dublin of communist Yugoslavia and in the North over the decision to play World Cup matches on Sunday, it was football that prevailed. Over time it has woven itself into the fabric of everyday life at every level – local, civic and national – and in recent decades its potential to encourage greater diversity has become even more apparent, with the game being used to help the integration of immigrants and allow women to participate more fully in sporting life.

Today soccer stands as a vibrant element of popular culture that arouses passion like few other international sports, allowing allegiances to be expressed with an intensity often greater than that seen at political gatherings. It is one of the few areas in life in which 'fanaticism' is generally encouraged, and the sport's capacity to provide an outlet for local and national pride is surely one of the main reasons behind its worldwide popularity. Football matches have provided many people with some of their most cherished memories, adding compelling drama and a strong sense of solidarity to everyday lives. In an increasingly atomised society, the powerful communal effect of supporting a football team helps people feel that they are part of something bigger than themselves. Those who founded association football were anxious to keep it apart from the grubby realities of politics and the wider world, but this was always wishful thinking: the more popular the game became, the more it was destined to reflect and reinforce an array of social, cultural and political identities.

1

Scuffles, Schools and Scots: The Genesis of Irish Association Football

Most sports, like nations, have their founding myths. These tend to ignore conflicting and ambiguous evidence in favour of a simple narrative with clearly identifiable milestones and personalities. So it is with Irish association football. The first game played in Ireland under association rules is usually said to have taken place on 24 October 1878, when two teams from Glasgow – Queen's Park and Caledonian FC – played an exhibition match at the Ulster Cricket Grounds on the Ormeau Road in Belfast. The match was said to have come about largely through the efforts of John Mecredy 'J.M.' McAlery (c. 1850–1925), manager of the Irish Tweed House in Belfast, who earlier in the year had witnessed this new form of football while on a visit to Scotland. (To add a little colour, it is sometimes claimed he was on honeymoon at the time, but he did not marry until the following year.) Not having seen the game before, McAlery was impressed and, on his return to Belfast, with the support of the Ulster and Windsor rugby clubs, he invited the two Glasgow teams to Belfast to introduce the new code to the city's sporting public.[1]

On closer inspection the truth is rather more tangled and complex, and it is difficult to pin down the sport's arrival in Ireland to a precise time and place.[2] Games of association football were actually taking place from the mid-1870s onwards, with one recorded on 11 December 1875 among members of the Ulster Cricket Club on its grounds in Belfast.[3] The players appear to have been experimenting with various rules prior to founding a football club and eventually plumped for rugby, setting up the Ulster Football Club in 1877. The cricketers of Alexander Cricket Club, Limavady, also tried out the new code in the early winter of 1876, as did the rugby players of Windsor FC, at Ulsterville, Belfast, in March 1877.[4]

Early variants of association football were also played outside Belfast, often involving British Army units based in Ireland: *The Westmeath Guardian* advertised a match in Mullingar on 20 November 1878 between a local team and one from the 15th Regiment.[5] Two teams from Sligo Foot Ball Club (probably a rugby club) played under association rules in Sligo on 17 March 1879 and further matches followed. Schools too were important nurseries for the game, introduced by the many teachers and students who regularly crossed the Irish Sea. On 28 November 1877 a match took place in Mallow, County Cork, between teams from the local school, Penn's, and Lismore College, County Waterford. It was played with teams of fifteen, but flexible rules were the norm at the time.[6] In the late 1870s the students of Clongowes Wood College in County Kildare played a form of association football that had no off-side rule, which apparently gave the game 'a very everyman-for-himself character'.[7] The association code also developed a nascent popularity in County Offaly, where St Stanislaus College and Tullamore played an association-style eleven-a-side game with two halves of 45 minutes on the college sportsground in March 1881, and did so again on 10 November 1881. On 31 March 1881, Tullamore also hosted a team from Banagher.[8] The likelihood is that many other matches took place that were not reported.

The match between Queen's Park and Caledonian on 24 October 1878 may not have been the first to be played in Ireland under association rules, but it was nonetheless an important milestone. It was watched by several hundred spectators, who paid an admission fee of sixpence, and appears to have had a sense of occasion about it.[9] The quality of the football was probably more advanced than anything those spectators had previously seen. The two visiting teams were among the game's finest practitioners and included several Scottish international players: Queen's Park had won three Scottish FA Cups in a row (1874–6) and would do so again (1880–2). Some spectators were clearly impressed by the Glasgow teams, with one predicting that the new game would 'soon commend itself to both players and onlookers'.[10]

While McAlery was not quite the sole father of Irish association football as he would later claim, he can probably be regarded as a midwife, who played an important role as a pioneering organiser, player and administrator.[11] Less than a year after the Queen's Park against Caledonian match, he and other enthusiasts founded Cliftonville Football Club on 20 September 1879 in north Belfast to allow members of Cliftonville Cricket Club to play another sport during the winter months. Initially opponents came mostly from Scotland, with the club hosting Caledonian on 17 October and a team from Ayr on 6 November 1879, but Cliftonville also encouraged the formation of other clubs in Belfast and helped found the IFA in the Queen's Hotel in Belfast on 18 November 1880. (Similar associations had already been founded in England (1863), Scotland (1873) and Wales (1877).) McAlery was appointed secretary of the new association, and seven clubs affiliated: Avoniel, Cliftonville, Distillery, Knock and Oldpark (from Belfast); Alexander (from Limavady) and Moyola Park (from Castledawson, County Derry). Other Belfast clubs such as Queen's Island, Ulster FC and Wellington Park joined soon afterwards.

At first, public interest in the association game, and all other football codes, was confined to small groups of enthusiasts. Even rugby, which had been played in Ireland since the 1850s, had a modest following. When the Irish rugby team beat Scotland in an early international fixture in February 1881, a supporter accepted that while he was proud of the team's victory, he was aware that 'there may be many who consider football a very small thing'.[12] At the time the sporting press was dominated by equestrian sports. Hunting and horse-racing had been popular in Ireland for centuries, well suited to a predominantly rural country with a strong military presence in which land ownership was concentrated in relatively few hands. By the eighteenth century, racing had taken on a more formal character, with irregular races over open fields giving way to more organised events. Permanent racecourses were laid out and an Irish Turf Club was founded in 1784 to regulate the sport.[13] While the upper realm of horse-racing was dominated by the gentry and aristocracy, interest was broad-based, and strong in urban as well as rural areas.

There was also significant interest in sports such as hare coursing, angling, athletics, boxing, billiards, rowing, sailing, shooting, lawn tennis and cricket. By the 1870s cricket was the most popular team sport in Ireland, attracting significant levels of elite patronage and popular participation. Played in various forms in England since the 1590s at least, it had become increasingly regularised during the eighteenth century and established itself as England's national sport. It came rather later to Ireland, where the earliest recorded game was played in 1792 between 'Garrison' and 'All-Ireland' teams in the Phoenix Park in Dublin. From the 1830s more and more clubs were formed, often by army officers and former pupils of English schools. In the years that followed, the sport's social base broadened to include the working classes in both urban and rural areas, and it continued to grow in popularity until the 1880s, when newly codified team sports, such as hurling and various forms of football, began to offer competition.[14]

These new codes replaced earlier forms of folk football that had been played throughout Britain and Ireland since the Middle Ages. Shaped by local traditions, they varied from place to place, but in most cases the players were many and the rules were few. Matches were often contested between different villages or opposing ends of a parish, and usually involved kicking or carrying a ball over a designated line or boundary, or between two markers such as trees, stones or posts to score a 'goal'. There was a carnivalesque element to these games, regularly held on religious holidays such as Christmas, Easter and Shrove Tuesday. The large numbers of participants were often watched by even larger crowds, who engaged in hard drinking and riotous behaviour and periodically joined in the football as the mood took them. At times the rowdiness could get out of hand and serious violence was done to life and limb, one sixteenth-century observer noting that 'sometimes their necks are broken, sometimes their backs, sometimes their legs, sometimes their armes, sometimes their noses gush out with blood'.[15]

The first reference to football in Ireland was in 1308, when John McCorcan, a spectator at a game in Newcastle, County Dublin, was charged with stabbing a player named William Bernard.[16] Thereafter mentions of the game occur occasionally in legal records, particularly when matches led to violence or public disorder. Secular and religious authorities looked on such games with displeasure, and they were frequently banned by official decree, when, as in 1518, the archbishop of Dublin forbade clergymen in his diocese from playing.[17] Football was most common among descendants of Anglo-Norman communities, particularly in the Pale and urban outposts of English settlements, such as Cork and Galway.[18] By the late seventeenth century the game had expanded into north Leinster and was occasionally mentioned in Irish-language literary sources. Séamas Dall Mac Cuarta's 'Iomáin na Bóinne' (c. 1715) describes a twelve-a-side game in County Meath between teams of English settlers and native Irish. Another poem by Matt Concannon the Elder recounts a rugby-like match interspersed with wrestling bouts played in Fingal around 1720 between six-a-side teams from Lusk and Swords, in which the ball could be carried or kicked along the ground. Twenty years later, in the poem 'Léana an Bhábúin' (1740), Redmond Murphy an tSléibhe described a twelve-a-side game in Omeath, County Louth, which lasted from midday to evening. Such evidence suggests that semi-regulated forms of football co-existed with more mob-like and anarchic versions.[19]

Matches were also reported in eighteenth-century Dublin, usually in green spaces on the fringes of the city at Oxmantown, Milltown, Drumcondra, St Stephen's Green and Merrion Fields. Most accounts report violent incidents, such as an affray near Finglas bridge in 1759 in which one player had his skull fractured and another his nose partly cut off, or the 'bloodshed and battery' that ensued during a contest near Three Rock mountain between 'mountaineers' and their Rathfarnham neighbours. Games were often dispersed by the lord mayor or city sheriff assisted by military detachments, and players were occasionally consigned to Newgate jail or pressed into the Royal Navy.[20] During the troubled years of the 1790s, football matches were sometimes used by disaffected groups as a cover for assembly and drilling, and elicited a sharp response from the military. This carried through into the early nineteenth century as the authorities clamped down on all forms of civil disobedience, and the game's popularity declined. The establishment's aversion to football was reinforced by growing evangelical disapproval of rowdy public gatherings, particularly when they occurred on the Sabbath, and by utilitarian economic doctrines that regarded most collective popular recreation as an excuse for idleness or mayhem.[21]

There were, however, places where rowdy recreation was indulged and even encouraged. During the nineteenth century, various forms of football were played in most English public schools to help develop qualities such as discipline, loyalty, teamwork, courage, initiative and 'fair play'. This was considered an essential part of the educational process and those who avoided it were often subject to sanctions. (At Eton, boys who did not play football were liable to be fined half a crown and receive a kicking from their schoolfellows.)[22] Rules were often determined according to where the game was played: schools with paved surfaces or stone cloisters such as Winchester and Charterhouse tended to adopt a 'dribbling' game in which players could be dispossessed without being upended, while those with large grassy playing pitches such as Rugby favoured a 'collaring' game in which players carried the ball in hand and could be tackled to the ground. Variations in rules did however militate against games between different schools. When these occurred there were attempts to agree common rules, but misunderstandings could always arise and lead to arguments or fights at odds with the high moral tone of public school sport.

The mid-Victorian era's passion for order and regulation was applied with particular rigour to sport. Boxing adopted the Marquess of Queensbury rules in 1863, and various forms of track and field athletics were regularised in the 1860s and 1870s and overseen by the Amateur Athletics Association (AAA). Established sports such as horse-racing and cricket also tightened up their rules and governance and assumed their modern forms. With football, attempts to agree common rules between different clubs and schools usually foundered on the insistence that 'our' particular code was the best, and others should simply adopt it. This prompted representatives from ten London football clubs to come together on 26 October 1863 at the Freemason's Tavern in Lincoln's Inn, London, to form a 'Football Association' to produce an agreed set of rules. Most of the discussion focused on whether or not to allow carrying the ball in the hands and 'hacking' (kicking an opponent's shins): the delegate from Blackheath FC argued that 'hacking was the true football game; if it was done away with all the courage and pluck of the game would disappear' and it would be taken up by 'a lot of Frenchmen who would beat you with a week's practice'. Others thought that players should concentrate on kicking the ball rather than their opponents and insisted that if hacking were allowed football 'will be entirely relinquished to schoolboys'. A month later, on 24 November 1863, a list of thirteen 'Football Association Laws' was agreed by the new Football Association, which banned hacking and carrying the ball in hand, although rugby-like rules, such as catching the ball and making a mark, were allowed. Since it was codified by an association rather than any single club or school, the new game became known as 'association football'.[23] At first though the new rules were often loosely interpreted, with some clubs continuing to carry the ball in hand. Confusion was eased somewhat when these formed their own Rugby Football Union in 1871, creating a permanent split between association football (often abbreviated in undergraduate slang to 'soccer' football or just 'soccer') and rugby football or 'rugger'.[24]

The importance accorded to the establishment of the Football Association (FA) in 1863 has lately been challenged by historians, who argue that it fails to acknowledge the significant contribution of working men to the sport's development.[25] Before the association's founding, various forms of football were being played as winter recreation by cricket clubs and teams organised around workplaces, military units and pubs; there is, for example, a record of Belfast millworkers playing in 1860.[26] Since the 1830s organised football had been played in the south Yorkshire steel-manufacturing town of Sheffield and a Sheffield Football Club, which played under its own 'dribbling' rules, was founded in 1857. Initially, Sheffield FC and other clubs in industrial parts of England and Scotland kept their distance from the London-based Football Association, but desire for a unified game and the attraction of competing in the FA's prestigious Challenge Cup (founded in 1871) proved irresistible. To take part, clubs had to agree to play by

FA rules, which were merged with the Sheffield rules in 1877 to produce the modern form of association football.[27] The 1877 rules helped create a simple and flexible sport that could be played by organised teams or at a more improvised level. Requiring nothing more than a ball (even a makeshift one of old paper or rags), it could be played almost anywhere, even in narrow city streets and alleys, by participants of varying ages and levels of strength and fitness. Injuries were less likely than in rugby and it required less time and equipment than cricket, all of which were important considerations for working men, who began to take up the new game in growing numbers.[28]

Sheffield's influence helped association football expand into the manufacturing towns of Lancashire, the English midlands and the industrial central belt of Scotland. The Scots took to the game with particular enthusiasm and left their mark on it. In its early days association football often resembled rugby as a rampaging pack of forwards lined up behind the ball and charged into opposing defenders. During the 1870s the Queen's Park club of Glasgow developed a more structured game, spreading out across the pitch and passing the ball to teammates in space. While some practitioners considered this to be an overly methodical and 'scientific' way of playing the game, it was undoubtedly effective and was soon widely adopted. The new style required changes in team formation, from packs of seven or eight forwards and two or three backs to a more ordered line-up of two full-backs, two half-backs and six forwards spaced across the front line. By the mid-1880s this had further evolved into the classic formation of two full-backs, three half-backs and five forwards, with speedy wingers and skilful inside-forwards complementing the efforts of a single centre-forward.[29]

These developments made soccer not just a better game to play, but also to watch, at a time when its potential pool of support was growing. From the 1870s the working class, especially the skilled and semi-skilled, had more disposable income and leisure time. An 1878 Factory Act stipulated that the working week should end at 2 p.m. on Saturday, and these free afternoons proved the ideal time for playing and watching football, which attracted ever larger crowds of followers, the game's excitement and unscripted drama providing welcome relief from the regimentation and monotony of factory or workshop. Although teams were limited to eleven players, spectators often became passionately involved and their presence on the sideline (and occasionally on the pitch) recalled some of the boisterous mass participation of earlier forms of folk football. Some clubs took the step of restricting casual access to their games by enclosing the playing area and charging an admission fee. This generated significant income for the more popular clubs and allowed them to offer furtive financial inducements to attract and retain the best players.

From the beginning, the payment of players (a practice largely confined to working-class clubs in the north of England) was strongly opposed by the London-based FA, who maintained that professionalism would corrupt the sport and undermine its ethos of 'fair play'. Working men though thought it perfectly fair that they should be compensated for loss of earnings, and as the game became more popular many were rewarded with 'expenses' and 'testimonials'. To try to bring some openness and order to an increasingly chaotic situation, the FA voted in 1885 to allow clubs to pay players in certain circumstances. Amateurs protested, but the FA was anxious to prevent the secession of leading clubs. (The refusal of the Rugby Football Union to countenance professionalism caused a permanent split between the union and league variants of rugby in 1895.) This paved the way for the foundation of the Football League in 1888, which consisted of twelve of the leading clubs from the north and midlands of England. Football clubs had already become an important focus for local loyalties and this was reinforced by the introduction of professionalism and regular league matches. With players bound by contracts, they were less likely to move on, and clubs became more stable entities. Followers identified with favourite players and settled teams, and began to develop that passionate devotion to their club that was so incomprehensible to outsiders. Although professionals represented only a small number of those who played the game, it was they who generated most public interest and whose deeds lived longest in popular memory.[30]

***

These developments took longer to happen in Ireland, where association football lagged behind rugby. A club playing under rugby-style rules had been founded in Trinity College Dublin in 1854, making it one of the world's earliest rugby clubs; others were founded by members of the North of Ireland Cricket Club in Belfast in 1868, and by the students of Queen's University Belfast in autumn 1869. The 1870s saw others formed in Carlow, Ballinasloe, Dungannon and Queen's College Cork, and the North of Ireland and Trinity clubs began to compete against Scottish and English opposition. Rugby-style games were also played in private schools such as Belvedere College, Dublin; Clongowes Wood in County Kildare; Tullabeg College in Tullamore; and Portora Royal School, County Fermanagh.[31]

An Irish Football Union (IFU) that adopted the rules of the English Rugby Football Union was founded in Dublin on 14 December 1874. Eight clubs affiliated: five from Dublin, and one each from Portora, Dungannon and Monaghan. In January 1875 a Northern Football Union of Ireland was founded in Belfast to cater for the game in the north-east and in 1879 it joined with the IFU to form the Irish Rugby Football Union (IRFU), which had affiliated clubs in Belfast, Dublin, Limerick and Cork.[32] There was, though, considerable crossover among the various codes with rugby players founding several association clubs. Opinion varied between those who saw the new code as a complement or a rival to rugby. One reporter who witnessed the exhibition game between Queen's Park and Caledonians in Belfast in October 1878 was not impressed by the novel sight of players 'butting the ball like a pack of young goats', and predicted that the Irish were unlikely to take to it; he advised prospective Irish footballers to stick to rugby, which he claimed required 'more wind, strength, pluck and endurance' than the new code.[33] The football correspondent of the Dublin newspaper *Sport* also considered the association game to be distinctly inferior, lamenting that it deprived rugby of some fine sportsmen, and hoped that in future football would be played 'in its best and manliest form under the good old rugby rules'. He dismissed soccer as 'too calculating and "canny" for the impulsive Irish temperament, and ... suitable to no-one but Scotchmen'.[34]

The Scottish influence on the Irish association game was indisputable, particularly in Belfast. On its foundation in November 1880 the IFA had adopted the rule book of the Scottish FA, which also donated £5 for the purchase of the Irish Cup in 1881. The close economic links between Belfast and the west of Scotland were particularly important. In 1879 Scottish employees of Dunville's distillery in Belfast founded Distillery FC, the most successful Irish club of the period, which won the Irish Cup four times during the 1880s. The Avoniel club that affiliated to the IFA in 1880 was also formed by Scottish workers who were building another distillery in the city. Queen's Island FC, which drew its players from the Belfast shipyards, won the Irish Cup in 1882 with an entirely Scottish team.[35]

The industrial city of Belfast and the surrounding Lagan valley provided the most fertile ground for the association code to take root. By the 1880s the pioneering clubs of Cliftonville and Distillery had been joined by up-and-coming challengers such as Glentoran and Linfield. Glentoran, founded in 1882, was based in East Belfast in the shadow of the shipyards, while Linfield FC was founded in Sandy Row in south Belfast in 1886 by workers from the Linfield Mill of the Ulster Spinning Company. By 1890 there were 124 active clubs affiliated to the IFA, clustered mostly in County Antrim and north Armagh. An Irish league was founded in 1890 with eight clubs: Cliftonville, Distillery, Glentoran and Linfield, along with the short-lived Clarence, Milford, Oldpark and Ulster clubs, all from the Belfast area. The Irish League was formed a week before its Scottish counterpart, making it the second oldest national league in the world after the English Football League.[36]

The creation of structured competitions with matches to be played by specified dates reflected the tighter controls of a commercialised industrial society in which time was money and deadlines were strictly enforced. For most players the founding of the Irish League changed the game from a hobby to a time-consuming activity that regularly interfered with their ability to earn a living. Motions to introduce professionalism were discussed at IFA conferences in 1890, 1891 and 1892, but were voted down. Finally, in May 1894, fearing that Belfast would lose its best players to English and Scottish professional clubs, the IFA voted to legalise the paying of players. Linfield, Glentoran, Distillery and the recently founded Belfast Celtic all turned professional, with only Cliftonville retaining its amateur status.[37]

Linfield dominated in the 1890s, winning five Irish League championships and six Irish Cups as well as many lesser trophies. After playing at several different venues, the club's growing popularity prompted a move to a new ground near Lower Windsor Avenue in 1905 and 'Windsor Park' in south Belfast became its permanent home. Although both Linfield and Glentoran were mainly supported by Protestants, they developed a keen rivalry based on geographical and occupational differences. Both became rivals of Belfast Celtic, founded in 1891 by the amalgamation of junior Falls Road clubs such as Milltown, Millvale and Clondara.[38] Supported largely by the Catholics of west Belfast (who formed roughly a quarter of the city's population), the new club was modelled on the Celtic Football Club of Glasgow, founded in 1887 to raise money for charitable causes and provide a focus for Glasgow's Irish Catholic community. Belfast Celtic played in the Irish League from 1896, giving a much-needed boost to a competition that had shrunk to only four teams two years earlier, and managed to win its first Irish League title in 1900. From the beginning its identity was closely intertwined with the nationalist politics of west Belfast. Joe Devlin, the nationalist MP for west Belfast, was a prominent shareholder, and two of his most important party lieutenants held senior positions at Celtic Park: Daniel McCann was the club's managing director and Hugh McAlinden its chairman, while a club director and leading nationalist solicitor, Joseph Donnelly, was elected a councillor for the Falls Division on Belfast Corporation in 1909 with the support of Devlin's machine.[39]

Political and sectarian differences added a sharp edge to club rivalries. The mid-1890s saw occasional violent incidents at matches and in 1899 a Belfast Celtic and Glentoran fixture sparked a 'disgraceful riot' at Celtic Park that was said to have introduced 'the curse of party bigotry' into football.[40] Such incidents were, however, rare enough before the political crisis of 1912–14 and Belfast Celtic's relationship with Linfield and Glentoran was not one of unwavering enmity. It was rather an uneasy blend of confrontation and co-existence, with occasional outbreaks of cordiality: in 1908 and March 1910 Celtic and Linfield played benefit matches for retired and injured players, with Joe Devlin performing the ceremonial kick-off.[41]

During the 1880s association football began to make progress in Dublin. The city's earliest clubs, Dublin FC and Dublin University, were founded in 1883 and played their first match on 7 November 1883, won 4–0 by Dublin FC. Both took part in the Irish Cup for the first time in 1884 but were quickly eliminated by more experienced Belfast teams.[42] Dublin FC did however manage to progress to the semi-final in 1890 before losing 4–2 to Cliftonville. By the 1890s the game had gained some popularity in colleges and secondary schools such as St Vincent's College, Castleknock, and had secured a foothold in some of the capital's rugby-playing schools, such as St Helen's, Montpelier, Chapelizod and Terenure Schools. In September 1890, students from the Catholic Medical School in Dublin and the Royal Hibernian Military School in the Phoenix Park came together with members of the Richfield Club, founded in 1887 by students of Bell's Academy in North Great Georges Street (a crammer for civil service exams), to found Bohemian FC, which became a focal point for Dublin association enthusiasts. There was though no escaping the influence of Belfast: the three Sheehan brothers, past pupils of the Belfast Mercantile Academy, were present at the founding meeting, and the club's first chairman, Alexander Blayney, a man memorably described as having 'a huge scrotum and a huge memory', had previously played in Belfast with St Malachy's and Cliftonville.[43]

Two years later, with the assistance of the IFA, a Leinster Football Association was founded on 27 October 1892 in the Wicklow Hotel in Dublin. Five clubs affiliated: Bohemian FC, Dublin University, Leinster Nomads and the school teams of Montpelier and St Helen's. A Leinster Senior League followed in 1894, a Leinster Junior Alliance in 1895 and a Leinster Minor Cup in 1898. The new provincial association gave a boost to the local game and the Leinster Cup final between Bohemians and Dublin University on 10 March 1894 roused considerable interest.[44] Bohemians went on to reach the final of the Irish Cup in 1895, but the gap in quality between Dublin and Belfast was clearly demonstrated when they were hammered 10–1 by Linfield. That year Shelbourne FC was founded in Dublin by players from the working-class suburb of Ringsend. Shelbourne reached the Leinster Senior Cup final in 1896, and the following year graduated to the Leinster Senior League, where it developed a keen rivalry with Bohemians.

By the 1890s association football was receiving growing attention in the press. Various state-sponsored initiatives, including the 1892 Education Act, which abolished fees in national schools and made attendance compulsory, had helped to raise educational levels and create a literate public that was keen to read about sports. Daily papers and specialised publications such as the *Irish Sportsman* (founded 1870) and *Sport* (founded 1880) began to give greater coverage to important club and international football matches. New papers devoted primarily to association football were launched, such as *Ulster Football and Cycling News* in 1887 and *Ulster's Saturday Night* (founded in 1894 and later renamed *Ireland's Saturday Night*). Press coverage expanded the game's following far beyond those who actually attended matches and played a key role in stirring up interest and shaping public perception.

The spread of the game in Ireland was also helped by developments in transport, particularly the growth of the railway network. By the time the first games of association football were being played in the late 1870s, the Irish rail system had over 2,000 miles of track and carried 16 million passengers annually. In the past the prohibitive cost and difficulty of travelling long distances had limited football matches to encounters between local rivals playing under local rules. With the development of railways, however, horizons began to broaden, and newly codified sports were among the chief beneficiaries.[45] By the 1890s it was possible to travel comfortably from Dublin to Belfast and back in a day and have time to play or watch a football match. The growth in railways was complemented by improvements in civic transport. In 1880 the Dublin United Tram Company integrated horse-drawn tram services across the city into a 32-mile network. Passenger numbers rose from about 10 million in 1881 to 25 million a year by the mid-1890s. At the end of the decade the system was electrified and by 1914 was carrying 58 million passengers annually and was acclaimed as one of the finest urban tram systems in the world.[46] Serving football grounds such as Shelbourne Park and Dalymount Park, it helped ensure that regular Dublin derby matches were accessible and well-attended.

The development of the bicycle also played its part in facilitating greater mobility. The first modern 'safety' bicycles (so-called because they had a chain drive and wheels of equal size unlike the unsteady 'Penny Farthing') were produced in England in the early 1880s and were greatly improved in 1888 by John Boyd Dunlop's development of the pneumatic tyre in Belfast, which made cycling safer and more comfortable. The 1890s saw a 'bicycle craze', as cycling became a popular sport in its own right and offered young men and women a convenient and affordable form of transport. It became easier for spectators to travel to fixtures and for players to attend training or games: the young Oliver St John Gogarty regularly cycled the 30 miles from Clongowes Wood College to Dublin to play for Bohemians, and then did the same in reverse after the game.[47]

Cumulative improvements in public and private transport made it possible for teams to compete for trophies on a national basis. They also allowed growing numbers of followers to travel to grounds outside their localities, boosting gate receipts and creating a noisier atmosphere that added to the sense of occasion. For dedicated supporters, travelling to games in large groups became an integral part of the experience of following a club that further reinforced identification and loyalty.

✳✳✳

Shortly after the founding of the IFA, association football found itself in competition with a new code that claimed to be more authentically rooted in Irish sporting traditions. In 1884 Michael Cusack and others founded the GAA to gain control over athletics in Ireland and to preserve and promote indigenous games. Cusack, an all-round athlete who also played rugby and cricket, had become disillusioned with the poor organisation and social exclusivity of established athletics organisations, and by the increasing prevalence of professionalism and gambling in Irish sport. The GAA was a national sporting body, open to Irishmen of all creeds, classes and political persuasions, but its close identification with nationalist Ireland was demonstrated by its choice of patrons: Charles Stewart Parnell, the recognised political leader of constitutional nationalism; Thomas Croke, the archbishop of Cashel and one of the most energetic and politically active members of the Catholic hierarchy; and Michael Davitt, leader of the Land League, who represented the agrarian agitation that underpinned the Irish Parliamentary Party (IPP) in the 1880s.

As well as reviving the traditional Irish game of hurling, Cusack and his colleague Maurice Davin (a well-known athlete and the GAA's first president) also sought to promote a uniquely Irish form of football. Since there was no agreed Irish version of the game, they created one, drawing up rules that were published in the Parnellite newspaper *United Ireland* on 7 February 1885. These were, however, rather vague and gave little indication as to how the game was played; even team size was uncertain, varying between fifteen and twenty-one. Cusack later instructed that the ball was 'not to be passed or carried in any way. It may be caught, but it must be kicked or put on the ground at once. It may also be hit with the hand. The passing and carrying is entirely foreign, having been imported from rugby.'[48] In attempting to differentiate Gaelic football from rugby, then the most popular form of football in Ireland, Cusack and Davin created a game that was rather closer to soccer: it was played with a round ball that was kicked rather than thrown, goals and not tries were scored, and tackling was (in theory) directed at the ball rather than the player. Like soccer it was designed to flow freely without regular set-piece plays such as scrums, line-outs and marks.[49]

An All-Ireland Gaelic football championship was contested from 1887 but was slow to take off, and by 1889 only six counties had entered. Interest from the general public was lukewarm and the crowds at early national finals were in the low thousands. Partly this was because of the inevitable teething problems of a new code, but the GAA also had to contend with wider political considerations. Members of the secret insurrectionary organisation the Irish Republican Brotherhood (IRB, popularly known as the Fenians) had welcomed the founding of the GAA, seeing it as an excellent vehicle to train and discipline Ireland's youth; the former Fenian leader John O'Leary was appointed one of its patrons in 1886. Several of the association's founders also belonged to the IRB and within a few years they dominated the GAA's national executive. When the Fenian candidate P.N. Fitzgerald was elected chairman at the annual GAA convention in Thurles in November 1887, he dramatically proclaimed that 'only men ready to die for their country should be at the head of the GAA'.[50] However Fenian domination provoked strong clerical opposition, particularly after the IPP split of 1890–1 in which the GAA largely sided with its patron Parnell. By 1890 the GAA had 875 affiliated clubs, compared with 124 for the IFA.[51] However, clerical disapproval and the embittered atmosphere in nationalist politics after Parnell's death in 1891 led to a decline in GAA membership, with some clubs abandoning Gaelic games to take up rugby or soccer.[52]

***

The first recognised international soccer match took place between England and Scotland on 30 November 1872 at Hamilton Crescent in Glasgow, watched by about 4,000 spectators. Matches grew steadily in popularity and by 1896 the same fixture was attracting over 50,000. On 18 February 1882, England provided the opposition for Ireland's first soccer international, at Knock Ground, Bloomfield, Belfast. The ubiquitous J.M. McAlery of Cliftonville captained Ireland, and Belfast clubs supplied the rest of the team: five from Knock FC, three from Cliftonville, and one each from Avoniel and Distillery. The inexperienced Irish eleven, which included the fifteen-year-old Samuel Johnston of Distillery (Ireland's youngest ever international debutant), suffered a 13–0 defeat – still to date England's biggest winning margin against any opponent. Other heavy defeats followed until Ireland managed to salvage some pride with a 1–1 draw against Wales at Ballynafeigh, Belfast, on 17 March 1883. Given the day, it was noted that several of the Irish players sported sprigs of shamrock in their shirts, and the draw was celebrated as a 'moral victory' by the local sporting press.[53]

The four national associations initially played under slightly different rules. For international games they usually adopted the home team's rules, but this led to occasional disputes. This prompted a meeting in Manchester on 6 December 1882 to agree uniform rules that paved the way for the establishment in 1884 of the world's first international soccer competition, the British Championship. (Rugby's equivalent had begun a year earlier and both would make important contributions to forging distinct national identities among the competing countries.) In the championship's first game, Scotland beat Ireland 5–0 at the Ulster Cricket Ground in Belfast on 26 January 1884. Ireland also lost that year to England and Wales, conceding nineteen goals and scoring just one in the three games. This rather set the pattern for the rest of the century. For the next twenty years or so, Ireland usually finished last, or occasionally beat Wales into third place, notably in 1887 when they defeated the Welsh 4–1 in Belfast to record their first ever win. The Irish though made little headway against the stronger international teams of England or Scotland, suffering regular heavy defeats, such as 7–0 and 9–1 thrashings to England in 1887 and 1890 respectively, and a 10–2 defeat to Scotland in 1888. There was also a humiliating 11–0 loss to Wales in Wrexham in 1888, which stands as Wales's record winning margin against any opponent, as does Scotland's 11–0 victory over Ireland as late as 1901.

Such heavy defeats were probably inevitable: the game was far more advanced in Britain than in Ireland, and England and Scotland had much larger pools of skilled and experienced players. In the twenty-five international matches played between 1882 and 1890, Ireland won one, drew one and lost twenty-three. This led some commentators to argue that Irishmen should confine themselves to playing their own games rather than allowing themselves to be humiliated in foreign sports.[54] However, in contrast to soccer, the Irish national rugby team had established itself early on as a competitive outfit, beating Scotland in 1881, England in 1887 and Wales in 1888. Ireland secured a share of the Rugby Championship in 1888 and won the tournament outright in 1894, 1896 and 1899. This success led to a certain 'nationalisation' of rugby, which was seen as a game at which Irishmen could excel.[55] Some argued that this was because the national team was more representative of the country as a whole than was the soccer team, while others claimed that the vigorous charging and full-blooded tackling of rugby was better suited to the passionate Irish character.[56] One observer attributed a decidedly 'Celtic' character to Irish rugby, arguing that 'impetuosity and torrential courage, not reasoned and scientific tactics, have carried the green jerseys to victory at rugby'; he contrasted this with soccer where success was determined by 'reasoned action, deliberation in method, and the union of individual and collective brilliancy'.[57]

The poor performance of the Irish soccer team created tensions between Belfast and Dublin. The national team selected by the IFA was usually composed entirely of northern players, occasionally supplemented by a single southerner.[58] Tom Kirkwood-Hackett, the representative of the Leinster Nomads club from Dublin, blamed Ireland's poor results on 'the prejudice of five men who select the team, preventing anyone outside the Belfast area being chosen to represent their country'.[59] Dublin newspapers took to referring to the 'Ireland' team in inverted commas, or even to 'Ulster' or 'Belfast', claiming that it was a regional rather than national selection of little interest to Dublin soccer followers.[60] They denounced the IFA for its failure to promote the game nationwide, claiming that 'if the association game was spread to the southern parts of Ireland, we could produce a combination which would hold its own against all-comers'.[61]

Although usually underdogs, the Irish were not complete no-hopers: even when outclassed they invariably fought hard, and in the 1890s their efforts began to yield results. On 7 February 1891 in Belfast they managed to beat Wales 7–2 and secured another four wins over Wales in that decade. There were also draws against England in 1894 and Scotland in 1896, and some near misses, including a narrow 3–2 defeat to England in 1898, which earned praise for Irish 'dash, pluck and speed'.[62] This though was followed in 1899 by heavy defeats of 13–2 to England and 9–1 to Scotland, greeted with the usual claims that a more genuinely Irish team would have done better.[63]

The Manchester conference of 1882 that agreed on a uniform set of rules for the British Championship heralded a period of greater co-operation among the four UK associations. However, difficulties arose in 1885, after the English FA legalised professionalism, and Scotland refused to face an English team that included professionals. The IFA attempted to mediate by proposing that the four associations should have an annual meeting to settle disputes and agree rule changes. The new body was called the International Football Association Board (IFAB) and met for the first time in London in 1886. All four UK associations had equal voting rights and its annual conferences were rotated among the four jurisdictions. Belfast hosted its first International Board annual conference in 1889, and thereafter these were held in Ireland at four-yearly intervals, usually in scenic coastal towns such as Portrush or Newcastle.

The IFA was proud of its status as a founding member of the International Board and prized its close ties with other members. The British Championship was its sole international focus: it would not play a full international match against a team from outside the UK until 1951. It also played an active role in shaping and refining the rules of the game. The replacement of umpires nominated by each team by neutral linesmen was an Irish initiative, as was the introduction of the penalty kick. In 1890, the IFA representative, J.M. McAlery, suggested that a clear shot at goal should be introduced to penalise fouls committed close to the goal. The measure was initially opposed by amateurs, such as the famous all-rounder C.B. Fry of the Corinthians club, who protested that 'it was a standing insult to sportsmen to have to play under a rule which assumes that players intend to trip, hack and push opponents and to behave like cads of the most unscrupulous kidney'. McAlery though eventually had his way and the penalty kick was adopted at the 1891 conference in Glasgow.[64]

In addition to full international fixtures, UK professional football also featured regular inter-league matches. From 1893 the Irish League played almost annually against the English and Scottish Leagues. There were occasional morale-boosting victories over the Scots in 1893, 1899 and 1903, but victory over the English proved elusive. The Irish League team invariably played its home matches in Belfast and did not host one in Dublin until October 1913. Closer UK links were also forged through club football. During the 1880s and 1890s, Belfast clubs regularly played English and Scottish opponents, and even competed in the English FA Cup, suffering occasional heavy defeats: Cliftonville went down 11–1 to Partick Thistle in 1887 while Distillery lost 10–1 to Bolton Wanderers in 1890. In 1888, however, Linfield did boost the reputation of Irish football by beating Nottingham Forest 3–1 in an FA Cup tie in Belfast. For many in Belfast, participation in the world's oldest cup competition was a matter of some significance, enhancing their sense of belonging to the wider British football community and even to the United Kingdom itself.

※※※

The society in which association football was taking root was a strictly gendered one, in which men and women were assigned their separate spheres: men took the lead in public life, while women were expected to create a domestic sanctuary that nurtured the family. When it came to sport, the main function of respectable women was to lend a degree of tone to the occasion. A notable feature of the match between Queen's Park and Caledonian FC in Belfast in 1878 was that female spectators were admitted free of charge. This was a common practice, and the presence of women – usually in reserved enclosures – was regularly noted at games.[65] Women though rarely ventured onto unreserved terraces, which were intensely male spaces, noted for shouting, swearing, drinking and general rowdiness. Soccer's origins, both public school and working class, were strongly shaped by contemporary concepts of gender, and its language and culture reflected the masculine values of the day. While sports such as archery, croquet and perhaps even golf and tennis were considered suitable for upper-class women, engaging in a vigorous contact sport such as football was regarded as taboo. Yet from soccer's earliest days, there were women who played the game.

In May 1881, Hibernian Park in Edinburgh, the home of Hibernian FC, provided the venue for an 'international' match between women's teams from Scotland and England (the Scots winning 3–1). However, some men saw women playing football as an encroachment on their domain and women's matches were regularly disrupted by jeering and taunting and even by pitch invasions and assaults on players. For the match at Hibernian Park, the club entrusted security to a 'guard' of Irish navvies and coal-heavers to ensure that the game passed off without incident.[66]

Just as in the male game, social class mattered in women's football. Working women would sometimes engage in informal kickabouts, but the best-known pioneering female proponents of the game tended to be from the upper or middle classes. Chief among them was Nettie Honeyball (almost certainly a pseudonym), who, in 1894, founded the British Ladies Football Club. The club's players, she noted, were 'all homely girls. We don't want any la-di-da members. We play the game in the proper spirit. We allow charging, but no bad temper is ever displayed, and I have never heard a cross word spoken.'[67] She was seen as a typical example of the 'New Woman' of the 1890s, which saw some independent middle-class women challenge gender stereotypes by earning their own living and taking a more active part in public life. Honeyball readily admitted that the motivation of the British Ladies FC went beyond sport. She herself was a committed suffragist who looked forward to proving that 'women are not the "ornamental and useless" creatures men have pictured ... I look forward to the time when ladies may sit in parliament and have a voice in the direction of affairs'.[68]

The Scottish suffragist Helen Matthews was also a keen footballer and played for the British Ladies in 1895. Their efforts were at first ignored and then opposed by the FA, which actively discouraged women from forming their own clubs. The press too was often scathing. After the British Ladies FC had played their first match in March 1895, *The Freeman's Journal* concluded that 'It is likely to be their last. The "New Woman" does not look to advantage in football costume, and the necessities of the game are not of a kind to enhance female gracefulness.'[69] Despite this, the club played dozens of matches throughout the UK in 1895–6. On 18 and 19 May 1896 it played before sizeable crowds at the City and Suburban Grounds at Jones's Road in Dublin, and in a farewell match on Saturday 23 May won 7–2 against a team of 'Dublin gentlemen'.[70] The visit though appears to have done little to help the women's game put down roots and it remained a marginal sport in Ireland for some time to come.

2

North and South:
Rivalry and Resentment 1900–14

By the turn of the century the Irish sporting landscape was changing. Sports that had dominated previously, such as horse-racing, hunting, boxing and athletics, were still popular but had to share the field with team games such as hurling and the various football codes. These were now organised on a national basis and their growth in popularity at a time of rising nationalism meant that they became intertwined with ideals of national sentiment and allegiance. This was perhaps most evident in the case of Gaelic games, which were seen as promoting a uniquely Irish form of culture. Association football had no such explicit cultural agenda, but it too was establishing itself as an important social activity. Local derby matches and cup finals were becoming firmly embedded in the sporting calendar, their significance heightened by the fact that they were often played on public holidays such as St Patrick's Day, Easter Monday or 26 December. Soccer also had an important international dimension, with annual matches continuing to stoke rivalries among the UK nations, and its importance as an expression of national sentiment would further boost its profile and support.

By the early years of the twentieth century, association football was becoming a genuinely international sport. When the first modern Olympic Games were held in Athens in 1896 (themselves a crucial milestone in the international standardisation of sport), they were dominated by track-and-field athletics. Soccer was included, but only as a minor exhibition event, haphazardly contested by club or scratch teams. It had a similar marginal status in Paris and St Louis at the 1900 and 1904 games but was included as a full sport for London in 1908, contested by the amateurs of England, France, Denmark, Sweden and Holland. Great Britain (represented by the England amateur team) beat Denmark in the final and did so again at the Stockholm Olympics in 1912.[1]

In the previous century conquest and commerce had secured for Britain the world's largest empire. Many aspects of its culture were exported or imitated abroad, including association football. However, the game's reception in the empire was fitful and uneven: it failed to put down strong roots in countries such as Australia, New Zealand, Canada and India, probably because most of the officers and officials of empire favoured higher-status sports, such as rugby and cricket, over the game of the British masses. Instead, soccer was most enthusiastically received in Europe and South America, suggesting that it was diffused most effectively through trade and informal cultural contact.

On the European continent, soccer gained its strongest footholds in France, Belgium, the Netherlands, Switzerland, Scandinavia and Germany, while in Latin America it was most eagerly adopted in Argentina, Uruguay and Chile, all places with significant commercial, educational or cultural links with Britain. It also made progress in the industrial north of Spain and Italy, where the first games were played by British visitors and expatriates. Soccer proved particularly attractive to local elites, who associated all things British with innovation and modernity, and often adopted anglicised names for their clubs.[2] The primacy of the UK's International Board was accepted by nascent football associations across the globe and the game's spread helped create an important sphere of British cultural influence.[3]

The early adoption of association football in Ireland meant that Irishmen played important roles in spreading it abroad. Among the earliest was the County Wicklow-born John H. 'Jock' Kirwan (1878–1959), an outstanding winger who won an FA Cup medal with Tottenham Hotspur in 1901 and seventeen caps for Ireland (1900–9). In

1910 he became the manager of AFC Ajax of Amsterdam, and remained so until 1915, helping to lay the foundations for its transformation into one of Holland's most important clubs. He later worked in Italy, where he managed Liverno (1923–4). Another leading pioneer was Dublin-born Arthur Johnson (1879–1929), who, after playing amateur football in Ireland and England, emigrated to Spain and played for Madrid Football Club months after it had been officially founded in March 1902 (on receiving royal patronage, the club would become Real Madrid in 1920). As well as coaching the team, he became captain in 1902 and team manager in 1910, helping to establish Madrid as one of the strongest clubs in Spain, winning four regional titles and the prestigious Coronation Cup (later Copa del Rey) in 1917; he also recruited several notable players such as the future club president Santiago Bernabéu, before moving on to Athletic Bilbao in 1920.

Madrid's great rival Barcelona also had an Irish connection. After a professional playing career that included six caps for Ireland (1912–19) and captaining Manchester United (1914–15), Dublin-born Patrick O'Connell (1887–1959) went to Spain and coached Racing Santander (1922–9; 1945–7), Atlético Madrid (1929–34) and Real Betis of Seville (1934–5; 1939–43). He achieved his greatest fame as manager of Barcelona (1935–9) through his strong identification with its Catalan heritage, and his efforts to help it survive the civil war of 1936–9 have ensured him a place of honour in the club's history. His achievement was also recognised in the place of his birth when a plaque was unveiled in 2015 at Fitzroy Avenue, Drumcondra.[4] Other notable figures included James Donnelly (1893–1959), who was born in Ballina, County Mayo, and moved to England in his childhood. After playing professionally in England in the 1920s, he embarked on a peripatetic career in which he coached several continental teams including Gradanski Zagreb (1933–5), the Turkish national team (1936–7), AS Ambrosiana-Inter (1937–8) (later Inter Milan), and Amsterdamsche FC (1938–40; 1944–5).[5] There were others who took the game even further afield, such as Paddy McCarthy (1871?–1963?), a boxer and footballer who was born in Cashel, County Tipperary, and moved to Buenos Aires in 1900 to work as a physical education teacher. In 1905 he helped found and coached the

Boca Juniors club, which would eventually become the most successful in Argentina.[6]

By the early twentieth century, association football was popular enough in continental Europe for international matches to take place, with Austria and Hungary meeting in October 1902. In 1904 seven countries – France, Belgium, Holland, Denmark, Sweden, Switzerland and Spain – came together to found the Fédération Internationale de Football Association (FIFA) in Paris. The game was at varying stages of development in the seven: some had no national associations, others had never played an international match, and the general standard of football played was often poor. (When the Freebooters club from Dublin toured Belgium in 1902, it won all six of the games played, including a 13–0 victory over a Brussels team considered to be one of the strongest in the country.)[7] However, as the game grew in popularity in Europe, FIFA continued to attract new members and spread its jurisdiction outside the continent, with South Africa joining in 1909, Argentina in 1912 and the USA in 1913.[8]

FIFA fully accepted the IFAB's rules and imperial measurements for playing pitch and goals, and its jurisdiction over the laws of the game. This cleared the way for the English FA to join FIFA in 1905, and the Scottish, Welsh and Irish associations followed in 1910. In 1913 the International Board agreed to admit four FIFA representatives, whose votes were balanced by one each from the UK associations. The UK associations though continued to regard FIFA as something of a foreign upstart, administering a game to which it had no real claim. The original IFAB members looked upon themselves as the founders and nurturers of association football and their board as the primary international authority. Their belief that the standard of football in the UK was far superior to anything played abroad was reinforced when England played its first internationals against continental teams in 1908 and 1909, trouncing both Austria and Hungary.

While the Scottish, Welsh and Irish national teams were happy to confine their efforts to the British Championship, some clubs were keen to test themselves against continental opposition. In 1912 Belfast Celtic undertook a tour of the Austro-Hungarian province of

Bohemia where, led by Prague-based clubs such as SK Slavia and AC Sparta, association football had flourished since the 1890s. This was in spite of the opposition of the government in Vienna, which feared the possibility of nationalist disturbances among large crowds.[9] The Belfast club played six games, winning five and drawing one. The fact that the Czechs of Bohemia, just like the nationalists of Belfast, were actively seeking political autonomy, gave an additional significance to the tour and both sides highlighted their distinctive national culture. The visitors' party included as team mascot Cathal O'Byrne (1876– 1957), a leading Belfast writer and advocate of Gaelic culture who, dressed in saffron kilt and playing the uillean pipes, led the Celtic team onto the pitch. An after-match dinner in Prague featured a display of Irish dancing and the recitation of poetry in Irish.[10] At an elaborate homecoming reception in Belfast, the Celtic players were praised by the parliamentarian Joe Devlin as 'one of the great and powerful athletic combinations of Europe. They had left behind them a record of which we all should be proud as Irishmen. The team created there an impression that not only exalted the Celtic organisation but brought honour and credit to the land to which you belong.'[11] Two years later the reputation of Irish, and especially Belfast, soccer was further enhanced when Celtic's rivals Glentoran, who had won the IFA Cup in March 1914, toured Central Europe the following May. They won most of their matches, including a 5–0 victory over a Vienna Select XI on 30 May, for which they were awarded the Vienna Cup, a trophy which remains in the club's boardroom to this day.[12]

**

By 1900 association football was on its way to becoming a mass sport in Belfast and a significant one in other cities such as Derry and Dublin. In January 1899 a crowd of over 7,000 watched the Leinster–Ulster interprovincial at Jones's Road in Dublin.[13] The game was making considerable progress outside Dublin, with competitive teams playing in Athlone, Dundalk, Longford, Kilkenny and Wicklow.[14] It was also beginning to spread to the south and, somewhat more tentatively, to the west: a Munster Football Association was founded in 1901 and a Fermanagh and Western Association in 1904. By 1904 there were 334 clubs affiliated to the various associations: 127 in the north-east, 90 in Leinster, 52 in mid-Ulster, 16 in Fermanagh and Western, 13 in the north-west and 29 in Munster, with many clubs fielding more than one team.[15]

In Munster much of the impetus came from the British military; several army regiments were stationed in the province and there was a large Royal Navy base in Cobh. The Munster Senior League usually featured as many army teams as civilian ones and the military often dominated the prestigious cup competitions. The 1914 Munster Cup final was contested by teams from the Rifle Brigade and the 24th Brigade of the Royal Field Artillery; previous winners included the Welsh Fusiliers, the Yorkshire Light Infantry, the 3rd Dragoon Guards, and the Gordon Highlanders.[16] The trophy was also won by civilian sides such as Cork Celtic, but soccer made slow progress in Munster, where the strength of the GAA and the game's close identification with the British military checked its popular appeal.[17]

While soccer's spread throughout the rest of Ireland was uneven, there were pockets where it flourished. In Athlone, for example, a club had been founded in 1887 by Orlando Coote, the son of a local landlord, who learned the game during his education in England. The game caught on locally and Athlone managed to win the Leinster Junior Cup in 1894.[18] The growing industrial city of Derry was also home to several soccer clubs and a Derry Football Association was founded in April 1886. The game received a boost in 1890 with the founding of St Columb's Hall, a club that enjoyed considerable success in the junior game and participated in the Irish League from 1900 as Derry Celtic.

Association football also enjoyed some early popularity in neighbouring Donegal. A match 'under the association rules' had been played between the villages of Castlefin and Croaghan in east Donegal as early as July 1881, and games were also played in the south of the county between teams from Mountcharles and Donegal town in 1882. Workmen from Derry who were laying the railway line from Donegal to Killybegs in the early 1890s brought football with them: a match between Dunkineely Wanderers and Inver Swifts was recorded on 29 June 1893 just six weeks before the line was completed.[19] In April 1893, the Derry FA broadened its jurisdiction to become the North-West FA, with seven affiliated clubs from Donegal. Soccer was particularly popular in the north-east of the county, with thriving clubs in Letterkenny, Milford, Ramelton and Kerrykeel. A County Donegal Football Association to which eight clubs affiliated was founded in Boyle's Hotel in Ramelton on 24 March 1894, and matches were regularly played against clubs from west Tyrone and Derry.[20]

Donegal's profile differed sharply from the usual soccer-playing area. The county was dependent on agriculture and fishing, which supported a scattered rural population and there were few substantial urban settlements (in 1881 only Ballyshannon and Letterkenny had populations greater than 2,000). However, the proximity of Derry city and the strong British military presence around Ballyshannon and Lough Swilly helped soccer gain a solid following.[21] Seasonal migration to Scotland was also crucial. Donegal developed particularly close links with the Celtic Football Club. Regular coming and going between Donegal and the west of Scotland forged a strong affinity between the two regions and made widespread support for Celtic one of the county's most distinctive sporting loyalties.[22]

However, some local newspapers, such as the Donegal News, exhibited a marked hostility to the association game. In 1905, it noted with regret that soccer was the dominant code in the Irish-speaking area of Gweedore and rather curiously blamed 'the women of Gweedore' for 'their adoption of West British habits and manners' which encouraged 'the shoneenism of those who play the imported British association game'.[23] In the early 1900s the GAA, recovering from the political factionalism of the previous decade, gained ground and Gaelic football grew in popularity, but soccer remained firmly established in the north-east and Inishowen peninsula.[24] Outside of these strongholds and Derry city, soccer remained under-developed in most of west Ulster, particularly in Tyrone, Fermanagh and Cavan. This was partly because of their poor transport links, scattered populations and competition from the GAA, but also stemmed from a lack of interest by the IFA, which focused predominantly on the east of the province.[25]

***

Although association football was played and watched by people from various backgrounds, it was increasingly identified with the urban working class. The founding of clubs by working men was an important part of the democratisation of Irish sport, allowing them to take greater charge of their own affairs and represent local areas or institutions with pride. For those whose lives were dominated by monotonous labour, grim surroundings and economic uncertainty, soccer offered a novel form of recreation and diversion. One Belfast commentator saw it providing 'a brief period of excitement and uplifting, which makes up for the weary and sordid days of the past week'.[26] The situation in Dublin was similar: when a crowd of 6,000 spectators saw Shelbourne defeat Bohemians 3–2 in the 1904 Leinster Cup final, a journalist noted that association football in Dublin 'rejoices in the fact that it is the chosen sport of the democracy, and is mainly of a plebeian nature'.[27]

This claim, although largely uncontested, was based almost entirely on casual observation: neither clubs nor associations recorded the social backgrounds of those who attended games. The only hard evidence we have comes from the rather grisly source of lists of the dead and injured at incidents in football stadiums, such as the Ibrox disaster of 1902 in Glasgow, in which a terrace collapsed and twenty-five people were killed and more than 500 were injured; most of the casualties recorded were young single males from the lower middle class and the skilled working class.[28] Those injured in the rioting at Celtic Park during the Belfast Celtic and Linfield game in September 1912 showed a similar profile: about two thirds were artisans, labourers or unskilled workers, while most of the remaining third were skilled workers.[29]

Anecdotal evidence also supports the claim. A keen soccer player and supporter such as Christopher Stephen 'Todd' Andrews (1901–85), born in Summerhill in Dublin and later a well-known figure in Irish public life, noted a strong correlation between sport and social class in the city. He recalled that soccer was the favoured sport of labourers, dockers, coal heavers, shop attendants, messenger boys and domestic servants, who had 'scarcely any amusements outside the pubs or an occasional soccer match'. The upper classes played golf, rugby, cricket, tennis, hockey and croquet; middle-class professionals and the wealthier shopkeepers and publicans generally confined themselves to rugby, cricket and tennis. Lower-middle-class shopkeepers and publicans (Andrews's own background) were closer in their tastes to the working class, regularly attending soccer matches at Dalymount Park or Shelbourne Park, while their children played soccer and cricket on vacant lots. Andrews claimed that most soccer supporters regarded rugby as the game of Protestants and 'Castle Catholics', and Gaelic games 'as fit only for country "goms"'.[30]

The large military and police presence in Dublin boosted sport, as did the wide-open spaces of the Phoenix Park. In 1901, in order to preserve existing cricket grounds, the Commissioners of Public Works laid out dozens of football pitches in the 'Fifteen Acres' area of the park; by 1906 there were thirty-one pitches, twenty-nine of which were being used for soccer.[31] The city's sporting culture was also strongly influenced by its two universities. By the mid-nineteenth century, Dublin University was one of the largest in the UK, with 1,500 students (compared to 1,300 at Oxford), many of whom were among the city's most active sportsmen.[32] The broad participation in Dublin sport of army officers, civil servants and students, could give it a socially exclusive tone, with most participants preferring to spend their leisure hours with those of a similar background. During the 1890s the popularity of association football in colleges and exclusive secondary schools, such as Clongowes Wood and St Vincent's College in Castleknock, led to criticisms from some nationalists that the game was socially elitist as well as 'west British'. However, the growing working-class popularity of the game soon retarded its development in elite schools, always keen to maintain their social distinctions. In 1895 the authorities at Clongowes banned the playing of association football on the school grounds, and in October 1907 pupils formally voted for a rugby-only policy, an example followed two years later by

Castleknock. For many private schools the playing of rugby would become a mark of exclusivity central to their identity.[33]

Middle-class interest in soccer in Dublin found outlets such as Freebooters FC and Bohemian FC. The Freebooters club was based in Sandymount and regularly featured players who had attended leading English public schools. It reached the final of the IFA Cup in 1901 but was relatively short-lived, dissolving in 1906. Bohemian FC proved rather more enduring. Several of its players were university students, professionals or white-collar workers: among the more notable were the senior civil servant A.P. Magill (1871–1941), who was private secretary to successive chief secretaries (1904–18), and the medical student and all-round sportsman Oliver St John Gogarty (1878–1957), who also played professionally with Preston North End reserves while studying at Stoneyhurst in Lancashire.[34] The presence on the Bohemian team of Protestant players (including one, John Curtis, who became bishop of Chekiang in China in 1929) and the club's refusal to play on Sunday (a stance that persisted until the late 1960s), led some to dub it Dublin's 'Protestant team'.[35] Bohemian FC drew its core following from the north inner city and the northside suburbs of Phibsborough, Drumcondra and Glasnevin, inhabited predominantly by lower-middle-class and working-class families. This support solidified when the club opened its own ground at Dalymount Park in Phibsborough on 7 September 1901 with a game against Shelbourne. From 1903 the stadium was used for cup finals and occasional international fixtures, further entrenching the popularity of soccer in the local area.[36]

Shelbourne's identification with its locality was similarly enhanced in August 1913 with the opening of Shelbourne Park in Ringsend.[37] The club drew support not only from the working-class areas of Ringsend and Irishtown in the south-east of the city, but more generally from the south-city working class and also some manual workers north of the Liffey. The club's players were themselves often casual labourers from the Ringsend area: the famous Irish international Val Harris (1884–1963), who played with Shelbourne (1903–8), was a docker known to report for games on Saturday afternoon caked in black dust after unloading a coal boat without having had a chance to wash. The distinction between Shelbourne and Bohemians was reinforced in 1905 when the former turned professional while the latter remained amateur. In a city in which subtle gradations of class were keenly observed, their rivalry was heightened by perceived social differences: matches between them were often termed 'the dockers versus the doctors'.[38]

While there were some occupational differences between players (though many working men also played for Bohemians), the supporters of both clubs were predominantly working class. As such, they found themselves caught up in the events of the 1913 Lockout when the two teams met on Saturday 30 August to play a match to celebrate the opening of Shelbourne's new stadium. Days earlier, the Dublin tram workers of James Larkin's Irish Transport and General Workers' Union had gone on strike, and Larkin's *Irish Worker* named a player from each side as a strike breaker and urged action to prevent the match going ahead. On the day a large crowd of striking workers gathered outside the stadium and tried to block spectators from entering, leading to violent clashes and a police baton charge on the picketers. Afterwards fifty people were treated for injuries and sixteen arrests were made. The violence anticipated events the following day, when police arrested Larkin to prevent him addressing a meeting in O'Connell Street and began brutally to disperse the large crowd. A pitched battle ensued, leaving behind two dead and over 400 injured on the first 'Bloody Sunday' of the century. However, the events of 30 August do not seem to have created any lasting ill-feeling between the strikers and soccer supporters: at another match between Bohemians and Shelbourne at the same venue five weeks later, it was noted that 'the popular parts of the ground were packed and the "Red Hand" man (Larkin's union organisers) seemed to be all over the place, either collecting for the unemployed or watching the match'.[39]

The rivalry between Bohemians and Shelbourne dominated Dublin senior football until the 1920s. Their clashes in the Leinster Senior Cup were a highlight of the season and between 1893 and 1917 these two clubs alone held the trophy, Bohemians winning it fifteen times and Shelbourne nine. The final was usually held on St Stephen's Day at Dalymount Park, attracting large crowds and becoming 'as much part of Dublin life during the Christmas holiday as the turkey and plum pudding'.[40] Bohemians and Shelbourne were, however, simply the most visible representatives of the game in Dublin. Elsewhere in the city there was a vibrant junior soccer scene, with local clubs springing up regularly. They arose from all kinds of social interaction that brought young men together: local neighbourhoods, parishes, schools, existing sports and social clubs, places of employment or worship, trade unions and pubs. They drew in not only those who played and watched but also officials, coaches, helpers and fundraisers. The situation was replicated in other urban areas, where clubs became important expressions of civic pride. Many adopted the coat-of-arms of their host town or city as their emblem and became integral parts of their communities, particularly through charity and benefit games which further cemented their local standing.[41]

***

In England the rise of association football coincided with a general decline in organised religious observance, particularly among the working class. Some attributed one to the other, claiming that football had displaced religion while at the same time mimicking its rituals, group singing and communal solidarity. The fall-off in religious observance in much of England was, however, a gradual and complex development and association football did not rush in to fill the vacuum. More often the two activities co-existed comfortably: in the early days of the game supporters often sang hymns and the communal rites of association football tended to complement rather than replace the fellowship and purpose of organised religion. Various churches recognised soccer's usefulness in promoting physical and mental fitness and offering young men an edifying alternative to the pub, bookmakers or street corner. In the industrial cities of the English midlands and north, clergymen and evangelical sportsmen founded clubs such as Aston Villa (1874), Bolton Wanderers (1874), Wolverhampton Wanderers (1877) and Everton (1878). The popular hymn 'Abide with Me' has been sung before English FA Cup finals for almost a century, and when the final was held at Wembley for the first time in 1923, the match programme helpfully informed the crowd that the new stadium covered the same ground area as the biblical city of Jerusalem.[42]

In Ireland too, where organised religion remained strong, many newly founded clubs were linked to religious institutions. Local leagues were often organised on a confessional basis, and for some young footballers it was unusual to play against opponents of a different religion. In Belfast there were thriving Protestant Church leagues, and the city's Central Presbyterian Association spawned several clubs. Many young players learned the game in the ranks of the Boys' Brigade, an organisation founded in Glasgow in 1883 to develop 'a true Christian manliness' in boys aged between twelve and seventeen through semi-military discipline, religious instruction and athletic activities. Brigade battalions had been founded in Belfast in 1888 and Dublin in 1891 and by 1900 were among the largest in the UK, with 740 and 1,132 members respectively. Membership was entirely Protestant and largely working-class, and soccer the most popular sport, played by dozens of clubs for current and past members.[43] In Dublin a large number of junior teams were linked to Catholic social clubs. Among the most notable was Pioneers, founded in 1908 by the Pioneer Total Abstinence Society and based in the Clontarf and Whitehall areas which was one of the city's most successful junior clubs. There were also several junior clubs based around the city's Church of Ireland parishes, such as St Barnabas from East Wall, which drew on a local colony of Ulster Protestant railway workers. The city's Adelaide Road synagogue also gave rise to a successful team, and members of Dublin's Jewish community such as Louis Bookman (1890–1943) and Robert Briscoe (1894–1969) made significant contributions to the development of the game in the capital.[44]

Workplaces too were important in spawning football clubs, a development that tended to reinforce the game's working-class character and root it more deeply in local communities. Three of Belfast's earliest clubs – Oldpark, Distillery and Avoniel – were formed by the workers at the Oldpark Printworks, the Royal Irish Distilleries and the builders of the Avoniel Distillery respectively, and the city's most successful club, Linfield, was founded by workers of the Ulster Spinning Company. Dublin also had its share of works' teams, often sponsored by leading employers. Chief among them was St James's Gate FC, founded in 1902 by the medical officer of the Guinness brewery to provide employees with healthy recreation. Generously supported by the brewery, and with a large workforce to choose from, the club thrived and in 1910 won both the Leinster Senior Cup and the Irish Intermediate Cup. The W. & R. Jacob & Co. biscuit factory, another of Dublin's largest employers, also spawned a successful team that played in the Leinster Junior League from 1914. One of their main rivals was Midland Athletic, founded in 1905 by employees of the Midland Great Western Railway based at the Broadstone depot in Dublin. In Dundalk, a railway and military town that attracted immigration from Britain and Ulster, rail workers founded the Dundalk GNR (Great Northern Railway) Football Club in 1885 to play rugby but switched in the 1890s to the association code and from 1906 played in the local Dundalk and District League.[45]

Most employers encouraged these developments and, like their employees, took pride in defeating a rival firm or factory, or in winning one of the many inter-company competitions, which helped to raise staff morale and promote industrial harmony.[46] Although clubs could outgrow workplaces, their origins were often reflected in club emblems and the attitudes and language of the factory floor continued to influence the game's culture. There were, though, trade unionists who were wary of works' teams supported and subsidised by major employers, seeing them as an attempt to sugar-coat exploitation and undermine class loyalty. This was echoed by a general suspicion of professional football by some on the political left, who condemned it as another opiate of the masses: a sporting circus orchestrated by the rich and powerful to distract workers from the grim realities of their lives and dissipate energies that might otherwise be harnessed by the labour movement.[47] However, such views risked alienating the class that socialists sought to represent and rather underestimated working-class discernment. Supporting a football club (even one established by employers) did not preclude supporting a trade union or a left-wing political party. During union marches and demonstrations, the flags and favours of football teams were often displayed to affirm local loyalties. Pride in the prowess and fighting spirit of a local team tended to buttress social solidarity, and football stadiums built in the hearts of working-class districts hosted a variety of social functions and formed important communal focal points.[48]

Some employers and clergymen who promoted association football did so for social or moral reasons, in the hope that it would encourage contact and friendships between those of differing classes and allegiances. People of varying backgrounds often came together on the pitch, in the committee room and on the terraces, though the game could also aggravate rather than overcome deeply held political and religious differences, and it made a significant contribution to the growing rivalry between Dublin and Belfast.

*** *** ***

As the seat of the British administration in Ireland and home to the country's social, legal and military elite, Dublin had a strong sense of itself as a capital city, which its inhabitants proudly proclaimed 'the second city of the Empire'. However, in terms of economic and commercial activity, Dublin fell far behind the industrial dynamos of Manchester, Birmingham, Glasgow and Belfast. Its manufacturing sector was dominated by the brewing, distilling and food processing industries, with well-established firms such as Guinness and W. & R. Jacob providing steady employment for some of the more fortunate of the city's manual workers. However, its economy relied more on moving than making goods, and few of its dockers, carters, hawkers, messengers and shop assistants enjoyed secure or well-paid jobs. In 1891, Dublin was overtaken in population by Belfast, which was, by some way, Ireland's leading manufacturing city, with thriving textile, tobacco, rope-making, engineering and shipbuilding industries that provided a range of employment opportunities. Belfast was the world's largest linen producer, a 'Linenopolis' that exported high-quality goods across the globe. Its shipbuilding industry was also of worldwide significance: by 1914 the city's Harland & Wolff shipyard employed over 12,000 men, and even its smaller competitor Workman, Clark & Co. had

10,000. The proportion of skilled workers was high, roughly a quarter of the male workforce, and they earned wages among the best in the UK. Belfast's employers and workers alike were proud of its industrial might and scoffed at Dublin's beer and biscuits economy, dismissing it as the second city of Ireland rather than the empire.[49]

Housing conditions were also generally better in Belfast. Its nineteenth-century back-to-back houses were small and basic, but they provided better accommodation than the decaying tenements of Dublin. Belfast was no workers' paradise: working hours were long (especially in textile mills), the labour often hard and monotonous, and trade unions were mostly weak. From May to November 1907 it experienced a bitter and occasionally violent strike of dock workers that spread to carters, coal-men and even members of the Royal Irish Constabulary (RIC), but employers held the line and the strikers gained little. However, the city's manual workers generally fared better than their Dublin counterparts. With its industrial economy and tightly knit working-class communities, Belfast was closer to the manufacturing towns of northern England and the west of Scotland. Workers moved regularly between Belfast, Clydeside and Merseyside in pursuit of better opportunities, and an interest in football, whether as a player or spectator, provided a ready means of making new friends and contacts.

The widely held belief of Belfast-based IFA officials that southerners were simply not 'men of business' reinforced their determination to keep control of the game in their own hands and provided another way to assert the city's superiority over Dublin. Across Europe, the founding of successful football clubs allowed thriving manufacturing centres to challenge the status of capital cities. Industrial cities provided a larger reservoir from which to draw working-class players and followers, and local elites were keen to act as patrons, as the rural gentry had done with other sports in the past. Just like Glasgow, Manchester, Liverpool and Milan, Belfast regarded itself as a thrusting, dynamic city that had overtaken the complacent national capital in sporting as well as industrial achievements.[50]

Soccer's popularity in Belfast added to that region's distinctiveness and was cited by some southern nationalists as evidence of its alien character.[51] Even soccer supporters in the South believed that the IFA was more anxious to cultivate links with England and Scotland than it was to spread the game throughout Ireland. After 1900, crowds at international games and cup finals staged in Dublin were similar to those in Belfast, but the IFA refused to cede any administrative control or try to develop the game more widely.[52] The Leinster FA complained that the IFA 'had done more to retard than advance the game in the province of Leinster. The latter had to make her own way, and work out her salvation as best she could.'[53] The situation outside Leinster was even worse, with Belfast clubs reluctant to venture beyond Dublin and incur heavy expenses to play against unproven teams in distant places such as Cork, Limerick and Waterford.

There were frequent disagreements between North and South over procedural and disciplinary matters, particularly on the vexed issue of Sunday football. The rules of the Protestant-dominated IFA prohibited playing on Sunday, but Leinster delegates argued that Sunday play was the norm in most of the country and would greatly assist the spread of the game. At the IFA annual general meeting (AGM) in Belfast in 1898, the Leinster FA sponsored a proposal to allow Sunday football, but this was rejected out of hand. Southerners claimed that the IFA's inflexible attitude was handing the initiative to the GAA, which generally played its matches on Sunday. The question was raised again in 1904, this time by Belfast Celtic backed by the Leinster clubs, but was again rejected.[54]

The Leinster FA chaffed at Belfast's administrative dominance and regularly complained that it was under-represented on the IFA Council. Its protests eventually had some effect: in 1900 the IFA Council was reformed to give the Antrim FA six of twelve seats, with Dublin receiving three and the North-West FA receiving the remaining three (the Antrim FA had the casting vote in the event of a tie).[55] The Dublin *Freeman's Journal* noted approvingly that the control of association football was no longer a monopoly of Belfast and that some recognition had been given to the game's growing popularity in the South. It welcomed the fact that for the first time the IFA's AGM was to be held in Dublin and was thereafter to be rotated among Dublin, Derry and Belfast.[56] In 1905 the IFA made another attempt to conciliate southerners, by holding the AGM of the

IFAB (rotated annually by the four UK associations) in Killarney, County Kerry, the only occasion when it was held outside of Ulster.

The question of professionalism also caused tensions. After the IFA had sanctioned the paying of players from 1895, most of the leading clubs in Belfast had turned professional. However, the game elsewhere was not popular enough to support professional clubs, and it would be 1905 before the Leinster FA followed suit. This contributed to the glaring difference in quality between Belfast and Dublin teams, vividly shown by Linfield's 10–1 victory over Bohemians in the 1895 IFA Cup final. *The Freeman's Journal* noted that the superior training and passing skills of the northern professionals prevailed over the 'undisciplined play' of Bohemians.[57] But as the game grew in popularity in Dublin, its leading clubs became more competitive and began a genuine footballing rivalry between North and South. When Bohemians beat Linfield 1–0 in an Irish Cup tie in April 1899, the newspaper *Sport* rejoiced that Dublin's energetic rushing game could prevail over Belfast's more 'scientific' professional style.[58] The following year Bohemians managed to reach the Irish Cup final, only to lose to fellow amateurs Cliftonville. In 1901 another Dublin club, Freebooters, also contested the final; they too were beaten by Cliftonville. From 1902 Bohemians began to compete in the Irish League; Shelbourne followed suit in 1904 and became Dublin's first professional club a year later. Finally, in 1906, Shelbourne beat Belfast Celtic 2–0 in the Irish Cup final to take the trophy to Dublin for the first time. On its return to the capital the team was greeted by 6,000 people at Amiens Street station and bonfires were lit in Ringsend and Irishtown.[59] In 1908, the final was an all-Dublin affair, with Bohemians beating Shelbourne 3–1 after a replay, marking the capital's arrival as a genuine power base of the game. This was confirmed after Leinster beat Ulster 3–0 in 1909, their first victory in an inter-provincial match, and by another all-Dublin Irish Cup final in 1911. When Shelbourne played Glentoran in an Irish Cup tie in Belfast in February 1913, *Sport* noted the advances made by the game in the capital and claimed that footballing rivalry 'has assumed the proportion of a struggle between the two cities'.[60]

***

While club and inter-provincial competitions pitted North against South, the national team had the potential to bring the two regions together. This, however, was rarely the case: there continued to be considerable resentment in Dublin at the running of the team and this was aggravated by its poor results. Soccer followers in Dublin were always quick to question the IFA's national credentials: after Ireland lost narrowly 1–0 to England in Belfast in 1902, *The Freeman's Journal* asked why the Irish team played in blue shirts rather than the national green which it insisted inspired far greater pride among Irishmen.[61] (The IFA team would continue to play in shirts of St Patrick's blue until 1931.) There were also regular complaints that Dublin did not receive its fair share of international matches: the first did not take place until 1900, when England came to Lansdowne Road on 17 March. The game roused considerable public interest and was attended by the Lord Lieutenant Earl Cadogan and 7,000 supporters, who were entertained by the band of the RIC. Ireland, captained by George Sheehan of Bohemians (the only southern-based player on the team, alongside eight from Ulster and two from English clubs), played well but were beaten 2–0. This, however, was taken as an encouraging result (the previous year they had lost 13–2), *The Irish Times* noting the 'marked improvement' in the team's performance and describing it as 'the best game of football ever witnessed in Dublin'.[62] Dublin gradually received more international games, particularly after the opening in 1901 of Dalymount Park, which hosted Scotland in 1904, 1906 and 1908, but had to wait until 1912 to hold the prestige fixture against England. Of the forty-two home internationals played in Ireland between 1882 and 1914, only six took place in Dublin.

From 1900 there was a notable improvement in Ireland's results. Previously, the IFA international selection committee, dominated by officials of northern clubs, relied largely on Belfast-based players. Its refusal to consider Irishmen who played professionally with British clubs deprived the team of some of the country's best footballers. However, crushing defeats to England and Scotland in 1899 eventually prompted the committee to begin selecting cross-channel professionals. When these were released by their English clubs, they usually provided a sterner test for opponents. Ireland beat Wales six times between 1902 and 1914, defeated Scotland for the first time in 1903 (and again in 1910), drew with England in 1905 and 1910, and eventually beat England in 1913. In 1903, the Irish managed to share the championship with England and Scotland, and the following year consolidated their standing by finishing runner-up to England. Even with this upturn in their fortunes, by the end of the 1912/13 season Ireland had won just fourteen international games out of a total of ninety played, with eleven of those victories coming against Wales. The team's poor showing did little to popularise the game outside its heartlands, and the IFA's 1903 annual report admitted that 'our repeated and consistent failings in the international encounters exercise a derogatory effect on the progress of the game'.[63]

National morale though was much improved by Ireland's first victory over England, on 15 February 1913 at Windsor Park. *The Irish Times* reported that '20,000 Irishmen yelled themselves hoarse' as England were beaten by 'Hibernian dash and determination'.[64] Another Dublin paper put the victory down to the fact that the team was more representative of the island as a whole, captained by the Dubliner, Val Harris, backed up by three other southerners: Peter Warren, Dinny Hannon and Bill McConnell.[65] Ireland beat England again on 14 February 1914, winning 3–0 at Ayresome Park, Middlesbrough, which meant that it had beaten England, Scotland and Wales in home and away matches. The Dublin sporting press concluded that 'all things being equal, an Irishman is as good and in many cases better in sport than his more favoured confrères across the channel', and heaped praise on southern-born players, such as the Bohemians full-back Bill McConnell and the former Shelbourne legend Bill Lacey.[66] Lacey had scored twice in the 3–0 victory over England and performed further heroics when he played in goal to help his team draw 1–1 against Scotland in Belfast on 14 March 1914. Combined with victories over England and Wales, the draw was enough to clinch the British Championship outright for the first time, an achievement celebrated North and South. Throughout the UK there was a strong belief that the Championship was the world's pre-eminent football tournament, and it was noted that the Irish team 'has rightly been acclaimed the World's Association Football Champions'.[67]

Attendances at international matches rose tenfold, from a modest 1,000 to 2,000 in the early 1880s to 10,000 to 20,000 in the 1910s. In exceptional circumstances they could be even higher: over 30,000 saw Ireland draw with Scotland in Belfast in 1914, a record attendance for a soccer match in Ireland. Cross-channel professionals such as Bill Lacey, Mickey Hamill, Patrick O'Connell, Val Harris, Billy Gillespie and Louis Bookman became heroes to Irish supporters. For once the team was seen as representative of the country, rather than just the north-east: of the fifteen players who played for Ireland in their title-winning season, five were born in Belfast (Hamill, Fred McKee, Sam Young, Dave Rollo and Rab Nixon), five in Dublin (McConnell, O'Connell, Harris, Ted Seymour and Harry Hampton), and two in Galway (Sandy Craig and Frank Thompson); Lacey was from Enniscorthy and Gillespie from Donegal, while Bookman was born in Lithuania and grew up in Dublin.[68]

Bookman is a particularly notable figure. Born Louis Buckhalter into a Jewish family in 1890, he and his family fled anti-Semitic persecution in Lithuania in 1895 and settled in the 'Little Jerusalem' area of south Dublin, where his father, a rabbi, anglicised the family name and became a cantor at the Lennox Street synagogue. The young Louis played for the Dublin Jewish team Adelaide (named after the Adelaide Road synagogue) and as a skilful outside-left helped them win the All-Ireland Under-18 Football Cup in 1908. Although his parents disapproved of him playing on Saturday, the Jewish Sabbath, Louis saw the game as his way into Irish society and also played for Frankfort (formed in the Frankfort Cottages area off Amiens Street) in the Leinster Senior League. After a brief spell with Belfast Celtic in 1910, he joined Bradford City (1911–14), becoming the first Jewish professional footballer to play in the English First Division. In Ireland's championship-winning season, he appeared in the 2–1 victory over Wales on 1 January 1914 and made a further three international appearances in 1921. He was also an accomplished cricketer who appeared in nine first-class matches for Ireland (1920–30). Always deeply proud to have represented his adopted country, he finished his football career with Shelbourne (1924–5) and until his death in 1943 had a small jeweller's shop in Pearse Street,

Dublin, where there was a standing invitation for fans to drop in and chat about the game.[69]

By 1914 British Championship games were keenly anticipated events in the sporting calendar that provided regular opportunities to express national pride and distinctiveness. The IFA team may have played in blue shirts, but these were emblazoned with a large crest of the head of a Celtic cross decorated with a harp and shamrocks. Although its most committed supporters were northern unionists, they were nonetheless 'prepared to display both a conspicuous Irish patriotism and a measured anti-Englishness'.[70] This, though, did little to undermine their identification with Britain. National rivalries were contained within the boundaries of the UK, whose component parts saw themselves as 'the four peoples, deserving of the title of the football nations'.[71] British identity was highlighted by flying the Union flag at all games, the attendance of members of the royal family or their representatives, and the playing of 'God Save the King' as the national anthem of all four countries. Most Irish unionists (just like those in Scotland and Wales) held complementary identities that allowed them to take great pleasure in beating England while at the same time celebrating the common cultural and sporting values that bound the UK together.

* * *

As nationalist politics settled down after the reunification of the IPP in 1900, a new generation of leaders was transforming the GAA into a more open broad-based organisation. While the new leadership distanced itself from physical force nationalism in an effort to attract mass support and clerical endorsement, it strongly affirmed the association as part of the broader nationalist cultural movement and gave precedence to promoting the uniquely Irish games of Gaelic football and hurling over its earlier concern with athletics. Rules excluding crown forces and those who played or watched the 'foreign games' of cricket, hockey, rugby and soccer that had been allowed to lapse during the 1890s were reinstated incrementally between 1901 and 1905.[72] One Munster Gaelic enthusiast characterised this as a declaration of war on English games, which he claimed 'were made to feel the shock so heavily that, one by one, soccer and rugby clubs began to disappear. In a few years there was not as much as a soccer ball outside the British garrison, in Cork County'. The resurgence of the GAA in Munster was so successful that by 1907 there were only ten clubs affiliated to the IFA in the province, compared with the GAA's 270.[73]

Many in the GAA believed that the association had a duty to 'de-Anglicise' Ireland. The call had first been made in a seminal address by the Gaelic scholar Douglas Hyde in 1892 when he observed that Irish sentiment 'continues to apparently hate the English, and at the same time continues to imitate them'. Hyde maintained that the only way to reverse Anglicisation was to recover as much as possible of Ireland's unique heritage, including its language, placenames, folklore, music, manners, customs and pastimes, and he praised the founding of the GAA as 'an enormous step in the direction of Irish nationhood'.[74] His address was a rallying cry for Irish Irelanders (the name often given to cultural nationalists) to adopt a holistic nationalism and GAA matches were increasingly accompanied by cultural displays, such as Irish music, dancing and poetry recitations.

By harnessing popular nationalist sentiment, while downplaying its earlier Fenian associations, the GAA attracted growing support, including the approval and assistance of much of the Catholic clergy. Both found common ground in extolling the virtues of the past and warning of the insidious moral dangers of foreign influences. Catholic priests often encouraged the foundation of GAA clubs and many sat on county boards; Gaelic games became the dominant sports in many Catholic schools and colleges.[75] The GAA was more democratic in its organisational structures than most other sporting bodies, including the IFA and IRFU, which tended to be dominated by small cliques of administrators, and it effectively used parish and county structures to establish itself throughout the country. (Soccer clubs in contrast were generally based around a more heterogeneous range of allegiances.) A network of county, provincial and national committees and regular congresses gave the GAA considerable popular vitality, but also ensured that much of its energy was absorbed by public disputes and controversies.

Among these points of contention were the very rules of Gaelic games. There was a recognition that Gaelic football in particular needed to be made more attractive to both players and spectators. Players rarely took up set positions, but contested for the ball in packs, and with no off-side rule, goalmouth melées were common. One former player complained in 1902 that it was being overtaken by 'the English game of association football' because 'the English game is safer and more scientific than Gaelic', and called for rule changes to make it less physical and more free-flowing.[76] Innovations such as the adoption of a lighter ball and greater use of the hand pass helped speed up play and in 1913 teams were reduced to fifteen players; goalmouth congestion was eased by the introduction of a 'square' into which outfielders could not enter without the ball. Gaelic football became a better game to play and watch and by 1914 was probably the most widely played team sport in the country.

Its adherents often claimed that not only was it a far superior game to association football, but that those who played soccer colluded in their country's cultural subordination. Soccer players were accused of social snobbery on the one hand for copying the pastimes of their colonial masters, and on the other of debasing themselves by playing a game popular with 'the lowest scum of England'.[77] The Sinn Féin founder, Arthur Griffith, claimed that soccer had been 'framed in accordance with the emasculated conditions of the Lancashire millhand' and was therefore unsuitable for the 'vigorous Gaelic temperament'.[78] Soccer was also dismissed as mercenary in motivation, with professional sportsmen seen as morally inferior to GAA amateurs, who played solely for the love of the game. For some, this illustrated the spiritual and sporting nature of the Gael, compared with the materialism and narrow self-interest of the English and their soccer-playing imitators, whose game was described by one nationalist as a 'gladiatorial pastime' that provided spectators with a 'pleasure of the lowest and least intellectual type'.[79] Such criticisms were echoed by the nationalist journalist D.P. Moran, who also argued that sports such as soccer and rugby were an integral part of British imperialist domination and that the close ties between the IFA and its English counterpart formed 'another link of the already too strong and heavy chain which binds us to the Saxon'.[80]

The connections between soccer and the British military formed another line of attack. From the 1890s army teams were among the best in the country, with the Gordon Highlanders beating Cliftonville to win the Irish Cup in 1890 and the Black Watch and Sherwood Foresters reaching the final in 1892 and 1897 respectively.[81] In 1899, the IFA welcomed the affiliation of the Army Association and acknowledged its role in introducing the game in the south of the country.[82] By this time most military sides had withdrawn from top-level football in Ireland (primarily because of the demands of the Boer War), but they continued to play in provincial and junior competitions, and military involvement in the game remained widespread: civilian teams employed army instructors for physical training, referees were often drawn from local regiments and military bands played at important matches. Outside of the north-east, however, army teams were not always welcomed and were occasionally excluded from competitions by the Leinster FA. Their facilities and opportunities for training were thought to give them an unfair advantage, and their winning of trophies ahead of civilian teams was often resented. These tensions would increase as the country became more politically polarised and nationally minded soccer supporters sought to keep their distance from the British state and its agents.[83]

Conflicts over sport were not unique to Ireland. Nationalists in other European countries also condemned association football as an alien import that insidiously advanced British cultural influence. German nationalists dubbed it 'the English disease' and advised their patriotic countrymen to stick to gymnastics, considered more suited to the national character, while Italians made a point of naming it 'calcio' to claim descent from the indigenous 'calcio Fiorentino', a form of no-holds-barred folk football played in Florence from the sixteenth century.[84] Ireland, though, was unique in having a popular nationalist sporting association that strongly discouraged playing soccer and promoted an alternative form of football. At its 1901 Annual Congress, the GAA pledged itself 'to resist by every means in their power, the extension of English pastimes to this country' and exhorted the 'young men of Ireland not to identify themselves with rugby or association football, or any form of imported sport'.[85] Sport became an important battleground in Ireland's culture wars, with many Irish Irelanders equating British sports with British rule. One GAA enthusiast argued that 'Next to language the distinctive games of a people are the purest indication of their nationality.' Enthusiasm for Gaelic games and the Irish language often went hand in hand, even if many found it easier to master the former.[86]

Gaelic football's kinship to soccer did mean that players could move with relative ease between the codes. Jock Kirwan, who won an FA Cup medal with Tottenham Hotspur in 1901, also won an All-Ireland Gaelic Football senior championship medal with Dublin in 1904; and Val Harris won an All-Ireland Championship with Dublin in 1903 before going on to play professional football with Shelbourne and Everton and captain the Ireland team that beat England in 1913. The similarity of the two games could, however, cause confusion, illustrated by a dispute in a match played in March 1913 by the attendants of Monaghan District Lunatic Asylum. Uncertain whether to play by association or Gaelic football rules, they eventually decided on the former, but when an advocate of Gaelic football illegally caught the ball, he was struck by an opponent. This led to a stand-up fight in which the two attendants traded blows until separated by one of the asylum's patients. When the matter later came before the resident medical superintendent, he decided that, to avoid further trouble, only Gaelic football should be played in the asylum as it was more likely to appeal to patients who enjoyed catching and handling the ball.[87]

✳✳✳

The political backdrop to the years 1912–14 was one of growing animosity between nationalists and unionists as the prospect of Home Rule for Ireland loomed. Politics was never too far from people's minds and could spill over into popular gatherings such as football matches. The IFA regularly proclaimed that politics had no place in sport, but reality often contradicted its rhetoric. The association was dominated by Belfast unionist businessmen and professionals, and its senior honorary positions were invariably filled by members of the unionist aristocracy. In 1897, Major Spencer Chichester (third son of the Marquess of Donegall) was succeeded as IFA president by the former lord lieutenant of Ireland (1886–9) and staunch Tory Charles Stewart Vane-Tempest Stewart, the 6th Marquess of Londonderry. Some southern Home Rulers, who recalled the IFA's refusal in 1892 to appoint Thomas Sexton, the Nationalist Party MP for West Belfast, as a vice-president of the association, saw this as a provocative and divisive decision.[88] Years later, nationalists were also alienated by the association's strongly imperial stance during the Boer war, in particular its decision to appoint as senior IFA vice-presidents the Irish-born Field Marshal Lord Roberts, the British commander-in-chief in South Africa, and General Sir George White, commander of the besieged garrison at Ladysmith, neither of whom was known to have any great interest in the game.[89]

Political divisions in Ireland intensified after the general election of 1910. Irish nationalists won the balance of power in the House of Commons and demanded a devolved parliament as the price for supporting a Liberal government. After two years of bitter wrangling the Liberals managed to curb the power of the Tory-dominated House of Lords, clearing the way for Home Rule. On 8 February 1912 Winston Churchill, then a leading Liberal minister, had intended to speak in favour of Home Rule at the Ulster Hall in Belfast. When unionists managed to thwart him, the nationalist MP Joe Devlin secured the use of Celtic Park in west Belfast. Angry unionists protested outside the ground but were unable to prevent Churchill from speaking. Celtic's stadium had, however, been irreparably politicised and in subsequent years would be used for other Home Rule rallies and the drilling of nationalist Volunteers.

When Celtic and Linfield met on 14 September 1912, they drew a crowd of 20,000 to Celtic Park (then the largest in the history of the Irish League), many of whom were primed for a political rather than a sporting confrontation. National flags and political banners were prominently displayed, and provocative songs and slogans traded. Fights broke out on the terraces and spread onto the pitch; hails of stones and 'Belfast confetti' (assorted nuts, bolts and rivets scooped up in the shipyards) were hurled and some rioters even discharged revolvers into the crowd. About 100 people were injured, many seriously, including several with gunshot wounds. The game was abandoned and teams locked in their dressing rooms for their safety. The trouble spread to local shipyards and factories, where Catholic workers were intimidated and attacked.[90]

The riot forced the IFA to convene an emergency meeting on 18 September and publish 'A Manifesto to the Football Public', which gave notice that no banners, flags or other emblems would be permitted at any football ground under their jurisdiction, and that any supporters found with firearms or explosives would be ejected and handed over to the police.[91] In December 1912 the IFA Management Committee further ruled that 'in all future League and City Cup games where revolver firing is resorted to by spectators, such games are to be abandoned and the replays to take place behind closed gates'. This had some effect, but crowd disorders continued up to the outbreak of the Great War, often accompanied by 'the inevitable demonstration of revolver music'.[92]

Such disturbances were not confined to Belfast. Crowd violence at a game in Derry in May 1912 between Institute and Derry Guilds also appears to have had political or sectarian roots. Institute had been founded in 1905 by the local Presbyterian Working Men's Institute, while Guilds had emerged from the Derry Catholic Young Men's Society. After a fight broke out between two players, it spread to the terraces and caused a full-scale riot. This had longer-term consequences: six months later Protestant clubs broke away from the Derry & District League to form their own City of Derry and District (Protestant) Alliance, dividing the game in the city along sectarian lines.[93] Soccer matches also provided the opportunity for political demonstrations in Dublin. When Scotland played at Dalymount Park on 15 March 1913, just two months after the Home Rule bill had been rejected in the Lords, the crowd of 12,000 gave the viceroy, Lord Aberdeen, a cool reception and the civilian band hired for the game refused to play 'God Save the King' (a British military band stepped in at the last moment). Such displays were a reminder to the government that nationalist loyalty could not be taken for granted and that there should be no back-sliding on Home Rule. However, they also confirmed the IFA's worst suspicions of southern disloyalty, and its international team would never again host a match in Dublin.[94]

Despite the Dalymount crowd's clear nationalist sympathies, most Irish nationalist politicians still kept their distance from association football. Victory over England in successive years in 1913–14 and winning the British Championship could possibly have been used to illustrate how a Home Rule Ireland could assert its own identity while remaining an integral part of the UK. The IPP, though, was wary of identifying too closely with soccer, probably fearing that it would allow Irish-Ireland opponents to tar them as West Britons. While leading IPP figures such as Joe Devlin in Belfast and Tim Harrington in Dublin were keen soccer supporters, recognising its popularity among their constituents, the party as a whole derived much of its influence from agrarian agitation and identified more with rural than with urban Ireland. There was therefore no attempt to use the national team as a rallying point, suggesting that soccer in 1914 was still seen by many nationalists as a sectional rather than a national sport, most strongly entrenched in the part of the country standing in the way of Home Rule.[95]

Even if more nationalist politicians had managed to overcome their misgivings about soccer's foreign origins and unionist links, it probably would have done little to bridge divisions. From 1913 the political crisis intensified, as both Ulster unionists and Irish nationalists created mass volunteer armies and imported thousands of rifles in spring and summer 1914. The country appeared to be heading for civil war, until events in Ireland were overtaken by those in Europe. The assassination of the Austrian Archduke Franz Ferdinand in Sarajevo on 28 June 1914 triggered a chain reaction of military mobilisations and declarations of war that within weeks drew in all of Europe's great powers, including the UK.

3

Things Fall Apart:
Conflict and Division 1914–21

After the outbreak of war in August 1914, the UK football authorities adopted the prevailing attitude of 'business as usual': international matches were suspended but the main club competitions continued as before. This stemmed partly from the widespread expectation that the war was likely to be short, and the difficulties of winding down a professional sport in which players were under contract. The move contrasted with that of the rugby union associations, including the IRFU, who immediately suspended all their main competitions for the duration of the war. The decision of the association football authorities to carry on was widely denounced. As British forces struggled to withstand German attacks on the Western Front in November 1914, an editorial from the unionist *Irish Times* noted that 'the streets of Dublin and Belfast are full of youths who are not in uniform' and complained that large crowds were attending football matches while under-manned army units were 'fighting desperately and dying grandly in the trenches of Flanders'.[1] In their defence, the football authorities argued that their sport provided ideal opportunities for further recruitment. Well-attended football matches were indeed magnets to recruiting officers, who repeatedly invoked the metaphor of 'The Great Game'; recruiting posters and leaflets proclaimed: 'Forwards wanted. No backs. Play up.'[2]

Among the tens of thousands of Irishmen who flocked to the colours in the early months of the war were footballers from all codes.

By December 1914 Bohemian FC had already contributed forty current and former players.[3] Those who joined up included some well-known Irish internationals, such as Billy Gillespie, Ireland's goal-scoring hero in the 1914 Championship, who served in France as a gunner in the Irish Horse Artillery (a harrowing experience that caused him to go prematurely bald). The action of such well-known figures was reported prominently in newspapers to encourage others to follow their example. It was estimated that half of the 20,000 men who enlisted in Belfast in 1914 were football supporters, while 1,400 followers of Glenavon FC in Lurgan were said to have joined up by early 1915. Within eighteen months more than half of the latter were killed, wounded or missing.[4] The IFA took considerable pride in their actions, noting in 1915 that 'the sport of association football in this country has made a really magnificent contribution to Kitchener's new armies'.[5]

'Business as usual' though could not stand the strains of prolonged war. At all levels the constant drain of young men undermined clubs and many folded. Even established ones such as Belfast Celtic, Linfield and Cliftonville lost many of their best players and found it difficult to field teams. By 1915 the number of clubs affiliated to the IFA had fallen from a pre-war figure of 393 to 221, while affiliates to the Leinster FA had fallen by half to about seventy. Crowds attending matches also declined and professional clubs struggled to pay wages. Fixtures were cut back, and the four UK associations voted to end all national competitions after the playing of the English FA Cup final on 24 April 1915. (The IFA was the only dissenting voice, continuing to cite the usefulness of matches for recruitment purposes.) The Irish League suspended operations from 1915 and was replaced by regional leagues in Belfast and District, Leinster and Munster. Matches continued in the Irish Cup (the sole national competition), Belfast City Cup, Leinster Senior League and various junior leagues. Less competition and a depleted pool of players caused the standard of football to decline and attendances at games in Dublin fell sharply during 1917–18.[6] With so many footballers in uniform, the strong military involvement in soccer revived and there were more games between army and civilian teams. The fundraising capacity of the game was exploited to the full and benefit games for soldiers' hospitals and charities were played regularly in Belfast and Dublin. Sometimes these had a national character, such as the game between Irish and Scottish regiments at Lansdowne Road on 14 April 1917 that featured several leading Scottish professionals. Rather more novel was a charity fundraising match between the top jockeys of Ireland and England played at Dalymount Park on 1 December 1917 that had the added attraction of a donkey derby at half-time.[7] Soccer provided a welcome distraction at the Front as well as at home. A Dublin officer serving in an Ulster regiment noted that the men rarely spoke of politics or Home Rule and that football was the main topic in their letters home. Newspapers featured stories of soldiers kicking footballs before them as they advanced into no-man's-land, while reports of matches played under the shadow of enemy guns reinforced the image of the happy-go-lucky Tommy bearing all his dangers and hardships with stoicism and good humour.[8]

The war gave a considerable boost to women's football, which had enjoyed some popularity among upper- and middle-class women in the 1890s before fizzling out. Women factory workers had long engaged in informal games during their breaks and, as their numbers grew during the war, female munitions workers in Britain and Ireland began to form more permanent teams and their own local leagues. As standards improved, their games began to attract substantial crowds. In late 1917, the Irish international Bill 'Offside' McCracken (1883–1979) helped arrange a match in Belfast between English and Irish 'munitionettes' to raise money for war charities. (McCracken's main claim to fame is that as a Newcastle United defender (1904–24) he became so adept at using the offside rule to frustrate opposition attacks (and opposing supporters) that in 1925 the International Board reduced the number of players required to play a forward onside from three to two.) The Irish players came from two existing teams, the Lurgan Blues and the Belfast Whites, while the English came from several different factory teams in the north-east. Billed as 'North of Ireland Ladies versus Tyneside Ladies', the game was played at Distillery's Grosvenor Park on 26 December 1917 and was watched by a crowd of 20,000 spectators who saw the English team win 4–1. Although not sanctioned by either the English FA or IFA, it has sometimes been considered the 'very first all-women's international'. Another match between the two sides held at St James's Park in Newcastle on 21 September 1918 drew a smaller crowd of 2,000.[9]

***

In the first year of the war, 80,000 Irishmen volunteered to serve with the British forces. However, by the autumn of 1915 enlistment was tailing off drastically as news sank in of the slaughter on the Western Front and at Gallipoli. The resurgence of nationalist feeling sparked by the 1916 Easter Rising diminished it further, and by the spring of 1918 the government planned to implement conscription in Ireland, as it had already done elsewhere in the UK. By this time most young Irishmen had no wish to play the 'Great Game', particularly away from home, and they prepared to resist; thousands joined the revived Irish Volunteers and support for Sinn Féin rose dramatically. After the European war ended, Sinn Féin won an overwhelming majority in the general election of December 1918 and convened the first meeting of an independent parliament, Dáil Éireann, on 21 January 1919. It declared the establishment of an Irish Republic and called for international recognition and support for Irish national independence. At the same time a unit of the Irish Volunteers (soon to be known as the IRA) shot dead two policemen at Soloheadbeg in County Tipperary, sparking an armed conflict that would last until July 1921.

Cultural conflict also raged in these years and arguments about national allegiance and identity took on a keener edge. As the conscription crisis deepened in May 1918, J.J. Walsh, honorary president of the Cork GAA, deplored that the same number (4,000) had attended a soccer match in Dublin as had attended a GAA hurling final. This moved him to ask: 'are we at war with England or are we not?'[10] During these years some GAA members saw the association as the sporting wing of Sinn Féin and condemned Irishmen who played non-native sports as traitors. Eoin O'Duffy, secretary of the GAA's Ulster council and commander of the IRA's Monaghan Brigade, denounced

soccer as 'the game of the foreigner' and claimed that 'the enemies of
Irish freedom patronise and finance it. Ireland asks her sons to play
and support our national games, and her enemies ask you to play
and support soccer – make your choice'.[11] Some seized on the rise in
national feeling as an opportunity to see off sporting competitors, with
the GAA Central Council exhorting county boards 'to take advantage
of the present feeling of the country ... with the object of completely
wiping out soccer'.[12] In response many soccer supporters feared for the
game's future, one noting 'there is an undercurrent to kill soccer here.
Hysteria is a dreadful disease when it grips the minds of otherwise
sensible people.'[13]

In later years some in the GAA would regularly claim that it had
nurtured the separatist ideals that had led to independence and that its
sportsmen had formed the backbone of the military campaign. In 1922,
J.J. Walsh, then postmaster general, told the Dáil that GAA members
'had been the principal contributors in the fight against England. I
think you will agree with that'.[14] This claim was not without foundation.
In 1913–14 GAA clubs contributed significant numbers to the newly
founded Irish Volunteers, with GAA president James Nowlan advising
every member to join and 'learn to shoot straight'.[15] GAA clubs often
served as recruiting grounds for the IRB and Volunteers, and after 1916
as fronts for Volunteer units. GAA matches were commonly used to
raise funds for republican prisoners and their dependants, and leading
revolutionaries such as Walsh, Harry Boland, Austin Stack and Eoin
O'Duffy were all closely involved in the GAA. They saw the association
as a powerful rallying-point that enabled nationalists to declare their
commitment to political separatism and their exclusive allegiance to
Gaelic culture. At a meeting of the GAA central council in April 1919,
Boland declared that the association 'owed its position to the fact that
it had always drawn the line between the garrison and the Gael', a claim
repeated by Michael Collins before the Leinster hurling final at Croke
Park on 11 September 1921.[16]

By the time Collins spoke, the GAA was inextricably bound up with
the events of 'Bloody Sunday', 21 November 1920. After the shooting
dead of fourteen suspected British intelligence agents in Dublin, crown

forces entered Croke Park and opened fire on a crowd watching a Gaelic football match, shooting dead thirteen spectators and one player, Michael Hogan of Tipperary, and wounding dozens of others. The atrocity became a defining event in the association's history, adding the GAA's own martyrs to the national pantheon, and would later be cited as evidence of the GAA's superior nationalist credentials.

Recently, however, some historians have cautioned against iden-tifying the GAA too closely with the independence struggle. While Dublin Castle often regarded the association as a Fenian front, its members included the apolitical, the apathetic and moderate Home Rulers as well as republican separatists, and there were many for whom social and recreational motives were more important than politics or cultural nationalism.[17] After the foundation of the Irish Volunteers in November 1913, some GAA clubs joined up en masse, but many held aloof and some officials refused to allow pitches, including Croke Park, to be used for drilling. When the Volunteers split in September 1914 after John Redmond's appeals to support the British war effort, most GAA members, like most Irish nationalists generally, backed Redmond, and many joined the British Army. Early historians of the GAA, however, preferred to concentrate on the far smaller number who fought with the Volunteers in 1916. About 300 of the approximately 1,800 insurgents were GAA members, mostly from a handful of highly politicised clubs. Seventeen of Dublin's seventy GAA clubs did not contribute a single participant, and many contributed three or fewer. After the Rising, the British government's Official Commission of Inquiry cited the GAA as one of the nationalist organisations behind it, leading to the internment of many GAA members (most innocent of any involvement). At the time, though, the GAA denied any responsibility for the Rising and issued a statement contradicting claims that it had assisted the Volunteers.[18] However, as separatist ideals gained broader currency, they naturally grew stronger in the GAA. On Sunday 4 August 1918 the association's decision to flout a government ban on public meetings by simultaneously playing matches across the country provided a nationwide demonstration of defiance. This though was as far as the association went, and it was significant that as the War of

Independence intensified and the Gaelic League, Sinn Féin, Cumann na mBan and the Irish Volunteers were all proscribed in November 1919, the GAA was allowed to carry on.

The more the political crisis intensified, the more soccer followers found themselves on the defensive, parrying accusations that their 'garrison game' encouraged fraternisation with the enemy and reinforced the British connection. The taunt clearly stung nationally minded soccer supporters, who insisted that their choice of sport did not define their patriotism. From 1917 the Leinster FA had tried to discourage games between civilian and military teams, and objected to the latter's admission to its competitions.[19] As civil unrest deepened, this opposition grew and in October 1920 the Leinster FA formally excluded military teams from the Leinster Junior Cup.[20] That same month the association made a point of cancelling all its games after the death on hunger strike of the republican Terence MacSwiney in October 1920, while the Leinster Junior Alliance of clubs moved a vote of sympathy to the relatives of six republican prisoners (some of whom were soccer players) hanged in Mountjoy Jail on 14 March 1921.[21]

Peadar S. Doyle, an Irish Volunteer sergeant who fought in the 1916 Rising, recalled that his comrades had a wide range of vocational and sporting backgrounds: 'They came from the staff of the Abbey Theatre, as well as from the ranks of the trades unions. There were soccer, and football and rugby men.'[22] Among the most prominent of the IRA's soccer men was Oscar Traynor, born into a strongly nationalist family in Dublin in 1886. As a young man, he played in goal for the Frankfort and Strandville clubs (both originating in the Amiens Street–North Strand area of Dublin), before moving to Belfast Celtic (1910–12) and took part in the club's tour of Bohemia in 1912. He fought in O'Connell Street during the Easter Rising and in 1920 became commander of the IRA's Dublin Brigade and a central figure in directing its operations in the capital, including the attack on the Custom House in May 1921.[23] One of his comrades was Robert 'Bob' Briscoe (1894–1969), a key IRA staff officer during the War of Independence who was later a vice-president of the Leinster FA.[24] Another member of the IRA's Dublin Brigade was Todd Andrews, a follower of Bohemian FC who regarded

Dalymount Park as his 'spiritual home'. His brother Paddy played league football with Bohemians and became a Free State international, while Todd himself was a tough-tackling right-half who captained University College Dublin (UCD) to a Collingwood Cup win in 1926. His nationalist sympathies briefly led him to play Gaelic football for Terenure Sarsfields, but he never really took to the game, dismissively claiming that it required only three skills: 'a capacity to field a ball, ability to kick it high and hard in the direction of goal, and at least elementary boxing skills'.[25] After receiving a suspension for practising the last of these, he quit Gaelic games for good.

There were also numerous less well-known figures. Traynor noted that soccer was often the game of choice of imprisoned republicans throughout the struggle and that when detained in Frongoch camp in 1916, he was 'amazed at the number of old soccer colleagues who were daily appearing there'. He observed that while Dublin soccer clubs such as Shamrock Rovers, St James's Gate, Brideville, Avonmore, Drumcondra and Jacobs had been seriously depleted by post-Rising arrests, there was many a Dublin-based Gaelic football team 'whose membership was in no way impaired as a direct result of the Easter fight'.[26] This was perhaps to be expected. In Dublin the IRA's most active members came largely from the better-off working class – the same group acknowledged as the most enthusiastic followers of association football. As the national struggle became more intense and divisive, some switched to Gaelic football or hurling, but many saw no reason to do so. Gerald Boland, a Dublin IRA battalion commander whose father James and brother Harry both chaired the Dublin GAA County Board, believed that 'more than half of the Dublin Brigade of 1918–21 were soccer men'.[27]

***

Despite the political turmoil of these years, most people went about their everyday lives as best they could, working, socialising, playing and spectating as before. After the war, soccer in the South revived as returning servicemen swelled the pools of available players and supporters hungry for entertainment. A crowd of 8,000 turned out for a game between Bohemians and Shelbourne at Dalymount Park in January 1919, an attendance all the more remarkable given the strict public health warnings in force owing to the virulent Spanish influenza epidemic of 1918–19 that had already claimed thousands of victims in the city. Despite the continued health risks, matches between northern and southern teams became more frequent, adding some edge to competitions, and a crowd of 14,000 attended an Irish Cup semi-final between Shelbourne and Linfield at Dalymount in March 1919.[28] Although games against northern opposition were popular, Bohemians and Shelbourne did not rejoin the Irish League for the 1918/19 season, claiming that after the disruption of the war they were unable to field teams of the required standard. Their decision, and the troubled political situation, ensured that the competition did not go ahead. The main Belfast clubs continued to play in the Belfast and District League, while their Dublin counterparts confined themselves to the Leinster Senior League.[29]

The withdrawal of southern clubs from the Irish League reinforced the provincial fissures already apparent in Irish soccer before the war. This was aggravated by the contrasting fortunes of the game's governing bodies, North and South. During the war soccer had fared better in Belfast than elsewhere. The city's main professional clubs largely weathered the downturn of 1914–15 and afterwards thriving war-time industries boosted workers' incomes and kept up attendance. There was also an exodus of English and Scottish professionals to Belfast, and the local soccer public eagerly responded to the opportunity to see well-known players in action.[30] This helped the IFA to maintain its strong pre-war financial balance of almost £2,000. In contrast the Leinster and Munster associations struggled. A request in 1918 from the Leinster FA for a grant of £300 to clear its debts met a tight-fisted response, the IFA giving only £50. The Munster FA fared even worse: the IFA regarded it as defunct and refused to provide any support. Aggrieved southerners compared their treatment to the £100 earlier given to Glenavon FC. The IFA did provide an additional £200 to the Leinster FA the following year, but the delay in coming up with the money confirmed the latter's belief that it had little interest in the game outside the north-east and was not prepared to share fairly its substantial financial resources.[31]

Severe financial problems gave a sharper edge to the long-standing grievances of the southern associations. Requests by the Leinster FA to host British Championship matches in Dublin in October 1919 and January 1920 were turned down, and it received nothing from the bumper gate receipts paid by the 30,000 spectators who saw Ireland draw 1–1 with England at Windsor Park on 25 October 1919. Leinster also complained of the poor recognition given to its players: in the six games played by Ireland in the 1919/20 and 1920/1 British Championships, only one southern-based player was selected, despite strong performances by both Shelbourne and Bohemians against Belfast teams in the Irish Cup.[32] Leinster also had minimal representation on important IFA committees such as those dealing with finance and international team selection, which meant that southern representatives were easily outvoted and often saw no point in attending meetings in Belfast.[33] The Leinster FA claimed that soccer in Ireland was focused far too much on the interests of professional Belfast clubs and that not enough attention was given to grass-roots amateur and junior leagues outside the north-east, which were crucial for popularising and developing the game. In these circumstances, the IFA's decision in January 1921 to move both Junior and Intermediate Cup semi-finals from Dublin to Belfast for security reasons seemed particularly insensitive and drove the two sides even further apart.[34]

During the post-war conflict football matches again provided ready opportunities to express political and sectarian allegiances, particularly in meetings between Belfast Celtic and its main rivals. Tensions came to a head at an Irish Cup semi-final against Glentoran on St Patrick's Day 1920 at Solitude in north Belfast, when rival supporters clashed; one discharged a revolver into the Glentoran crowd, wounding several people, including a police sergeant, and violence also spilled out onto nearby streets.[35] The IFA responded by abandoning the competition and awarding the Irish Cup to Shelbourne, who had already qualified for the final. The association put most of the blame on Celtic, fining the club and closing Celtic Park for a month, even though the riot had occurred at a neutral ground. More violent incidents followed and at the end of May 1920 the Celtic directors thought it best to withdraw from the Irish League and the main cup competitions and confine their efforts to the safer Falls Road League. It was a prescient decision: from the summer of 1920 civil disorder intensified in Belfast, and over the next two years widespread violence left hundreds dead and thousands injured.[36]

Violent scenes in football grounds were not confined to Belfast. When Ulster took a 5–0 lead against Leinster at Dalymount Park in October 1919, the home crowd invaded the pitch and assaulted an Ulster player. Cup games involving the leading Dublin and Belfast clubs were often tense affairs and, as both were increasingly reluctant to play outside their own cities, the Irish League was again postponed for the 1920/1 season.[37] The IFA was also wary of staging international games in Dublin, its reservations reinforced by an incident in February 1921 when the Ireland amateur team, composed mostly of northerners, played France in Paris. An IFA official noticed the presence of Irish tricolours (described as 'Sinn Féin flags') among the crowd and threatened to order the team off the pitch unless they were removed, which they were.[38] The decision was badly received in the South, with the *Irish Independent* noting that 'the greater number of the members of the Irish team hold evidently political opinions different from those of the majority of the Irish people'.[39] The ultra-nationalist *Catholic Bulletin* went considerably further, claiming that the incident showed the 'bitter anti-Irish atmosphere of association football' and the air of 'slavery in which all important association matches are played'.[40]

At the next meeting of the IFA council in March, the matter was raised by the Leinster official Larry Sheridan, who argued that insistence on the removal of the Irish tricolour risked undermining the game's fragile popularity in the South. In response his IFA colleagues accused him of engaging in party politics. While the IFA was always quick to deprecate the mixing together of politics and sport, the unionist sympathies of its leading figures were by this time even more pronounced than before the war. Captain James Wilton, who was the association's president (1914–45), had been a prominent member of the Ulster Volunteer Force (UVF) in Derry, while Thomas Moles, a member of the IFA council and its international selection committee, was close to the Unionist Party leader Sir Edward Carson and had helped to arm the UVF in 1914. Moles was also a unionist MP at Westminster (1918–29) and the Northern Ireland parliament (1921–37) and, as a leader writer for the *Belfast Telegraph*, was one of Ulster unionism's main champions.[41]

∗∗∗

From the summer of 1920 sporadic actions by the IRA gave way to a sustained campaign of attacks on RIC barracks; dozens of policemen were killed and many more resigned. Their ranks were filled by newly recruited 'Black and Tans' whose reckless indiscipline irrevocably alienated nationalist civilians. As the conflict intensified, unionists called for even stronger action to defeat the IRA. Addressing an Orange Order demonstration on 12 July 1920, Carson had declared that, if the British government was unable to protect loyal subjects, 'we will take the matter into our own hands'. This precipitated another series of concerted attacks on Catholic workers (and leftist Protestants) in Belfast shipyards and factories: thousands were forced out of their workplaces, hundreds injured and over a dozen killed. Two years of bloody sectarian violence followed.

In August 1920 the Dáil cabinet responded by ordering a boycott of Belfast businesses, driving a further wedge between North and South. By 1921 most of the nationalist population supported the separatist policies of Sinn Féin (the party won a massive majority in that year's national election) and were keen to assert their country's independence in all aspects of Irish life. The Leinster FA increasingly regarded the IFA as a biased, anti-national organisation and baulked at accepting its authority. (By then the Leinster FA was the only functioning provincial body outside of Ulster: the Munster FA no longer operated and the game in Connacht was loosely organised in local leagues.) In this polarised atmosphere a routine procedural dispute had serious and lasting consequences. After Shelbourne had drawn an Irish Cup

semi-final against Glenavon in Lurgan in March 1921, they expected
the replay to be held in Dublin. Glenavon though were unwilling to
travel south, citing violent incidents at a game against Shelbourne in
Dublin the previous year. They argued that serious disorder was even
more likely on this occasion, since three days after the proposed date
for the replay six republican prisoners were to be hanged in Dublin
on 14 March 1921. The IFA decided therefore that the game should be
replayed in Belfast. Shelbourne refused to travel, claiming that they too
feared for their safety since Belfast was no less troubled than Dublin.
Shelbourne's stance was supported by the Leinster FA, but the IFA was
unmoved and awarded the tie to Glenavon. Dubliners were outraged,
with the local *Sport* newspaper claiming that 'no greater insult has
been known in the annals of Irish football' and insisting that it would
be far better for Dublin clubs 'to be a self-contained and independent
association unit within small confines than to be the tail of a weak and
moribund association'.[42]

Amid rising suspicion and recrimination, the treatment of Shelbourne became a defining issue, crystallising long-held grievances and
confirming the belief of many southerners that the IFA would always
favour northern clubs.[43] At a meeting on 4 May 1921 the Leinster FA
proposed severing relations with Belfast, claiming that with so few
games being played between northern and southern clubs, its affiliation
to the IFA was effectively redundant and a new association would do
much more to develop the game outside the north-east. On 1 June
1921 eight leading Dublin clubs came together to form a new Football
League of Ireland. A week later at a council meeting on 8 June 1921 in
the Molesworth Hall in Dublin the Leinster FA proposed the creation
of an independent Football Association of Ireland (FAI), which was
formally founded ten days later. Its administrative structure was largely
that of the Leinster FA: Jack Ryder was appointed secretary, and the
newly appointed chairman, Robert Richey, wrote to Belfast to inform
the IFA of their action.[44] While the decision to secede was supported by
most Leinster clubs, some had misgivings. Dundalk, for example, which
drew players and support from the North, had no wish to cut itself
loose from the IFA. Neither did Bohemians and Shelbourne, Dublin's

two leading clubs, who feared the loss of lucrative games against Belfast rivals and the prospect of their players being denied selection for the national team.[45]

The IFA was taken unawares by the speed of Leinster's action. Over the years it had grown used to complaints from the South and believed that they could be appeased as in the past. To this end, it made some conciliatory gestures, offering Dublin the next IFA Senior and Intermediate Cup finals, which afterwards would alternate between Dublin and Belfast. It also offered to hold more international games in the capital, improve Leinster's representation on the IFA Council and discuss the rotation of council meetings between Dublin and Belfast. When southern officials rejected these concessions as insufficient, the IFA adopted a more coercive approach, warning the FAI that its affiliated clubs would be blacklisted. In an effort to crush the breakaway association at birth, the IFA successfully lobbied the English, Scottish and Welsh FAs to deny it any form of recognition: British clubs were prohibited from playing against any FAI affiliates and it would not be awarded any international fixtures.[46] The IFA also began to court the wavering Bohemian and Shelbourne clubs but, after some deliberation, both decided that it was impracticable to submit to an authority in another political jurisdiction and they joined the FAI in August 1921, agreeing to take part in its new league competition the following month. The FAI received a further boost when twenty-eight clubs from the Falls and District League in west Belfast applied to join and were accepted, which enabled it to present itself as an all-island association whose jurisdiction straddled the newly created political border.[47]

These developments ran parallel to the island's political partition. December 1920 saw the passing of the Government of Ireland Act which provided for the creation of separate twenty-six-county and six-county states each with their own devolved parliaments. Elections for these were held in May 1921, resulting in almost a clean sweep by Sinn Féin in the South (124 of 128 seats) and a clear majority by unionists in the North (40 of 52). On 7 June the northern assembly voted Sir James Craig prime minister of Northern Ireland, and its new parliament was officially opened on 22 June 1921 in Belfast City Hall by King George V.

While these events were not the direct cause of the split between the Dublin- and Belfast-based football authorities, they clearly influenced it, providing the Leinster FA with both example and opportunity. For its part, the IFA had no doubt that Leinster's action was political, its president James Wilton later claiming that 'the Dublin seceders are under the thrall of Sinn Féin politics, with its ridiculous motto of "Ourselves Alone"'.[48] The political partition of the island suggested to aggrieved southerners that its fractious sporting relationship with Belfast could be similarly resolved, and the Leinster FA eagerly seized the moment.

The question is often asked as to why association football split, while the administration of most other sports survived political partition and retained some level of all-Ireland organisation. For the GAA, Ireland's largest sporting organisation, the border imposed in 1921 was usually an irrelevance to its administration and competitions: it prided itself on being a thirty-two-county association, which was clearly facilitated by the fact that its games were largely confined to nationalists. But amicable relations could also be maintained in sports whose adherents differed in politics and allegiance, such as cricket, hockey and rugby. All were assisted by federated structures that allowed for local autonomy and minimised the potential for administrative friction. The Irish Hockey Union allowed considerable independence to its provincial associations and largely confined itself to the selection of international teams. To cater for players, officials and followers of all political persuasions, its international teams played under a four-provinces flag and adopted 'The Derry Air' as a national anthem. In the case of cricket, partition actually seems to have prompted closer ties, with the Irish Cricket Union and Northern Cricket Union uniting in 1923 under a representative committee to oversee international selection and the all-island dimension of the game.

Rugby was the sport with which association football was most often compared, its administrative unity often held up as a reproach to soccer's partitionist bickering. There were, however, significant differences among those who ran, played and watched the two games. Most of the leading officials of the IRFU, North and South, were upper-class, often Protestant and unionist. The IRFU's headquarters was in Dublin and its spacious stadium at Lansdowne Road was the accepted venue for international matches. Its international selection committee was broadly based and most Irish rugby XVs usually featured a good mix of players from North and South. It also helped that the IRFU's main all-island focus was on the national team. Unlike the IFA, it did not administer all-Ireland league and cup competitions; instead the four provincial unions ran their own club tournaments (a situation that persisted until 1990), which avoided the worst of the recurrent friction and recrimination that eventually frayed the bonds between North and South in soccer. There were of course occasional differences of opinion among those who administered rugby, but they were generally resolved by like-minded men who generally shared many of the same sporting, social and cultural values.

There was little such fellow-feeling in soccer. Regular disputes aggravated the administrative and geographic tensions caused by the location of the sport's headquarters outside the capital. Different conceptions of national allegiance also came into play: by 1921 most of the leading officials of the Leinster FA were nationalist in sympathy and found it impossible to accept the authority of a body whose political and cultural loyalties differed from those of the majority of people on the island. In seceding from IFA control, many southern administrators saw themselves as finally throwing off the shackles of an anti-national governing body in favour of a form of self-determination that would better serve their needs and reflect their identity.

4

Football on a Divided Island 1921–39

The FAI's new league championship started on 7 September 1921 with eight clubs: Bohemian FC, Dublin United, Frankfort, Jacobs, Olympia, St James's Gate, Shelbourne and YMCA, all based in Dublin. The first FAI competitions took place in difficult circumstances, in the troubled interval between the end of the War of Independence in July 1921 and the start of the Civil War in June 1922, when real or threatened violence was never too far away. The FAI Cup began in January 1922 and concluded when St James's Gate beat Shamrock Rovers 1–0 in a replay at Dalymount Park on 8 April 1922. Rovers' supporters were incensed at the result and attacked the opposing team as they left the field. Some Rovers' players joined in the mêlée and pursued their opponents to their dressing room, but backed off when IRA man Jack Dowdall, brother of the Gate player Charlie Dowdall, produced a revolver; some accounts say that he actually discharged it into the dressing room ceiling.[1]

Most football supporters just wanted a return to normality. The founding of the FAI gave a psychological boost to football in the South and in the year after the split it experienced a 25 per cent growth in affiliated clubs, mostly from Dublin. Clubs outside the capital were few and often unaffiliated, and the greatest challenge facing the FAI was to transform itself into a truly national association. The July 1921 truce eased security and transport restrictions and opened the way to bringing more regional clubs into the fold. Over the next three years the FAI managed to create qualifying competitions for the FAI Cup in Westmeath, Offaly, Tipperary, Cork, Waterford, Limerick, Galway,

Roscommon and Sligo, while dozens of clubs from outside the capital took part in the national Junior Cup competition. The association also worked to improve regional structures, initiating plans in September 1921 to create an Athlone and District Association that included nine teams from Athlone and one each from Clara, Mullingar, Moate, Castlerea and Ballinasloe.[2] In 1922 the game in the midlands received a considerable boost when Athlone Town became the first club from outside Dublin to be elected to the League of Ireland (colloquially often known as the Free State League).

The FAI's jurisdiction had yet to be precisely defined and it sought to cast its net as wide as possible. It planned to form a new Belfast District Association to include nationally minded clubs in Belfast, as well as others in Derry, Fermanagh, Antrim and Down, to support its claim that it was a genuinely all-Ireland body. However, by 1923 it was clear to the FAI that accepting affiliations from clubs based across a national border was impractical and contrary to FIFA regulations. To gain international recognition the FAI was compelled to adjust its administration in line with partition and confine its activities to the twenty-six counties. It was also the case that some southern administrators from the leading Dublin clubs had been rather discomfited when Alton United of the Falls Road League (a team that included several former Belfast Celtic players) had won the FAI Cup final against Shelbourne at Dalymount Park on 17 March 1923, providing a jolting reminder of the continued strength of Belfast football.[3]

The FAI's mission to spread the game was assisted by its decision to permit the playing of football on Sunday, the main day of leisure for most working people, which opened the way to greater participation in GAA strongholds. The Munster FA had ceased to function soon after the outbreak of the war in 1914, with the wholesale withdrawal of military teams, and the political violence of 1920–2, particularly acute in the province, provided a formidable barrier to its revival.[4] Late in 1922 the FAI dispatched a delegation to Cork to re-found the Munster association, to which ten clubs affiliated: Fordsons, YMCA, Tramways, Barrackton, Clifton (all based in Cork); Tipperary Town, Tipperary Wanderers, Clonmel and Cahir Park from Tipperary; and Limerick. By

1925 there were over 100 affiliated clubs in Munster, mostly clustered in the cities of Cork, Limerick and Waterford.[5]

As early as 1924, the FAI could point to the fact that the cup final was contested by two teams from outside Dublin: Athlone Town and Fordsons, the works' team of the Ford Motor Company in Cork. Athlone won, and on their return home were greeted by thousands of proud supporters, the victory further entrenching soccer's popularity in the town.[6] Two years later, it was Fordsons' turn: watched by a crowd of 26,000 at Dalymount Park, they beat Shamrock Rovers 3–2 in the 1926 final to become the first Munster club to take the trophy. The win inspired a joyous celebration of civic identity, the victorious team parading through the city in a torchlight procession behind local bands. To demonstrate local soccer's solid nationalist credentials, the evening ended with a rendition of Thomas Davis's anthemic 'A Nation Once Again'.[7] The victory gave an enormous boost to both the Fordsons club and soccer in Cork, prompting *The Cork Examiner* to make the rather exaggerated claim that 'at the moment Association is the most popular game in the Free State'.[8] Clubs such as Glasheen, Grattan United and Rockmount were founded that year, while others such as Greenmount Rangers (1930) and Evergreen (1932) followed soon afterwards. Playing in local senior and junior leagues, they helped create a vibrant soccer culture in working-class areas such as Shandon Street, Blarney Street and Gurranabraher on the northside of the city and Turner's Cross, Ballyphehane and Togher on the southside.[9]

During the 1920s association football experienced a steady growth in popularity, with cup finals and important league games regularly attracting crowds of over 20,000 spectators. By 1926 fifteen counties were represented in Free State cup competitions, compared with only six counties three years earlier. The launch in August 1925 of *Football Sports Weekly*, a publication largely devoted to the association game, testified to a growing appetite and audience. The new paper lauded the spread of soccer into towns such as Waterford, Wexford, Longford, Drogheda, Tullamore and Navan, and insisted that association football was 'the coming game amongst the youths'.[10] However, at the top level most clubs struggled to find the resources or support-base needed to survive in a largely semi-professional national league. During the early 1920s Dublin clubs such as YMCA, Frankfort, Rathmines, Dublin United and Olympia were forced to drop out, and were replaced by others such as Midland Athletic, Pioneers, Rathmines Athletic, Brooklyn and Shamrock Rovers. Of these, only Rovers would go on to generate widespread support and have a lasting impact in the league.

By 1926 the Free State League had taken on a more representative national character, with four of its ten clubs based outside the capital (Athlone Town, Fordsons, Bray Unknowns and the newly elected Dundalk GNR). The game was gaining a greater foothold in the west midlands and across the Shannon, with clubs springing up in Counties Sligo, Galway and Mayo, and in September 1928 a Connacht Football Association was established.[11] Finding opponents of sufficient standard though could be a problem for the more advanced teams in the west, such as Sligo Rovers, founded in 1928 in a town with a strong passion for the game. In 1932 it joined the Leinster Senior League for regular competitive games, and managed to win the competition in 1933/4, ensuring election to the Free State League in 1934. In some cases support for regional clubs was not just confined to their host town itself but drew in players and spectators from rural hinterlands. Dundalk FC (as the club was known from 1929) attracted followings in areas such as mid-Louth, east Monaghan, south Armagh and south Down, and provided an outlet for regional as well as civic allegiance.

The ability to field a team in the Free State League was, though, only one measure of soccer's popularity. In parts of the country there were thriving amateur and junior leagues that served local enthusiasts better than a club struggling to survive in a senior national competition. During the 1930s some even claimed that the election of clubs from Sligo and Limerick to the Free State League had weakened the junior game in those areas. However, the FAI's efforts to popularise soccer were showing results. At the 1929 annual meeting of the Leinster FA, Osmond Grattan Esmonde, beginning his tenure as president (1929–36), declared the game to be in 'a flourishing and prosperous condition' with over 300 clubs taking part in its competitions the previous season.[12] Within a few years, Waterford, Limerick, Drogheda, Dundalk,

Athlone, Navan, Tullamore, Kilkenny, Enniscorthy, New Ross, Wexford, Longford, Mullingar, Sligo and Donegal all had competitive local leagues that attracted significant numbers of players.[13] By 1932 there were 470 clubs affiliated to the FAI: 369 in Leinster, 85 in Munster, 15 in Connacht, but just 2 in Ulster. The Ulster counties of Cavan and Monaghan proved particularly resistant to soccer, and even when clubs did form, they were reluctant to affiliate to national or provincial associations. In some cases partition had separated them from their natural hinterlands and membership of the FAI risked interfering with playing teams from across the border. The strength of the GAA also provided a formidable barrier: by the 1920s Gaelic football had established itself as the dominant sport in both counties. As late as 1934 only one soccer club from the area, Monaghan United, was listed in the FAI's annual report.[14]

In areas of west Ulster under FAI jurisdiction the situation was more encouraging. The pre-war popularity of soccer in Donegal continued, despite some opposition. After the foundation of the Irish Free State in 1922, the GAA redoubled efforts to promote its games in Donegal, successfully establishing new clubs in the south and west of the county, but in areas such as the north-east and the Inishowen peninsula soccer was so strongly entrenched that it remained the dominant football code. By 1934 it was estimated that there were 103 soccer teams in the county, compared with sixty-seven playing Gaelic football.[15] Some local GAA activists argued that this reflected badly on the county's patriotism, with one claiming in October 1928 that the county's soccer enthusiasts would be happy to see the return of British rule. In response Henry McGowan of Ballybofey Athletic FC insisted that 'we, who are carrying on the association football game here, do not want the British back and have sense enough to know that association football would be as useless a weapon in bringing them back as Gaelic football was in putting them away'. He further observed that most GAA county board members were ill-qualified to speak on such matters since, unlike himself, none had seen active service in the War of Independence.[16]

While the FAI was keen to promote soccer at the local level, it recognised that national competitions were its most important showpieces and attracted most public and press interest. During the 1920s the league was dominated by the Dublin 'Big Three' of Shelbourne, Bohemians and Shamrock Rovers. Founded in Ringsend in 1901, Rovers established a strong reputation in the Leinster Senior League before joining the Free State League in 1922 and winning the championship at their first attempt. They went on to win six league titles in the interwar years, and the much-coveted league and FAI Cup double in 1925 and 1932, building up strong support across the city. Although their heartland was in Ringsend and Irishtown, after entry to the league they played in Milltown in south-east Dublin, where their new stadium of Glenmalure Park was officially opened on 19 September 1926 with a friendly against Belfast Celtic that attracted 18,000 spectators. Rovers' success soon helped them draw additional support from the surrounding suburbs of Dundrum, Terenure, Ranelagh and Kimmage, areas not served by any existing league team.[17]

Dublin clubs had telling advantages over their regional counterparts. The latter faced higher travel costs for away games and were unable to rely on the bumper gate receipts provided by regular local derbies. Towns and cities outside the capital were usually capable of supporting only one local team, which often struggled to stay solvent. Athlone had to withdraw from the league in 1928 (and would not be readmitted until 1969), while Fordsons was largely dependent on the sponsorship of the Ford Motor Company in Cork; when this ceased in 1930, the club, renamed Cork FC, faced a serious shortfall. Despite such difficulties, other regional clubs became key members of the league: Dundalk GNR (1926), followed by Waterford FC (1930), Cork Bohemians (1932), Sligo Rovers (1934) and Limerick FC (1937). Dundalk managed not just to survive, but to thrive, winning the league championship in 1933 (the first team from outside Dublin or Belfast to take a national senior league title). Regional teams generally became more competitive in the 1930s: Sligo Rovers won the league in 1937; Dundalk finished runner-up in 1931 and 1937, as did Cork FC (1932 and 1934), Waterford (1938) and Sligo Rovers (1939). Cork and Waterford also managed to win FAI Cups in 1934 and 1937 respectively, victories that attracted massive popular support: a Cork newspaper claimed that 'for enthusiasm and sheer love of a great game ... a cup final to soccer followers is worth a hundred league games'.[18] By the end of the 1930s the League of Ireland could claim to be a genuinely nationwide competition, with half of its teams from outside the capital.[19]

The FAI could also take pride in the performance of League of Ireland representative teams, which during the 1920s and 1930s generally held their own in matches against the Irish and Welsh Leagues, and even beat the Scottish League in their first meeting in 1939. Interest in domestic league football was solid and attendances mostly held up well. With the earnings of English professionals capped by a maximum wage, outstanding Irish players such as Sacky Glenn and Paddy Moore of Shamrock Rovers spent all or most of their careers at home and before the Second World War the FAI national team usually fielded a majority of home-based players. Local talent was supplemented by experienced cross-channel English professionals, such as Jimmy Turnbull, who played with distinction for Cork FC in 1935–6; and the renowned England international centre-forward William Ralph 'Dixie' Dean, who joined Sligo Rovers in 1939 and often added thousands to attendances. However, while these imports could give clubs a temporary fillip, they did little for long-term sustainability, and the transfer fees and bonus payments needed to secure them could plunge clubs into serious debt.[20] Club owners and officials rarely planned for the future and the interwar popularity of the game masked endemic structural weaknesses, particularly poor pitches and inadequate accommodation for spectators. Most grounds were rudimentary or even unsafe – in January 1929 over thirty people were injured when a hoarding collapsed in Tolka Park in Dublin during a match between Drumcondra and Shelbourne.[21]

***

One of the most notable features of the Free State League was the presence of so many teams founded in workplaces. This was perhaps all the more remarkable given the country's small industrial base: the 1926 census recorded 164,000 industrial employees (13.5 per cent of the workforce; two-thirds of whom were engaged in the processing of food and drink), compared with an agricultural workforce of 644,000. The first winner of the Free State League in 1922 was St James's Gate FC, the team of the Guinness brewery, and that year it also claimed the FAI Cup and the Leinster Senior Cup, the country's two most prestigious knock-out competitions. Guinness's variant of welfare capitalism, which provided generous health, educational and recreational benefits for employees, made its jobs among the most sought-after in a city where secure employment was scarce, and also helped attract some of the country's best footballers. Works' teams could sometimes blur the line between amateur and professional: players were not usually paid to play but turning out for the team was understood to be part of their duties and they received time off for training. Guinness's management welcomed the publicity and the improved staff morale that came from sponsoring a successful team, and in 1928 spent £20,000 to build the club's Iveagh sports grounds in Crumlin.[22]

During the 1920s St James's Gate seldom had to go outside the brewery to find players, but this began to change when the onset of the Great Depression in 1929 curtailed recruitment. An ageing workforce struggled to supply enough players to sustain the club's position in a national league. From the early 1930s it began to recruit professional footballers from outside the firm, which helped it to stabilise its position and win the FAI Cup in 1938 and the league championship in 1940. Despite these successes and the support of Guinness employees and soccer followers in the Liberties, James's Street and Crumlin areas, the club's attendances never matched those of its main Dublin rivals and the capacity of its new stadium was rarely tested. It remained strongly dependent on its parent firm, which was seriously affected by the 1940s' wartime economic downturn, and its funding was cut. In 1944 St James's Gate finished bottom of the League of Ireland and failed to gain re-election for the following 1944/5 season, dropping back into the Leinster Senior League.[23]

The other most successful works' team of the 1920s, Fordsons of Cork, suffered a similar fate. The Ford Motor Company, which had begun production in Cork in 1919, became the city's largest employer,

with 7,000 workers by 1930. In 1921 it founded Fords FC, later renamed
Fordsons FC after the tractor model that was Cork's main output. In
1926 Fordsons began to play in the Free State League, but as one of only
two Munster clubs in the league, its travelling expenses were heavy and
had to be defrayed by Ford. When economic depression hit in 1929–30,
the firm cut its sponsorship and advised the club to confine its efforts to
local competitions. However, Fordsons was keen to maintain national
league football in the Free State's second city and in 1930 severed ties
with Ford, renamed itself Cork FC and played in the League of Ireland
until replaced by Cork City FC in 1938.

Most works' teams, particularly when restricted to employees,
found it difficult to survive at the highest level. Jacobs, the team of
the W. & R. Jacob & Co. Biscuit Factory, was a founder member of
the League of Ireland in 1921. Never a leading club, they struggled to
find players of the required ability and finished bottom of the league
in three consecutive seasons (1930–2), after which they failed to gain
re-election. For many years afterwards, though, Jacobs continued to
provide a valuable sporting outlet for employees in the Leinster League,
winning the FAI Intermediate Cup in 1950 and three Leinster Senior
League titles in a row (1953–5).

Midland Athletic, founded by employees of the Midland Great
Western Railway in Dublin, was one of six new teams to join the League
of Ireland in 1922, but lasted only three years before returning to the
Leinster Senior League. Other clubs such as Dolphin FC also had a strong
vocational component: it was founded in 1921 by a group of butchers,
some of German origin, associated with the Butchers Club in Gardiner
Street, and took its name from Dolphin's Barn in south-west Dublin
where it played home matches. Its election to the League of Ireland in
1930 necessitated a move to Tolka Park in Drumcondra, after which
the club enjoyed some success, appearing in FAI Cup finals in 1932 and
1933 and winning the league championship in 1935. However, its small
support base could not sustain the costs of national league football and
it was forced to drop down into the Leinster Senior League in 1937.

In Dundalk the growth of soccer owed much to the town's main
employer. After falling into abeyance during the Great War, Dundalk

GNR (Great Northern Railway) FC was refounded by railway employees in 1919 and joined the Leinster Senior League in 1922 and the League of Ireland in 1926. The support of its parent firm was crucial to the club's development and success: it provided steady employment for local players and spectators and subsidised travel for the team. The club recruited professional players, often from across the border, and soon became one of the strongest teams in the league. As the club's popularity grew, it became less reliant on the Great Northern Railway and in 1929 dropped the 'GNR' from its name. As Dundalk FC it won the league championship in 1933 and its first FAI Cup in 1942.[24]

***

While some employers were happy to assist the development of soccer in the new state, the same could not always be said of its political leaders. Many had been influenced by the ethos of Griffith's Sinn Féin and prioritised the promotion of native culture. The state's first minister for education, Eoin MacNeill, insisted that 'if Irish nationality were not to mean a distinctive Irish civilisation, I would attach no very great value to Irish national independence'.[25] The new Free State government and its agencies generally showed a marked preference for Gaelic sports: in the National Army and An Garda Síochána only Gaelic games were played, and most politicians were wary of identifying with soccer.[26] When the League of Ireland managed to secure games against the Welsh and Irish Leagues in the mid-1920s, no leading political figures attended. Soccer followers had little doubt that their absence was politically motivated, and lamented that 'not one prominent public man took the smallest notice ... They felt, probably, they might lose caste, political or otherwise'.[27]

The game also faced strong opposition from the GAA, whose attitude to soccer had in no way been softened by the FAI's secession from Belfast. In fact the GAA's hostility became even stronger after independence: the new association was denounced as a partitionist organisation and its relaxation of rules against Sunday play made it appear a more dangerous rival. The GAA insisted that the FAI and all other bodies that fostered non-native sports were 'antagonistic to the national ideals of the GAA'.[28] Irish Irelanders had always insisted that 'colonial culture' in Ireland was propped up by the British presence, and that once its agents had departed the Irish people would be free to create a truly Gaelic state. However, in the immediate aftermath of independence there was disappointment at the slow progress of Gaelicisation and considerable dismay that 'garrison games' had not gone the way of the garrison. The fact that soccer had not only survived, but appeared to be thriving in Leinster and spreading into Munster and Connacht, was considered an affront.[29] In 1923, one GAA official claimed that while 'men were sacrificing their all to drive the English out of Ireland, the adherents of rugby and soccer were fighting vigorously, through these games, to keep them here ... men of this calibre were, and are, the biggest enemies of the country'.[30] Such rhetoric was probably encouraged by the fact that the bitter Civil War of 1922–3 had opened up divisions in the GAA as in all nationalist organisations, and opposition to 'foreign games' provided a convenient unifier for pro- and anti-Treaty factions. Soccer could be portrayed as not just a rival code, but an obstacle to true cultural self-determination.[31]

Association football probably faced more sustained opposition in the Free State than in any other European country. There was no place for it in July 1924 when the government staged the Tailteann Games, an ancient Irish festival in honour of the legendary Queen Tailte said to date back to 1896 BC. Having accepted something less than a sovereign thirty-two-county republic with the Anglo-Irish Treaty of 1921, the new Cumann na nGaedheal administration was intent on showing that the Free State was a proud and independent Gaelic entity, and not the West British satellite of anti-Treaty propaganda. While often criticised for its lack of vision and drab parsimony, the new government showed considerable ambition in staging the Tailteann Games and was even prepared to loosen the state's purse strings, providing £16,000 in grants, mostly to renovate Croke Park and enable it to host a range of cultural and sporting events.

The festival provided the opportunity for the first significant co-operation between the GAA and a native government, and J.J. Walsh, the minister for posts and telegraphs and a senior GAA official, was given responsibility for its planning. Since the intention was to represent all that was best and most distinctively Irish in an emergent nation, sports subject to the GAA ban, such as soccer, rugby, cricket and hockey, were excluded. Besides the GAA sports of Gaelic football, hurling, handball and camogie, a wide range of other sports and activities were considered acceptable, including athletics, swimming, diving, cycling, rowing, boxing, rounders, golf, tennis, gymnastics, wrestling, weightlifting, yachting, horse-racing, billiards and chess. To show that the Free State looked to the future as well as the past, there were races for motor-cycles, cars, motor-boats and aeroplanes, which proved the most popular attractions.

Competitors represented Ireland, England, Scotland, Wales, the USA, Canada, Australia, New Zealand and South Africa. Although events were supposedly open only to those of Irish birth or descent, some athletes with no Irish connections who had just competed in the Olympic Games in Paris took part. Among these was Johnny Weissmuller, who had won three gold medals in the Olympic freestyle swimming events and would later become world famous as the star of the Tarzan films. Weissmuller competed in the swimming competitions in the pond at Dublin Zoo, much to the delight of local spectators. Some Irish practitioners of soccer, rugby, cricket and hockey may have wondered how a place could be found at the games for Weissmuller and not for them, but most agreed that the festival provided some much-needed colour and excitement and it was lauded by the *Irish Independent* as 'a triumph beyond expectation'.[32] It was held again in 1928 and 1932, but was rather less successful, with fewer foreign participants and lower attendances. The Fianna Fáil government that assumed office in March 1932 was never enthusiastic about this inheritance from its predecessor and it was never held again after 1932.[33]

Opposition to soccer came not just from the state, but also from the state's republican opponents. The Sinn Féin newspaper *An Phoblacht* was notable for its extreme attitude, condemning soccer and rugby as 'games imported here by those who raped and robbed and ruined those whose blood flowed in our veins'.[34] When in 1936 the Donegal socialist-republican Peadar O'Donnell suggested that the *Irish People*, the new paper of the left-wing Republican Congress, should have a 'Soccer Notes' column to appeal to working-class readers, he was quickly slapped down by the radical republican and former editor of *An Phoblacht* Frank Ryan.[35] Attitudes to soccer though varied widely among republicans. The writer Brendan Behan, for example, who came from a staunchly republican Dublin family and was himself imprisoned for his part in an IRA bombing campaign in England in 1939, was a supporter of the game, which his father and brothers played enthusiastically in local leagues. Behan enjoyed the company of footballers and was particularly proud of his friendships with renowned England players such as Stanley Matthews and the former England captain and Wolverhampton Wanderers manager Stan Cullis.[36]

In the newly independent state, public discourse was often dominated by strident displays of nationalist zeal as politicians, officials and publications attempted to outdo each other in their denunciations of foreign influences.[37] Such over-the-top rhetoric is temptingly quotable, but it should be borne in mind that the GAA was far from monolithic in its attitude to competing sports and extreme statements often expressed the view of a zealous and vociferous minority. There was an element of nationalist posturing in frenzied denunciations of 'foreign games', which could be employed by sharp-elbowed GAA officials to boost their Gaelic credentials and assist their rise through the ranks. Supporters of association football and GAA were not always divided into sharply defined camps: there were many who took a broad interest in sport and were happy to play and watch a variety of games. Those who did so rarely issued public statements or wrote to newspapers, and easy-going tolerance inevitably draws less attention than shrill prejudice. Many GAA members did not support the ban and unsuccessfully called for its removal at annual congresses in 1924, 1925 and 1926. Some also acknowledged that those who played sports other than Gaelic games had contributed to the achievement of Irish independence and the formation of national identity. Dan McCarthy, GAA president (1921–4) and a former Irish Volunteer, recalled in 1924 that when he was imprisoned in Knutsford jail after the Easter Rising he was struck by the fact that 90 per cent of his fellow prisoners were soccer players and reminded delegates that 'they had not got a monopoly of patriotism in the GAA'.[38]

The soccer community often made the point that it too had played its part in the national struggle. It stressed the military records of leading figures such as Oscar Traynor and Emmet Dalton (an important lieutenant of Michael Collins and former Bohemians player) and those of many lesser known players who had also played noteworthy parts and in some cases given their lives.[39] Soccer followers claimed that it was nonsensical to assert that 'the playing of foreign games tended to sap one's national outlook … if a man loves his country, no sport, foreign or otherwise, will alter that love … Faithful to Eire, we have answered her call, soccer men, Gaelic men, rugger and hurley men, true-hearted sporting men – Irishmen all'.[40] Traynor himself argued that 'some of the highest executive officers of the Republican movement, from 1916 onwards, played the despised foreign games and I never heard any of them apologising for doing so'. He invoked the memory of the young IRA martyr Kevin Barry, who had played rugby and cricket, insisting 'that the game a man played did not influence his convictions one iota'.[41]

The belief of many soccer followers that their sport was treated unfairly seemed confirmed when the Cumann na nGaedheal government passed a Finance Act in 1927 that imposed income tax on the earnings of all sports except Gaelic games. The situation was compounded in 1932 when the new Fianna Fáil government reimposed an entertainment tax on all sports except those of the GAA, which was given preferential treatment on the basis that it was engaged in an important national service by promoting distinctively Irish games.[42] This led to complaints that such distinctions were discriminatory and divisive, the FAI protesting that it 'regards all preferential treatment in sport as tending to create and perpetuate schism and antagonism among our fellow countrymen, who deserve and need unity for so many sporting purposes'.[43] It also stressed soccer's importance to the working class, claiming that it 'provides health-giving exercise for all classes among the youth of our country and open air entertainment for the poorest of our people. Of all team games, it is best entitled to be described as the people's game'.[44]

In the Dáil debates on these taxation decisions, several TDs took the opportunity to proclaim their strong commitment to Gaelic games and their disapproval of non-native sports, with some claiming that they had never even seen rugby and soccer being played.[45] One Fianna Fáil deputy maintained that the crowd at an All-Ireland hurling final represented 'the real Ireland in miniature' and that 'the epic struggles' of these games showed the Gaelic ideals of the new state at their best. He thought it only right to give preferential treatment to the GAA since it supported 'the language and liberation of the Gael' in a way that neither soccer nor rugby ever could.[46] Others maintained that while they had no hostility to non-native games, the fact that soccer was played on a professional basis made it a commercial activity that should be taxed as such.[47] One rural Labour Party TD spoke of the owners of soccer clubs as 'speculators [who] ... buy and sell young men and make profits by getting the gate money. That is not the position of Gaelic football.'[48] In the Seanad the former soccer player Oliver St John Gogarty, who tended to cast a cold eye on the pieties of nationalist Ireland, took a rather different view, insisting that 'there is no such thing as national Irish football' and that Gaelic football 'ought to be doubly taxed because it is a bastard of soccer and rugby'.[49]

Introducing the 1931 Finance Bill, Minister for Finance Ernest Blythe announced his intention to continue the GAA's exemption from tax but made clear his disagreement with the association's 'policy of branding a man as a bad Irishman or a bad citizen if he happens to play a particular game of football'.[50] Deputies representing urban constituencies insisted that the tax would fall most heavily on the hard-pressed working-class. Blythe's ministerial colleague Patrick McGilligan argued that 'if there is any game which ... destroys the tedium of work for the working man, it is association football, the game to which he looks forward on Saturday and Sunday ... [and] carries him through the winter, the most discontented period of the year'.[51] He was supported by fellow party members such as J.J. Byrne, who argued that the entertainment tax was a vindictive and discriminatory levy 'framed for one object ... to wipe out the playing of soccer in the Irish Free State'. He maintained that although soccer operated mainly on a semi-professional basis at the top level, it was played primarily for the love of the game and produced no significant dividends or profits; indeed most of the clubs in the League of Ireland had crippling debts, which additional taxation was bound to aggravate.[52]

The 1932 entertainment tax put an extra penny on the standard sixpence admission to a game and pro-rata increases on the more expensive charges. In a period of falling wages and rising unemployment, attendances declined and in 1932 it was noted that Dundalk, Cork FC, Dolphin, Drumcondra and Jacobs were all struggling to stay solvent. For its part, the FAI kept up criticism of the tax which it claimed held back soccer's development and prevented investment in pitches and stadiums. Other sporting bodies also protested strongly against the tax which, in the end, raised considerably less revenue than the government had hoped. This consideration was probably foremost in the decision to remove it in the budget of 1934, a move strongly welcomed by the FAI.[53]

During the mid-1920s the profile of several sports was raised by growing press coverage and by radio. The BBC began transmitting in Northern Ireland in 1924 and broadcasting in the Free State began with the state-controlled Dublin Broadcasting Station (2RN) in 1926. By 1938–9 there were 139,000 licensed sets in the Free State and 124,000 in Northern Ireland, suggesting that about half of all households in the North had a radio, compared to about a quarter in the South. (In both jurisdictions there was widespread licence evasion, with the number of sets considerably exceeding the number of licences.) 2RN (known as Radio Éireann from 1937) saw itself as an important body in disseminating official culture through Irish language broadcasts and programmes devoted to traditional music and Gaelic games.[54] The first live broadcast of a sporting event was the All-Ireland hurling semi-final between Galway and Kilkenny on 29 August 1926, while the first soccer match broadcast was the FAI Cup final between Bohemians and Drumcondra on 17 March 1928, prompting the inevitable complaints that the station was promoting foreign culture. Thereafter coverage was sparing: important international or domestic games occasionally received partial live broadcasts but mostly had to make do with after-match reports.[55]

The FAI rarely protested, believing that regular live broadcasts would discourage supporters from attending games and lead to falls in gate receipts that the association and clubs could ill afford. However, even modest radio coverage multiplied Irish soccer's audience, making it a topic of conversation for many who never passed through a turnstile. Important matches also featured on newsreels, raising soccer's profile among the country's large cinema-going public. During the 1930s, 45 per cent of Irish items shown on Pathé newsreels in Irish cinemas were related to sport (compared to 17 per cent on politics): soccer featured strongly, particularly Irish international matches, as well as the major English club and international games. Gaelic games received rather less coverage, but the balance was later redressed when the Irish-language organisation Gael Linn launched its Amharc Éireann newsreels in 1956: these ran until 1964 and featured local news for Irish audiences; Gaelic games were given priority in sporting items, while soccer was excluded.[56]

The belief of many soccer enthusiasts that their game did not receive fair or fitting coverage in the national press led to the founding of *Football Sports Weekly* in August 1925. It regularly addressed the game's position in Irish life, conceding that the GAA ban on 'foreign games' may have had some justification when the country was under British rule, but had no place in a free and independent nation: 'Sport is sport, and if Eire is to take her place with any success among the athletic nations, then let our youth indulge in any game they choose ... God knows we have the stuff. Let us use it.'[57] Pleading for 'the right of every young Irishman to play any game he chooses', it expressed the hope that 'Ireland one day may be able to challenge all nations on the football field ... But that day will not come till bans and other antediluvian devices are consigned to the scrapheap.'[58]

This, though, was a society in which 'bans' of all kinds were liberally employed against any form of behaviour that ran counter to national, social or religious norms. While the new state proudly proclaimed that the Irish people had finally won their freedom after centuries of oppression, it was often rather proscriptive as to how that freedom should be exercised. One of its first legislative measures was to pass a Censorship of Films Act (1923) to protect the Irish public from creeping 'Californication' and other pernicious foreign influences. A state-sponsored Committee on Evil Literature attempted to prevent the import of indecent foreign books and periodicals, and a stringent Censorship of Publications Act (1929) banned the works of many leading twentieth-century authors. In taking these measures the state had the full backing of the Catholic Church, which added a few prohibitions of its own. Clergy mounted regular attacks on immodest dress, 'company-keeping', modern music and the 'lascivious dancing' that accompanied it. Jazz in particular was denounced as a pagan cacophony that threatened both public morality and indigenous culture, and there were regular calls for it to be banned from the national airwaves. Independent Ireland, traditionalists believed, was a place apart, and Church and state stood united to defend it from the evils of cosmopolitan Anglo-Saxon culture.[59]

Such attitudes meant that much of the urban working class was often unsure of its place in the new dispensation: the rural Gaelic idyll promoted by the state's founders was a foreign country to many. Attending domestic soccer matches allowed them to express a sense of kinship not just with the supporters of their own team but with the followers of the game generally. Incessant attacks on their favoured sport reinforced their sense of being at odds with official cultural orthodoxy and this found its way into the works of urban writers, such as James Plunkett's semi-autobiographical *Farewell Companions*, a coming-of-age novel set in Dublin between the world wars. The protagonist's father, a British Army veteran, regards Gaelic enthusiasts as 'half-cracked' and at family gatherings in Ringsend he and his brothers animatedly discuss local soccer and bemoan the hostility of teaching orders such as the Christian Brothers 'to a game every kid in Dublin starts playing the minute you lift him from his cradle'.[60]

***

After partition, the Irish League differed from its southern counterpart in some important respects. It was one of the oldest national leagues in the world, with some of its oldest clubs. There were, however, only six of them: Cliftonville, Linfield, Glentoran, Distillery, Glenavon and Queen's Island. The 1921 split deprived Irish football of the Dublin–Belfast rivalry that had been one of its most compelling features. The Irish League largely became again what it was on its foundation in 1890 – a competition for Belfast clubs. Derry Celtic had resigned in 1913 (partly because many of its players took up Gaelic football), and by 1921 the only non-Belfast club remaining in the league was Glenavon of Lurgan, County Armagh. Like Dublin, Belfast too had a 'Big Three', made up of Linfield, Glentoran and Belfast Celtic (from 1924); it was they who drew the largest crowds and swept up the main trophies. Their goalscoring stars, such as Joe Bambrick of Linfield and Glentoran, Fred Roberts of Glentoran and Sammy Curran of Belfast Celtic, spent most or all of their careers in the Irish League and became genuine folk heroes. Most other Irish League clubs, however, drew modest crowds and usually found it difficult to attract or hold on to the better players. Often their main ambition was just to remain in the league and every season was a new struggle to survive.[61]

The 1920s was a rocky time for the export-oriented Northern Ireland economy, as countries across the globe raised trade tariffs after the post-war slump. The flagship industries of shipbuilding and linen were hit by sharp falls in demand and laid off thousands of workers. In 1926, a quarter of the insured workforce was unemployed, and the figure rarely fell below this level until 1939.[62] These difficulties were aggravated by the 1929 stock market crash, which sparked the century's most severe and prolonged economic depression. Jobs in Belfast shipyards fell from 20,000 in 1924 to 2,000 in 1933, and the long-established firm of Workman & Clark went out of business in 1934. Those lucky enough to keep their jobs had to accept wage cuts and there was less disposable income available for leisure activities such as attending football matches. Queen's Island FC, founded by Belfast shipyard workers, and the only club to break the grip of the 'Big Three' by winning the Irish League in 1924, was seriously affected and forced to drop out of the competition in 1929. Newly established league clubs, such as Ballymena Football and Athletic Club (founded in 1928), struggled to survive as gate receipts fell; the club was forced to replace its Scottish professionals with local amateurs and folded in 1934.[63] By 1930 there were just 226 clubs affiliated to the IFA, down from 325 in 1926.[64]

In the early 1920s economic distress had been aggravated by political turmoil and serious violence. By June 1922 there had been 416 violent deaths in Belfast alone, as well as at least 2,500 serious injuries, 600 businesses destroyed and 20,000 people forced to flee their homes. The city's religious divisions became even more bitter and entrenched. Northern nationalists felt abandoned by the partition settlement of 1921–2 and many chose to ignore the existence of the new state, with nationalist elected representatives often refusing to sit in the Northern Ireland parliament on the grounds that this only gave legitimacy to a discriminatory and oppressive government. The easing of violence did, however, allow Belfast Celtic to return to league football in 1924 after a four-year absence. This provided an important focus for Belfast nationalists, whose opportunities for asserting their separate identity were few.[65] Nationalist pride was reinforced by Belfast Celtic's near domination of Ulster football in the interwar years. The club won eleven of the twenty-one league championships it contested, including four consecutive titles (1926–9), and another five (1936–40) under the management of the legendary Elisha Scott. Born in the Shankill district to a Protestant family, Scott (1894–1959) made his name as a goalkeeper with Liverpool and won twenty-six caps for Ireland (IFA) (1920–35). Having played briefly with Belfast Celtic in 1918, he became player-manager in 1934 and epitomised the club's professionalism and will to win.

Although Celtic had an open recruitment policy, with many Protestants players and an estimated 10 per cent Protestant support, there was no denying its nationalist orientation.[66] Seeing itself as a beleaguered outpost that faced discrimination from the northern football authorities and hostility from fellow clubs, it forged close links with southern clubs, particularly Shamrock Rovers, and also aligned with its Glasgow namesake. A strong triangular relationship between the two Celtics and Shamrock Rovers linked Belfast, Glasgow and Dublin together in an informal alliance that had considerable overlapping support. Belfast Celtic was much admired in the South for its professional approach and skilful football, and it attracted large crowds whenever it crossed the border for regular friendly, charity and testimonial games. The Dublin-based *Football Sports Weekly* featured a 'Northern Notes' section in its pages, almost entirely devoted to the fortunes of the Belfast club.[67]

Celtic's willingness to play in the Free State with such frequency was exceptional. After the 1921 split, football supporters North and South focused primarily on their own league and cup competitions. But, while relations between the IFA and FAI could be frosty at an official level, those between clubs, players and supporters were often rather more friendly. Contact was maintained by trophies such as the Condor Cup (1924–32), contested by Bohemians and Linfield, with matches played alternately in Dublin and Belfast. There were also officials on both sides who tried to keep lines of communication open, particularly through matches between the Irish League and the League of Ireland. In the absence of regular international fixtures, these contests were eagerly anticipated and 18,000 spectators attended the first inter-league game at Dalymount Park on 13 March 1926; the teams would play again on six occasions over the next thirteen years. When they met at Windsor Park in 1927, supporters from both parts of the island mingled with ease and sang 'The more we are together'.[68] However, jurisdictional disputes between the two associations soured official relations and in 1930 led to the suspension of inter-league matches for eight years. They resumed on 17 March 1938 before 30,000 spectators at Dalymount Park. Holding such games on St Patrick's Day was motivated by strong practical considerations and helped draw large crowds, but it also aligned soccer in the South with national culture and allowed supporters to display their patriotism on Ireland's national day. The Welsh League was also a regular visitor, and in 1937 the League of Ireland hosted the Yugoslav League. On 17 March 1939 the star-studded Scottish League side visited Dublin for the first time. Since the English and Scottish FAs were still not prepared to sanction full international matches against the FAI team, in Dublin it was almost regarded as such and a crowd of 35,000 at

Dalymount Park roared the League of Ireland to a 2–1 victory. This gave a massive confidence boost to a league that had often struggled but had at least managed to survive two decades of economic uncertainty and administrative turmoil.

**

After its upsurge during the First World War women's football faced many barriers. There were many (men and women) who did not approve, believing that football was not suitable for females, and there was even some spurious medical opinion that claimed it could damage their child-bearing capacity. The English FA maintained that women's football was undermining the status of the game and in December 1921 prohibited women from using its pitches and threatened with suspension men who coached women or officiated at their games.[69] Women's football was, however, strongly entrenched in some areas, particularly the industrial towns of Lancashire, where the best-known team of the era was Dick, Kerr's Ladies of Preston (Dick, Kerr's was a former locomotive works that became a large munitions factory). The team gained a reputation for its skilled and exciting play and drew large crowds, most notably on 26 December 1920 when their game against St Helens Ladies (another munition workers' team) at Goodison Park in Liverpool attracted a capacity crowd of 53,000 spectators.[70]

If Preston was the centre of the women's game in England, then Belfast was its equivalent in Ireland. Women's participation in the game outlived the war and the IFA did not follow the English FA in banning women from using its pitches. During the 1920s the city boasted several strong women's teams, mostly based around factories, such as Ropeworks, York Street Mill, Owen O'Corks and Roebucks. (Danny Blanchflower's mother, Selina Ellison, played centre-forward with Roebucks, and it was she who nurtured Danny's and his brother Jackie's interest.) Visiting teams also added to the popularity of the game and on 23 May 1925 Dick, Kerr's won 2–0 against a French Ladies XI at Windsor Park. There were also occasional matches in the South. In Dublin a Shamrock Rovers Ladies XI managed by the Rovers legend

Bob Fullam took on a Rutherglen XI from Glasgow on 25 May 1927. The Scots were one of the strongest women's teams in Britain, having recently beaten Dick, Kerr's, and outclassed the home team to win 8–1 before 12,000 spectators.[71]

Rutherglen featured the outstanding Irish player of the day, the Belfast-born Molly Seaton (1905–74). The Glasgow team toured Northern Ireland in 1928 playing in Larne, Ballymena, Derry and Belfast, with Seaton the star attraction. A strong, tough-tackling centre-half, she was a superb all-round player who led by example, covered the entire pitch and usually managed to get on the scoresheet. After Rutherglen returned to Glasgow, she remained in Belfast to play with York Street Factory Girls and various Irish women's XIs based in the city. On 27 July 1931 she captained the Irish team that lost 3–2 to England at Windsor Park before a crowd of 4,500, giving a superb display and scoring both goals. A match report described her as 'a magnificent general' and concluded that Ireland would have won easily 'if there had been another Molly'.[72] A Belfast team, 'Molly Seaton's Ladies', was built around her, and contested a one-off Irish Ladies Football Cup at Grosvenor Park on 19 August 1932, beating Ropeworks Ladies 5–0.[73] Thereafter the women's game in Belfast declined somewhat in popularity, although an Irish XI that featured Seaton did take on a French team at Grosvenor Park in 1936, losing 4–1 before a crowd of 2,000 in the last major women's match staged in Ireland in the interwar period. The IFA offered little encouragement, but some leading male players were more supportive: the match against the French selection on 4 August 1932 was refereed by the former Irish international captain Mickey Hamill, and the linesmen were Joe Bambrick and Fred Roberts, the two top goalscorers in the Irish League, and all officiated again at subsequent women's games.

Women's contributions to the game often went unheralded. Sean Fallon, who played for Glasgow Celtic (1950–8), attended the Sisters of Mercy school in Sligo in the 1930s and was always grateful for the valuable coaching he received from one of the nuns who was herself a useful footballer and regularly joined in the boys' matches.[74] All too often women were consigned to peripheral roles: Cork FC for example had a Ladies Committee, but this was largely limited to fundraising activities.[75] From photographs of the crowds attending matches it is clear that soccer continued to retain a female following. The actress Maureen O'Hara was a keen Shamrock Rovers supporter and a regular visitor to Glenmalure Park during the 1930s; many years later she could still clearly recall the fierce tackling of Sacky Glen and the mercurial brilliance of Paddy Moore. There were also some pioneering women involved in the administration of the game. Mary Jane Cunningham, the wife of Joe Cunningham, was appointed a director of Shamrock Rovers in 1936, becoming the first female director of an Irish football club. She was one of the key personalities in the Irish game, taking an active part in the running of the club and the signing of new players until her retirement in 1972.[76] In all, the growth in popularity of the women's game after the First World War was more significant than the brief upsurge of the 1890s and rather more rooted in working-class communities. Although women's football went into eclipse from the mid-1930s, it still managed to plant seeds of real interest that would later flourish when circumstances proved more congenial.

5

Leagues of Nations:
International Football 1921–39

After secession from the IFA in June 1921, the FAI's overriding ambition was to seek international recognition. Initially this was rather difficult, as for seven months after its founding it was an association without a state, the Irish Free State only coming into being after ratification of the Anglo-Irish Treaty and the election of a provisional government by Dáil Éireann in January 1922. Determined to look beyond the UK, in early 1922 the FAI contacted the Fédération Française de Football (FFF) to seek a match against the French national team. The French federation declined, regretting that the fixture could not be arranged as the FAI did not belong to FIFA and advised it to seek membership.[1] The FAI's subsequent application to FIFA was, however, refused on the grounds that the world body could not recognise two separate national associations from the same country (even though at the time the IFA was not actually a member of FIFA). The outbreak of civil war in Ireland in June 1922 also complicated the matter, with FIFA concluding that the country's political situation was too unstable to admit a new association.[2]

The strained relationship between FIFA and the UK associations added to the complications. When FIFA attempted to revive international football after the end of the war, British officials insisted that Germany and Austria be excluded. FIFA demurred, and the UK associations withdrew (only rejoining in 1924). This was a serious blow to FIFA, which believed that the prestige and expertise of the UK associations were crucial to the global development of the game. However, it and the main continental federations hoped that the UK could be brought back within the fold and were reluctant to alienate its associations by recognising the newly founded FAI, a body that had yet to prove itself viable and carried little weight internationally.

With the route to FIFA blocked, the FAI applied for membership of the IFAB in June 1922, but IFA opposition meant its application was immediately rejected. While the IFA held the upper hand, it had been damaged by the split and could not completely ignore the new association, which represented hundreds of clubs outside Northern Ireland and dozens within it. In February 1923 it agreed to meet the FAI to discuss their differences at the Shelbourne Hotel in Dublin.[3] The FAI presented the northern delegates with an eight-point document that effectively partitioned the administration of association football in Ireland, proposing that the FAI should have control in the twenty-six counties of the Irish Free State, while the IFA, which should rename itself the 'North of Ireland Football Association', would oversee the six counties of Northern Ireland. Should the two associations agree to unite, their headquarters would be based in Dublin. It further advocated that both associations would be represented on international bodies such as the IFAB and FIFA. IFA representatives were outraged. At most they were prepared to concede that, providing the FAI dissolved itself, meetings of IFA executive committee could alternate between Dublin and Belfast, and more international games could be held in Dublin. With such a glaring gap between the two sides, the meeting broke up without agreement.[4]

Within days, the IFA contacted the English, Scottish and Welsh FAs and successfully lobbied for sanctions against the FAI: the British associations agreed that they would play no international games against its teams and their clubs would not be allowed to play within its jurisdiction. With Britain firmly closed off, the FAI renewed its efforts to forge links with the Continent and in March 1923 managed to persuade the French Athletic Club of Gallia to come to Ireland. Gallia, which included some French international players in its line-up, drew

1–1 with Bohemians on Easter Saturday (31 March) and 0–0 with a League of Ireland selection at Dalymount Park the following day. The league team had to be renamed a 'Pioneer FC XI' at the last minute to downplay the game's representative significance and conform with the terms of Gallia's permit from the Fédération Française. The visitors though were warmly received and after the Sunday match Gallia's officials were presented with the Irish and French tricolours that had flown over the stadium. Highlighting the symbolic aspects of the game, newspaper reports recalled the presentation seventy-five years ago of the Irish tricolour to Young Ireland nationalists in Paris in 1848.[5]

Such matches were not enough to sustain a new national association, which would clearly struggle to survive without the income and prestige provided by regular international fixtures. Since the Irish Free State had become an internationally recognised polity on 6 December 1922 (a year after the signing of the Anglo-Irish Treaty) and the Civil War was coming to an end, the FAI renewed its application for FIFA membership in May 1923, arguing that an independent state was entitled to its own football association. Mindful of the grounds for FIFA's refusal the previous year, it adopted the title of the Football Association of the Irish Free State (FAIFS) to define the limits of its territorial jurisdiction.[6] It also enlisted the help of government, accompanying its application with a letter from Osmond Grattan Esmonde (1896–1936), assistant secretary at the Department of External Affairs (and later president of the FAIFS), who confirmed that the association was acting with the consent of the Free State government and was entitled to all the rights and privileges enjoyed by national associations under FIFA rules.[7] The application was considered at FIFA's Annual Congress in Geneva in 1923 and, with the support of the influential Fédération Française, the FAIFS was admitted to provisional membership of FIFA on 10 August 1923. There were, however, some conditions: membership was granted pending clarification of the political status of the Free State from the British Foreign Office, and the association's jurisdiction was confined to the twenty-six counties of the new state, which meant that it could no longer accept affiliation from clubs in Northern Ireland.[8]

FIFA's decision to admit the Free State to membership prompted the IFAB to take the Irish split more seriously and organise a conference with the FAIFS in Liverpool in October 1923 to make a renewed attempt to resolve Irish differences. Buoyed up by FIFA recognition, Dublin demanded that the IFA explicitly recognise FAIFS jurisdiction over the twenty-six counties, that it be allowed play international matches on the same basis as the IFA, and that the IFA alter its name in keeping with its territorial jurisdiction, as the FAIFS had recently done. The IFA was prepared to accede only to the first of these, but it and other IFAB delegates agreed to recognise the FAIFS as an association with 'Dominion' status, equivalent to those from other Commonwealth countries such as Canada and South Africa. The practical effects were to lift the boycott on players registered with the FAIFS, sanction inter-league matches against UK teams, and allow clubs affiliated to the UK associations to play in the Free State. These were welcome concessions, but the FAIFS had still received only partial recognition and the IFA was the real winner. The British associations continued to recognise the latter as the only body competent to represent Ireland in international football, and all its powers remained intact, including the right to select players from its neighbouring 'Dominion' association and to use the title 'Ireland' for its team. The FAIFS had hoped for matches against British international teams, but requests in subsequent months to play against England, Wales and Scotland were rejected.[9] Mostly, the British associations continued to regard the FAIFS as a rather troublesome body that sought to drag them into political arguments. An FAI team would not play full international fixtures against England until 1946, Wales until 1960, Scotland until 1961 and Northern Ireland until 1978. This isolation represented a serious setback to the fledgling association and has been described by a leading historian of the game as 'a calculated act of political spite ... [and] a sure way of starving the nation's Lilliputian football culture of competition, income and support'.[10]

Many knotty issues remained to be resolved, which the conference was happy to leave to bilateral negotiations between the two Irish associations. When they met again in Belfast on 8 March 1924, the IFA suggested that the Ireland international team be selected by a committee on which the two associations would have equal representation but would be permanently chaired by an IFA member. The FAIFS asked that the chair should be rotated in alternate years, but this proved unacceptable to the IFA and the negotiations foundered, Dublin insisting that it was not prepared to accept Belfast's permanent supremacy. It drew the conclusion that its future in international football lay with FIFA and continental Europe.[11]

***

To secure a first taste of international competition, the FAIFS looked to the upcoming 1924 Olympic Games in Paris. Since FIFA was an organiser of the Olympic soccer tournament, and the FAIFS a provisional member of the world body, it was entitled to send a team. In the past Irishmen had participated in Olympic Games for the UK, and for American and South African teams, but this was their first opportunity to do so under their own flag and Irish nationalists were anxious that their country's independence should be acknowledged internationally. The FAIFS assumed it would have official support for its efforts, but soon found otherwise. The president of the Irish Olympic Council, John J. Keane, was a leading GAA official who was markedly unsympathetic to the FAIFS, regarding it as a partitionist body that promoted a foreign sport. Rather than supporting the FAIFS bid, the Olympic Council of Ireland called on the two Irish soccer associations to combine their resources and send a united team to Paris. The IFA, however, had no interest in any such co-operation. After much argument the FAIFS eventually managed to mitigate the objections of the Olympic Council by recruiting a player from Northern Ireland, which allowed the team to be portrayed as an all-Ireland selection that could compete under the flag of the Olympic Council of Ireland.[12]

The council, though, remained grudging in its attitude and offered no financial assistance. The estimated cost of sending a team to Paris was over £800 and the FAIFS's own coffers were almost empty. To raise the required funds it launched a public appeal and arranged a series of exhibition games. The best-attended of these was played between a

Free State League selection and Glasgow Celtic at Dalymount Park on 22 February 1924 and attracted 22,000 spectators who paid gate receipts of £1,200. However, after expenses (including a substantial payment to Celtic) and the deduction of the government's entertainment tax, only £250 remained.[13]

Eventually, with donations from private citizens and various football clubs, the funds to send a team to Paris were raised. On 24 May a squad of sixteen players, most of whom played for Bohemians, St James's Gate and Athlone Town, the leading amateur clubs in the domestic league, were seen off by well-wishers at Dublin's Westland Row station. Although no political or civic dignitaries were present to confer any official endorsement, the FAIFS was determined to invest the party with the dignity of national sporting ambassadors and on their arrival in Paris on 27 May players and officials laid a wreath (inscribed in Irish and French) at the tomb of the Unknown Warrior.

Twenty-two national associations had accepted FIFA's invitation, eleven for the first time, including other newly independent nations such as Lithuania, Latvia and Estonia. The tournament was to be played on a knock-out basis, and the Irish team received a bye to advance to the last sixteen. On 28 May 1924 they faced Bulgaria in their opening game at the Stade de Colombes near Paris, the first time that Irishmen had competed under their own flag in an Olympic event. The Free State had no official national anthem at this stage and on the advice of the Department of External Affairs used Thomas Moore's 'Let Erin Remember'. To avoid a colour clash with the Bulgarians who wore green, the Irish wore light-blue shirts. It proved a successful start to international competition, the Irish winning 1–0 with a goal from Paddy 'Dirty' Duncan of St James's Gate. Unfortunately, there were few spectators present to witness this piece of Irish sporting history: the official attendance in the 45,000-capacity stadium was just 1,659 (1,137 of whom had received complimentary tickets).[14] The Free State progressed to meet Holland in the quarter-final at the Stade de Paris on 2 June, when an even smaller crowd of just under 1,500 saw them eliminated from the competition after a 2–1 defeat. Holland gave Uruguay a tough game in the semi-final, losing 2–1, and Uruguay went on to win the tournament, beating Switzerland 3–0 in the final before a crowd of 40,000.[15]

To make the most of the trip, the Irish arranged a challenge match on 3 June at the Stade de Colombes against Estonia, which they won 3–1. The following evening the Cercle athlétique de Paris club hosted a formal dinner for the Irish delegation attended by the long-serving FIFA president Jules Rimet. Newspaper reports referred to 'The Soldier's Song' (which had become the unofficial Irish national anthem) being sung, after which the party returned home in good spirits, arriving in Dublin on 6 June. Their performance was one of the highlights for the Irish Olympic team, which did not win any medals in athletic events, although the former Bohemians winger Oliver St John Gogarty brought home a bronze medal for his poem 'Tailteann ode' in the mixed literature competition.[16]

On their return the team received no official recognition. There was some press coverage, but even that was sparing; the Free State still had no radio station of its own and the absence of domestic radio coverage of the tournament limited its public impact. The unionist *Irish Times*, in the process of accommodating itself to the new state, provided the most laudatory commentary, congratulating the FAIFS on its achievement in getting a team to the Olympic Games and praising the team's displays. Many southern unionists feared that the new regime would take the nationalist slogan of 'Ourselves Alone' to an extreme, creating an autarkic and culturally insular Gaelic state in which they would struggle to find a place. *The Irish Times* therefore made a particular point of welcoming the fact that the Free State had not entirely rejected 'those Saxon sports that have become the inheritance of the whole civilised world'.[17] Players and officials were, however, well aware that although they had represented their country with pride, they had done so with little support from the government or the Olympic Council of Ireland.

A coda to the event was that on 14 June the Free State team played the USA, who were returning from the Olympics having also been eliminated in the second round. The Irish team was largely composed of the same amateur players who had gone to Paris. A modest crowd of

3,700 in Dalymount Park gave a warm welcome to the visitors, who took to the pitch carrying the Irish tricolour and the Stars and Stripes. For the first time at a soccer international the national anthem played was 'Amhrán na bhFiann' ('The Soldier's Song') and, thanks to a hat-trick from Ned Brooks of Bohemians, the home team won 3–1, recording the Free State's first win on home soil.[18]

*** *** ***

The team's solid Olympic performances further convinced FAIFS officials that soccer's international dimension was a trump card that could be used to gain greater acceptance for the game at home and greater recognition abroad. Playing international football would proclaim to the world that the Free State was a sovereign nation rather than a British province, and that, unlike the UK, it was keen to forge sporting links with the rest of the world. The association and its supporters, therefore, often stressed that soccer was a genuinely global sport. Major Bryan Cooper TD, the unofficial leader of an independent group of ex-unionist Dáil deputies, argued that 'soccer is THE international game and is being played in lands where the English language has hardly ever been heard'.[19] International matches, though, proved difficult to secure. In 1925, the FAIFS invited the French, Belgian and German national teams to play in Dublin but all declined, partly because of the expense involved in travelling to play an unproven team and partly because of the risk of offending the UK associations.[20] Eventually the efforts of the FAIFS bore fruit and the Italian football association agreed to host a senior international against the Free State in Turin in March 1926. The team was drawn from Free State League players, mostly semi-professionals, and on 17 March a squad of fourteen and officials departed for Italy, facing an arduous boat and train journey of four days. Along the way they met delegations from the Fédération Française in Paris and the Swiss FA in Lausanne, and on arrival in Turin on Saturday 20 March were greeted by Italian officials.

During the interwar period soccer grew significantly in popularity in most European countries. After the carnage of the Great War, sporting idealists hoped that international matches might allow states to settle their differences on football fields rather than killing fields and that FIFA would be the sporting partner of the League of Nations founded in 1920. Such hopes though were often disappointed as aggressive nationalism co-opted soccer for its own ends. This was particularly so with authoritarian regimes, who believed that it was the winning rather than the taking part that mattered, and boasted of sporting success as evidence of racial or political superiority. Fascist Italy, intent on promoting the cults of youth and virility, was among the first European states to harness soccer, using it to train and discipline prospective warriors at home and project its sporting prowess abroad.[21] Italy's performance in the 1924 Olympic Games had been rather disappointing: the team was eliminated in the quarter-finals (like the Free State), but since then they had improved, beating France 7-0 in Turin in March 1925. They would go on to win the bronze medal in the 1928 Olympics and dominate international competitions in the 1930s, winning the 1934 and 1938 World Cups and the 1936 Olympics.

The Free State approached the game on 21 March 1926 with some confidence. Most of the team had played in a 3-1 victory over the Irish League a week earlier and had high hopes of beating the Italians; they were further encouraged by the cool and misty weather – it had rained all morning but stopped just before the game. As the Italians wore savoy blue (in honour of the ruling House of Savoy), the Irish wore green shirts for the first time. FAIFS officials insisted on the Irish tricolour being flown in the stadium, and on being told that none was available, produced their own. Once the game started it became clear that the long journey had taken a toll on the Irish and that they had under-estimated their opponents. The Italians were three goals up by half-time and coasted to a 3-0 win.[22]

The return fixture in Dublin on 23 April 1927 was eagerly antici-pated and the visitors were accorded a degree of official recognition: on 22 April they were received by Governor General T.M. Healy at the viceregal lodge in the Phoenix Park. Healy described the Italians as 'a powerful lot of boys' who would take some beating but regretted he could not attend the game 'owing to a prior engagement'. However, Kevin O'Higgins, the influential minister for justice who would be assassinated three months later by IRA dissidents, accepted an invitation to attend.[23] The *Irish Independent* commented that 'The recognition extended to the game by the government, the reception accorded the Italian visitors by ... the Governor General, and many other ceremonies connected with the match marked it as something out of the ordinary in our soccer world.'[24]

The FAIFS had expected a large crowd and, with Dalymount Park still in need of substantial development, the IRFU allowed it to use Lansdowne Road. An enthusiastic crowd of over 20,000 saw Italy win 2–1. Afterwards the visiting party was entertained at a dinner in the Royal Hibernian Hotel. The government was represented by O'Higgins, flanked by an eclectic mix of dignitaries, several of them Italophiles or Fascist sympathisers. They included the independent Dublin TD Alfie Byrne, a regular attender of soccer matches; Osmond Grattan Esmonde, a government TD and keen supporter of both soccer and Mussolini; the pro-Fascist Professor Walter Starkie, who lectured in Italian literature at TCD; and General William Richard English Murphy, deputy commissioner of An Garda Síochána, who had served with the British Army on the Italian front in the Great War. The proceedings were marked by considerable nationalist hyperbole on all sides. In 1927, the more brutal aspects of Italian Fascism were often overlooked and many took a benign view of Mussolini as a strong leader who had imposed order on a fractious country. Grattan Esmonde described the match as 'an epoch-making event in the history of association football in the Irish Free State' while General Murphy paid tribute to the football skills of the Italian players and the fighting spirit of Italian soldiers, which he had witnessed himself at the Piave River in 1918. On behalf of the Italian delegation, Paolo Ingenere Graziani, spoke of the two countries' long struggles for independence and of how sport could 'help the two peoples to defend the freedom they had won'. The Italian national anthem and the Fascist anthem 'Giovinezza' were loudly sung and applauded. There were similar scenes the following day as the Italian party sailed from Dún Laoghaire; a large crowd sang Fascist songs and 'all gave the ancient gladiatorial and modern Fascisti salute, the right hand outstretched'.[25]

***

Over the next five years, the Free State played six more matches (three against Belgium, two against Spain and one against Holland); only two were at home and they won four, drew one and lost one. Although infrequent, they provided opportunities for FAIFS officials to remind the government of their efforts to promote the Free State abroad, and they assiduously recorded the diplomatic courtesies extended to the Irish team in its away matches, noting with pride the flying of the Irish tricolour and the playing of 'Amhrán na bhFiann'. In the Dáil, Grattan Esmonde, by this time president of the FAIFS (1928–36), argued that soccer should receive far greater credit for its valuable ambassadorial role. He recalled that some weeks earlier (on 26 April 1931) when the Free State played Spain in Barcelona the unfurling of the Irish flag 'created a very great sensation among the Spanish people ... To say that association football is anti-national, anti-Irish or anti-patriotic is not a fact ... The soccer association is there to uphold, in the international language of football, the honour of our country'.[26]

The FAIFS gave serious consideration to participating in the inaugural FIFA World Cup in Uruguay in July 1930, unlike the UK associations, which were again in dispute with FIFA. However, at a time of severe economic depression, it could not raise sufficient funds to send a team. There was also considerable uncertainty surrounding the new competition: two months before it was due to begin, no European team had committed to taking part, and it took the intervention of FIFA president Jules Rimet to persuade four teams from Europe – France, Belgium, Romania and Yugoslavia – to make the long sea voyage to Montevideo. In the end thirteen teams competed, and the tournament was won by the hosts, who defeated Argentina 4–2 in the final, watched by a crowd of almost 70,000.

The Great Depression made it harder still for the FAIFS to secure international opposition. The Free State played only once in 1932 (beating Holland 2–0 in Amsterdam) and not at all in 1933. However, as the world economy improved, international matches became more frequent, with Ireland (FAI) playing twenty-two matches between 1934 and 1939 (ten at home). This was primarily because a credible international tournament now existed. Thirty-two countries had applied to compete in the 1934 FIFA World Cup, and qualifying rounds were required to determine the sixteen finalists who would travel to Italy. The Free State was placed in a group with Belgium and Holland, with the top two to qualify. On 25 February 1934 it played its first competitive international in Dalymount Park, against Belgium. The Irish had previously won three consecutive friendly matches against Belgium and the game attracted an expectant crowd of 28,000. The Belgians proved speedy and skilful opponents and were two up after 20 minutes, but the Irish fought back, with Paddy Moore of Aberdeen FC scoring four goals to earn a 4–4 draw (the first time in World Cup history that a player had scored four goals in a match).

Moore was like most footballers of the era – an accessible and down-to-earth figure. Before walking to the game in Dalymount he joined some young boys in a kick-about in Ballybough during which one of the boys put the ball through the window of a nearby house and, although Paddy agreed to compensate the irate householder, a garda was called. Once the matter was settled, the prescient garda immediately hailed down a car and asked the driver to 'take this man to Dalymount Park, he's late for the big game and God knows we need him'.[27] Although Moore scored again in the Free State's next qualifier against Holland in Amsterdam on 8 April 1934, this was not enough to save the Irish from a 5–2 defeat that eliminated them from the competition.[28]

The home match against Belgium had though been accorded a novel level of official recognition, with Éamon de Valera, president of the government's executive council, warmly welcoming the Belgian players to Government Buildings. De Valera's Fianna Fáil administration had come to power in 1932. The party received substantial working-class support and some of its leading figures were keen soccer supporters. De Valera himself, although often regarded as a cultural chauvinist, had a relatively open attitude to sport. In his youth he had taken up a wide range of sports including boxing, cycling, cricket and athletics. His preferred form of football was rugby, a game he had played with some ability as a full-back (he was a Munster trialist in 1904) and which he thought particularly suited to the Irish temperament.[29] He also had a pragmatic awareness of the propaganda value of international sport, clearly highlighted months after he came to power by the worldwide publicity received by two Irishmen, Bob Tisdall and Pat O'Callaghan, when they won gold medals in the 400 metres hurdles and hammer-throwing events respectively at the 1932 Olympic Games in Los Angeles. De Valera's appreciation of the uses of association football, the most internationally popular of all team sports, in promoting a greater international awareness of Irish sovereignty, led him to develop cordial relations with the FAI and formally welcome several visiting national soccer teams during the 1930s.[30]

However, most FAIFS invitations to political dignitaries to attend its international games and functions were declined. The poor response from members of the Oireachtas to attend the post-match banquet with Holland in 1935 led the FAIFS to conclude that there is 'a section of Irish political life which is unable or unwilling to grasp the significance of the football "split" and the role the new southern-based Association could play in promoting the Irish Free State abroad'.[31] Soccer in the Free State was not quite the pariah sport that some supporters claimed, but most serving politicians, although prepared to tolerate and occasionally acknowledge the game, were wary of endorsing it. Until the late 1930s, those who attended games regularly in an official capacity were a rarity and tended to be rather singular figures, such as Alfie Byrne, a colourful independent TD who represented several different Dublin constituencies and served as honorary president of the Junior Football Association. In his youth Byrne had played for Strandville (based in the North Strand) and later served as vice-president of Shamrock Rovers while also maintaining a close association with Bohemian FC.[32] As lord mayor of Dublin (1930–9), he welcomed the Hungarian team in December 1934 and often argued the case for soccer in the Dáil, deploring that we 'have in our midst a certain small bigoted narrow-minded section who believe that we can only play one game without violating our national feelings'.[33]

***

In its post-independence relationship to the new state, soccer had some similarities with rugby. The two codes were those most directly in competition with Gaelic football, and both were regularly reminded of their foreign origins. There were those who played and watched soccer and rugby, and sometimes even excelled at them, such as the brothers Kevin and Michael O'Flanagan, who represented Ireland in both codes in the 1940s. This, though, was unusual. For the most part the core constituencies of the two sports differed and, in a society where class differences mattered, their respective governing bodies usually kept their distance. The IRFU was proud that it had managed to remain a thirty-two-county body and that its international team represented both Irish jurisdictions, but this carried its own strains: the difficulties involved in maintaining harmonious relations between unionist and nationalist members often necessitated compromises, which attracted censure on both sides of the border. The question of which flag to fly at international games at Lansdowne Road proved particularly contentious: the IRFU's decision in 1925 to use a four-provinces flag at matches in Dublin, rather than the national tricolour, led to criticism from clubs in Munster and Connacht. Eventually pressure from nationalist rugby supporters and the Irish government compelled the flying of the tricolour at Lansdowne Road from 1932 (in Belfast the Union flag was flown, and at away games the IRFU's own four-provinces flag). The IRFU administration still valued its links with the British Commonwealth, toasting King George V at their annual dinner in Dublin in 1933 and cancelling games on his death in 1936. In contrast, those who ran and supported association football in the Free State were generally more nationalist, and had few worries about alienating or upsetting unionist sensibilities. As in politics, partition permitted the South to exercise independence on its own nationalist terms, and the FAIFS proudly displayed the emblems and symbols of the new state.

This contributed to strained relations between the Dublin association and Belfast, which mirrored that of their respective states. Since partition they had viewed each other warily: Northern Ireland saw the aggrieved Free State as a possible threat to its existence, while the latter saw the former as a reproach to its nationalist ideals. By the mid-1920s they had managed to reach a *modus vivendi* that prevented open conflict, but the accession to power of Fianna Fáil in 1932 brought louder denunciations of partition and the progressive loosening of the constitutional constraints that bound the Free State to the Commonwealth, and in 1937 de Valera's new constitution explicitly laid claim to 'the whole island of Ireland'. Unionists viewed this as an outrageous act of aggression and North–South relations deteriorated.

Hostile political rhetoric often carried over into the sporting sphere and created an atmosphere in which the generosity and goodwill required to bring the opposing camps together was lacking. The FAIFS was especially irritated by the IFA's claim that its jurisdiction extended to the entire island and its insistence on calling its international team 'Ireland'. FAIFS officials raised these matters at the June 1927 FIFA Congress in Finland, requesting that the IFA should be redesignated the 'Football Association of Northern Ireland'. This was unanimously accepted by delegates from the twenty-one national associations present, but ignored by the IFAB, whose members continued to refer to the IFA's international team as 'Ireland'.[34] The matter was again broached with FIFA in 1929 but, without the IFAB's support, FIFA claimed that it was powerless to insist on any name change.[35]

Much of the FAIFS's dissatisfaction stemmed from its exclusion from the British Championship which provided the IFA with regular lucrative games against England and Scotland. For thirty years after the 1921 split the IFA's international team competed only against its British neighbours. Home games were almost always played in Windsor Park (although Celtic Park was used for a match against Wales in 1930) and attracted crowds ranging from 20,000 to 40,000. When the British Championship resumed in 1919, most of the outstanding pre-war Irish players had either retired or were past their best and the IFA team struggled; it would be 1958 before it won the Championship again.

Northern Ireland and Wales generally fought to avoid the wooden spoon, but the former did have occasional successes: in 1926 and 1928 they finished as runner-up, scoring impressive wins against both England and Scotland in 1927/8. Victories over England were particularly prized. After a 2–0 success against England in October 1927, Northern Ireland's centre-forward Hugh Davey recalled that it was 'impossible to put into words the emotion and delight you feel when winning against England in front of your own countrymen'.[36]

Just like the Northern Ireland state, the IFA looked eastwards for kinship and support. It was content with its status as an integral part of the UK, an attitude reinforced by annual fixtures against exclusively British opposition. Home Championship matches allowed the public expression of bonds of fellowship that had been forged at such great cost during the Great War. An observer at a fixture against Scotland in a jammed Windsor Park in February 1929 was struck by the fact that 'there was something essentially British in the scene which took place, even in the tense moments before the ball was set in motion. The teams lined up facing each other, and led by the [Royal Ulster] Constabulary band, the whole assembly joined in the singing of the national anthem'.[37]

While the IFA cherished its British connections, it also had a strong sense of itself as the original and legitimate governing authority for football in Ireland. It affirmed its authority by continuing to use the name 'Ireland' and selecting players from all thirty-two counties, as if the split had never occurred. (Its insistence that Ireland was one – at least in football matters – was a notion generally dearer to nationalist than unionist hearts.) Since the FAIFS was unable to secure any international games in the early 1920s, southern-born players such as Bill Lacey of Liverpool FC, Patsy Gallacher of Glasgow Celtic and Tom Farquharson of Cardiff City, continued to line out for the IFA team. However, all three switched allegiance to the FAIFS when it began to play international matches in the late 1920s. Other notable southern-born players, such as Jimmy Dunne of Sheffield United and Arsenal, Harry Duggan of Leeds United, Paddy Moore of Shamrock Rovers and Aberdeen, Alex Stevenson of Everton, Jimmy Kelly of Derry City and Tommy Breen of Belfast Celtic and Manchester United, also played for both teams. It sometimes seemed that the IFA was more inclined to select southern-born players after the split than before it; altogether thirty-two players appeared for both countries between 1926 and 1950. Most did so without qualms, claiming they were sportsmen who were proud to take the field with other Irishmen, often friends and clubmates, at a time when there were few opportunities to play international football. Many southern supporters enjoyed seeing their favourite players compete against the best and were prepared to lend their support to the IFA international team. When Jimmy Dunne was selected to play for Ireland (IFA) against Wales in February 1928, this was welcomed in the South on the grounds that 'today he will play for his country'.[38] Large numbers of southerners often travelled to these matches: when Northern Ireland beat Scotland 2–1 at Windsor Park in 1934 before a crowd of almost 40,000, it was reported that 'football followers in all parts of Ulster and the Irish Free State were strongly represented in the large crowd'.[39]

Such support though was not universal: the west Belfast-born Mickey Hamill, who had captained Ireland to their Championship win in 1914, believed that the IFA discriminated against Catholic players and refused to play for its team after 1921. FAIFS officials were also unhappy to see southern-born players representing the IFA and in November 1930 relations between the two associations frayed when the IFA selected three Bohemian FC players – Alec Morton, Fred Horlacher and Jimmy Bermingham – for an amateur international against England in Belfast. This was the first time the IFA had selected players from a club affiliated to the FAIFS, which immediately forbade them to take part in the fixture. The three players though informed the FAIFS that as amateurs they believed themselves to be free to play. Criticised in the southern media for acting unpatriotically, they received threatening letters and were suspended by the FAIFS. The case ended up in the High Court in Dublin in December 1930 and was eventually settled when the suspensions were lifted and the three agreed to affirm their allegiance to the FAIFS.[40] The episode seriously damaged relations between the two associations: most fixtures between northern and southern clubs were discontinued, as were inter-league games, which were not resumed until 1938.

The incident was thrown into sharp focus by the decision of Dublin-born goalkeeper Tom Farquharson to refuse an invitation from the IFA to play for its team in September 1931. Farquharson, a staunch nationalist, had won seven IFA caps (1923–5), but announced in 1931 that he would never play for the IFA again. To reward his stance, the FAIFS presented him with a framed parchment and offered to cover any financial loss; one official suggested that his portrait be hung in the association's offices as an inspiration to his fellow players.[41] Farquharson's example was followed by Jimmy Dunne, then probably the best-known Irish footballer of the day, who declined to play for Northern Ireland against Wales in Belfast on 5 December 1931, and afterwards made fifteen appearances for the FAI team.[42]

In an attempt to resolve outstanding disputes and improve relations, the two associations met in Dublin in February 1932. They made some progress, the IFA agreeing in principle to the establishment of a joint committee with equal representation for both associations to oversee international affairs. The FAIFS then requested a seat on the IFAB to give it full equality in international matters. The IFA baulked at this, arguing that as a FIFA member the FAIFS was already represented on the International Board. Negotiations broke down and the subsequent recriminations left the two sides further apart than ever.[43] Afterwards the IFA lobbied the English FA to ask English clubs not to release Free State players for international duties in the hope of forcing the FAIFS back to the table. Wolverhampton Wanderers cited friction between the FA and the FAIFS for refusing to allow Charlie Greene to play in a friendly game against Hungary on 16 December 1934, and Arsenal, Leeds and Everton followed suit. The FAIFS criticised the English FA as unhelpfully partial to the IFA, and relations between Dublin and the IFAB associations suffered.[44]

In March 1936, the FAIFS appointed an energetic new general secretary, Joe Wickham (1890–1968), an experienced official who had already served as president of the Free State League and chairman of the FAIFS. Wickham was intent on asserting the association's authority at home and gaining greater recognition abroad. To try to force FIFA into action on the IFA's exclusive claim to 'Ireland', he changed the international team's name from the Irish Free State to Ireland for a game against Switzerland on 17 March 1936 and renamed the FAIFS the Football Association of Ireland (FAI).[45] (Most supporters of the FAI team simply referred to it as 'Ireland' throughout its history.) Wickham became a familiar figure at FIFA conferences, tirelessly handing out bundles of miniature maps of Ireland to convince delegates of the anomaly of the IFA claim to control football on the whole island while only having effective jurisdiction over a sixth of its territory. However, many foreigners remained confused by the precise details of the Irish dispute and Wickham was eventually told in blunt terms that FIFA did not have the authority to issue directives to the IFAB or its constituent members.[46]

Wickham also tried to turn the tables on the IFA by selecting players born in the North for the FAI team. When Ireland (FAI) beat France 2–0 in Paris in May 1937, the goals were scored by Davy Jordan (Wolverhampton Wanderers) and Jackie Brown (Coventry City), both born in Belfast and the latter already capped by Northern Ireland; the Newry-born Johnny Feenan of Sunderland also featured on that team. This provoked protests from the IFA and for upcoming games it insisted that players declare allegiance to one team. In response the Drogheda-born Manchester United goalkeeper Tommy Breen withdrew from the FAI team for a World Cup qualifier against Norway on 7 November 1937 to play for Northern Ireland against Scotland three days later. Such decisions could have serious consequences for players, and Breen was not selected again by the FAI for another eight years.[47] Insistence by both associations on capping the same players continued to cause friction and also damaged relations between the FAI and English clubs, who disliked releasing players for two different international teams. When Belfast-born players such as Jackie Brown, Harry Baird (Manchester United) and Walter McMillen (Chesterfield) were selected to play for the FAI team against Czechoslovakia in Prague on 18 May 1938, McMillen was said to be ill, while Baird and Brown were withdrawn by their clubs after instructions from the English FA.[48]

The situation in which both associations fielded teams called 'Ireland' was given an additional edge by the promulgation of the new

Irish constitution, *Bunreacht na hÉireann*, by de Valera's government in 1937, which effectively created an Irish republic in all but name. The term 'Free State' was never much liked by Irish nationalists and the first article of the new constitution insisted that 'the name of the State is Éire, or in the English language, Ireland'. This boosted Wickham's determination to lay exclusive claim to the name 'Ireland' and in November 1938 he and two other high-ranking FAI officials, Myles Murphy and Jim Brennan, travelled to London to ask the Irish high commissioner (effectively ambassador), John Dulanty, to bring political pressure to bear on the English FA to recognise its claim.[49] The timing was significant, with the FAI attempting to take advantage of a recent thaw in Anglo-Irish relations. On his accession to power in 1932 de Valera had begun to chip away at the 1921 Treaty to make it clear that the Free State was no loyal Dominion. He abolished the oath of allegiance to the crown, downgraded the office of governor general and ceased payment of land annuities owed to the British Treasury, the last triggering a trade war. These, and further moves to expand the Free State's independence, were interpreted as breaches of the Treaty by successive British governments and strained relations. By the late 1930s, however, the threat of war in Europe and the economic damage caused by protective trade tariffs made a resolution in the interests of both states. This came about after a series of constructive meetings between the heads of government in 1938, which led Prime Minister Neville Chamberlain to conclude of de Valera that 'queer creature as he is in many ways, he is sincere, and ... no enemy of this country'.[50] Such goodwill led to the signing of an Anglo-Irish agreement in April 1938 that settled the financial and trade disputes, and transferred to Dublin three strategic 'Treaty ports' that Britain had retained in 1921. Hoping to take advantage of these improved relations, Dulanty wrote on several occasions to the Dominions Office asking it to intervene on the FAI's behalf, but the British government and the English FA were clearly reluctant to become involved and the initiative came to nothing.[51]

***

While the FAI was often disappointed by the tepid recognition received from the Irish government, this became somewhat warmer as the decade progressed. In May 1937, Minister for Finance Seán MacEntee became the first member of the Fianna Fáil cabinet to accept an official invitation from the FAI when he attended the post-match banquet for the Swiss national team.[52] When Ireland (FAI) played Norway in an important World Cup qualification match in Dublin in November 1937, three government ministers – MacEntee, Oscar Traynor and Frank Aiken – attended the game, as did the attorney general, Patrick Lynch. The game was broadcast on Radio Éireann, and the Fianna Fáil-sponsored *Irish Press* praised the Irish players and FAI officials as important ambassadors for the state.[53]

Soon after the inauguration in June 1938 of Douglas Hyde as Ireland's first president under the new constitution, the FAI invited him to a match against Poland on 13 November 1938 at Dalymount Park. Hyde agreed to attend and, flanked by de Valera and Traynor, enjoyed seeing the Irish team secure a 3–2 win. The president's secretary, Michael McDunphy, had anticipated some form of protest from the GAA since Hyde had been one of the association's patrons since 1902. However, he believed that it was neither advisable nor practical for the president to ignore a sport as popular as association football: procedural notes for presidential attendance at sports fixtures stated that 'there is no question that preference should be given to national games, such as hurling and football, but such a preference does not mean the complete exclusion of games and sports of an international character'.[54] Hyde himself appreciated that soccer was popular with 'a very large section of the Irish people, a big number of whom are and have been earnest workers in the National Movement' and was keen to take up the invitation.[55]

The GAA Central Council, though, had little sympathy for the niceties of the president's position: a majority believed that he had publicly flouted its rules by attending the game and voted to remove him as a patron. Hyde refrained from comment to avoid stoking the controversy, but de Valera was incensed. He had envisaged the presidential office as above party politics and factional disputes, and complained strongly to the GAA. His indignation was widely shared. Hyde was a much-respected figure who had always managed to promote Gaelic culture without resorting to denigration. Many condemned the GAA's attitude as arrogant and bigoted, *The Irish Times* observing that 'the belief that the national soul is injured by the presence of the head of state at a game of this kind is cant of the worst kind ... A connection of thirty years' standing is to be broken by a display of intolerance which it would be difficult to parallel even in those countries in which party zeal passes for patriotism.'[56] While some GAA members thought that the association had over-reached itself, its leading officials were unrepentant. To charges of 'intolerance' the GAA president Pádraig MacNamee responded that 'My only complaint is that we are not half intolerant enough. We and all Irishmen, who value the inheritance of the Gael must always be intolerant of everything foreign in this country. We can never rest until the last vestige of foreign domination is gone beyond recall.'[57]

In Northern Ireland, the incident was eagerly seized on by unionists. One claimed that the GAA seemed to spend more time denouncing 'foreign games' than promoting its own, and dismissed these 'fanatics' as 'perpetual disturbers [who] prepare the soil for the extremists'.[58] They denounced the South as a narrow and intolerant state, where even one's choice of sport was subject to sanction.[59] Hyde's removal as a patron of the GAA was condemned as 'symptomatic of the spirit of primitive tribalism that passes current for enlightened nationalism in Southern Ireland. It is a travesty of patriotism and of culture; it engenders sectional hatreds, restricts and distorts the outlook of thousands and makes its advocates the laughing stock of more advanced and progressive nations.'[60]

In the end the GAA lost most from the incident. Hyde remained a popular figure and the FAI, which wisely said very little, appeared for once to be closer to the government than the GAA. Association football had been granted official recognition by the Irish head of state and subsequent presidents would ensure that this continued.[61]

***

From the mid-1930s, FAI international matches became more frequent, averaging about four a season. They usually attracted crowds of over 20,000, and the level of press coverage and public interest was significantly greater than a decade earlier. To qualify for the 1938 World Cup in France, the FAI team was drawn against Norway. The amateur Norwegians were a strong side, having finished third in the 1936 Berlin Olympic Games and beaten the hosts Germany 2–0 (said to be the only international football match ever attended by Adolf Hitler). They also proved too strong for the Irish, beating them 3–2 in Oslo on 10 October 1937 and drawing 3–3 in Dublin on 7 November to secure qualification. Such disappointments caused some recriminations in Irish soccer, including complaints from provincial associations that the FAI was overly focused on Dublin, particularly when selecting the national team.[62]

The FAI team was chosen by a selection committee of five officials, usually drawn from the established Dublin clubs, who tended to plump for the players they knew best. The FAI, no doubt aware that similar complaints had in the past driven a wedge between Belfast and Dublin, made an effort to respond. In 1939, it arranged for the national team to play their first game outside the capital, at the Mardyke in Cork. The opposition was a strong Hungarian team who had finished second to Italy in the 1938 World Cup final. A capacity 18,000 crowd saw the teams draw 2–2 on 19 March, although the veteran *Irish Independent* sportswriter W.P. Murphy was scathing about the lack of vocal support from spectators, describing them as 'one of the most apathetic crowds I have ever seen at an international', and put this down to the absence of Cork players on the Irish team.[63] The association clearly did not regard the experiment as a success, and it would be 1985 before another full international was held outside Dublin.

With the World Cup still in its infancy, most of the matches the FAI team played in the 1930s were friendlies; these were viewed as important opportunities for teams to enhance their reputation and were keenly contested. As the decade progressed, so too did Irish fortunes, and in 1936–8 Ireland (FAI) achieved wins against strong teams such as Germany, France, Switzerland and Poland. In the fraught atmosphere of the 1930s, international sports fixtures were often complicated by politics. After Hitler's accession to power in Germany, the Nazi state exercised tight control over sport and ruthlessly used it to promote the Third Reich, most notably at the 1936 Olympics. The increasingly politicised nature of international sport would lead commentators, such as George Orwell, to characterise it as 'war minus the shooting' in which national enmities were aggravated 'by sending forth a team of eleven men, labelled as national champions, to do battle against some rival team, and allowing it to be felt on all sides that whichever nation is defeated will "lose face".'[64]

The FAI was, however, keen to assert its independence and secure matches, and showed little concern about such politicisation. Its team played Germany three times between 1935 and 1939, which created some invidious situations. To wring the maximum propaganda value from international matches, the German FA encouraged visiting teams to give a pre-match Nazi salute as a courtesy to their hosts.[65] Irish players obeyed the request in Dortmund on 8 May 1935, but did not repeat the gesture in the return fixture against Germany in Dalymount Park on 17 October 1936, although some FAI officials did rather awkwardly comply. When a German photographer tried to cajole spectators to give the required salute, most of the Dublin crowd responded with a variety of one- and two-fingered gestures instead. The Irish players were similarly defiant and tore into the visitors to secure a 5–2 win, probably the high point of Ireland's first decade of international football.[66]

When Ireland and Germany met again in Bremen on 23 May 1939, the political situation was rather more tense. Two months earlier, Germany had invaded Czechoslovakia in defiance of the Munich agreement and heightened the prospect of war with Britain and France. Violent Nazi persecution of German Jews had intensified since the *Kristallnacht* pogrom of 9–10 November 1938 and was widely reported by the international press. Some questioned the wisdom of playing in Germany but as ever the FAI was anxious for the match to go ahead. The FAI secretary recorded the 'lavish hospitality' extended to his party and noted with pride that 'the Tricolour and the Swastika flew side by side in the stadium'. He also recorded that the Irish players and officials were 'very cordially welcomed' by the German sports minister, who 'paid special tribute to us playing the match as arranged despite ... untrue press reports regarding the position in Germany and their intentions'.[67] The Nazi's bellicose nationalism was rather more evident than in Dortmund four years earlier. For an hour before the kick-off, the Irish team had to stand on the pitch listening to Nazi speeches and chants that worked up the German crowd and players. On the instructions of the Irish embassy the Irish players gave the Nazi salute during the German national anthem but as they did so their staunchly nationalist captain, Jimmy Dunne, exhorted them to 'Remember Aughrim! Remember 1916!', rousing them into a fervour that matched that of their opponents and helped them secure a hard-fought 1–1 draw.[68]

Just over three months later, the histrionics witnessed in Bremen assumed a more deadly form when German tanks rolled into Poland on 1 September. Europe was again at war and international football was put on hold. Ireland (FAI) would not play another international match for seven years. In thirty international games between 1926 and 1939, the team had won eleven, drawn eight and lost eleven. It had failed to qualify for the 1934 and 1938 World Cup tournaments but had forged amicable relations with leading European football associations in France, Germany and Hungary, and consolidated the FAI's position in the international game. This allowed Irish soccer followers to argue that their country was no chauvinist insular state but one open to the outside world. The very fact that the Irish national team was participating in international football was probably far more effective than most government propaganda in alerting other countries to its independent status. On the pitch the FAI team had managed to establish itself as a credible force, capable of matching and even beating some of the best sides in Europe. This was a matter of considerable pride to Irish soccer supporters and provided much-needed encouragement to a country beset by the post-revolutionary disillusionments of political division, economic stagnation and stubborn poverty.

6

National Service:
War and Its Aftermath 1939–55

On 2 September 1939, the day after the German invasion of Poland, Taoiseach Éamon de Valera announced that his country would remain neutral in the European war. The policy was a popular one, overwhelmingly supported by the parliamentary opposition and the electorate, most of whom believed that any other decision risked fanning the embers of civil war. The response in Northern Ireland was predictably different. In a BBC radio broadcast, Prime Minister Craig declared, 'We are King's men', and announced his government's unqualified support for the war effort. Éire's neutrality reinforced Northern Ireland's strategic importance and the ports of Belfast, Derry and Larne would prove crucial in helping Britain win the hard-fought Battle of the Atlantic.[1] The province's shipbuilding, engineering and textile industries also proved invaluable: firms that had struggled in the 1930s were reinvigorated to produce hundreds of ships, thousands of aircraft and vast quantities of uniforms and fabrics for military use. Belfast's importance to the war effort made it a prime target for the Luftwaffe, which mounted devastating bombing raids on the city in April and May 1941 that destroyed hundreds of homes and claimed almost 1,000 lives.[2]

North or South, there was little of the euphoria of 1914: nobody expected the war to be over by Christmas or described it as a 'Great Game'. The pre-war hope that sport could mitigate or even prevent international conflict now seemed naive. All across Europe, national sporting competitions were abandoned as combatants feared aerial bombardment or gas attacks on crowded sports stadiums. The English FA suspended the Football League in 1939 and replaced it with regional competitions. While football could not be seen to absorb too much national energy, the British government accepted that a scaled-down game would serve as a morale booster for soldiers and civilians and a useful fundraiser for war charities.

With the suspension of the English Football League, many Irish-born professional players returned home to avoid their wages being reduced to £1 a week or the prospect of military conscription. Some though stayed to play in regional leagues, take up civilian employment or join the roughly 50,000 volunteers from the twenty-six counties who served with the British armed services. In Éire too many sportsmen joined the Defence Forces. The country's regular and reserve forces had amounted to fewer than 20,000 men in 1939 but after an intensive recruitment campaign by Minister for Defence Oscar Traynor, the regular army was increased to over 40,000 by May 1941 with an additional 106,000 serving in the Local Defence Force. Many new recruits were soccer players and, anxious to encourage physical fitness and maintain morale, the Defence Forces relaxed its insistence on playing only Gaelic games. The young Con Martin, who would become a distinguished international footballer, played Gaelic football, soccer and basketball for various army and Air Corps teams. This brought about the inevitable protests, with the general secretary of the GAA describing the decision as 'a national betrayal and a nullification of the natural order' and demanding Traynor's dismissal.[3] Some however thought that the Defence Forces had more pressing concerns and Sean O'Faolain was moved to write: 'With a world war raging at our shores, boiling up from the Papuans to the Aleutians, from Iceland down to Madagascar, I think that this is, of all recent Celtic lunacies, the most lunatic that I have ever met.'[4]

While the different approaches of the two Irish states to the war had compounded partition, soccer occasionally eased tensions. After the destruction wrought by the Belfast Blitz, which began in April

1941, several clubs crossed the border to play fund-raising matches. Among these was St James's Gate (the previous year's League of Ireland champions), who played against Glentoran at the Oval for the 'Unity Cup' on 28 April 1941 in a gesture widely praised in Belfast.[5] A week later the Oval was virtually destroyed when the Luftwaffe targeted east Belfast. With the usual paths to international and representative football closed off, it made sense for the two Irish associations to work together, and inter-league matches were played with greater regularity: there were eleven meetings between the two sides (1940–5), held twice-yearly at Dalymount on St Patrick's Day and Windsor Park on Easter Monday (the Irish League won five, the League of Ireland won three, and three were drawn). The pitting together of the country's best players roused considerable popular interest in both jurisdictions, sometimes attracting crowds of over 30,000. A generally friendly spirit prevailed during these games, with the fact that the teams represented different leagues rather than different states toning down their national significance.

**

Neutrality had been a forthright expression of Éire's independence but came at the cost of political and diplomatic isolation. After the war the FAI was eager to renew its contacts with the wider world: international matches were its main form of income and the team had gone seven years without playing one. Largely owing to the energetic efforts of its general secretary, Joe Wickham, Ireland (FAI) was among the first countries in Europe to resume international football, with away matches in June 1946 against Portugal and Spain. The choice of opposition was significant: the fact that both countries had been neutral during the war minimised the possibility of diplomatic friction. Having also suffered from wartime isolation, they too were keen to return to the international sporting arena and they provided the opposition in six of the first seven post-war matches played by the Irish between 1946 and 1948.

Like other authoritarian regimes, the right-wing dictatorships of Spain and Portugal readily exploited the propaganda opportunities offered by sport, using their national football teams to create greater unity at home and gain greater recognition abroad. Franco had outlawed the separatist symbolism of clubs such as Barcelona in Catalonia and Athletic Bilbao in the Basque country, and strongly favoured the country's leading Castilian team Real Madrid, whose players formed the backbone of the Spanish national side. In Portugal, Salazar's regime similarly encouraged devotion to the national team, elevating it to one of its three main patriotic symbols with the slogan 'Fatima for religion, Fado for nostalgia, and Football for the glory of Portugal'.[6]

For its Iberian tour, the FAI was keen to include northern-born players and selected four Northern Ireland internationals: Billy McMillan and Jackie Vernon of Belfast Celtic, Josiah 'Paddy' Sloan (Arsenal) and Jimmy McAlinden (Portsmouth, previously Belfast Celtic). The IFA, rather surprisingly, agreed to facilitate the request. This was partly a result of the wartime improvement in relations between the associations and partly because the IFA's president was Austin Donnelly of Belfast Celtic, who was happy to see present and past players from his club gaining international honours.[7]

The Irish went down 3–1 to Portugal on 16 June but, a week later, inspired by a heroic display by their stand-in goalkeeper Con Martin, beat Spain 1–0 on 23 June, the best away result the team had ever achieved. General Franco had greeted the Irish officials and attended the game, while the Irish ambassador in Madrid held a reception for the team. The FAI considered the tour to be a great success and Jackie Carey recalled it as the most satisfying of his career, crediting the important contribution of the northern players. This was the first time that the team had travelled by aeroplane, and the post-war growth of air travel would transform the world of international soccer, significantly increasing the options of peripherally located teams such as the two Irelands.[8]

By 1946, the FAI team was in the unusual position of having played throughout Europe, but never against any of its nearest neighbours. This was a state of affairs that the association was anxious to change, and with England due to play Northern Ireland in Belfast on 28 September

1946 to mark the post-war resumption of the British Championship, Joe Wickham saw an opportunity. In August he contacted Stanley Rous, his counterpart in the English FA, reminding him that 1946 marked the twenty-fifth anniversary of the FAI's founding and suggesting that a senior international game against England in Dublin would be a fitting celebration. He assured Rous that the first English national team to visit Dublin since 1912 would receive a warm welcome from the Irish public.[9]

The English FA accepted, agreeing to play at Dalymount Park on 30 September. The FAI and the Irish government were determined to make the most of the visit, which was seen as an ideal opportunity to mend bridges after the strains of the war years. The decision of Éire, still a member of the Commonwealth, to remain neutral during the war and deny Britain the use of its strategic ports had prompted bafflement and exasperation in Britain. In practice de Valera's administration had adopted a pro-Allied neutrality, but this received little acknowledgement, largely owing to de Valera's punctilious observation of public protocols. In particular, his decision in May 1945 to express his government's condolences to the German ambassador in Dublin on the death of Hitler triggered an outpouring of anger in Britain: de Valera was widely denounced as an insular nationalist bigot who had spent the war sheltering safely under Britain's defences, while all the time harbouring a bitter enmity to his protector.

Resentment towards the Dublin government was however somewhat mitigated by the actions of the many thousands of its citizens who volunteered for the British armed services. These included high-profile footballers, such as Alex Stevenson of Everton and Jackie Carey of Manchester United, both of whom lined out against England at Dalymount Park. Stevenson joined the RAF and served as ground crew, while Carey enlisted with the Queen's Royal Hussars and served in the Middle East and Italy, mostly as a physical fitness instructor and coach of army football teams. Although a patriotic Irishman with a great love of the Irish language, Carey saw no contradiction in joining the British Army, maintaining that 'any country which gives me a living is worth fighting for'.[10]

To allay accusations of Anglophobia, de Valera insisted on hosting a pre-match reception at Government Buildings for the English team and officials, who were presented with a glass replica of the Ardagh chalice. President Seán T. O'Kelly attended the match, while Tánaiste Seán Lemass led the government delegation, and Sir John Maffey, the UK representative in Ireland, was also present. Radio Éireann broadcast coverage of most of the game, with a commentary by Eamonn Andrews.[11] England's visit was regarded as a major event: they were regarded as one of the best teams in the world and players such as Billy Wright at centre-half and Tom Finney, Raich Carter, Tommy Lawton and Wilf Mannion in the forwards were well-known to Irish supporters. Two days earlier in Belfast they had easily overcome Northern Ireland by a score of 7–2.

Facing England aroused a national passion like no other and the capacity crowd roared on the home team, who dominated the play. The Irish, though, could not put the ball past the imposing figure of the England goalkeeper Frank Swift, who recalled how they bombarded his goal and how Kevin O'Flanagan, Alex Stevenson and Jackie Carey all outshone their English counterparts. Against the run of play, Tom Finney scored for England in the eighty-second minute. Swift later wrote that the goal 'broke the hearts of the crowd and the Irish players and it gave England one of the most hard-earned wins in their entire history. Long after other memories of this game have died, I shall remember the silence which followed Tom Finney's winner.'[12]

At the post-match dinner (which the English visitors, still subject to wartime rationing, remembered as 'the best any of us had eaten in years'), the Irish players were generously praised by their opponents who expressed the hope that there would be many more meetings between the teams.[13] The match had proved a highly successful venture for the FAI, its friendly atmosphere helping to improve Anglo-Irish relations and serving as a reminder of soccer's diplomatic importance. FA officials agreed to a return match and the two teams met again in September 1949 (the English League also visited Dublin in 1947). In between there was an unexpected jolt in Anglo-Irish relations when Taoiseach John A. Costello, who had replaced de Valera after sixteen years of Fianna Fáil rule, in September 1948 announced his inter-party government's intention to withdraw from the Commonwealth and declare Ireland a republic, which was given legal effect the following April. The name 'Republic of Ireland' took some time to gain international currency and most people in Britain, having become accustomed to 'Éire', continued to use it for both the state and its national football team for many years to come.

Constitutional manoeuvrings did not stand in the way of the Republic's first away game against England on 21 September 1949 at Goodison Park, Liverpool. The Irish though were not especially confident. Only seven players were released by their clubs in time to attend a pre-match training session in Southport, and Con Martin remembered his feelings of trepidation before the game, 'looking around and fearing the worst. For my money, there were too many small lads, too many square pegs in round holes to have any real chance against a team which we reckoned was one of the best in the world.'[14] England were indeed a formidable team who could ruthlessly exploit the opposition's weaknesses: two years earlier they had beaten Portugal 10–0 in Lisbon and eight weeks after playing the Republic they inflicted a 9–2 defeat on Northern Ireland.

The match at Goodison was the reverse of the earlier encounter in Dalymount: England dominated, but their attacks foundered on a strong Irish defence in which Martin, Carey and goalkeeper Tommy Godwin of Shamrock Rovers were outstanding. This time the Irish took their chances, Martin converting a penalty in the first half and Peter Farrell of Everton sealing a 2–0 victory in the eighty-fifth minute. The English reaction was one of surprise mingled with admiration: one newspaper noting that 'Eire, small and weak by soccer standards, triumphed where the great European teams in their pre-war heydays always failed ... they set about [England] with keen, swift, direct action and flayed the hides off them.'[15] This was the first time a team from outside the UK had beaten England at home. However, owing to English familiarity with the Irish players (nine of whom played for English clubs) and a vague understanding of the exact constitutional status of 'Éire', the Irish were not regarded as genuinely foreign opposition, and England's first home defeat to foreigners was usually attributed to the great Hungarian team that won 6–3 at Wembley in 1953.

The win at Goodison was the FAI team's greatest achievement in twenty-five years of international football. After such an encouraging result (and a cheque for over £3,000 for its half-share of the gate receipts), the FAI hoped that more lucrative games with England would follow. There were amateur internationals in Dublin and Shrewsbury against England in 1951 and 1952, but it was to be another eight years before the two teams played a full international match (a World Cup qualifier at Wembley on 8 May 1957) and fifteen years before they played another friendly (on 24 May 1964 at Dalymount Park).

Seven weeks after their win in Goodison, the Republic played Sweden in a World Cup qualifying match on 13 November 1949, needing a win to force a play-off for qualification. A large and expectant crowd of 41,000 turned up at Dalymount, but the Irish defence was unable to cope with Sweden's twenty-year-old striker Calle Palmér (later signed by Juventus), who scored a hat-trick to secure a 3–1 win and qualify his team for the tournament in Brazil. The Irish had fallen short again, but they could still have played in the final stages. After several qualified teams withdrew, the FAI received an invitation from FIFA to send a team, but it declined. Having already lost £500 on a short Iberian tour in May 1948, the association feared that the estimated £2,700 required to send a team to Brazil would bankrupt it.[16]

***

When all four UK associations rejoined FIFA in May 1946, after a break of seventeen years, the IFA policy of selecting players born outside Northern Ireland came under additional scrutiny. This had already been highlighted when England played the two Irish teams within a couple of days in September 1946. Beforehand the FA secretary Stanley Rous had written to both IFA and FAI seeking assurances that they would only field players born within their territorial jurisdictions. The FAI agreed, but the IFA refused to change its policy, claiming that it was in line with IFAB rules, and two southern-born players, Jackie Carey and Bill Gorman, played in both matches.[17] The game against England also played a part in reversing the FAI's recently adopted policy of selecting players born in Northern Ireland (and the IFA's brief acquiescence in this). Derby County and Portsmouth had agreed to release Peter Doherty and Jimmy McAlinden respectively for the match in Dublin, but after the intervention of the IFA these offers were rescinded.[18] Afterwards the FAI made no further attempts to select northern players and its attitude towards the IFA hardened.[19] The IFA though persisted in its policy and selected seven southerners to play against Scotland on 27 November 1946 – Bill Gorman, Con Martin, Peter Farrell, Jackie Carey, Davy Walsh, Alex Stevenson and Tommy Eglington – and until the 1949/50 season continued to select roughly half of its team from the South.

The FAI renewed its protests, insisting that this was a clear breach of FIFA regulations. But so long as its leading players continued to accept the IFA's offer to play for Northern Ireland, the FAI thought better of forcing a public confrontation with much-admired sportsmen. For their part, the players saw representing Northern Ireland as an opportunity to compete against the best players in Britain and, since they were subject to a maximum wage at their clubs, the international match fee was a welcome addition to their income. Carey, for example (who played twenty-nine times for the FAI team and nine for the IFA), argued that football was 'his profession', which he was entitled to practise whenever possible. Players such as Carey and Martin were also influenced by friendships with Northern Ireland teammates and by the hope that their actions could mitigate the partition of Irish football, keeping alive the possibility of North and South coming together one day.[20]

At the FIFA congress held in London in July 1948, the FAI again vigorously protested against the IFA selection policy. FIFA though had re-admitted the UK associations in 1946 on the understanding that there would be no interference with their domestic competitions and insisted it had no authority to intervene in the British Championship. This changed when Northern Ireland, along with the other three IFAB teams, agreed to take part in the 1950 World Cup and FIFA used the 1949/50 British Championship as a qualifying group, with the top two eligible to go to Brazil. When Northern Ireland drew 0–0 with Wales in Wrexham on 8 March 1950, the team was captained by the Dubliner Con Martin, and included three other southern-born players (Tom Aherne,

Reg Ryan and Davy Walsh). The match was technically a World Cup qualifier, and all four southerners had already played for the Republic in earlier qualifiers against Sweden and Finland. The FAI protested to FIFA that players were now representing two different teams in the same competition. FIFA though was still reluctant to act, so in April 1950 the Shamrock Rovers chairman, Joe Cunningham (a member of the FAI selection committee), decided to take the initiative: he wrote to all the FAI's English-based players asking them to commit only to the Republic in future. Cunningham insisted that he took this action primarily to bring pressure to bear on the IFA to join forces with the FAI and field a genuinely all-Ireland team for international matches.[21]

Other than Carey, Con Martin was the best-known dual player of the period, winning thirty caps for the Republic and six for Northern Ireland. Before the game against Wales the FAI had asked him to withdraw, but, unwilling to let down his Northern Ireland teammates, he went ahead and played. Afterwards he came under additional pressure from both the FAI and his club Aston Villa to declare solely for the Republic and even received threatening letters calling him a Judas. Reluctantly, he gave in and agreed not to play for Northern Ireland again. On 5 April 1950 the FAI council congratulated Martin on his 'spirited action', but it was a decision he made with some regret, having made many good friends in Belfast.

Taking their cue from Martin, others followed suit and announced that they too would play only for the FAI team, heralding the end of the dual international. The IFA, however, was not willing to give up without a fight and selected the Sligo-born Sean Fallon of Glasgow Celtic to play for Northern Ireland against England on 7 October 1950. Fallon had earlier played for a Northern Ireland XI against the British Army in Belfast on 14 September 1950 and was keen to do so again, but he received a letter from Cunningham asking him to withdraw. There were also family considerations: Fallon's father John was a British Army veteran and secretary of the British Legion in Sligo; he served on Sligo Corporation and County Council and a controversy was likely to damage him politically. Sean's mind was finally made up when he learned of a threat to burn down the family home in Sligo, allegedly from local elements of the IRA. Like Martin, he declined the IFA's offer with a heavy heart, believing he had failed his Northern Ireland teammates. This finally brought an end to the IFA's attempts to select southern-born players and led to a sharp deterioration in relations between the two associations.[22] When the IFA celebrated its seventy-fifth anniversary by hosting a match between a Europe and a Great Britain selection at Windsor Park on 13 August 1955, the FAI was not invited, although Oscar Traynor and Joe Wickham attended in a private capacity.[23]

***

The withdrawal of southern players weakened an IFA team already on a poor run. In the 1946/7 Championship, Northern Ireland had finished as runner-up to England, beating Scotland and drawing with England, but afterwards the team's form declined: the 0–0 draw against Wales in March 1950 was the first time it had avoided defeat in ten matches. Danny Blanchflower, a talented wing-half who made his debut for Northern Ireland in 1949, was critical of the air of amateurishness and defeatism around the team, recalling that 'there was no plan, no policy, no encouragement and very little hope'.[24] Recognising the need for change, in September 1951 the FAI appointed the Magherafelt-born Peter Doherty (1913–90) to manage the national team on a part-time basis. Doherty, a skilled inside-left, was the outstanding Northern Irish footballer of his day, who had a highly-successful career in England, scoring 198 goals in 402 Football League matches (1933–53), as well as three goals in sixteen matches for Northern Ireland (1935–50). Much admired by fellow professionals such as Bill Shankly, Stanley Matthews and Billy Wright, he was described by his contemporary Len Shackleton as 'the genius among geniuses'.[25] In 1940 he volunteered to serve with the RAF and became a physical training instructor sergeant at its Loughborough Rehabilitation Centre for injured fliers. The war robbed him of his best playing years and in 1949 he became player-manager of Doncaster Rovers, leading them to promotion to Division Two in his first season.[26]

Described as 'a simple, direct and unevasive man with an Ulster accent and bright red hair that always caught attention on the field',

Doherty brought a new professionalism to the Northern Ireland team.[27] European club tours with Manchester City and Derby had opened his eyes and convinced him that better-coached continental teams would soon overtake their British counterparts. When an international player, Northern Ireland's poor form was galling for such a fierce competitor and it rankled with him that England always played Northern Ireland at provincial venues (they did not play at Wembley Stadium until 1955); he was convinced 'that we are included in the International Tournament merely "to make up the number".'[28] Doherty sought to compensate for his team's modest resources with intensive coaching, organisation and discipline. Although the IFA's selection committee still picked the team, Doherty's opinions carried weight. He encouraged the selectors to choose younger players and stick with them rather than changing the team after every defeat. He soon won the respect of his players for his meticulous preparation and inspiring motivational skills, with one recalling that his team talks 'could make eleven footballers go out and give their lives for Ireland'.[29] Although Northern Ireland lost their first three games in the 1951/2 British Championship, the team played well and promised better things to come. The next season saw real improvement, with draws achieved against both England and Scotland.

While the IFA team was making progress on the pitch, the FAI was rather more concerned with administrative and jurisdictional matters. Having stopped southern-born players from playing for Northern Ireland, it turned to its other great bugbear – the continued use of the name 'Ireland' by the IFA. The IFA still clung tenaciously to this and, in a motion tabled at FIFA's annual Congress at Lisbon in 1954, reminded the world body that 'the IFA remains the National Association and indeed the only association entitled to use the title "Ireland". Its territory may be reduced in size but in every other respect it remains unaltered. It carries the confidence of the other British associations and it takes its place in the British International Championship as "Ireland" and is the only body competent to do so.'[30]

FAI secretary Joe Wickham was, however, determined to wrest the name away from Belfast and rarely let a FIFA conference pass without raising the matter. In Helsinki in July 1952, he lobbied intensively for the FAI to be given exclusive rights to the name 'Ireland', backing up his arguments with the usual maps of Ireland and explanatory leaflets in English, French and Spanish.[31] As ever, FIFA was reluctant to become involved and the matter had still to be resolved when both teams entered the qualifiers for the 1954 World Cup. Drawn in a group with Luxembourg and France, the Republic was eliminated after home and away defeats to the French in autumn 1953. For Northern Ireland, the 1953/4 British Championship was again its qualifying group and, although it managed a victory over Wales in Wrexham in March 1954 (the first under Doherty), the top two qualifying places were taken by England and Scotland.

Some months afterwards, FIFA finally directed that when competing in the World Cup the FAI team was to be called the Republic of Ireland and the IFA team Northern Ireland. This, though, did not bring the matter to an end. The IFA continued to call its team 'Ireland' in the British Championship and was generally known under that name in Britain. One unintended result was that English stereotyping of the Irish was often applied to the IFA team, much to the irritation of many of its supporters. The Pathé News commentary of Northern Ireland's 3–2 victory over England at Wembley on 6 November 1957 described a successful Irish attack in its usual brisk tones: 'Before you can say begorrah, McCrory has landed a beauty.'[32] The IFA continued to use the name Ireland until the politically-charged 1970s, when northern officials and supporters became uncomfortable with its thirty-two-county implications, and from 1973 adopted Northern Ireland as the team's official description in all competitions. Old habits died hard, however, and many in Britain would continue to call the IFA team 'Ireland' for some years to come.

***

After elimination from the 1954 World Cup qualifiers, the Republic of Ireland found itself in the familiar position of having to make do with friendly matches for the next three years. One of these, against Yugoslavia in October 1955, would prove to be among the most

controversial it ever played. When, in 1950 and 1952, the Yugoslav FA
had offered to play in Dublin, the FAI showed an uncharacteristic
reluctance to accept.[33] Yugoslavia was a communist country, which was
regularly accused by Irish Catholic publications and the mainstream
press of persecuting Catholic clerics. In 1950 the FAI declined the
invitation on its own initiative but in 1952 thought it advisable to seek
the advice of John Charles McQuaid, the Catholic archbishop of Dublin
and the most influential member of the hierarchy.[34]

McQuaid was a meticulous administrator who closely supervised
the social and cultural life of his diocese and expected to be consulted,
and deferred to, by organisations of all types. In 1943 he had written
to Shelbourne FC deploring the practice of holding matches at Tolka
Park on Good Friday within earshot of the archbishop's residence,
and the club immediately desisted. When asked his opinion on
playing Yugoslavia in 1952, he rather dismissively claimed to have
no interest in soccer but advised the FAI not to proceed with the
game. His opposition centred on the imprisonment in 1946 by the
Titoist government of Archbishop Aloysius Stepinac of Zagreb for
co-operating with pro-Nazi Croatians during the war. Stepinac was
released from prison in 1951 but remained under house arrest. His
case was well known in Ireland and on 1 May 1949 over 100,000
people gathered in O'Connell Street in Dublin to protest against
his treatment and that of Cardinal József Mindszenty of Hungary.
After Stepinac was elevated to cardinal by Pope Pius XII in 1952, his
treatment had received further publicity and, on the archbishop's
advice, the FAI declined the Yugoslavs' offer.[35]

However, when the request was renewed three years later, the FAI
decided to accept, without referring the matter to the archbishop.
Circumstances had changed: by 1955 Stepinac was rarely mentioned in
Irish newspapers and, as both Ireland and Yugoslavia had affiliated to
the recently founded Union of European Football Associations (UEFA),
the FAI was keen to cultivate friendly relations with a fellow member.
It also seems that the dismissive attitude to international soccer
shown earlier by McQuaid had rankled with Joe Wickham. After the
announcement that Yugoslavia would play at Dalymount Park on 19

October 1955, Wickham was contacted by Fr John O'Regan, chancellor of the Dublin diocese, who made clear his unhappiness that the match had been arranged without consulting the archbishop and suggested the invitation should be rescinded. Wickham reminded O'Regan that the archbishop had claimed to have no interest in soccer matches when contacted three years earlier and insisted that it was now too late to cancel.[36]

This set in motion a train of events that revealed much about the power of the Catholic Church (and its limits) in 1950s' Ireland. Taken aback by the attitude of the FAI, McQuaid instructed his flock not to attend and privately contacted Taoiseach John A. Costello, a pious Catholic and Knight of Columbanus, who readily agreed that the government, a Fine Gael and Labour Party coalition, would publicly oppose the match. Even before McQuaid's intervention there was some disquiet in official circles about the game: a memo circulating in the Department of External Affairs noted, 'Had we been consulted in advance regarding the advisibility [sic] of inviting a Yugoslav team here, I think it safe to say we would have advised against the proposal having regard to the persecution of the Church and imprisonment of Cardinal Stepinac which formed the subject of numerous references in the Dáil and protest notes to the Yugoslav government.'[37] Costello advised President Seán T. O'Kelly to cancel his earlier acceptance of the FAI's invitation to attend, and two other government ministers also cancelled, including the Labour Party Tánaiste William Norton. O'Kelly, although himself a devout Catholic and a Knight of Columbanus, was deeply unhappy at this turn of events: on receiving the invitation, he had consulted the government before accepting and no objection had been raised. He could not though defy Costello's advice without creating a constitutional crisis. In private, he wrote to his long-time friend Oscar Traynor, then president of the FAI, to assure him that 'it distresses me that any action of mine might contribute in the slightest to the embarrassment and discomfiture of your friends in the Football Association of Ireland. They are a body I hold in considerable esteem, and I have always received from them the utmost consideration ... You may have an opportunity to assure them privately of my continued esteem.'[38]

An earlier inter-party coalition led by Costello had already shown its willingness to bend before clerical pressure, having capitulated to McQuaid's opposition to the Minister for Health Noël Browne's scheme to introduce free medical care for mothers and children in 1951. There may also have been wider political considerations at stake: the Irish government was seeking admission to the United Nations, which eventually happened two months later, and was looking for support from anti-communist members.[39] Pressure was immediately brought to bear on the FAI by the Department of Justice, with Wickham and Traynor summoned to a meeting. Thomas Coyne, the departmental secretary, advised that proceeding with the match was unwise and that he was reluctant to grant entry visas to the Yugoslavs who might take the opportunity to defect to the west. The FAI delegation argued that the Yugoslavs were 'good friends who had always fought the Irish cause in football' and that cancellation was likely to create an international incident that would tarnish the country's image. Rather grudgingly, Coyne agreed to grant the required visas, but insisted that the FAI guarantee to cover the expenses of any Yugoslavs who might choose to remain in Ireland.[40]

In the event, the visitors managed to resist the temptations of 1950s' Dublin and returned to Belgrade with a full complement. Far from being prospective defectors, the Yugoslav football team were the pride of Tito's state and enjoyed a highly privileged status. They were one of post-war Europe's most consistent teams, reaching the quarter-finals of three successive World Cups (1954–62), and winning silver medals at three successive Olympics Games (1948–56) and gold in 1960. At home, they were regarded as important international ambassadors, their willingness to play all-comers forming a conspicuous part of Yugoslavia's non-aligned foreign policy that set it apart from the Soviet bloc. In a country ripped apart by bloody ethnic warfare in the 1940s, their success was highlighted by Tito as evidence that former enemies could unite and work together.

The Yugoslavs were rather taken aback by the controversy and insisted that they had travelled the world without encountering any similar protests. Their ambassador in London issued a statement critical of McQuaid's intervention, while his press attaché added that 'It is a great pity ... that a sporting event intended to make two nations, who know so little about each other, get to know each other a little better is now over-shadowed by a campaign of intolerance and mixing of politics and sport. There is no doubt that the whole character of the match has been spoilt by this intervention.'[41] During their visit the Yugoslavs studiously avoided becoming involved in any further controversy, claiming that politics and religion had no place in sport. Their team members came from a variety of backgrounds: Liam Tuohy of Shamrock Rovers, who was making his international debut, recalled that several of the Yugoslav players crossed themselves as they ran onto the pitch and that 'there were nearly more Catholics on their side than there were on ours'.[42]

The Irish state made its disapproval of the match clear in various ways. Not only was there to be no presidential or government representation, but the Army Band was instructed not to attend. The Irish team trainer Dick Hearns, who was a member of the gardaí, also withdrew his services. The Radio Éireann commentator Philip Greene declined to cover the match (with the backing of his employer) and it went ahead without radio commentary. There was also opposition from some members of the public: well-known players such as Con Martin were stopped in the street and asked not to play. While McQuaid was careful to remain outside of the fray, Catholic lay organisations weighed in. An Ríoghacht (The League of the Kingship of Christ) claimed that the Yugoslavs represented 'a tyrannous regime of persecution'. The chief scout of the Catholic Boy Scouts of Ireland accused the FAI of entertaining 'the tools of Tito ... in the capital city of Catholic Ireland' and warned young people not to go to the match on pain of mortal sin. The FAI also received letters of protest from the Catholic Association for International Relations, the Knights of Columbanus and the Guilds of Regnum Christi. The papal nuncio, Archbishop Albert Levame, described McQuaid's intervention as 'magnificent and splendid'.[43] Joe Wickham (a practising Catholic, two of whose sisters were nuns) was denounced from the pulpit by his parish priest in Larkhill as 'a Judas who had sold Christ the King for a mere game of football'.[44]

Commandant W.J. Brennan Whitmore, an Irish Volunteer staff officer in the General Post Office (GPO) in 1916, who had adopted strong pro-Axis views during the Second World War, saw the FAI's decision as evidence that the nation had turned its back on the ideals of the Easter Rising and was accepting 'an alien philosophy and mode of life. Since the game of soccer is an alien mode, it is part and parcel of the alien facade behind which we have been committing national hari-kari for generations.' However, the 1916 veteran Alasdair Mac Caba differed, maintaining that 'the whole episode is disturbing from a democratic point of view. For the decreasing few who continue to entertain hopes of winning over the North by an earnest [show] of tolerance on this side of the border, it is decidedly discouraging.'[45] Inevitably, the controversy was picked up in Northern Ireland: one Belfast newspaper claimed that the incident 'is further proof of the power that the Roman Catholic Church claims in the 26 counties and justifies Ulster's fear that Dublin rule would mean Rome rule', while the anti-Catholic minister of education, Harry Midgley, described McQuaid's action as 'one of the most monumental pieces of clerical interference yet seen in Ireland'.[46]

In the face of so many protests, the FAI held an emergency meeting of its council on the Saturday before the game. Most of those present spoke against any form of political or religious interference in sport: Leo Clery of the Leinster FA summed up the general mood by remarking that 'it would be a sorry day for Ireland when visiting players and officials were asked their politics or religion'. The majority concluded that cancellation would seriously damage Ireland's standing in international football and voted for the game to proceed; they also agreed to forward a letter of explanation to Archbishop McQuaid. There was though some opposition to playing: the representatives of the Army Football Association and Transport FC demurred, and the chairman of Dundalk FC, Peadar Halpin, refused to attend the game or any associated functions.[47]

On the day of the match, fears of large-scale protests from Catholic groups did not materialise: outside Dalymount Park there was a small picket from members of the Legion of Mary carrying anti-communist signs and a solitary protestor waved a yellow and white papal flag. Since no government figures attended, Oscar Traynor was presented to the teams and he and the Yugoslav team were loudly cheered. The official attendance was 22,000, supplemented as usual by the lithe legions who scaled the perimeter wall without paying, and they saw the skilful visitors thoroughly outplay the Irish and win 4–1. Newspaper reports of the match made little mention of the controversy, generally confining themselves to pointing out the glaring gap in ability between the two teams and calling for the immediate appointment of a team manager to replace the FAI's obsolete selection committee.[48]

The attendance was probably less than would have been expected for a match against top-class opposition. Comparisons are complicated by the fact that it was a friendly and was played on a Wednesday, which tended to attract smaller crowds than matches played on a Sunday. The only other home internationals played on Wednesdays around this time were World Cup qualifying matches in 1953 against Luxembourg and 1956 against Denmark, which were watched by crowds of 20,000 and 32,600 respectively. The two previous friendly internationals played on Sundays at Dalymount against Norway in 1954 and lowly-rated Holland in 1955 attracted official crowds of 34,000 and 16,800; a friendly against Spain on Sunday 27 November 1955 five weeks after the Yugoslavia match drew 35,000. While the controversy had probably reduced the crowd, it had not done so drastically, and thousands of soccer supporters had been prepared to defy the wishes of the country's most powerful Catholic cleric. Many simply wanted to see one of Europe's best teams in action but, for some at least, there was probably more at stake. The numbers who attended to make a point cannot be definitively ascertained, as the opinions of spectators were not canvassed and received little public expression at the time, but there was some surprise at the size of the crowd. The Republic in 1955 was, after all, a deeply religious country: 95 per cent of the population was Catholic and attendance at Sunday Mass was almost universal. Large crowds attended Catholic religious processions, festivals and pilgrimages. The previous year had been designated a 'Marian year' by the Church and had seen numerous public devotions to the Blessed Virgin, including a large procession of over 25,000 people in the centre of Dublin, in which trade unions featured strongly.[49] Catholic values permeated everyday life and those seen to oppose them risked denunciation and isolation. In 1954 Archbishop McQuaid established a 'Vigilance Committee' to monitor communist activity in Ireland and, in the polarised atmosphere of the Cold War, some clergy took every opportunity to rail against the evils of Godless communism and stoke the 'Red Scare'.[50] While tangible targets for their wrath were scarce, the net was cast widely: a delegation of Irish writers and artists that included James Plunkett and Anthony Cronin who visited the Soviet Union in January 1955 were strongly denounced by militant Catholics.

However, it was also the case that not everyone bowed to clerical dictation. There had always been an anti-clerical dimension to Irish republicanism and the fact that Fianna Fáil was in opposition in 1955 allowed it greater leeway to defy McQuaid: even the legendary IRA gunman Dan Breen, a GAA devotee who professed little interest in soccer, attended the match to show solidarity with Traynor and 'fire his last shot for Ireland'.[51] McQuaid received considerable correspondence, much of it critical of his intervention, including a letter from 'a Cheerful Heretic of no particular denomination' who suggested that 'since you are required to love your enemies, may I suggest that there are worse – and bloodier – ways of doing it than taking them on at football? And giving them the father and mother of a hiding. If you can.'[52]

Most of those who disobeyed McQuaid were probably practising Catholics. But while prepared to accept their Church's teaching in matters of faith and morals, and its firm control of a network of educational, health and correctional institutions, many believed that it was not the business of Church or state to dictate what sporting events they should attend. Ireland in the 1950s was a deeply conservative country, but it was also a long-standing parliamentary democracy in which civil rights such as freedom of association and assembly were broadly accepted. Any attempt to interfere with these rights was always likely to provoke some opposition. There were no anti-Catholic political banners or placards displayed at Dalymount Park on 19 October, but the presence of over 20,000 people at a football match condemned by McQuaid represented a rare act of public defiance and a forthright reminder to the Catholic Church to confine itself to its proper sphere.

Characteristically, though, this was not the lesson drawn by McQuaid. Having been compelled to take a greater interest in soccer, he now appreciated that it was a popular activity among altar boys and clerical students in his diocese and decided that he needed to exert greater control over the FAI. He set up a committee of four priests under the chairmanship of Fr George Finnegan to attend to the spiritual needs of players and bring influence to bear on FAI council members. The former objective had some success and McQuaid was encouraged by the growing numbers of young footballers he saw attending religious retreats.[53]

Two years later there was the possibility of a rerun of the controversy when the FAI agreed to play a B-international match against communist Romania in October 1957. In the weeks before the game some extreme Catholic organisations began to highlight the persecution of Catholics by the government in Bucharest. Dismissing claims that they were bringing politics into sport, P.E. Feighan, the general secretary of Fírinne (formerly Maria Duce), asked 'since when did the pillage and plunder of churches and the murder of God's holy anointed get the name of politics and since when did the kicking around a leather ball with the representatives of a godless regime which indulges in such practices become a form of sport?'[54] Archbishop McQuaid again took an interest, concluding that the FAI had learned nothing from the Yugoslavia match, and asked Fr Finnegan to approach the association to ensure that no further games would be arranged against communist opposition.[55] Fearful of offending McQuaid, the Department of Justice held off issuing visas to the Romanian party but was left with little choice when they received 'peremptory instructions' to do so from the new minister for justice, Oscar Traynor, who had taken up office in March 1957 and threatened to issue the visas personally if the department delayed.[56] In the end, the game went ahead without incident on 20 October 1957 at Dalymount Park, where a crowd of 21,500 saw the teams draw 1–1. The following year, Ireland played home and away against Poland, and did the same against Czechoslovakia in 1959. These and all subsequent matches against communist countries passed off without controversy.

7

A Cold House:
The Irish League 1939–72

The Irish League season continued after the outbreak of war in September 1939, when the title was won for the fifth successive time by Belfast Celtic. However, the province's direct involvement in the conflict meant that league football was on borrowed time. Clubs struggled to field teams and in 1940 the authorities suspended the competition: according to one club official, 'football had become secondary in the fight for basic existence and freedom'.[1] The Irish League was replaced by the North Regional League, in which player registration was looser and games less frequent; Belfast Celtic remained the dominant team. The Irish Cup continued and was won by Ballymena in 1940 with Belfast Celtic and Linfield sharing the next six titles. The domestic game was enlivened by the presence of well-known English League players such as Les Bennett (Tottenham Hotspur), Jack Rowley (Manchester United), Dick Kemp (Liverpool), Ron Greenwood (Chelsea) and George Drury (Arsenal), who had been posted to Northern Ireland with the armed services and turned out for local clubs. Matches against military teams provided the nearest thing to full international games, and during 1941–3 an IFA selection played the British Army on three occasions and a Combined Services team twice.[2]

The Irish League resumed in 1947 and was won by Belfast Celtic, who between 1926 and 1948 won fifteen titles. Fielding legendary players such as Jackie Vernon, Billy McMillan, Jimmy McAlinden and

Charlie Tully, the team of the late 1940s was often recalled as the best ever seen in the Irish League, providing glamour and excitement at a time when there was little enough of both. Its continued success was a matter of considerable pride to nationalists in Belfast, and indeed across Northern Ireland: a former Derry City player recalled the eager anticipation of Celtic's visits to the Brandywell – even though this usually meant defeat for the home side.[3] The club was also much admired in the South. When the FAI selected northerners for its national team, these were usually past or present Celtic players, such as Vernon, McMillan and McAlinden. The presence on the Celtic team of FAI internationals, such as Tom Aherne, Robin Lawler and Johnny Campbell, also encouraged greater interest and identification from southern supporters. While such links helped sustain the club's nationalist identity, they also aggravated the suspicions of unionists, who maintained that its real loyalties lay across the border.

Between August 1947 and March 1948 Celtic swept all opponents aside, winning a record thirty-one consecutive matches. Their Belfast rivals, Glentoran and Linfield, looked with envy at the quality of their team and on learning that Celtic's young free-scoring centre-forward Jimmy Jones (1928–2014) was a Protestant, the Linfield secretary Joe Mackey tried to convince him that Windsor Park was his natural home and that he 'shouldn't be over there playing with those Taigs'. Jones, though, was happy at Celtic Park, where he maintained that religion was irrelevant: 'no one cared what you were. I wasn't interested in hearing that kind of sectarian rubbish and I told him to stuff his money and stormed out slamming the door behind me. Mackey never forgave me for that.'[4]

The 1948 title was the last Belfast Celtic would win; within a year the club had withdrawn from the Irish League. This was not brought about by the financial problems that had plagued so many other clubs, but by the intense sectarian rivalry of Belfast soccer. The catalyst was a crowd disturbance at a league match between Linfield and Celtic at Windsor Park on 27 December 1948. At the time the title race between the two teams was carefully poised, with Linfield three points ahead, and the atmosphere before the game was even more tense than normal.

Political developments in the South may also have contributed: on 21 December 1948 the inter-party government legislated to leave the British Commonwealth and declare a republic. While most Belfast football supporters rarely paid much attention to the deliberations of the Dáil, the measure was widely reported in northern papers and fuelled unionist fears about the future constitutional status of Northern Ireland.

Relations between Celtic and Linfield were often volatile and there had been scuffles between players when they met two months earlier at Celtic Park. Some spoke of a 'palpable sense of foreboding' before the game on 27 December, which attracted a near capacity attendance of 27,000. The already tense atmosphere was heightened in the first half when Jimmy Jones collided with the Linfield defender Bob Bryson, who had to be carried from the field. During the interval the Linfield secretary Joe Mackey made a PA announcement that Bryson had suffered a broken leg. This inflamed some of the Linfield support, who became even more aggrieved when another Linfield player was injured and could not continue. Anger on the terraces expressed itself in ever louder abuse of Celtic players, and the ill-feeling spread to the pitch, with a player from each side sent off for fighting. Celtic took the lead but Linfield, with only eight players on the field, fought back and scored a late equaliser that prompted wild celebrations. Celtic's Scottish forward George Hazlitt was disconcerted to see Royal Ulster Constabulary (RUC) men reacting to the Linfield goal by throwing their caps in the air: 'Even with my background of growing up in a tough area in Glasgow, I had never seen anything like it ... I realised we were not going to have much protection at the end of the game.'[5]

When the final whistle sounded, hundreds of Linfield supporters poured onto the pitch and attacked the Celtic players. Most managed to fight their way to the dressing room, with some, such as goalkeeper Kevin McAlinden and Robin Lawler, receiving injuries (McAlinden did not play again for three months). However, Jimmy Jones was the crowd's main target. Isolated from his fellow players, he was set upon and thrown over a pitch-side parapet onto the terracing where he was kicked unconscious. Clearly intent on ending his football career, his attackers jumped heavily on his leg, breaking it in five places. Only the intervention of Sean McCann, a former Celtic teammate then playing for Ballymena United, saved him from further injury. McCann, who had attended the game as a spectator, fought his way to the prostrate Jones and tried to protect him. He recalled that 'they were kicking him up and down the terrace steps like a rag doll. Jimmy was screaming in pain and I could see his right leg was horribly mangled, his heel sticking out where his toes should have been.' He appealed for help to a policeman standing nearby but was ignored. (Before he lost consciousness, Jones, whose father was an RUC sergeant, recalled hearing a policeman say: 'Stop kicking him or I'll use my baton.') McCann shielded his friend as best he could until medical attention arrived. Jones's injuries were so severe that he was taken immediately to the nearby Musgrave Clinic where the surgeon who examined his shattered leg thought at first that it would have to be amputated, although it was eventually saved after four operations.[6]

Jones was a well-known and popular player and football supporters throughout the province were appalled. The nationalist *Irish News* described his attackers as 'a frenzied crowd of primeval savages', and unionist papers also contained letters of condemnation from Linfield supporters who had torn up their season tickets in disgust.[7] The Celtic directors issued a statement which described the violence as 'without parallel in the annals of football' and implicitly criticised Linfield and the RUC for failing to protect their players. The incident highlighted the issue of partisan policing, which for many nationalists was a recurrent grievance; the fact that the RUC had failed to intervene and made no arrests during the riot seemed clear evidence that Celtic's players could no longer rely on police protection and were risking life and limb by playing in hostile stadiums.[8] Some Celtic supporters advocated a permanent boycott of Windsor Park and called on their club to withdraw from the Irish League and play in the South.[9]

The incident was raised in the Northern Ireland parliament when it reconvened in January 1949. The nationalist member for mid-Derry, Eddie McAteer, argued that it clearly showed that the RUC was a partisan police force that preferred to use its batons on peaceful political protestors than on violent thugs. Harry Diamond, the Socialist Republican Party MP for the Celtic heartland of the Belfast Falls constituency, claimed that the attacks had been planned before the game and that the RUC had been instructed to stand aside. There was a sharp clash between long-time enemies Jack Beattie, the anti-partition Labour MP for Belfast west, and the labour unionist Harry Midgley, who three years earlier had traded blows on the floor of the house. Beattie claimed that Midgley, who was chairman of Linfield FC, had helped to incite the violence by singing 'bitter sectarian songs' at Christmas functions in the days before the game. Midgley condemned the violence but insisted that he and Linfield bore no responsibility, describing those involved as a fringe hooligan element rather than genuine supporters. To uproar from the unionist benches, Beattie questioned the even-handedness of the RUC, claiming that if the players being attacked had worn Linfield shirts, the police would have intervened vigorously.[10] In response the Minister of Home Affairs Edmond Warnock accused opposition members of exploiting the incident for political gain and denied any failure by the RUC, insisting they were a 'strictly impartial force who did their duty well' and had simply been outnumbered at Windsor Park.[11]

On 4 January 1949 the IFA's central committee met to consider the referee's report; it concluded that Linfield bore some responsibility for the riot and ordered the closure of Windsor Park until 1 February. The result was that Linfield had to switch its next two home games to Solitude in north Belfast. Celtic officials denounced this minor sanction as adding insult to injury and as further evidence of the IFA's institutional sectarianism. They insisted that over the years the IFA had treated their club unfairly in matters such as crowd behaviour, player suspensions and the scheduling of fixtures. On several occasions beforehand Celtic's board had considered withdrawing from the Irish League in protest at discriminatory treatment but had baulked at taking such drastic action. The latest violence had though brought matters to a head and the club believed that it had been failed by both the football and civil authorities.[12] Its misgivings were confirmed in March 1949 when Celtic's request for the postponement or cancellation of an upcoming league match against Linfield at Celtic Park on 2 April was refused.[13]

The IFA's failure to act decisively against the violent attacks on Celtic players was the final straw for the club's directors and they decided to withdraw from the Irish League at the end of the 1948/9 season, as they had done in 1918/19 and 1920–4. Celtic finished second to Linfield in their final championship season, but after the events of 27 December, gave the impression of simply going through the motions. After the club played its last league match at Celtic Park on 21 April 1949 the directors notified the Irish League of its intention to withdraw from next season's competition. Even before this, they had already begun to dismantle their team, making arrangements to transfer key players such as Johnny Campbell, Robin Lawler and Tom Aherne to English clubs. *The Irish News* announced that in May the club would undertake a ten-match tour of North America, and that no announcements on its long-term future would be made until it returned.[14]

On 4 May the Celtic players and officials were warmly received at New York City Hall by the Irish-born city mayor William 'Bill-O' O'Dwyer and the Irish consul-general Garth Healy. Although the club's policy was to avoid overt displays of nationalism that might embarrass its Protestant players, most Americans assumed that it represented nationalist Ireland and before their first match in New York on 8 May the team paraded behind an Irish tricolour. This was strongly criticised by unionist papers in Northern Ireland, and manager Elisha Scott and most of his players felt compelled to issue a statement that the flag had been produced without their prior knowledge and the incident would not be repeated; they also pointed out that while in Toronto they had toasted King George, stood for 'God Save the King' and accepted a presentation from the Veterans' Association of the British Army's 36th Ulster Division.[15]

The highlight of the tour was a match on 29 May at Triborough Stadium, New York, against a Scotland team that had beaten England 3–1 at Wembley a month earlier to win the British Championship. To the surprise and delight of their supporters, Celtic upset the odds by winning 2–0. While many saw the victory as the most glorious in the

club's history, it made little difference to its future. A day earlier, the
IFA council had held its monthly meeting at which it accepted Celtic's
request to withdraw from the league. Once the decision was made,
neither side was prepared to back down. It may have been, as a club
historian suggests, that 'the Celtic board was embarking on a game of
brinkmanship with the IFA', hoping for an apology that never came.
The IFA was, however, not in the habit of issuing apologies, particularly
to Belfast Celtic, and the club was lost to the league.[16]

Once the American tour was over, Celtic unloaded its remaining
players and never again played a competitive match. Given the severity
of the violence directed at their players on 27 December and the half-
hearted response of the authorities, the directors were genuinely
worried that a future riot would lead to fatalities.[17] The club's withdrawal
was a serious blow to football in Belfast, ending the compelling three-
way rivalry that had existed with Linfield and Glentoran. Within weeks
of the beginning of the 1949/50 season, there were complaints that the
standard of football had fallen and overall gate receipts had certainly
declined.[18] For the province's nationally-minded soccer supporters,
Celtic's departure left a huge void. Some transferred their allegiance
to Distillery, a club that played at Grosvenor Park in west Belfast and
drew cross-community support. Distillery, however, only ever attracted
modest crowds, which fell further after Grosvenor Park was destroyed
in an arson attack in 1971. Many turned their backs entirely on the
Irish League and focused their support on Glasgow Celtic, while others
turned to Gaelic games.[19] Celtic's withdrawal also soured relations
between North and South, and the Dublin and Belfast Intercity Club
Cup that had been played every year since 1941 came to an abrupt halt
in 1949.[20]

The fact that Belfast Celtic left the league with no formal announcement led many to believe that it was a temporary move like
that of the early 1920s. There is some evidence that the Celtic directors
intended their absence from senior football to be short-lived: they
retained their affiliation to the IFA and the County Antrim FA, and
Elisha Scott remained as club manager and attended to administrative
duties until the mid-1950s. The club even played occasional friendly

matches for charitable purposes, including one against Shamrock Rovers at Dalymount Park on 24 July 1951 for the family of Jimmy Dunne, who had died suddenly in 1949; there was also a home match against Glasgow Celtic on 17 May 1952 which attracted 30,000 spectators to Celtic Park. But if the intention was to return at a more propitious time, this never happened. Anger at the events of 1948/9 ran deep and proved stronger than any desire to rejoin the Irish League. The loss to west Belfast, particularly its sense of pride and identity, was immense. Over sixty years later one supporter lamented: 'It was like a black cloud coming down, as if there was nothing to live for or look forward to on a Saturday. It's a grief which never went away.'[21]

Celtic Park remained in use as a greyhound stadium until 1985, when it was demolished and replaced by a shopping centre. Those who can recall seeing Celtic play get fewer with each passing year, but the club is not forgotten. Its triumphs and troubles spawned several excellent histories and the club is remembered in the folklore of west Belfast; a dedicated Belfast Celtic Society was founded in 2003 and works assiduously to keep its memory alive.[22] The circumstances of its demise undoubtedly reinforced nationalist alienation from the IFA and even from the northern state itself, highlighting the wider question of whether nationalists in the province could ever really be treated with fairness.

***

Celtic was replaced in the league by Crusaders FC, a club that drew its core support from the Protestant areas of north Belfast and Newtownabbey. In Celtic's absence the competition was usually dominated by Linfield and Glentoran, although in 1952 Glenavon of Lurgan became the first club from outside Belfast to win the trophy. Glenavon (a team with predominantly Protestant support) was a beneficiary of Celtic's demise and was managed by former Celtic players Harry Walker (1950–4) and Jimmy McAlinden (1954–68). It also attracted Celtic players such as Jackie Denver and Jimmy Jones. The latter, who grew up in Lurgan, recovered from the horrific injuries he sustained at Windsor Park and joined Glenavon (1951–62), quickly regaining his form to become the Irish League's all-time top scorer. In 1957 he helped Glenavon become the first non-Belfast club to win the league and cup double; another league title followed in 1960 and IFA Cups in 1959 and 1961, as well as a host of lesser trophies. There were also other competitive teams across the province, with Derry City, Ards, Distillery, Ballymena United, Coleraine and Portadown challenging for major trophies, and even occasionally winning them, to ensure that the Belfast 'Big Two' did not entirely have things their own way. However, the followings of clubs outside Belfast remained modest and localised.

With few other forms of entertainment available, the popularity of Irish League football held up well in the 1950s and early 1960s. Matches between the leading sides attracted good crowds and were enlivened by notable characters and keen personal rivalries such as those between Tommy Dickson of Linfield and Wilbur Cush of Glenavon and Portadown. With a maximum wage of £20 a week in English football until 1961, some of the best domestic players chose to stay at home. Indeed some renowned English professionals, such as the great Jackie Milburn, ended up in the Irish League: Milburn played centre-forward with Linfield (1957–60) and was the league's top scorer in the 1957/8 and 1958/9 seasons and Ulster footballer of the year in 1958, his presence often attracting thousands of additional spectators. Northern Ireland's performances in the 1958 World Cup had raised soccer's profile and the participation of Irish League clubs in European competitions from 1957 added novelty and excitement to the domestic game, even if they were usually outclassed by European opposition. There were, however, enough good results to give supporters an occasional lift and kindle hopes for future fixtures. During the 1960s Glentoran had a solid record in Europe, achieving creditable home draws against Panathinaikos in the European Cup (1964), Antwerp in the Fairs Cup (1965), Glasgow Rangers in the Cup Winners' Cup (1966) and Anderlecht in the European Cup (1968), but lost the away legs. They almost went one better in the European Cup in 1967/8 when they drew 1–1 with Benfica at the Oval and 0–0 in Lisbon, but unfortunately became the first team in the competition to be eliminated on the away goals rule, while Benfica went on to reach the final of that season's competition. Linfield also achieved European success by beating FC Aris of Luxembourg and Vålerenga of Norway to reach the quarter-final of the 1966/7 European Cup.

From the mid-1960s onwards the Irish League came under increasing pressure. Rising living standards offered supporters alternative entertainment and domestic football could seem workmanlike and parochial in comparison with televised highlights of cross-channel games. Moreover, an undercurrent of sectarian tension remained. Although there were no incidents as violent as the attack on Jimmy Jones, the possibility of a repeat could not be entirely discountenanced: when the Dubliner Terry Conroy scored twice to give Glentoran a 2–0 win over Linfield in the 1966 IFA Cup final, he enraged the Linfield supporters to such an extent that the referee gave him advance warning of the final whistle and advised him to get off the pitch as quickly as possible.[23]

As public unrest grew in the later 1960s many people became wary of gathering in crowds, particularly those that included violently partisan elements. From 1967 nationalist demonstrations demanding full civil rights for all in Northern Ireland gathered momentum. The government responded with a combination of tentative reforms and heavy-handed policing that aggravated unionist fears and nationalist grievances. This led to severe inter-communal violence in the summer of 1969, especially in Derry and Belfast, and the arrival of the British Army on the streets. The army's presence reinvigorated a moribund IRA, which by the early 1970s had embarked on a full-scale campaign of violence to force a British withdrawal. Loyalist paramilitaries stepped up attacks on Catholics and the province descended into an even bloodier spiral than the early 1920s, with almost 500 violent deaths in 1972 alone. An already divided society experienced new levels of polarisation, mistrust and hostility.

By this time the only Irish League team with predominantly nationalist support was Derry City, and it was here that the effect of the Troubles on football was felt most dramatically. As an industrial working-class city, Derry had always been a soccer hotbed, represented in the Irish League by Derry Celtic (1900–13) and after 1929 by Derry City. During the 1930s the club offered the main opposition to the Irish League dominance of Belfast Celtic, finishing as runner-up on four consecutive occasions (1935–8) and enjoying a sizeable and loyal local support. On its founding, the name 'City' had deliberately been chosen as more inclusive than 'Celtic', and for a time the club did have some Protestant support. It was, however, generally identified with the nationalist community, and its Brandywell stadium was located on the Lone Moor Road, just south-west of the Bogside in a strongly nationalist part of the city.

Even before the outbreak of the Troubles, Derry City's insistence on playing at the Brandywell led to friction with the IFA. After the club won the league title for the first time in 1965, it became the first Irish League team to win a European Cup tie over two legs by beating FK Lyn of Norway 8–6 on aggregate in 1966. However, the IFA refused to allow it to play its second-round tie at the Brandywell, claiming that the ground was not up to European standard and would reflect badly on the league. Derry believed that the IFA was motivated primarily by political spite and withdrew from the competition rather than play at another venue. The IFA's stance confirmed many nationalists in their view, as the Derry journalist Eamonn McCann put it, that the IFA was 'almost the sporting wing of the Stormont government'.[24]

During the Troubles there was regular rioting in the vicinity of the Brandywell and in the early 1970s matches were regularly postponed; ties between Derry City and Linfield in particular became flashpoints for sectarian riots. After the postponement of a match between the two on 19 August 1971, the Brandywell was used by the Social Democratic and Labour Party (SDLP) and the Northern Ireland Civil Rights Association for a rally urging civil disobedience, adding to the reluctance of other teams to play there.[25] The approaches to the ground were often barricaded and on 11 September 1971 the Ballymena United team bus was hijacked and burned. The RUC declared the area unsafe and other clubs refused to risk the safety of their players and spectators by playing there. From September 1971 Derry was forced by the IFA to play its home games in the predominantly Protestant town of Coleraine, over thirty miles away. Most supporters were unwilling to make the journey and crowds shrank, leaving the club facing bankruptcy.

At the start of the 1971/2 season, Derry's request to return to the Brandywell was rejected by the league. Months later, the city experienced the worst incident in the Troubles so far, when on 30 January 1972, 'Bloody Sunday', British troops opened fire on the crowd after a civil rights march, killing thirteen civilians in the Creggan district. The ensuing shock and anger made it even more difficult for the city to host football matches and the club withdrew from the league on 13 October 1972.[26] Although the circumstances were different from the departure of Belfast Celtic over two decades earlier, many nationalists saw Derry's predicament in a similar light, as another refusal of an unsympathetic unionist establishment to accommodate nationalists, in sport as in other areas of the province's life.

After Derry's departure, there was no Irish League club with a predominantly nationalist following and there were fewer direct confrontations on the terraces. Despite this, the atmosphere in grounds could still be tense and threatening. Deterred by the possibility of violence and the probability of sectarian profanity, many supporters drifted away until only a hard-core remained and abusive chants echoed around near-empty stadiums.

8

Rise and Fall:
The League of Ireland 1939–72

National league football continued in the South throughout the war. However, fuel rationing and reduced rail services made it difficult to fulfil fixtures and some regional clubs struggled: Sligo Rovers was forced to withdraw (1940–8), as was Waterford FC (1941–4). In 1943 the FAI secretary reported a decline in the number of affiliated clubs (from 228 in 1942 to 193) owing to the large numbers of young men who had either joined the Defence Forces or emigrated to Britain, but in spite of all the prevailing problems, football was holding up reasonably well.[1] With the general narrowing of the entertainment options, the top-level game became more popular than ever. Attendances at FAI Cup finals exceeded 30,000 throughout the war years and a record crowd of over 44,000 saw Shamrock Rovers beat Bohemians 1–0 in the 1945 final.

In the league, the balance of power shifted. Clubs from outside Dublin strengthened their teams by signing up professionals who had returned from Britain. Cork United (formed in 1940 after the dissolution of Cork City FC, who had replaced Cork FC in 1938) dominated the wartime league, winning five of the six league titles between 1941 and 1946 by blending new signings with a nucleus of local players. Other regional clubs, such as Dundalk and Limerick, were also bolstered by professional returnees and performed strongly.

Having weathered the war years, the League of Ireland looked forward to a return to normality. But even normality entailed serious challenges for Irish soccer. It was a sobering thought that by the 1945/6 season only two founding clubs (Bohemians and Shelbourne) were still playing in the league, which had contracted to eight teams. Many others had come and gone, dropping back into regional competitions or simply dissolving. Their fate demonstrated the practical difficulties faced by semi-professional soccer in a country where there was strong competition from other codes and minimal state and municipal support. In 1945 Dublin had four teams in the league, with one each from Cork, Waterford, Dundalk and Limerick, but much of the country lacked representation, including areas where the game was strong at junior level. In 1948 the withdrawal of Cork United showed that even sustained success was not enough to secure a club's position. Afterwards, Dublin clubs reasserted themselves: from 1947 to 1959 the league championship was dominated by Shamrock Rovers, Drumcondra, Shelbourne and St Patrick's Athletic; only the recently formed Cork Athletic took the trophy away from the capital in 1950 and 1951. St Patrick's Athletic, based in Richmond Park, Inchicore, and drawing support from the surrounding west Dublin suburbs, showed that newcomers could successfully challenge established clubs, winning the league title at its first attempt in 1952 and adding further titles in 1955 and 1956.

Rivalries between teams were keen but seldom aggressive. Supporters mingled together on the terraces and trading banter was a central part of the experience of attending a match. League of Ireland football was one of the few bright spots in 1950s' Ireland, its success aided by the moribund economy. The decision of successive governments to persist with economic protectionism into the late 1950s had proved disastrous. With high levels of poverty, unemployment and emigration, and a society that was often drab and conformist, league football provided some much-needed excitement: urban social life, as one former player put it, 'revolved around the football ground, the cinema and the dancehall'.[2] The lack of alternative entertainment and affordable admission prices ensured healthy (and occasionally enormous) crowds at most games, adding to the atmosphere and sense of occasion. During the 1950s the installation of floodlights at several stadiums allowed matches to be held on winter evenings and contributed to strong mid-week attendances. The most glamorous and best-supported team was Shamrock Rovers, whose rivalry with Drumcondra, pitting the north of the city against the south, became the most intense of the period. Their league derbies drew crowds of over 20,000 to Milltown and Tolka Park, while their FAI Cup final meetings in 1948, 1955 and 1957 were all watched by over 30,000 people. Other clubs too attracted impressive attendances: the 1951 final between Cork Athletic and Shelbourne drew 39,000 spectators.

The standard of football was generally good, with domestic league clubs featuring some of the best Irish players. The wage ceiling of £20 per week in the English Football League meant part-time professional footballers with good day jobs could earn as much in Ireland. International selections regularly featured home-based players and in November 1956 the Republic of Ireland beat world champions West Germany 3–0 at Dalymount Park with a team that included seven League of Ireland players. The domestic game was full of keenly-contested individual rivalries, such as the celebrated clashes between the Shamrock Rovers winger Liam Tuohy and the Drumcondra full-back Bunny Fulham; characters such as Eamonn 'Sheila' Darcy, a long-serving goalkeeper with both Rovers (1956–62) and Drumcondra (1962–8) who combined spectacular saves with crowd-pleasing antics, added to the entertainment value.[3]

The latter 1950s was the era of 'Coad's Colts': Paddy Coad, a former Shamrock Rovers inside-forward had become team coach in 1949 and assembled an adventurous and exciting young side. Players such as Tuohy, Paddy Ambrose, Gerry Mackey and Ronnie Nolan packed stadiums and established Rovers as the pre-eminent club side in the Republic. In a highly competitive environment, they won nineteen trophies (1954–9), including three league championships and two FAI Cups, and established themselves as one of the league's best-ever teams. When Rovers became the first League of Ireland team to enter the European Cup in 1957, it was fitting that their first-round opponents should be Manchester United's renowned 'Busby Babes', to whom they were often compared. An official crowd of 46,000 filled Dalymount Park (then the largest ever to attend a club game in Ireland) and saw

United's superior skill and fitness prevail as they ran out 6–0 winners in a performance that lived long in the memory of those who were there. Coad's team did rather better in the away leg at Old Trafford, when they ran United close with a 3–2 defeat that restored some pride.[4]

An important strand of domestic football was regular matches between the five professional leagues in Britain and Ireland. There were two a year (1946–50) between the League of Ireland and Irish League, none in 1951–2 and then usually one a year (1953–70). Although playing for one's league was considered a lesser honour than playing for one's country, the appearances were nonetheless valued and provided a useful means of granting international representative honours to home-based players not selected for the full international team. They were also used to acknowledge the important contributions of the league's best English-born players, several of whom, such as Johnny Matthews, Dave Bacuzzi, Bobby Tambling and Peter Thomas, played for League of Ireland XIs during the 1970s.

For most of this period both northern and southern leagues were in a reasonably healthy state, and matches between them attracted good crowds, as did their occasional games against the English and Scottish Leagues. These allowed Irish supporters to see the best cross-channel players and were very popular with the football public, even if the League of Ireland was usually outclassed by full-time professional opponents and suffered some crushing defeats, such as losing 9–1 to the English League at Maine Road on 10 February 1954 and 11–0 to the Scottish League at Celtic Park on 28 November 1962. There were, however, occasional good home results, such as a 1–1 draw with the Scots on 6 September 1961 and a 2–1 win against the English League on 2 October 1963 at Dalymount Park, providing much-needed boosts to both the domestic league and national pride.

✳✳✳

Throughout these years the urban working class continued to provide soccer's most dedicated supporters. The sport's important place in working-class life was well demonstrated in May 1952 by the visit to Dublin of Doncaster Rovers to play a benefit match against a Drumcondra XI for the Workers' Union of Ireland's Jim Larkin Memorial Fund. A half-century earlier, as a trade union organiser in Scotland and Belfast, the Liverpool-born Larkin had seen at first-hand how soccer could help to make workers' lives more enjoyable and endurable. After moving to Dublin in 1908 and founding the Irish Transport and General Workers' Union, he encouraged the setting up of football teams for union members and went on to serve as a vice-president of the Leinster FA.[5] His 'bread and roses' philosophy insisted that trade unions should demand more than the necessities of existence for their members and in his later years he planned the creation of a new cultural, educational and recreational centre for Dublin workers and their families. After his death in 1947, his Workers' Union of Ireland (WUI) colleagues set up a memorial fund to realise his dream. Some of these had close associations with Drumcondra FC, a club that drew strong support from the northside dock-working community in East Wall (southside dockers were more likely to support Shamrock Rovers or Shelbourne). East Wall had long been one of Dublin's main soccer nurseries, its passion for the game and popular street leagues forming the backdrop to Sean O'Casey's anti-war play *The Silver Tassie* (1928).

Doncaster Rovers played in the English second division but were a team of interest in Ireland: their player-manager, the Northern Ireland international Peter Doherty, was a much-admired figure among Irish supporters and in 1951 had signed two Drumcondra players, Christy Giles and Christopher Lawlor. When the secretary of the memorial fund committee, Charles Phipps, approached Doherty, he readily agreed to bring his team to Dublin without payment of a match fee. On the evening of Friday 9 May 1952, a crowd of 12,000 spectators gathered in Dalymount Park to see an entertaining game that was won 2–1 by the visitors and raised £1,000 for the fund.[6]

Despite its popularity in some quarters, soccer still occupied a rather ambivalent position in Irish life, viewed by some as a sport that had no place in an independent Ireland. The GAA's ban remained in force and, although often evaded, it was far from a dead letter. 'Vigilance committees' policed GAA members with zeal and those who played or watched banned sports risked expulsion. Falling foul of the ban was a rite of passage for many young Irish footballers. Jackie Carey and Kevin O'Flanagan played Gaelic football at school and were selected for the Dublin minor team but were dropped when found to have played soccer. Con Martin helped the Dublin senior Gaelic football team win a Leinster title in 1941, but when the GAA discovered he was playing soccer for Drumcondra, he was expelled from the association and his medal withheld. (He eventually received it in 1973.) In 1948 the future Celtic player Sean Fallon was beginning to make a name for himself as a Gaelic footballer with Sligo but gave up the game when reprimanded by his County Board and forced to choose between it and soccer.

Condemnation of 'foreign games' was still ritualistically employed by GAA officials to boost their nationalist credentials. In 1953 the association's president, M.V. O'Donoghue, argued that the ban was essential 'to curb the baneful activities of Anglicisation and to prevent the infiltration into the GAA of saboteurs and fellow travellers ... Its duty was to expose, counter and nullify anything inimical to the accepted national ideal.' Referring to the FAI's appointment of Scot Dugald Livingstone as national coach in 1951, O'Donoghue denounced him as 'the chief of the new Saxon recruiting campaign' who 'had been busy enticing young Irish boys by various inducements to become happy little English children and heirs to the joy of a soccer paradise'.[7]

In his account of growing up in Dublin in the 1950s, the journalist Gene Kerrigan recalled that the soccer-supporting working class were considered by many in authority as 'less than properly Irish. There was Real Ireland, a Gaelic-speaking, GAA-playing, predominantly rural, genuflecting nation, respectful of the old gunmen who presided over the state. And there was the rest of us, who in one aspect or another, or in several, didn't quite measure up ... We were not native speakers. We were not – not quite – natives. To us, GAA games were games, not badges of national pride ... we made a hero of Stanley Matthews and when the Manchester United plane crashed at Munich we mourned Busby's Babes, not least because one of them, Liam Whelan, was a northsider ... It wasn't that we were Anglophiles, we just preferred the bright to the grey, the exciting to the dull.'[8]

While some soccer supporters took an interest in Gaelic games, others were indifferent or decidedly hostile: Eamon Dunphy recollected that when growing up in Drumcondra many of his soccer-playing friends were contemptuous of the GAA and looked down on its games. He recalled that 'the ban and the idea that theirs was a foreign game was a source of bitter amusement to soccer people. Country people were dismissed as "culchies" or bogtrotters, and their sport was accordingly derided as unsophisticated'. Fearing ridicule, he kept his enthusiasm for Gaelic games to himself.[9]

Antipathy to soccer in schools proved enduring, particularly in those run by the Christian Brothers, an order that prided itself on its nationalist zeal.[10] When in the early 1950s the talented young soccer-player John Giles went to Brunswick Street secondary school in inner-city Dublin, his father was compelled to sign a document pledging him to play for the school's Gaelic football team. Giles recalled that 'the schools were very anti-soccer in those days' and that some teachers saw his ability at the game as evidence of a lack of national commitment: 'the level of hostility to the "soccer men" or "corner boys" from the authority figures at the school was astonishing'. The fact that authority figures regarded an important part of working-class culture with such contempt had a strongly alienating effect on many young soccer players. Even though he came from a republican background, Giles noted that 'the idea of soccer as the foreign game was drilled into us to such an extent that, for a few years after I left school, I didn't feel Irish at all'.[11]

Other Republic of Ireland managers, such as Mick Meagan and Eoin Hand, had similar experiences in Christian Brothers schools in Dublin, recalling that teachers would regularly resort to corporal punishment to discourage the playing of soccer, even outside school hours.[12] Such attitudes persisted into the 1970s. In April 1971, the talented young footballer Liam Brady was made captain of the Irish schoolboy team to play Wales. At the same time he was selected for the Gaelic football team of his school St Aidan's in the north Dublin suburb of Whitehall and was told that he faced expulsion from the school if he did not play. The seventh son of a Dublin docker, Brady was steeped in football: his brothers Ray and Paddy played professionally in England (Ray made six international appearances for the Republic (1963–4)), another played with Shamrock Rovers, and his great-uncle Frank was capped for the Free State in the 1920s. In defiance of his school, Brady went ahead and played for his country and never returned to St Aidan's.[13]

Throughout his long career, the FAI secretary Joe Wickham insisted that the playing of soccer was entirely compatible with Irish patriotism. He repeatedly pointed out that 'soccer is not an English game now. It is an international sport that is the national game of countries like France, Germany and Italy, so you do not lose your Irish nationality by playing it. We are all Irishmen too.'[14] The FAI rarely missed an opportunity to assert its national credentials. Since its foundation it had regularly used the Irish language version of its name (Cumann Peile na hÉireann) on official correspondence and match programmes, and for a World Cup qualifier against Czechoslovakia in October 1961, the association asked Radio Éireann to include an introduction in Irish before its live broadcast.[15] The fiftieth anniversary of the Easter Rising, which was commemorated by numerous local and state-sponsored events, was marked by the FAI with a ceremony before the Cup final at Dalymount Park on 24 April 1966. The association took out press advertisements to contact soccer supporters who held Irish Volunteer/IRA 1916–21 military service medals and received hundreds of responses.[16] On the day, 200 veterans of the Easter week fighting in Dublin (roughly a third of the surviving total) stood to attention on the pitch to welcome President Éamon de Valera, who was loudly cheered by the 27,000 crowd. After inspection by Minister for Education and FAI President Donogh O'Malley, ranks of veterans marched around the ground to martial airs. 'The last post' was sounded as the tricolour was lowered by Captain Tom Scully, a member of the Boland's Mill garrison in 1916 and a long-serving FAI council member.[17]

***

Many of the national schools attended by working-class pupils were under-resourced and made little provision for sport of any kind: they lacked pitches, equipment and teachers with the required abilities and interests. Lack of resources, coupled with the anti-soccer attitude of schoolteachers (both lay and religious) intent on promoting official Gaelic values, ensured that very little soccer was played in the schools of the twenty-six counties. This was a matter of some frustration to the FAI which in 1938 sought a meeting with the minister for education to address the matter. Five years later the association was still bemoaning 'the hostile attitude of some schools and colleges to football' and seeking an explicit confirmation from the Department of Education that there was no official objection to the game being played in schools. Such approaches yielded few results, and into the mid-1960s Joe Wickham admitted that he was saddened by the fact that 'even now, soccer is not accepted by most Irish schools and boys have to organise themselves outside the schools'.[18]

This though spurred the FAI to encourage the formation of parish leagues to cater for young players, particularly in expanding Dublin suburbs such as Ballyfermot, Crumlin, Walkinstown, Cabra, Finglas and Whitehall – areas that would become strongholds of the game and supply many future international players.[19] Soccer enthusiasts also took their own initiatives. In the mid-1920s locals in Drumcondra had set up a street league which in 1928 evolved into Home Farm FC. This went on to develop thousands of young players, including several who won international honours such as Jackie Carey, Kevin O'Flanagan, Joe Haverty and Liam Whelan. The Manchester United manager Matt Busby praised Home Farm as the best organised amateur sports club he had ever seen. It became central to the development of Irish soccer and even made efforts to align itself with the state's cultural values, coaching some of its teams through the Irish language.[20] In Dublin its work was complemented by other leading clubs such as Stella Maris, Johnville, Belvedere, St Joseph's Boys, Lourdes Celtic and Bulfin United, who contributed to a thriving culture of youth football and the founding of the Dublin and District Schoolboys League in 1944. Under-age soccer also made good progress outside the capital and formal Schoolboy Leagues were founded in Cork and Waterford in 1948. In 1947 Ireland (FAI) played its first under-15 international against England at Dalymount Park and demonstrated the strength of Irish schoolboy football with an 8–3 win, following this up with another victory over England in London in May 1948.[21]

Schoolboy leagues and clubs became important parts of communal infrastructure throughout the country. Some grew into enduring institutions that catered for generations of young players, many of whom would go on to become the coaches and officials of the same clubs, keeping alive a strong sense of continuity and community. In many working-class areas soccer clubs were often among the most vibrant institutions, drawing on a reservoir of voluntary effort that made an important and underrated contribution to local civic society. Volunteers gave freely of their time to organise teams, coach players, mark pitches, arrange games, transport players and raise funds. Such activities played a crucial role in binding local communities together, particularly in the new suburbs of towns and cities where there was often little else in the way of social infrastructure.

These efforts were often assisted by the minority of politicians who were enthusiastic soccer supporters. Fianna Fáil ministers such as Brian Lenihan senior and David Andrews (the son of C.S. 'Todd' Andrews) were keen players (Lenihan was an amateur international) and later held prominent positions with the FAI. After the death of Oscar Traynor in 1963, his successor as FAI president, Donogh O'Malley, was another leading Fianna Fáil minister. The dynamic O'Malley was representative of a new breed of Irish politician, more concerned with shaping a modern prosperous country than observing the shibboleths of the past. An all-round sportsman who had played inter-provincial rugby for three provinces and amateur international soccer for Ireland, he believed that any form of sporting sectarianism was damaging to the Republic's international image and as minister for education (1966–8) sought to provide a wider range of sports in schools. He criticised the GAA ban as narrow and outdated, maintaining that 'rugby and soccer people were sick and tired of having the finger pointed at them as if they were any worse Irishmen. When Ireland was asked for sons to call to the colours we were not asked what shape of a ball we used.'[22] O'Malley's promising career was cut short by his death in 1968 aged forty-seven, but the Fianna Fáil hold on the FAI presidency continued when he was succeeded by the strongly nationalist Neil Blaney, Fianna Fáil TD for Donegal North-East and Minister for Agriculture and Fisheries.

Blaney's election testified to soccer's continued importance in Donegal, where it had considerable cross-party support. Local Fine Gael TD and Minister for Local Government (1954–7) Patrick O'Donnell noted the immense pride across the county when the Aranmore-born Matt Gallagher of Hibernian FC made his international debut for the Republic on 7 March 1954 and made the point that 'I have seen soccer in my own native Rosses where not one word of English was spoken.'[23] For all its popularity, though, soccer in Donegal could seem detached from the game in the Republic, with clubs often having closer connections across the border in Derry and Tyrone. An FAI conference held in Lifford in 1952 highlighted the proximity of the border and a scattered population as the main barriers to the game's development.[24] Although Donegal was a stronghold of junior soccer and both Swilly Rovers and Ballybofey-based Finn Harps had won the FAI Junior Cup, it took almost half a century for the county to have a club in the League of Ireland. Not long after the foundation of Finn Harps in 1954, its chairman, Patsy MacGowan, approached the FAI to explore the possibility of playing in the league and found himself pushing at an open door. Joe Wickham had long believed that Donegal should be represented in the national league and was strongly supportive. After Finn Harps had performed well in junior soccer for several years, they were elected to the League of Ireland in 1969 ahead of the applications of Athlone Town and Home Farm.[25]

During the 1960s there was increasing tension between the modernising aspirations of the state, anxious to open the Irish economy to outside influences and investment, and the rhetoric of cultural exclusion still sometimes voiced by the GAA. These tensions crystallised in lively debates over 'the ban', or Rule 27 as it was officially known, and were often subsumed into a wider debate about the opening up of Irish society. GAA modernisers saw the ban and its appendages as relics of a mean-spirited chauvinism that reflected badly on the association. A lifelong member, Breandán Ó hEithir admitted that he found 'any rule or law that set one group of Irishmen to spy on another set of Irishmen, in the name of a superior national purity, distasteful in the extreme'.[26] For many years a group of GAA members had been working to abolish the ban, most notably Tom Woulfe of the Civil Service club, and finally in April 1971 their efforts bore fruit, with Congress voting to revoke Rule 27. It was an important milestone for the GAA and for Irish society, but attitudes did not change overnight and some suspicion between the respective associations and their codes remained.

***

During the early 1960s the dominance of the League of Ireland by clubs from the capital continued, their grip on the title broken only by Limerick in 1960 and Dundalk in 1963. Dublin clubs won the FAI Cup from 1958 to 1970, with Shamrock Rovers achieving a notable six in a row (1964–9). The standard of play remained strong and a League of Ireland XI that contained five Rovers players beat the English Football League side 2–1 at Dalymount Park on 2 October 1963. But after Drumcondra's league win in 1965, the balance of power shifted, and between 1965 and 1983 the only Dublin club to win the title was Bohemian FC (1975 and 1978). Waterford led the way, winning six out of eight championships from 1966 to 1973.

While the success of clubs such as Waterford, Dundalk, Cork Hibernians, Cork Celtic, Sligo Rovers, Limerick United and Athlone Town made the league a truly national competition, the decline of Dublin clubs was a worrying development in the game's heartland. When Shamrock Rovers won their fourth consecutive FAI Cup final in 1967, beating St Patrick's Athletic in a Dublin derby, the match was watched by only 12,000 spectators, one of the smallest ever to watch a final. When Rovers won their next two FAI Cups against Waterford and Cork Celtic in 1968 and 1969 there were much larger attendances of 39,000 and 28,000 respectively but, while some teams brought massive followings to cup finals, many of these were occasional supporters who rarely attended league matches.

By the early 1970s attendances were falling for all clubs. The reasons were many and often rooted in wider developments in society and culture. During the 1960s the encouragement of greater economic competition and free trade gathered momentum and in an expanding world economy, employment and productivity increased and emigration fell. Living standards improved, with higher incomes allowing greater access to consumer goods. By 1966 most Irish homes had a television set which was often the centre-piece of family leisure and English channels could be received along the east coast. In 1964 the BBC began broadcasting its *Match of the Day* programme on Saturday nights, while its commercial rival ITV began its *Big Match* Sunday afternoon coverage in 1968, clashing directly with League of Ireland games. Domestic football, often played on poor pitches and in ramshackle surroundings, compared badly with the televised highlights of English matches, and fewer people were prepared to stand on the terraces to watch their local team. English soccer was also proving more attractive to Irish players. The abolition of the maximum wage in England 1961 and the introduction of greater freedom of contract from 1964 opened up new opportunities for talented players, most of whom aspired to play for an English club. The loss of players lowered domestic standards and attendances, and Irish clubs became increasingly dependent on transfer fees from abroad to survive. The quality of League of Ireland football declined, and from the early 1970s onwards its players rarely featured on the international team.

European club competitions did, however, offer the possibility of playing at a higher level. Irish clubs began to contest European trophies in 1957 but had to wait until 1963 to eliminate foreign opposition, when Drumcondra beat a Danish Odense Select XI home and away to progress to the next round of the Inter-Cities Fairs Cup. For the rest of the decade Shamrock Rovers did most to vindicate the League of Ireland's reputation, achieving home draws and one-goal away defeats to top continental teams such as Valencia CF (Fairs Cup, 1963/4), Real Zaragoza (Fairs Cup, 1965/6) and Bayern Munich (UEFA Cup Winners' Cup 1966/7), all of whom reached the final or won the respective competitions. In 1969 Rovers also managed a 2–1 home win over FC Schalke 04 in their Cup Winners' Cup tie before losing 3–0 in Germany.

Even when results were disappointing, European matches could still be memorable occasions. In the first round of the European Cup on 18 September 1968, Waterford were drawn against Manchester United, who four months earlier had become the first English club to win the competition. No Irish soccer stadium could cope with the demand for tickets and the game was played at Lansdowne Road. It drew a crowd of 48,000, the largest to attend a soccer match in Ireland, attracted by the rare opportunity to see the 'United Trinity' of George Best, Denis Law and Bobby Charlton in competitive action. Although the game was a great financial success for Waterford, it again revealed the chasm between the two leagues. United won 3–1 in Dublin, with Law scoring a hat-trick, and added another four goals in the second leg at Old Trafford to secure a 7–1 victory.[27]

Qualification for European tournaments added a new dimension to domestic Irish football. For clubs there was the possibility of securing an attractive draw and bumper gate receipts; for players the opportunity to play the best teams in Europe before large crowds; for supporters the opportunity to see the Continent's best players and, for the truly dedicated, the chance to travel to far-flung places to support their team. For all three there was the tantalising possibility of causing an upset against one of the giants of European football. Domestic rivalries were usually set aside for these matches and the club involved became the national standard bearer, drawing support from across the league. However, there were also drawbacks. Games sometimes involved heavy travel expenses that already hard-pressed clubs struggled to recoup. League of Ireland part-timers were usually outclassed and occasionally suffered demoralising defeats that showed how far domestic Irish football had fallen behind and confirmed local critics in their poor opinion of domestic football.

By the early 1970s it was clear that the League of Ireland was in serious trouble: between 1969 and 1973 gates declined by 60 per cent.[28] The fall in attendances was self-perpetuating: the smaller the crowd, the more muted the atmosphere and the less enjoyable the experience. Many casual supporters drifted away. Some retained a sentimental attachment to their club and might occasionally attend an important cup tie or a big European game, but their regular support could no longer be relied upon. The League of Ireland found itself locked into a vicious cycle of small crowds, dwindling resources and falling standards. Respected families such as the Proles and the Cunninghams, who had owned Drumcondra FC and Shamrock Rovers respectively, sold their interests and withdrew from direct involvement in the game. Drumcondra folded in 1972 and took with them a half-century of tradition. Many were bewildered at the speed and sharpness of the league's decline. The Irish international Paddy Mulligan recalled that when he left Shamrock Rovers to go to Chelsea in 1969 the domestic game was in a reasonably healthy state, but on his return to Glenmalure Park a decade later he found himself playing in a 'withered' league.[29]

Jackie Carey of Ireland (FAI) challenges Tommy Lawton of England in the first ever meeting between the two teams at Dalymount Park in 1946. Con Martin and Bill Gorman of Ireland look on. © PA Images/Alamy Stock Photo

Northern Ireland's Peter Doherty, guesting for Brentford in the Wartime League during the Second World War. © PA Images/Alamy Stock Photo

Northern Ireland vs Czechoslovakia during the 1958 World Cup in Sweden.
© Archive PL/Alamy Stock Photo

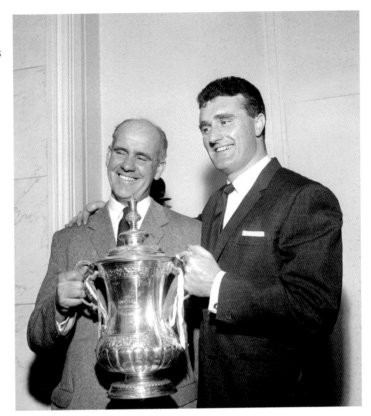

Jackie Carey and
Noel Cantwell, past
and present captains
of Manchester
United, with the FA
Cup won by United
in 1963.
© PA Images/Alamy
Stock Photo

Northern Ireland's Gerry Armstrong (right) scores against Spain in the 1982 World Cup.
© PA Images/Alamy Stock Photo

Two of Northern Ireland's greats – Danny Blanchflower and George Best.
© BNA Photographic/Alamy Stock Photo

The Shamrock Rovers All-Ireland XI for a friendly v Brazil at Lansdowne Road on 3 July 1973. Back row, l–r: Miah Dennehy, David Craig, Paddy Mulligan, Martin O'Neill, Derek Dougan, Alan Hunter and Liam O'Kane. Front row, l–r: Bryan Hamilton, Pat Jennings, Tommy Carroll, John Giles, Don Givens, Terry Conroy and Mick Martin.
© Connolly Collection/SPORTSFILE

Alan McDonald of Northern Ireland tries to stop Elzo of Brazil during the 1986 World
Cup in Mexico. Norman Whiteside and Mal Donaghy look on.
© PA Images/Alamy Stock Photo

Liam Brady and Jack Charlton after the 2–2 draw with Belgium in the European
Championship qualifier on 10 September 1986. © Inpho

The Republic of Ireland starting line-up against Italy for the 1990 World Cup quarter-final. Back row, l–r: Kevin Moran, Paul McGrath, Pat Bonner, Mick McCarthy, Andy Townsend and Steve Staunton. Front row, l–r: John Aldridge, Niall Quinn, Kevin Sheedy, Chris Morris and Ray Houghton. © Trinity Mirror/Mirrorpix/Alamy Stock Photo

A mural painted at Carnforth Street in east Belfast for the UEFA European Championship in 2016. © DMc Photography/Alamy Stock Photo

A mural painted in St James's Crescent in west Belfast to mark the sixtieth anniversary of the demise of Belfast Celtic. © Extramural Activity

The Republic of Ireland's Robbie Keane beats Germany's Oliver Kahn to score a late equaliser in the 2002 World Cup. © PA Images/Alamy Stock Photo

Katie McCabe of the Republic of Ireland is tackled in a friendly against the USA in Austin, Texas, on 8 April 2023. © Bob Daemmrich/Alamy Stock Photo

9

One Long War and Three World Cups: Northern Ireland 1956–86

For the 1958 World Cup, FIFA decided not to use the British Championship as a qualifying group. This meant that Northern Ireland would not have to overcome England and Scotland to qualify. The draw, though, did them no favours, placing them in a group with Italy and Portugal, two of Europe's strongest teams. Northern Ireland had little experience of continental opposition, having only played their first full international against a non-UK team in May 1951, drawing with France in a friendly match in Belfast and then losing to them in Paris in November 1952.

By the time the qualifiers for the 1958 World Cup in Sweden came around, manager Peter Doherty had assembled a settled, well-coached team, with some exceptional individual players, such as Harry Gregg in goal, Danny Blanchflower at wing-half, and Jimmy McIlroy and Peter McParland in the forward-line. In the team's first qualifier in Lisbon on 16 January 1957, they secured a draw, and then proceeded to beat Portugal and Italy in Belfast to qualify. England, Scotland and Wales all qualified as well. This meant that the 1957/8 British Championship was highly competitive: Northern Ireland drew with Scotland and Wales and beat England 3–2 at Wembley on 6 November 1957 to share the championship. The win over England (the first since 1927) was a particularly important milestone: Peter McParland recalled it as a day that would always be 'stamped across every Irishman's heart'.[1]

In Northern Ireland there was considerable pride in the team's achievements: despite being the smallest of the fifty-three nations that had entered the World Cup, it had managed to qualify where many others had failed. (It remained the least populous country to play in a World Cup tournament until Trinidad and Tobago reached the finals in 2006.) Qualification had, however, given rise to a difficult dilemma for the IFA. Playing in Sweden raised the possibility of playing on Sunday, which was expressly forbidden by its constitution. This was a real predicament in a province in which much of the Protestant population regarded Sunday as a day for religious worship, rest and reflection. At the time such attitudes were not uncommon in those parts of the UK where Protestant Dissenting religions remained strong, but they were held with particular fervour in Northern Ireland, where cinemas, shops, pubs, parks and playgrounds were closed on Sundays. However, for most Catholics, Sunday was for both religious observance and sport, and the usual day for GAA matches. This was regarded as offensive by some Protestants and, after complaints in 1934 (including one from Prime Minister Craig), BBC Ulster ceased broadcasting the scores of Gaelic games on Sunday. When it resumed in 1946, it was careful to delay until Monday to avoid causing offence.[2]

The question of Sunday football was complicated by the composition of the IFA. Its affiliates included many clubs from various Church leagues who were strongly opposed to playing on Sunday. A 75 per cent majority was needed to change the IFA rule, and with seventy-six of its clubs affiliated to the main Churches League, this was never going to be easy. However, most IFA senior officials had no wish to throw away hard-earned qualification and on 28 January 1958 the IFA council voted to approve Northern Ireland's participation by twenty votes to eight. At the same time it also forwarded a request to the FIFA Organising Committee that the team be given an exemption from Sunday fixtures.[3]

FIFA refused to countenance any special treatment and when the draw was made in Stockholm on 8 February 1958, Northern Ireland found itself in a tough group alongside Czechoslovakia, Argentina and West Germany, with the matches against the Czechs and Germans scheduled for Sundays 8 and 15 June. The IFA issued a statement that the decision to play would be left to individual players, but this did little to appease strict Sabbatarians, who regarded it as a principle far too important for private judgement. Opponents of Sunday football held a large rally in Belfast's Assembly Hall on 16 February 1958 (a Sunday) that included representatives of all the main Protestant churches and some leading IFA officials. Rev. Rupert Gibson of the Presbyterian Church argued that 'if the commandments were binding in one place – Ulster – they were equally so in another – Stockholm', and the meeting issued a strong statement calling on the IFA council to reverse its decision.[4]

Most Northern Ireland players had little difficulty playing on Sunday, having already done so on pre-season club tours. Harry Gregg was the most notable exception: brought up to believe in strict Sunday observance, he gave the matter prolonged consideration and only committed to play after consulting a clergyman who raised no objection. Others, both Catholic and Protestant, regarded opposition to Sunday football as behind the times and misguided: the Aston Villa forward Peter McParland noted that such a situation 'could only happen in Ireland, and it looked like making us the laughing stock of the football world'.[5] Jimmy McIlroy of Burnley spoke of how frustrated the players were 'to win against the foreigner on the field, yet lose to Irishmen off it'. He observed that 'the majority of senior clubs want us to play on Sundays. The majority of players want us to play on Sundays. The majority of spectators want us to play on Sundays ... Hundreds of insignificant clubs voted against it ... The opinions of the amateur leagues should be recorded ... and ignored! Such men are millstones to Irish international prestige.'[6]

The IFA eventually cobbled together a compromise. On 13 March it met representatives of the Churches League, who agreed to withdraw their opposition in return for an IFA commitment not to enter a team in any future competition that required playing on Sunday.[7] (The IFA later resiled from this position, but the issue remained contentious, and Windsor Park did not host an international match on a Sunday until 2015.) The controversy was the second time in three years that there had been a serious clash in Ireland between playing football and religious strictures. The intervention of Archbishop McQuaid in the South and the Sunday football controversy in the North clearly illustrated that partition had produced two conservative states in which dominant religions were used to getting their way. It was, though, significant that in both cases the disputed football matches went ahead despite the opposition of powerful individuals and institutions.

Northern Ireland's build-up for the World Cup was probably more seriously affected by the crash of the aircraft carrying the Manchester United team at Munich in February 1958. The international team lost Jackie Blanchflower, their first-choice centre-half, who was seriously injured and never played again. Harry Gregg was also on the crashed plane but suffered only minor injuries and heroically returned to the wreckage to carry injured passengers to safety. He was soon playing again for Manchester United and made his way to Sweden by boat and train when his teammates flew out in June.

The Northern Ireland party were based at Tylösand, a small, pleasant seaside resort near the city of Halmstad; appropriately, the nearby river was called the Lagan. From the start, they were accessible and friendly, attended numerous civic receptions and adopted a local boy as their team mascot. The Swedes were much taken by their informality and readiness to break into popular songs, such as 'When Irish eyes are smiling', 'The Mountains of Mourne' and 'How can you buy Killarney?'; many locals supported the Irish as their second team. Their relaxed demeanour did not however imply any lack of competitiveness. Astute observers, such as the English sportswriter Brian Glanville, recognised that Doherty had assembled an impressive team; it lacked a goal-scoring centre-forward, but he expected it to do well nonetheless.[8]

Glanville was proved correct, and the team adapted well to tournament football. Like its southern counterpart, it suffered in one-off games from the reluctance of British clubs to release players and the lack of time for training and preparation. In Sweden the team was together for several weeks, which allowed Doherty time for the intensive coaching at which he excelled. The climate also suited: it was the first time the World Cup had been held in such a northern latitude and the summer of 1958 was cooler than normal. Even the squad's limited resources (Doherty had only brought seventeen players rather than the permitted twenty-two) initially proved an advantage, facilitating a settled and closely-knit team. There were no religious tensions: on the Sunday of their first game both Protestant and Catholic players and staff attended a service at the small Lutheran church in Halmstad and together sang the hymn 'Fight the Good Fight'. Peter McParland recalled their strong camaraderie, maintaining that 'once an Irishman pulls on that green shirt, he becomes twice the player' and that Doherty's rousing team talks reminding them they were playing 'for the glory of Ireland' had a powerful effect on players from all backgrounds.[9]

In their opening game in Halmstad on 8 June, Northern Ireland battled hard and played some skilful football to beat Czechoslovakia 1–0, impressing the local crowd and the Swedish press. This was followed by a 3–1 defeat to Argentina (the first time they had faced a team from outside Europe), which left them needing at least a draw against world champions West Germany on 15 June 1958. The game was attended by King Gustav of Sweden and the Governor of Northern Ireland, Lord Wakehurst, and proved to be one of the most exciting of the tournament. Northern Ireland secured a 2–2 draw, with Gregg making a series of superb saves. The much-respected German coach Sepp Herberger described them as 'the cleanest team we have fought in the tournament so far. They are tough tacklers and rough fighters, but they never go beyond the rules.'[10] The Irish then had to meet Czechoslovakia again in a play-off in Malmö on 17 June. In another outstanding performance they beat them for a second time (2–1) to reach the quarter-final, but this was as far as they would go. Two days later they faced France in Norrköping, 400km to the north, after a long and tiring coach journey. Three games in five days proved too much for the small squad: with most players fatigued or carrying injuries, they went down 4–0 to a strong French side that was beaten in the semi-final by Brazil, the eventual winners.

The team was disappointed, but not overly despondent. They had reached the last eight in the world and along the way had played with style, celebrated with gusto and lost with grace. Their commitment, skilful play and sporting attitude won admirers across the board. Gregg and Blanchflower featured in the team of the tournament, and others such as Bertie Peacock, Billy Bingham and Peter McParland (who weighed in with five goals and later had a public park named after him in Newry) performed brilliantly. Perhaps the team's most characteristic player was the diminutive Leeds United midfielder Wilbur 'Billy' Cush, whose work-rate, courage and tough-tackling embodied the spirit of a fearless underdog and endeared him to the Swedish crowd.[11] A proud Peter Doherty maintained that 'no country in the history of world soccer has earned greater glory from ultimate defeat'.[12]

Throughout the tournament, interest at home in Northern Ireland had been strong. The games had been broadcast in part or in full on radio by the BBC NI Home Service and attracted huge audiences – an estimated 250,000 tuned in for the play-off against Czechoslovakia on 17 June. While some of Northern Ireland's games were covered by Swedish television and seen on the Continent, technical difficulties prevented them being relayed to Northern Ireland. Some of the tournament highlights were shown by Pathé News though and press coverage was considerable, with match reports and related stories making the front pages of the province's main newspapers: a *Northern Whig* editorial noted that 'our players have already done the province proud, not only by their skill, but by their bearing as ambassadors of sport for their native land'.[13] The team's achievement was all the more notable since Scotland and England failed to qualify from their groups, and the only other UK side to reach the quarter-finals was Wales (who had an easier route). Claims that Northern Ireland 'have proved themselves the best in the British Isles'[14] were not confined to the province itself: British papers such as the *Daily Mail* lauded the team's 'comradeship, unselfishness and friendliness' and noted that 'they have made friends with the world'; while the *Daily Express* described them as 'Britain's top ambassadors' who 'made the greatest impression on the field and off it'.[15] A French journalist described Northern Ireland as the 'true revelation of the tournament'.[16]

The team's performances were appreciated far beyond their usual following. Lady Wakehurst, wife of the Governor of Northern Ireland, who had been on a fishing holiday in Norway during the tournament, noted how it had done more to promote the province 'than anything else we could possibly have done ... Everywhere we went people asked us questions about Northern Ireland – seemingly because of the magnificent performance of the team ... The players were tremendously brave, courageous and brilliant.'[17] The nationalist *Irish News*, often critical of the IFA, was generous in its praise, especially for Doherty's skilled leadership.'[18] There was also admiration from south of the border, whose government habitually dismissed Northern Ireland as an illegitimate statelet. Dublin had earlier advised the Irish Legation in Stockholm that since Northern Ireland would be playing under the British flag they should 'plead diplomatic illness and not attend any matches'. If pressed for comment they 'might express pleasure, or regret, at the victory, or loss, of the Northern Ireland team, adding a remark regretting that the team is not representative of all Ireland as in the case of rugby football'.[19] For most people, the team's performances soon dispelled such diplomatic equivocation. The Fianna Fáil-sponsored *Irish Press*, while adhering to its usual convention of referring to the team as the 'six counties', was full of praise for its exploits, hailing Peter Doherty 'as the master strategist and Danny Blanchflower as the great tactician'; it was further noted that the team's success had created 'wild interest' in Donegal.[20]

Since its foundation Northern Ireland had rarely featured in international news. When it did, it was usually for reasons such as political division and sectarian conflict. However, during the World Cup Northern Ireland presented an image of normality and harmony, reinforced by the demeanour of a team whose sportsmanship on the pitch was matched by their good humour off it. Most agreed that the tournament had served the province well, advertising its existence in a positive and progressive light, and going some way to ease divisions, with Catholics and Protestants such as Doherty, Blanchflower, Gregg, Peacock, McIlroy and McParland admired across the sectarian divide. One newspaper noted that 'in three weeks the 17 footballers have earned more valuable publicity for Northern Ireland than would years of pamphlet propaganda'.[21]

In purely sporting terms too the tournament was important. Jimmy McIlroy noted that it had transformed Northern Ireland from 'soccer nonentities' into a 'world soccer power ... those three weeks in Scandinavia did more for Irish football than all the seventy-odd years that had gone before'.[22] After decades of playing the same three teams in the British Championship, year in and year out, the IFA had engaged with the rest of Europe rather hesitantly, and not without incident, most notoriously in the 'Battle of Windsor' on 4 December 1957. The match had originally been arranged with Italy as a World Cup qualifier, but bad weather prevented the arrival of the Hungarian referee and the two sides agreed to play a 'friendly'. When this was announced just before kick-off, many supporters voiced their annoyance, believing they had been short-changed. The ill-tempered mood spread to the pitch, with a succession of niggling fouls by both sides. The game ended in a 2–2 draw and, as the Italians left the pitch, some were attacked by spectators and sustained minor injuries; only the intervention of the home players and the police prevented more serious assaults. Italian officials and press were outraged, one journalist commenting that 'now I know why the Romans never came here'. There were protests in the Italian Senate and the match gained extensive media attention across Europe. The Irish government was deeply concerned at these reports of hooliganism in 'Ireland' by the followers of a team called 'Ireland' and instructed embassies to set the record straight. The Irish embassy in Rome stressed that the incident had happened in Belfast, which was 'the principal city of the six counties which constitute so-called Northern Ireland, still held by Britain against the will of the great majority of the people on the whole of the island'.[23] The province's leading football journalist Malcolm Brodie wrote after the match that Northern Ireland's 'reputation tonight stands at zero throughout the world following those disgraceful scenes ... Now comes the task of rebuilding it from the debris of that disastrous day'.[24] The unremittingly positive coverage of Northern Ireland's World Cup adventure in June 1958 did so with something to spare.

The joyous reaction of many in Northern Ireland to the World Cup campaign was understandable in a state that was often defensive and insecure. From its foundation in 1921, roughly a third of the population regarded it as illegitimate, as did the only state with which it shared a border. In its first two decades Northern Ireland struggled to establish itself amidst constitutional uncertainty, economic decline and sectarian strife. The IRA remained active into the 1950s, mounting raids on Gough and Omagh military barracks in 1954, and in December 1956 began its 'Border Campaign' with attacks on police stations and customs posts. Over the next six years this cost the lives of eleven republicans and six RUC men and caused considerable material damage; in 1957 alone over 300 incidents were reported. The Stormont government responded by interning hundreds of suspected republicans and by summer 1958 the IRA campaign was fizzling out. It had enjoyed little support from northern nationalists and never seriously threatened the Northern Ireland state but had put unionists on their guard and sharpened political and sectarian tensions.

When, therefore, Northern Ireland featured in the news for reasons other than IRA attacks, the government was keen to make the most of it. It distributed promotional information on Northern Ireland throughout Sweden and invited foreign journalists on fact-finding tours. Some nationalists though remained sceptical. Cahir Healy, the veteran MP for South Fermanagh, asked if the Swedish people were receiving information on matters such as sectarian discrimination and the gerrymandering of political constituencies.[25] Despite the team's success, its relationship to the wider nationalist community remained fraught. One nationalist newspaper observed that 'the Unionist aim to make political capital out of the showing of the Six County soccer team in the World Cup was as palpable as it was typical. Evidently it was as much a propagandist as a football game to the partitionist mind.'[26] Many footballers from a Catholic/nationalist background represented Northern Ireland with distinction, their sporting competitiveness, team spirit and desire to play international football taking precedence over any political reservations. But for some, these reservations persisted, particularly the belief that the IFA discriminated against Catholic players. Charlie Tully, a west Belfast Catholic who played with Belfast Celtic and Glasgow Celtic in the 1940s–50s and was one of the province's most gifted footballers, appeared only ten times in ten years for Northern Ireland (1948–58). Left out of the 1958 World Cup squad, he believed his omission was primarily motivated by sectarian bias. While some nationalists were prepared to support Northern Ireland during the tournament, many others kept their distance, believing that the team did not represent them, no matter how well they performed. Some insisted that the image of unity given by the World Cup was deceptive, papering over deep-seated bigotry. Nationalists who made their way to Windsor Park rarely felt at home. As a young man, the inter-county Gaelic footballer and future SDLP politician Seamus Mallon went to an international match to support his friend Peter McParland; he was dismayed to hear him being subjected to sectarian abuse and never returned.[27]

***

The 1958 World Cup had been such an enjoyable experience for players, officials and supporters that all were eager to repeat it. Some argued that the team should prioritise qualification for future tournaments even if this risked re-opening the controversy about Sunday play.[28] However, little was done to build on the achievement. For all Doherty's success, the IFA insisted he carry on in a part-time capacity, claiming they did not have the resources to employ him full-time.[29] Northern Ireland shared the 1958/9 British Championship with England, but then rather lost their way and finished last for the next four seasons. After Doherty resigned in February 1962, his successors, Bertie Peacock (1962–7), Billy Bingham (1967–71), Terry Neill (1971–5), Dave Clements (1975–6) and Danny Blanchflower (1976–9), all struggled to make an impact. Form through the late 1960s and early 1970s was patchy, with roughly two defeats for every win. The mainstay of the season was still the British Championship, and although there were notable results such as 1–0 victories over Scotland in Glasgow on 18 May 1971 and over England at Wembley on 23 May 1972, the team usually struggled to avoid the wooden spoon. As well as competing in the World Cup, Northern Ireland began playing European Nations' Cup qualifiers in 1962 but failed to make the finals of any international tournament through that decade and the next. This was despite the presence from 1964 on the team of George Best, often regarded as the most naturally gifted Irish footballer of all time. His sublime skills, pop-star looks and troubled personal life made him more globally famous than any other twentieth-century Irish sportsman, even though he never graced the finals of an international tournament. He occasionally played magnificently for Northern Ireland, scoring nine goals in thirty-seven appearances, but as his personal problems mounted his effectiveness waned and he rarely featured from 1973 onwards.[30]

In the bloody political violence of the early 1970s, large public gatherings were often judged too dangerous and from October 1971 to March 1975 no international matches were held in Northern Ireland: the team was forced to play its 'home' games in England.[31] Northern Ireland still proved a tough opponent throughout the decade, with notable wins in qualifying groups over Sweden, Yugoslavia, Belgium and Denmark, but was not consistent enough to reach the final stages of any international tournaments. In March 1980 Billy Bingham became manager for the second time and would remain in charge for the next thirteen years. Under his leadership the team enjoyed its greatest period of sustained success, winning the British Championship outright in May 1980, the first time it had done so since 1914. Unfortunately, it was prevented from defending its title when the upsurge in violence that accompanied the republican hunger strikes of 1980-1 prompted England and Wales to refuse to travel to Belfast. The team did, however, manage to fulfil their fixtures in the preliminary rounds of the 1982 World Cup, securing victories over Portugal, Sweden and Israel to qualify for the final stages in Spain.

Before the tournament, Northern Ireland's expectations were modest. There were few star players on the team, several of whom played in the lower divisions of English football, and the squad was padded out with Irish League part-timers. In the four games played prior to the World Cup, Northern Ireland drew with Scotland and lost to England, France and Wales, conceding twelve goals and scoring just one. When their tournament started on 17 June, they had rallied sufficiently to secure a 0-0 draw with Yugoslavia and a 1-1 draw with Honduras four days later. This left them needing a win against the hosts and group favourites Spain to progress to the next round. Against all the odds, they managed it on a memorable night in Valencia on 25 June 1982. The decisive goal was scored by Gerry Armstrong after 47 minutes and, despite having defender Mal Donaghy sent off (and several other unfavourable refereeing decisions), Northern Ireland managed to hold out for a famous 1–0 victory.

The win came at a time when the province had experienced thirteen years of the Troubles, which showed no sign of ending, and it provided a welcome respite. The journalist Ed Moloney described it as an 'all too rare event when a battered community could temporarily forget its woes and take a special sort of pride in a magnificent achievement', and believed that it had – even fleetingly – improved cross-community relations. Sammy Duddy, the press officer of the Ulster Defence Association (the largest loyalist paramilitary organisation), welcomed the fact that Protestant supporters were cheering for Catholic players such as Gerry Armstrong and Martin O'Neill, and optimistically maintained that when Northern Ireland were playing 'there's no such thing as religion'.[32]

The team's victory was widely celebrated, *The Irish Times* noting that 'not just the Shankill Road and Newry, not just the sundered six counties, but the whole island cheered Northern Ireland's victory over Spain ... To call the Valencia victory the high point of Northern Ireland football history, or even of a century of Irish soccer, was no flight of fancy.'[33] Telegrams of congratulation were sent to the team by the Catholic Primate of Ireland Cardinal Tomás Ó Fiaich, the nationalist SDLP, and Taoiseach Charles Haughey. There were also reports that the team was cheered on by a mixed crowd of loyalist and republican prisoners in the Maze. It was noted that the World Cup coincided with a temporary easing of violent conflict. At a time when there was a politically motivated killing almost every three days, there were none between Northern Ireland's first match on 17 June and their last on 4 July, and for almost another two weeks afterwards.[34]

The win even prompted the Sinn Féin newspaper, *An Phoblacht: Republican News*, to take a more conciliatory attitude to the IFA team and to soccer generally. While noting that most republicans saw the existence of separate Northern Ireland and Republic teams as deeply partitionist and that many 'have a traditional antipathy to soccer as not just a foreign game but a British game', *An Phoblacht* was nonetheless prepared to celebrate the outstanding performance of a 'Fall's Road man Gerry Armstrong' and to acknowledge that the 'six counties team undoubtedly has a wide and sympathetic support north and south'. The paper's television critic watched the game in a pub in the Dublin suburb of Cabra and was taken aback by the 'white-hot atmosphere' and enthusiastic support for Northern Ireland.[35]

Advancing into the second round, Northern Ireland kept hope alive with a draw against Austria before eventual elimination on 4 July after a 4–1 defeat to France. While disappointed that their tournament had ended, the team were proud to have matched the achievement of 1958. As in the earlier tournament, Northern Ireland's spirit on the pitch and friendliness off it earned them many friends among neutrals. When their convivial post-match celebrations and raucous sing-sings sparked rumours that the Irish players were boozing between matches, the Spanish manager wryly noted that perhaps he should have encouraged his team to do the same.[36]

Players attributed a great deal of their success to the coaching and motivational skills of Billy Bingham, who, with his assistant Bertie Peacock, provided strong links with 1958. The team's talented young centre-forward Norman Whiteside, who, aged seventeen years and forty-one days was the youngest player ever to appear in a World Cup tournament on 17 June 1982, recalled that Bingham's team talks were 'tailored for the ... team and were about our country, its people, what they'd gone through over the past decade and what our being out there meant to them'. Whiteside, who had played his earliest competitive football with the Boys' Brigade, was proud of his roots in the Shankill, a community he saw as 'an entrenched, embattled people who have been let down by everybody'.[37] Others focused on the team's wider representation, noting that it usually contained seven Protestants and four Catholics, a ratio close to that of the Northern Ireland population as a whole. Players such as Armstrong and Donaghy came from the nationalist Falls Road, and much was made of the fact that they were lining out alongside others who had grown up on the Shankill. Bingham believed that the team's mixture of religions was one of its strengths, encouraging the players to make an additional effort to get along and try harder for each other on the pitch. He recalled that they 'all sang each other's songs, we rejoiced together and we commiserated with each other when we lost. The team could not have done what it had if it had eleven Protestants ... or eleven Catholics.'[38] Bingham was full of praise for the efforts of his captain, Martin O'Neill, who in 1980 became the first Catholic to lead Northern Ireland since Jackie Vernon in 1951. O'Neill's appointment had, however, been greeted with protests, and both player and manager received abusive sectarian letters.[39] While players of both religions got on well together and gave their all for the team, they did not entirely forget their political backgrounds: at a reception for the team at Stormont in November 1983, Whiteside noticed that Protestant players went straight to Ian Paisley of the Democratic Unionist Party (DUP), while Catholics clustered around John Hume of the nationalist SDLP.[40]

Northern Ireland's final game in Spain was watched by Jim Prior, the secretary of state, who claimed that 'all of Northern Ireland has supported this team and it has brought a new pride and unity to the country'. Prior sought to encourage this unity by investing in the infrastructure of Northern Ireland football and provided a £1 million grant to improve Windsor Park. But this was a gesture that was unlikely to win cross-community support: for nationalists, Windsor Park was indelibly associated with the ultra-Protestant support of Linfield FC and that club's refusal to employ Catholic players, and some dismissed Prior's grant as a subsidy for bigotry.[41] Most in the nationalist community remained suspicious of the IFA, with many regarding support for its team as tacit recognition of the Northern Ireland state.[42] Others had enjoyed the tournament, but believed that it had changed nothing, concluding that 'when the moment of glory which we all can share has passed, the cancer of sectarianism which makes this society ultimately so difficult to unite, lives on'.[43]

Northern Ireland's World Cup exploits assumed an even greater importance owing to the uncertainty that surrounded the British

Championship. After the temporary abandonment of 1980/1, the competition was resumed in 1982 and continued for another two years. Much to the delight of their supporters, it was won by Northern Ireland in its centenary and final year in 1984. While the IFA still valued the competition and prized its links with the other UK associations, this was not always reciprocated. By the early 1980s attendances had declined sharply at most Championship games other than England against Scotland, and their two FAs believed the competition had outlived its usefulness. They had bigger fish to fry and the Championship was brought to an end in 1984. With its demise, qualification for major international tournaments became even more important for Northern Ireland.

Two years later the team emerged from a group that included England, Romania, Turkey and Finland to qualify for the 1986 World Cup in Mexico, beating a strong Romanian team home and away. Qualification was assured on 13 November 1985 with a 0–0 draw against England at Wembley, celebrated with great enthusiasm by the 15,000 Northern Ireland supporters present. In Mexico the team was drawn in a tough group based in Guadalajara. With an ageing team, they were unable to repeat the heroics of 1982 and, after drawing with Algeria, lost to Spain and Brazil. The tournament failed to match the excitement of four years previously but was again watched by large crowds at home, who remained proud of their team. Bingham summed up the general mood when he remarked: 'It's always disappointing to lose but if there is a consolation we did it with dignity.'[44] For many supporters, the team's sustained achievement in these years – winning the British Championship in 1980 and 1984, and qualifying for successive World Cups – outshone even the deeds of 1958, and made 1980–6 the golden age of Northern Irish football.[45]

Just like four years earlier, playing in the 1986 World Cup had contributed to a greater sense of normality in day-to-day life and provided a respite from the Troubles. Violent deaths again declined temporarily, with none at all during the team's three games between 3 and 12 June, even though there were sharp political tensions. In November 1985, the British and Irish governments had concluded an

agreement that gave the latter a new consultative role in the affairs of
Northern Ireland. Outraged Unionists denounced the agreement as
the thin end of the wedge that would lead to a united Ireland. There
were protests on the scale of those that had greeted the Home Rule
Bill of 1912, including mass rallies and civil disobedience. In a nod
to the huge 'Ulster Says NO!' banner displayed on Belfast City Hall,
Northern Ireland fans used their international platform in Mexico to
unfurl a large 'Guadalajara Still Says NO!' at the game against Algeria
on 3 June.[46] By this time, the Northern Ireland team had become an
important symbol for much of the province's unionist population. They
were deeply proud of its achievements and determined to maintain its
autonomy. With Northern Ireland clearly outperforming the Republic,
the IFA president Harry Cavan was moved to ask 'who needs a united
Irish soccer side?'[47] By the mid-1980s the prospect of unity in Irish
soccer seemed further away than ever.

10

Thirty Years of Hurt:
The Republic of Ireland 1955–85

After the Republic's defeat to Yugoslavia in October 1955, the FAI appointed Jackie Carey as team manager. Before retiring from playing in 1953, Carey had been the team's most influential player and coach in all but name. The change was not therefore a dramatic one, and FAI officials continued to pick the team. Carey started well on 27 November 1955, with a 2–2 draw at home to Spain, and won his next three games (all friendlies), including a celebrated 3–0 victory over world champions Germany at Dalymount Park on 25 November 1956. Drawn in the same qualifying group as England for the 1958 World Cup, they approached the campaign with some confidence. In the first competitive match between the two teams, England avenged their 1949 loss in Goodison with a 5–1 victory at Wembley on 8 May 1957, but the Republic still had a chance of forcing a play-off when England arrived in Dublin on 19 May 1957.

Cheered on by a record crowd of 47,600, the Irish took the lead after three minutes and dominated a strong England team that included Duncan Edwards, Tommy Taylor, Billy Wright, Tom Finney and Johnny Haynes. The match was an enthralling one and as it drew to a close the expectant crowd 'were clearing their throats for a Dalymount roar to end Dalymount roars and tell the world that we had beaten England's soccer stars for the first time on an Irish pitch', when England scored a last-minute equaliser.[1] The 1–1 draw ended the

Republic's hopes of qualification and stunned the Dalymount crowd. Most made no effort to leave the ground but remained rooted to the spot in mute disappointment: the Radio Éireann commentator Philip Greene observed that 'You could hear the silence at Nelson's Pillar.'[2]

England's late goal was remembered for many years afterwards as a crushing setback, and the overwhelming sense of shared disappointment was more frequently recalled by Irish supporters than the 2–0 win over England in 1949. The results of the national team during the 1950s were mixed: in thirty-two games, it won fourteen, drew six and lost twelve. The team though were never no-hopers: there were enough victories and good performances in friendlies to raise hopes before qualification campaigns, even though these were invariably dashed. Despite repeated disappointments, attendances at international matches held up well, and the Republic was one of the best supported football teams in Europe per head of population. When almost 50,000 people crammed into Dalymount Park, they could create a spine-tingling atmosphere in the compact stadium, and the famed 'Dalymount roar' was more than just a media cliché. After his team's win in 1957, the England manager Walter Winterbottom expressed his astonishment at the Irish support, noting that 'if we had a crowd cheering for us like that we would beat the world. We never get that encouragement. In fact I have never heard anything quite like it.'[3]

Irish supporters revelled in their team's underdog status, which chimed with the popularly held view of their country's history. An official narrative of Ireland's past that stressed persecution, suffering and unending struggle was taught in schools, invoked by public figures and generally accepted by most of the population. This was summed up in de Valera's reply to Churchill's disparagement of Irish neutrality in 1945, when the taoiseach spoke of 'a small nation that stood alone ... for several hundred years against aggression ... that was clubbed many times into insensibility, but that each time on returning consciousness took up the fight anew; a small nation that could never be got to accept defeat and had never surrendered her soul'.[4] It was a view that could easily be transmuted into sporting terms: an underdog that fought hard against stronger opponents, suffered repeated misfortunes, but never gave up, and the football stadium often became an arena in which historical conflicts were reframed and re-enacted. England's late equaliser was seen as yet another injustice in a long line of injustices inflicted on Ireland by 'the Saxon'.[5] Irish supporters often referred to England as the 'Auld Enemy', mostly in jest, but a jest with an edge nonetheless; national reputation was at stake, and these contests were more than just games of football.

When Northern Ireland won new friends and recognition in Sweden in 1958, the Republic's players and supporters looked on with envy. They had, after all, been playing against continental opposition from the mid-1920s and had entered every World Cup since 1934 without qualifying. The team could at least console themselves that they would not have to wait too long to play competitive international football, after UEFA had created the European Nations' Cup in 1958. Seventeen teams entered the inaugural competition, among them the Republic of Ireland. (England and Northern Ireland waited until the 1964 qualifiers, and Scotland and Wales until 1968.) The first competition was run on a knock-out basis and the Republic faced Czechoslovakia in the preliminary round, winning 2–0 in Dublin on 5 April 1959 but were eliminated after a 4–0 defeat on 10 May in Bratislava. They then won four of their next six friendly matches (including a 1–0 victory over West Germany in Düsseldorf on 11 May 1960), but again form deserted them when they needed it most. They lost all four matches against Scotland and Czechoslovakia in the 1962 World Cup qualifiers; the last game was a crushing 7–1 defeat in Prague on 29 October 1961 (still the team's worst defeat in a competitive fixture).

This succession of disappointments did little for national self-confidence. Many supporters blamed the team's poor results on its selection by a committee of five FAI officials, the 'Big Five', a procedure long since abandoned by most international teams. In criticisms that mirrored those made by Dublin when the Irish team was selected by a Belfast-dominated IFA committee, players and supporters of regional League of Ireland clubs claimed that they were discriminated against by Dublin officials. Even established international players such as Sean Fallon from Sligo (eight caps, 1950–5) and Frank O'Farrell from Cork (nine caps, 1952–9) believed that they would have been selected more often had the 'Big Five' not been biased towards players born or based in Dublin. While the committee probably favoured those they knew, players from outside of Dublin still formed a significant presence on the national team: of the eighty-nine players from the twenty-six counties selected by the FAI (1946–59), twenty-nine were born outside the capital, with the cities of Cork (10), Limerick (6) and Waterford (4) leading the way.[6]

Supporters also claimed that some English-based players performed better for club than country, and their commitment to the national team was questioned. This though was usually unfair: the Republic played most of their matches on Sunday, and cross-channel players had often turned out for their clubs a day earlier. Arthur Fitzsimons, a skilful inside-forward who won twenty-six international caps (1949–59), recollected how he would rush to catch a boat immediately after playing for Middlesbrough on Saturday to get to Dublin for an international game. Despite the poor pay, kit and facilities provided for the Republic's players, he was adamant that 'nothing would stop him getting home to play for his country'. Like many players who were based abroad, playing in England reinforced his sense of national identity and he loved the noise and excitement in Dalymount on big match days, recalling that 'when I stood for the national anthem, I felt ten feet tall, and as strong as ten men. We feared no-one. I never played for money or fame, but for my country and I'd do it all again in a heartbeat.'[7]

Notwithstanding their commitment, players arrived in Dublin fatigued, often after a rough sea voyage. Most gave their all, but they could rarely give their best. For the next match, they could find themselves replaced by League of Ireland part-timers who at least had a better chance to rest before games but were often outclassed by continental professionals. The selectors would then revert to English-based players and the cycle of complaint and experimentation would begin again.[8] With much of the team often arriving for matches within hours of the kick-off, there was little time for preparation, and Carey generally gave them only the most basic tactical instructions.

Carey was a popular and respected figure among Irish players, many of whom had idolised him in their youth, but his tenure as manager was disappointing. Some believed he could have done more to challenge the FAI bureaucracy and improve the international set-up. However, during his fourteen years in charge, the easy-going Carey never insisted on selecting the team and was probably personally too close to leading officials to shake up the complacent administration of Irish international football.[9]

After the humiliations of 1961, the Republic's fortunes recovered somewhat. The team eliminated both Iceland and Austria in 1962/3 in the European Nations' Cup, before finally going out to Spain after home and away defeats in March and April 1964. In between there was a morale-boosting 1–0 victory in a home friendly against a strong Scotland team on 9 June 1963. But again the team was found wanting in key competitive matches. In 1965, the Republic was paired with Spain in a two-team qualifying group for the 1966 World Cup. Spain, European champions in 1964, provided a formidable barrier, but in a surprise result the Irish managed to win at home on 5 May 1965 before losing in Spain on 27 October. They were finally eliminated with a 1–0 defeat in a play-off at the Stade Colombes in Paris on 10 November. The FAI had originally suggested Wembley Stadium as the venue for the play-off, but agreed to hold it in Paris after the Spanish Federation had offered the Irish association its share of the gate receipts.[10] The decision to play in Paris, where Spain had much more support than Ireland, came in for serious criticism from players and supporters, who believed that the FAI had put its own financial interests ahead of those of Irish soccer. It was especially disappointing to lose out on qualification for a World Cup tournament to be held in England, where the Irish would have enjoyed significant support.

By this time popular engagement with the game was beginning to be strongly influenced by television. Previously, those who did not attend matches were largely dependent for their impressions on radio, still photography and newspaper match reports: all conjure up their own mental images, but none capture the game quite like moving pictures. Newsreels conveyed some of the excitement of big games, but their coverage was usually fleeting and failed to replicate the sport's real-time drama. Television, however, was a transformative technology that massively expanded football's audience. Televised coverage had begun to come into its own in the 1950s: BBC broadcasts of FA Cup finals attracted millions of viewers and boosted the reputation of epic games such as the 'Matthews' final' of 1953. The 1960 European Cup final between Real Madrid and Eintracht Frankfurt was the first to be broadcast live across the Continent and saw a star-studded Madrid team win 7–3 with a memorable performance.[11] By then, Ireland still lacked its own television channel, but some areas could pick up British broadcasts, which encouraged the Irish government to set up Telefís Éireann (later RTÉ) in 1961. The new channel was a resounding success and it was estimated that over half of the Republic's 680,000 homes had television sets by 1966.

During the 1960s, World Cups became global events watched by hundreds of millions.[12] The 1966 tournament was the first to be televised by RTÉ and attracted the curious as well as the committed. Without a team of their own to support, many Irish viewers backed England, admiring the skills and demeanour of players such as Bobby Charlton and Bobby Moore (although this support rather waned in later years). The sports journalist Con Houlihan maintained that showing the 1966 World Cup on Irish television 'effected a quiet revolution in our island: it opened windows and blew away cobwebs – and implanted soccer in almost every parish'.[13] Houlihan was exaggerating somewhat: soccer's progress into rural Ireland was rather more tentative, and there were still some who accused RTÉ of promoting foreign culture, noting that the World Cup was producing 'disturbing effects here among those followers who contaminate their minds with such world-disturbing, unnatural and degrading recreations'.[14]

Watching World Cup matches on television made the dream of qualifying for an international tournament even more attractive to Irish football supporters, but this seemed destined to remain a dream. In the qualifiers for the 1968 European Championship (the renamed Nations' Cup), the Republic managed only a single home win, against Turkey. The team was already eliminated before it faced Czechoslovakia at Dalymount Park on 21 May 1967 in front of 8,500 spectators, the venue's smallest ever crowd for a full international. Carey had stepped down as manager three months earlier, and the position was shared by the senior players Noel Cantwell and Charlie Hurley. The team did even worse in the 1970 World Cup qualifiers, gaining only a single point in six games. Morale plummeted: players and officials traded recriminations, blaming each other for the team's failings, while supporters became increasingly disillusioned with both. In the past Irish supporters had accepted the team's defeats and disappointments with resignation and continued to attend games in good numbers, but many were now losing interest.[15]

Players claimed that the FAI cared little for the national team. Some suggested that the association's readiness to play friendly matches against Poland (six times between 1964 and 1970) stemmed from officials' ability to make easy profits by exchanging western currencies for black market zloties and live royally on the proceeds. When the team played in grim industrial cities such as Katowice, some 'blazers' would stay in good hotels in Warsaw and not bother travelling to the game. Little thought was given to the players. When, in May 1970, the team travelled by rail to West Berlin after a game in Poland, the train was overbooked; the few available seats were given to FAI officials while players stood in corridors or sat on suitcases a day before they were due to represent their country. As the future Irish manager Eoin Hand noted, the attitude seemed to be that anything was good enough for the players.[16] When they returned to their clubs in England and related such incidents, their managers were usually horrified and increasingly reluctant to entrust their players to an association that seemed indifferent to their welfare.[17]

The hierarchical structures of the club game were replicated, and even accentuated, at international level: players were treated as hired hands and were expected to put up and shut up. In the circumstances it is perhaps surprising that more did not become disillusioned, but generally they swallowed their reservations and performed as best they could. Experienced players such as John Giles were frustrated by the contrast between the professionalism and confidence of his Leeds United club team and the haplessness and defeatism of the national side. While international football had moved on elsewhere, Irish football remained stuck in a rut. By the late 1960s, players' morale was at its nadir: Giles noted that there was 'no sense among the players that we were ever going to qualify ... It was back to the old Irish thing, always champions at moral victories. As a nation, we didn't expect to win ... If we won the occasional match that was good, but there was no real drive or feeling that we were going to do anything.' This lack of ambition and acceptance of mediocrity sapped his pride in representing his country, and he admitted that there were times when he and other players found it difficult to motivate themselves: 'Not through any lack of patriotism, but through professional despair at the shambles.'[18]

Eventually, after a run of abysmal results, senior players approached the FAI to request that the international team should be chosen by the manager, as was the norm in most other countries. Somewhat reluctantly, the FAI agreed and in 1969 appointed Mick Meagan as the first manager with control over team selection. Meagan, a Dubliner who had played in the League of Ireland with Drogheda and Shamrock Rovers and in England with Everton and Huddersfield Town, was a popular figure who had won seventeen caps for his country (1961–9). However, his part-time appointment did not address any of the team's deep-rooted weaknesses: after failing to win any qualifying games for the 1970 World Cup, the Republic suffered five successive defeats in the 1972 European Championship qualifiers. Liam Tuohy replaced Meagan for the last game of that campaign when the Republic was defeated 6–0 by Austria in Linz on 10 October 1971. (Unable to secure the release of cross-channel players, Tuohy had been forced to field ten League of Ireland part-timers.) This capped the team's worst ever run of form: since November 1967 it had gone twenty games without a win, and for many soccer supporters had become a national embarrassment. It was one thing to be an underdog, but even underdogs were expected to win occasionally.

Results improved somewhat under Tuohy, respected by players for his enthusiasm, tactical nous, man-management and dry sense of humour. In June 1972 the team entered the Independence Cup in Brazil (marking the 150th anniversary of Brazilian independence) and won its first games in over four years, beating Iran and Ecuador. There was also a notable 2–1 win over France at Dalymount on 15 November 1972 in a World Cup qualifier. As an international player (1955–65), Tuohy had experienced the FAI's amateurism at first hand and was determined to make changes. One of his most important innovations was to insist that important qualifying matches be played midweek rather than on Sunday, which gave players some time to rest and prepare. English clubs, though, remained reluctant to release players and Tuohy could rarely field his strongest eleven. During the 1972-3 qualifying campaign the Republic stumbled again, with home and away defeats to the Soviet Union. However, some progress was made, and for the first time since 1957 the team did not finish last in its World Cup qualifying group.

The team's form had contributed to a view that soccer was a marginal working-class game that did little for the country's international reputation. Many Irish businesses were reluctant to associate with it in any way, as was shown when the League of Ireland XI secured its first ever win in seventeen attempts against the English Football League at Dalymount Park on 2 October 1963, beating a strong team managed by Alf Ramsey that included future World Cup winners such as Bobby Moore, Martin Peters and Roger Hunt. The scorer of the winning goal, Ronnie Whelan senior, who played with St Patrick's Athletic, worked for the Finglas-based electrical firm Unidaire and received a warning from company management for taking unauthorised time off to play the game.[19] Paddy Mulligan of Shamrock Rovers had a similar experience. While working for the Irish National Insurance Company in 1966, he received a call-up to join the Republic of Ireland squad for a week-long tour in Austria and Belgium. When his employer refused his request for leave, he decided to go without permission. On his return he was hauled up before the board of directors, given a stern reprimand and warned that he would lose his job if he ever took unauthorised leave again. He was staggered that an Irish company would take such a petty attitude to an employee selected for his country and reflected that 'representing your country – to me it was the greatest honour ... But that was soccer in Ireland in those days. The poor relation.'[20]

The FAI often believed itself to be the poor relation in its dealings with RTÉ, regularly criticising the national broadcaster's soccer coverage. Even when games were broadcast on radio, they were often on local rather than national wavelengths, seriously curtailing their

availability, and although commentaries on soccer matches and programmes such as Radio Éireann's *Soccer Survey* drew large audiences,
there remained a sense that there was little interest and even some
antipathy to soccer within the station.[21] Politicians such as Senator
Tomás Ó Maoláin and the Dublin Fianna Fáil TD Seán Moore raised
this issue in the Oireachtas, with the former maintaining that the station's coverage amounted to 'apartheid in sport'.[22] The FAI made regular complaints to RTÉ about its poor coverage of the national team
and League of Ireland soccer, and in protest occasionally refused it
permission to broadcast international games.[23]

When it came to television, the FAI was torn between the desire
to promote the game by reaching a new audience, and the fear that
it could discourage spectators from attending and rob the association
of much-needed revenue. Since there was no competition for
broadcasting rights, sports associations were generally paid a pittance
that rarely made up for lost gate receipts. When RTÉ broadcast its first
full live soccer match on 8 April 1964 (a home European Championship
qualifier against Spain), the FAI allowed it to do so only because the
game was a sell-out, and thereafter television coverage of international
games was intermittent.

Soccer's low standing was reflected in its poor facilities and
infrastructure. Since the opening of Dalymount Park in 1901, it had
been developed by Bohemian FC into a serviceable stadium, hosting
five international matches against Scotland and England between 1904
and 1913. After partition, it became the de facto 'national stadium'
while continuing to serve as Bohemians' home ground. It was though
a rather humble venue and in 1929 Bohemians hired the renowned
Scottish engineer and draughtsman Archibald Leitch to oversee its
redevelopment. Leitch was the foremost stadium architect of his day,
having already designed grounds such as Hampden Park and Ibrox in
Glasgow, Hillsborough in Sheffield, and Goodison Park and Anfield
in Liverpool. His signature style was to fit as many spectators as
possible into a small space by creating an enclosed stadium that had
a covered stand on one long side of the pitch and open terraces on
the other three. This was the basic plan used for Dalymount, with the

addition of a reserved standing enclosure in front of the main stand
(which had seating for 2,355), creating a compact stadium that could
hold about 40,000 spectators. By 1940 Bohemian FC, a club owned by
its members, had spent almost £20,000 on improvements and had to
borrow extensively. It received little help from the FAI and was kept
afloat only by vigorous fundraising.[24]

While Dalymount could usually cater for domestic league and cup
games, it was often inadequate for major international matches. When
Spain played there in March 1947, there was a record official attendance
of over 42,000; many others gained admission without paying and the
crowd spilled onto the pitch and delayed the kick-off. Such incidents
were not unusual and Dalymount gained the reputation of being one of
the most chaotic venues in international football, described in 1952 by
the French manager as 'plain hell'.[25] When Sweden visited in September
1949, their press commented on the stadium's 'primitive condition'
and the general run-down state of Dublin, which it characterised as
teeming with beggars and Catholic churches.[26] Plans for a thorough
redevelopment of Dalymount were drawn up in the 1950s, but the
estimated cost of £30,000 was prohibitive and in the years that followed
the stadium was often a work in progress that made little progress.[27]
Accordingly, the Republic continued to play its games in an unsuitable
and unsafe venue, illustrated yet again in a European Championship
qualifier against Austria in October 1963, when 'gates were broken
down. Many got in for nothing, the pitch was inundated any time
anything of note occurred or when there was a stoppage in play, giving
the youth of Dublin a chance to show how undisciplined they were.'[28]

***

During the 1960s players from both sides of the border were often
frustrated by the failings of their national teams. The fact that both
seemed at least half a team short of international standard suggested
that an all-Ireland eleven could compete more effectively. There was also
the hope that bringing together players and supporters from different
backgrounds might help heal some of the island's communal divisions.

However, neither the IFA nor the FAI showed any real interest in creating a united team. The latter's aspirations to unity were often more rhetorical than real and by the late 1960s even these had waned: at a meeting of the FAI Senior Council on 14 November 1969, a motion for discussions on fielding an all-Ireland team was defeated by fourteen votes to twelve.[29]

Frustrated at administrative inertia, the veteran internationals John Giles and Derek Dougan discussed the possibility of putting together a team that would represent North and South. Dougan was one of the most singular figures in the game. A prolific goalscorer, he had played for several English clubs and gained a reputation as a flamboyant and outspoken individualist, on and off the pitch. He was a vocal chairman of the English Professional Footballers' Association (PFA), one of the best-known soccer pundits on British television, and wrote several books scathingly critical of those who ran the game. In an era when footballers generally steered clear of political or religious controversy, Dougan readily acknowledged the sectarian aspects of life in Northern Ireland. A Protestant from east Belfast, he had observed how Irish footballers of all backgrounds got on well together in England and believed that this goodwill could be harnessed.[30] In 1973 he and Giles enlisted the help of the latter's brother-in-law, the Dublin businessman Louis Kilcoyne, who lobbied the head of the Brazilian FA and soon-to-be FIFA president João Havelange for the world champions Brazil to come to Ireland. In return, Kilcoyne promised him the FAI vote in the forthcoming election for the FIFA presidency. Brazil had already planned a European tour to prepare for the 1974 World Cup in West Germany and its coach was persuaded by Havelange to finish with a game in Dublin.

When Dougan sought IFA support for the match, he received a cool response from the influential IFA president and FIFA vice-president Harry Cavan. A strong defender of the IFA's powers and independence, Cavan was wary of any moves towards all-Ireland unity. (Dougan never subsequently played again for Northern Ireland and was convinced that Cavan was responsible.)[31] It also seems that the FAI, which had not been involved in organising the match, had its reservations.[32] Dougan and Giles nevertheless managed to put together a team of six players from Northern Ireland and five from the Republic to face Brazil at Lansdowne

Road on 3 July 1973. Calling the team 'Ireland' risked further complications and instead it lined out in green and white hoops as a 'Shamrock
Rovers XI' (Kilcoyne had recently bought the club) and adopted 'A Nation
Once Again' as its 'national anthem'. In an exciting game, televised live on
RTÉ, the makeshift Irish team provided a stiff test for the Brazilians, losing 4–3 before an appreciative crowd of 34,000, which Dougan claimed
'gave the best vocal support I have ever heard in fifteen years'.[33]

Seldom has defeat in a football match prompted such celebration
and hope, but this was seen as a genuine moral victory and public and
press responded with enthusiasm: headlines proclaimed 'Brazilians
rocked by United Irishmen' and there were widespread calls for the
FAI and IFA immediately to begin discussions on creating a united
team.[34] The two associations were prompted to discuss pooling their
playing resources at conferences in 1973 and 1974, but there was little
progress. By this time, they had been separated for over half a century
and had developed distinct structures, priorities and identities. Most
IFA officials saw the border as a bulwark rather than a barrier and were
determined to maintain their autonomy in football as in politics. They
despaired of the attitude of southerners who seemed to think that
unity could be decreed without taking into account the bitter divisions
in Northern Ireland and on the island as a whole, and insisted that
without a political settlement a cross-border team was just a dream.[35]
When tentative negotiations on unity with the FAI broke down in
1980, a clearly relaxed Harry Cavan observed: 'The plain truth of the
matter is that the people of Northern Ireland do not want an all-Ireland
team. And we are acting on their behalf.'[36] Cavan and his southern
counterparts were also aware that greater unity might entail major
administrative changes, including a need for fewer officials. Since the
negotiations were carried out by those who had most to lose, it was
perhaps not surprising that they made little headway. In subsequent
years the question of unity was raised periodically, but northern
opposition, southern half-heartedness and a fraught political situation
combined to maintain the status quo.

✳✳✳

In October 1973 John Giles took over as the Republic's team manager and set about transforming its mentality. He refused to countenance talk of defeat or damage limitation, and encouraged his players to believe that they played in one of the world's strongest leagues and could match any international opposition. One recalled that 'John had an aura of confidence ... When we faced big players, John was not scared; when we faced great sides, he was not intimidated. That rubbed off on us. The past was forgotten: there would be no more notching up of moral victories.'[37] The team's preparation was significantly improved when Giles persuaded the FAI to align the dates of the Republic's matches with those of the England national team. This made English clubs more likely to release players and provided Giles with a stronger and more settled squad. On a short South American tour in May 1974, the Republic performed well, losing 2–1 to Brazil and gaining a rare away win, against Chile. Better was to come. For the Republic's first competitive game under his management, against the Soviet Union at Dalymount Park on 30 October 1974, Giles had worked assiduously to secure the release of players and was able to field his strongest team. They stunned the football world by beating the Soviets 3–0, the Irish centre-forward Don Givens scoring the first hat-trick by an FAI international player since Paddy Moore in 1934. Con Houlihan maintained that 'Ireland's albatross around the neck is the national sense of inferiority; at Dalymount yesterday the men in green shattered that.'[38] More strong performances followed, but the team lost crucial away games to the Soviet Union and Switzerland in May 1975 and again failed to qualify.

This rather set the pattern for the Giles era, which marked a considerable advance, but ultimately promised more than it delivered. At home the Irish were capable of beating any opponent on their day, but poor away results meant that qualification was still elusive. (In the thirty years from 1955 to 1985 the Republic managed only four away wins in competitive matches, against Czechoslovakia, Cyprus, Malta and Iceland.) The team still struggled with a lack of confidence in crunch games and on several crucial occasions suffered from dubious refereeing decisions. After the controversial disallowing of a goal scored against Bulgaria in Sofia on 1 June 1977 that resulted in a 2-1 loss and failure to qualify for the 1978 World Cup, the French manager Michel Hidalgo had no doubt that 'the referee had deprived Ireland of victory'.[39]

This was not an isolated case: looking back on dubious decisions that played a part in depriving the Republic of qualification for the 1978 and 1982 World Cups, the Irish midfielder Liam Brady was convinced 'there was a lot of skulduggery going on'.[40] In these years many Irish supporters developed the habit of immediately looking to the officials when their team scored to confirm that the goal would stand. Similar complaints about refereeing standards were also made by other countries – particularly smaller countries whose protests could be easily ignored. Suspicions about some officials were probably well-founded: the quality of refereeing in international football was uneven and in many places the venality of officials was taken for granted. (In the Soviet Union during the 1970s and 1980s the bribing of referees was so common that one official who refused to take money became a celebrity.)[41] In the Soviet bloc, sports organisations were important arms of the state and were encouraged to show communism's physical and moral superiority by defeating capitalist opponents whenever possible. Most were not fastidious about the methods employed. At the time FIFA and UEFA showed little interest in investigating refereeing irregularities and neither was itself a model of probity.

The Republic also failed to qualify for the 1980 European Championship, during which it was drawn in the same qualifying group as Northern Ireland. The two international teams had never played each other by choice, but, pitted together by UEFA, they had no option and faced each other for the first time at Lansdowne Road on 20 September 1978. Amid fears that their meeting might be accompanied by crowd trouble, or even paramilitary violence, there was little celebration. Violence still continued in Northern Ireland, claiming over 400 lives in 1976-7, and many feared its spread across the border. An estimated 8,000 Northern Ireland supporters travelled to Dublin and gardaí mounted the largest security operation ever seen for a sports event in the city. While there were no serious violent incidents during the match, afterwards there were scuffles and stone-throwing incidents around Lansdowne Road, quelled by a garda baton charge.[42]

The game itself was a dour 0–0 draw that failed to match the fixture's historic significance. Liam Brady, one of the Republic's most influential players, found it 'stupid and senseless' that two Irish teams were trying to deny each other qualification for an international competition, and recalled that the players were rather intimidated by the occasion and played within themselves.[43] When the return leg was played in Belfast on 21 November 1979, the game was more open and Northern Ireland won 1–0. Few southern fans attended and there was no serious crowd trouble (although the Republic's midfielder Gerry Daly was struck on the head by a coin). Northern players and supporters celebrated the victory over their nearest neighbours but, for the most part, both teams seemed happy to put the game behind them.

Under Giles's management the Republic established itself as a respected international outfit, strengthened by the emergence of new talent, particularly the Dublin-born Arsenal trio of Liam Brady, David O'Leary and Frank Stapleton. But qualification for an international tournament still proved elusive. By March 1980, increasingly involved with his other job as player-manager of Shamrock Rovers, Giles believed he had taken the Republic as far as he could and resigned. He was succeeded by Eoin Hand, who as player-manager of Limerick United (1979–83) had won the League of Ireland title in 1980 and gained a reputation as a promising young coach. Hand took charge for the 1982 World Cup qualifiers, the first campaign in which the FAI invoked the UEFA rule that clubs were compelled to release players for competitive international games, which considerably strengthened the Irish squad.[44] In a tough group Hand gained notable home victories over Holland and France, the latter attracting a crowd of 54,000 to Lansdowne Road. However, the Republic eventually finished second on goal difference to an outstanding French team that reached the semi-finals of the World Cup in Spain and won the 1984 European championship.

***

These years saw a development which would have significant consequences for Irish soccer and lay some of the foundations for the team's
later successes. This was the ability to recruit players of Irish descent born
abroad, which substantially increased the pool available for international
selection. In 1956 the Dáil passed an Irish Nationality and Citizenship
Act to make Irish citizenship more accessible to the descendants of
Irish emigrants and those born outside the state. This was a response
to the massive exodus of the 1950s and was intended to make it easier
for emigrants and their descendants to return to Ireland. According
to its provisions, the child or grandchild of any person born in Ireland
could claim Irish citizenship and an Irish passport. When combined
with FIFA's Article 18 which ruled that 'any person who is a naturalised
citizen of a country in virtue of that country's laws shall be eligible to
play for a national or representative team of that country', this meant
that the children and grandchildren of Irish-born emigrants were eligible
to represent the Republic of Ireland soccer team. However, the FAI was
slow to respond and had to be prompted into action. In April 1964, the
Manchester United manager Matt Busby notified the association that his
defender Shay Brennan, born in Manchester to County Carlow parents,
would be a valuable addition to the Republic.[45] Brennan would go on to
win nineteen caps (1965–70), but at the time there was little appreciation
of how the new broader qualification criteria would eventually transform the Republic's position in world football.

This can be partly explained by a reluctance in Ireland to
acknowledge emigrant communities in Britain, often seen as an
unwelcome reminder of the state's poor economic performance since
independence. The 1940s and 1950s had seen a massive outflow of
young men and women, as the Irish economy failed to provide them
with a living. In Britain the situation was different: the demands of
the wartime economy, post-war reconstruction and the growth of
the National Health Service created employment opportunities that
attracted droves of Irish immigrants. By 1951 there were almost 700,000
Irish-born people living in Britain, a number that increased as the rate
of emigration accelerated through the 1950s.[46] These predominantly
working-class immigrants were concentrated in industrial regions in

which association football was the most popular sport. Some played the game at various levels and many more supported a league team or became involved in the running of a local club. Their children took it up with even greater enthusiasm and by the 1960s and 1970s there were dozens of professional footballers of Irish descent playing in Britain who were eligible for selection for the Republic.

The FAI though made no systematic effort to identify them and the team's persistent under-achievement did little to attract footballers with international ambitions. However, after John Giles became manager in October 1973, he made it clear that he welcomed any suitably qualified players. Giles's professional approach and the team's improved results began to attract talented players, such as Mark Lawrenson of Preston North End, a promising young defender born in Preston to an English father and an Irish mother, who declared for the Republic in April 1977. The Republic fielded an entire team of Irish-born players for the last time against Turkey in October 1975, and by the time Hand led the team into the 1982 World Cup qualifiers, a third of the twenty-four players he used were born outside Ireland. Not everyone in Ireland was happy at this development, at least initially, and Hand received some abusive letters and phone calls, with one caller threatening that 'If you play any more of these English bastards, the only capping they'll get will be knee-capping.'[47] Such extreme views became even more marginal as players from the diaspora such as Lawrenson, Seamus McDonagh, Tony Grealish, Michael Robinson and Chris Hughton (who in 1979 became the first black player to be capped for the Republic) represented the team with distinction.

***

In May 1982 the Republic was scheduled to tour South America to play against top-class opponents such as Argentina and Brazil. However, by the time it was due to depart, Britain and Argentina had been at war for over a month after the Argentinian military junta had ordered the invasion of the Falkland Islands. Hand strongly questioned the wisdom of playing Argentina, arguing that it would be deeply unpopular in

Britain and sacrifice the goodwill of the English FA and its clubs (who were not compelled to release players for such tours). This was not the first time that the FAI had undertaken a controversial South American tour. On 12 May 1974 the Republic became the first foreign international team to play in Chile after General Augusto Pinochet had overthrown the leftist government of Salvador Allende in September 1973. The match was played at the Estadio Nacional in Santiago, which, after the coup, had been used by Pinochet's forces as a detention camp and was the scene of torture and executions. The Soviet Union had been scheduled to play a World Cup qualifier there on 21 November 1973 but refused, claiming that the stadium was 'stained with blood'. In Ireland there were strong protests about the FAI's decision to play in Chile from Amnesty International and the Labour Party, but to no avail.[48]

On both occasions, the FAI insisted that politics had no place in sport and that Ireland was a neutral state that did not take sides in other countries' wars or internal affairs. In 1982 its attitude chimed with the Anglophobic leanings of some government figures, particularly Taoiseach Charles Haughey, who rarely missed an opportunity to tweak the lion's tail. Hand believed that the FAI was pressurised to proceed with the tour by the Irish government, determined to display its neutrality and independence. After a Royal Navy submarine sank the Argentinian cruiser the General Belgrano in the South Atlantic on 2 May with the loss of over 300 lives, Haughey called for European Community sanctions against Argentina to be lifted, seriously alienating the British government and attracting widespread condemnation in the British press.

None of this helped Hand secure the release of players. He first contacted the Manchester United manager Ron Atkinson, who was staggered to learn that the Republic planned to play Argentina in the middle of a war and plainly told him to 'fuck off'. Pressing Atkinson for an official response to relay to the FAI, Hand was told: 'That is my official response, Eoin: tell them to *fuck off*.'[49] Other club managers replied in similar terms. This led the FAI to cancel the game against Argentina, but to go ahead with the rest of the tour. Several clubs still refused to release players and Hand was compelled to call on uncapped and League of Ireland players to supplement his weakened squad.

The tour itself showed FAI planning at its worst. The cheapest travel options had been chosen, resulting in long, uncomfortable flights that left players drained. In their first game on 21 May the Republic were beaten 1–0 by Chile in Santiago. Fatigue really caught up with them six days later in out-of-the-way Uberlândia, when a Brazil team that included world-class footballers such as Falcao, Socrates and Zico ran riot against their jaded opponents and racked up a 7–0 victory; it was the Republic's record defeat. Liam Brady, then playing his club football with Juventus and regarded as one of the best midfielders in Europe, was devastated by the humiliation and resolved to take no further part in the tour. He was eventually prevailed on to play in the final game on 30 May against Trinidad and Tobago in Port of Spain, but soon regretted doing so, as the Republic put in another inept performance to lose 2–1. The tour was the most disastrous in the Republic's football history, demoralising the players, generating fierce resentment in Britain and forfeiting much of the respect the team had built up in the previous decade. Hand himself described it as 'a shambles'.[50]

When the preliminary rounds of the 1984 European Championship began less than four months later, the team had still not recovered its confidence and failed to qualify from a group that included Spain and Holland. The 1986 World Cup qualifiers were even worse, with just six points taken from a possible sixteen. Players and supporters were deeply disenchanted and, after a depressing 0–0 home draw with Norway in May 1985 that scuppered the Republic's chances of qualification, Hand was seen to bow his head and lament 'it's never going to fucking happen for this country'.[51] After that game Hand was physically threatened and spat on by supporters.[52] The campaign ended on 13 November 1985 in a 4–1 home defeat to Denmark, watched by a small despondent crowd of 15,000. Public disillusionment mirrored that of the late 1960s. In contrast to Northern Ireland, who had just qualified for back-to-back World Cups, the FAI team had gone nineteen campaigns since 1934 without qualifying for a major tournament.

11

Coming of Age:
The Charlton Years 1986–95

The Republic's collapse against Denmark in November 1985 convinced the FAI that drastic action was required, and in a bold move in February 1986 it appointed an Englishman as manager: Jack Charlton, an experienced club manager and World Cup winner as a player in 1966. Supporters greeted the appointment with a mixture of wary approval, vocal scepticism and outright opposition; at his first home game one banner read 'Go Home Union Jack'. His tenure began slowly with a home defeat to Wales in March, but wins against Czechoslovakia and Iceland in the Iceland Triangular Tournament in May 1986 showed some improvement. Most supporters remained to be convinced and waited to see how the team would fare in the more testing preliminary rounds for the 1988 European Championship in West Germany. In a group that included Scotland, Belgium and Bulgaria, the Republic's performances were steady rather than spectacular (a 1–0 away win against Scotland on 18 February 1987 was the highlight), and yet again they looked to have missed out. However, an unexpected Scottish win in Bulgaria in November 1987 secured the team's first ever qualification for an international tournament.

When the draw was made for Euro '88, the Republic was pitted against England in its first game, with tough matches against the Soviet Union and Holland to follow. The excitement of qualifying was mixed with considerable trepidation: many believed that the team had been fortunate to qualify and feared it would struggle against such strong opponents. The pessimism induced by decades of failure died hard: in an eight-team tournament that included seven of the great powers of European football, the Republic were 33/1 outsiders to win, and the most popular football bet made with Irish bookmakers was that the team would not score a single goal.[1]

Still, many thousands immediately began preparations to travel to Germany. When the Republic and England met in the Neckarstadion, Stuttgart, on 12 June 1986, Irish supporters outnumbered the English in the 51,000 crowd. The Irish got off to a dream start when Ray Houghton scored after six minutes, and then spent most of the game stoutly defending against repeated attacks. Goalkeeper Packie Bonner of Glasgow Celtic pulled off a string of remarkable saves and, after one of the most nerve-wracking games in Irish football history, the Republic emerged as 1–0 winners. To have beaten England in the first major tournament game in the team's history was beyond the expectations of all but the most optimistic Irish supporters. Among those who celebrated was the veteran RTÉ commentator Philip Greene, who had been flown out to Stuttgart by the FAI in recognition of his contribution to Irish soccer. Having seen so many Irish defeats and near misses over the years, he was moved to tears by Ireland's victory, and recalled, 'We laughed and cheered and hugged each other like liberated people who had escaped from tyranny.'[2]

The result dispelled the fear that Ireland might be embarrassed on the international stage and many with little previous interest were drawn in: the next two matches were keenly watched in homes, halls, pubs and clubs across the country. On 15 June the Irish played some superb football against the Soviet Union and were somewhat unfortunate to concede a late equaliser to draw 1–1. This though kept hopes alive of making the semi-finals, and thousands of additional supporters travelled to Gelsenkirchen for the match against Holland on 18 June in which the Republic needed only a draw to progress. As against England, the game was notable for the team's last-ditch defending, but this time they conceded in the 82nd minute to go down to a 1–0 defeat to the competition's eventual winners. Despite their deep disappointment, thousands of Irish supporters stayed in the stadium after the game to salute the players. They did so with a fervour that moved many neutrals (including German police officers) and in the days that followed pride in the team's achievement grew. There was a sense among Irish players that what they had done had transcended sport: team captain Frank Stapleton described Euro '88 as 'something we will never see again in the history of Ireland'.[3] Many recalled the tournament as a week-long national carnival. The writer Nuala O'Faolain observed that 'the whole feel of living here was different, because there was something exciting and happy to think about'. People were 'able to say "we" and "Ireland" without feeling embarrassed ... Maybe the good humour and self-belief of the last week will come back to us in other ways ... As it is, the success of the Ireland team has palpably improved the quality of life for all of us. I note, for example, that the president of the GAA congratulated the soccer team on their achievements, and by just such small increments civilisation is made.'[4]

Soccer-supporting Fianna Fáil government ministers such as Brian Lenihan, Michael O'Kennedy and Bertie Ahern attended the games in Germany, and politicians who had previously kept their distance recognised that the sport was now too popular to ignore. Among the large crowd greeting the team on its return to Dublin airport was the Taoiseach Charles Haughey, who praised the team's exploits and noted that 'the country feels better this lovely Sunday morning than it has felt for a long time'.[5] During the decade large crowds had turned out to salute the achievements of other Irish sportsmen, such as Barry McGuigan's world boxing title in 1984, Eamonn Coughlan's gold medal in the 5,000 metres at the World Championships in 1985 and Stephen Roche's Tour de France win in 1987, but the country had never seen anything like this. An estimated 250,000 people lined the streets of Dublin to applaud the team as it paraded in an open-topped bus and was given a civic reception by the lord mayor. Looking out on the vast crowd celebrating the team's achievements, the FAI president Fran Fields was convinced that 'the game in this country had, at last, come of age'.[6]

Had Euro '88 been a one-off, it is likely that much of the Republic's new political and public support would have dissipated or moved on to other sports. Instead, it marked the beginning of the most successful period in the team's history, and a year later Ireland qualified for the 1990 World Cup in Italy. Again, excitement and expectation were heightened when the Republic was drawn to play England in the first game in Cagliari, Sardinia. Among supporters there was some foreboding that England would take revenge for Stuttgart, but in the end honour was saved with a hard-fought 1–1 draw. A dreary scoreless draw against Egypt followed, which kept open the Republic's hopes of qualification but otherwise provided little reason for celebration. Criticisms of the team's style that had been voiced since Charlton took over became louder. The respected sportswriter Hugh McIlvanney dismissed the Ireland v. England match as 'yob football' and noted that 'even for someone as pro-Irish and as fond of Charlton as I am, loving the way his teams play is an impossibility'.[7] After the draw against Egypt the RTÉ pundit and former international footballer Eamon Dunphy passionately condemned the team's style as a betrayal of the traditions of Irish soccer. There were many in that soccer community who agreed with him, but in the celebratory atmosphere of the time such views were not popular and Dunphy suffered considerable verbal abuse on his return to Dublin.

Charlton though made no apology for the way his team played, insisting that since his time with the squad was limited, it was essential that they had a clear and simple game-plan. As a player he had always been proud of his ability to stop opponents from playing and carried this through into his coaching. He observed that most international teams played the same way, building slowly from the back with short passes before working the ball through midfield and only then bringing the forwards into play. To counter this, he went for a hard-running style in which his team defended by relentlessly harrying opponents, even in their own half of the pitch, gleefully noting that 'ball-playing defenders were used to having all the time in the world. So we went after them. And they didn't like it.'[8] The team's attacking plan was equally direct. Charlton's main priority was that players should avoid losing possession in their own half and, rather than patiently probe for openings, he instructed them to play the ball behind opposing defenders and chase it down. International opponents struggled to cope with the Republic's unorthodox tactics and the team became notoriously difficult to beat.

The team's direct style was fully evident when it secured a 1–1 draw with a goal by Niall Quinn against Holland on 21 June to ensure a second-round tie against Romania on 25 June in Genoa. Public interest was by then almost universal. The game had an afternoon kick-off and most employers bowed to the inevitable by allowing or encouraging staff to take time off work. A tense game was scoreless after extra-time and then went to a nail-biting penalty shoot-out in which both teams scored their first four kicks. After Packie Bonner saved the Romanians' fifth penalty, David O'Leary coolly converted to put his team into the quarter-final of the World Cup. Those few minutes remain imprinted on the minds of all who saw them, and a 2017 RTÉ poll voted the Genoa penalty shoot-out the single greatest moment in the country's sporting history.

The team's victory was boisterously celebrated throughout the country. In Dublin thousands of cars converged on the city centre, blaring horns and flashing lights, while supporters sang and danced in the streets. The game coincided with the last days of Ireland's presidency of the European Council and a meeting of the then twelve heads of government in Dublin Castle; many journalists covering the summit had at least one eye on the match. Taoiseach Charles Haughey, already revelling in the European presidency, interrupted a press conference to watch the final stages of the shoot-out and demonstrated his new-found fluency in soccer-speak by declaring himself 'over the moon'.[9] Foreign journalists and politicians were taken aback by the unbridled celebrations of their Irish counterparts; a photograph of the veteran journalist John Healy shedding tears of joy summed up the national mood.

In its first ever World Cup, the Republic had managed to reach the quarter-final, equalling the achievement of Northern Ireland in 1958. The reward was a game in Rome against the host nation on 30 June 1990, for which thousands of additional supporters, including Haughey, flew out to Italy. In a tight game at the Stadio Olimpico, the Republic lost 1–0 but made the Italians work hard for their victory, and there was immense pride at their performance and never-say-die attitude. Both Haughey and a rather more sheepish Charlton did laps of honour around the stadium waving the tricolour to celebrating Irish fans. A visibly moved Charlton claimed that the tournament was an even better experience for him than winning the World Cup with England in 1966 and expressed his pride that the team had 'put Irish football on the world map ... Everybody played with great bravery, great dedication and great spirit. I think the Irish people will be proud of them and that pleases me very much.'[10]

While some recoiled from the team's unsophisticated style of play, others admired their heart and fearlessness, one Italian journalist praising them as expressing 'all the character, force and honesty of the brave Irish nation'.[11] An English observer lauded the Republic's courage, work-rate and tactical nous, noting they had 'a collective spirit which should make the British Isles proud this morning on their behalf'.[12] Just as many from the South had supported Northern Ireland in 1982 and 1986, so the Republic enjoyed considerable support and goodwill in the North, and not just from nationalists, with the unionist *Belfast News Letter* unreservedly praising the achievement of the team and the conduct of the supporters.[13]

The team's return to Dublin prompted celebrations that exceeded those of 1988. A massive crowd (including half the government) greeted them at Dublin airport and, as they made their way in an open-topped bus to a civic reception at College Green, the streets were lined with an estimated 500,000 people in the largest gathering ever seen in the city. Most supporters were happy to cheer honourable defeat and celebrate the achievements of a team that had given its all. Looking out on the cheering crowds, Packie Bonner observed, 'It's like we won. In a way we did when you see this.'[14]

* * *

By reaching the quarter-final of the 1990 World Cup, the Republic had announced itself as a serious force in international football. There was, therefore, considerable disappointment when the team failed to qualify for the 1992 European Championships in Sweden, finishing a point behind England and counting themselves unlucky not to beat

England when they met at Wembley on 27 March 1991. They were soon involved in trying to qualify for the 1994 World Cup, to be held in the United States, from a difficult group that included Spain, Denmark (the 1992 European champions) and Northern Ireland. On 13 October 1993 the Republic suffered its first competitive home defeat in eight years against Spain, which left it needing at least a draw in the last qualifying game against Northern Ireland.

In a spectacularly ill-judged instance of fixture planning, the final match in the group had been set for Belfast on 17 November 1993. It could not have come at a worse time. Peace negotiations by John Hume of the SDLP, Gerry Adams of Sinn Féin and the British and Irish governments were moving towards a conclusion, stirring up long-standing unionist fears that the British government would abandon them. While the negotiations proceeded, so too did the violence: the year had already seen dozens of killings when on Saturday 23 October 1993 an IRA bomb exploded at a fish shop on the Shankill Road and killed ten people. Six days later members of the loyalist Ulster Freedom Fighters sprayed with gunfire the Rising Sun Bar in Greysteel, County Derry, leaving seven customers dead.

Although the sporting context bears no comparison to such atrocities, it too added to the edge. Since 1986 Northern Ireland's fortunes had declined while the Republic's had prospered. In August 1993 the FAI team was placed sixth in the FIFA world rankings, its highest ever position. By November 1993 Northern Ireland had no chance of reaching the 1994 World Cup but knew that victory over their neighbours would prevent them from qualifying. Never before in their history had the teams played for such high stakes. They had met earlier in Dublin in March 1993 in a one-sided game which the Republic won 3–0. As their team coasted to victory, the home supporters' chant of 'There's only one team in Ireland' had rankled with their opponents, who eagerly awaited the return match. Northern Ireland Manager Billy Bingham made little secret of his desire for revenge and stoked tensions by adding that 'at least our team is of Irish extraction and not full of mercenaries'.[15] Expecting a hostile reception, the FAI declined to take up its ticket allocation and advised supporters not to travel.[16]

The match attracted 10,000 supporters, policed by about 1,000 RUC officers. Long before kick-off, sectarian songs and chants echoed around Windsor Park, including some mocking the victims of the Greysteel shootings. The heightened atmosphere gripped some of the Northern Ireland players and staff, who belted out 'God Save the Queen' with even greater fervour than normal, and Bingham whipped up a crowd that needed little encouragement. All of the Republic's players were roundly abused, but some were singled out for particular treatment, particularly those connected with Glasgow Celtic such as Packie Bonner and Tony Cascarino, and black players such as Paul McGrath and Terry Phelan.

The intense atmosphere exploded after 73 minutes, when Northern Ireland took the lead with a spectacular volley by Jimmy Quinn. The Windsor Park crowd were still celebrating when five minutes later Alan McLoughlin equalised for the Republic. The game ended in a 1–1 draw that allowed the Republic to equal Northern Ireland's achievement and qualify for successive World Cups. Celebrations were, however, muted: the Republic's players and few supporters were taken aback at the hostile atmosphere and there was a sharp exchange between Charlton and Bingham. *The Irish News* described it as 'a night of shame for soccer', while another report noted that the game 'laid bare for 90 minutes or so the horrible undercurrent of poisonous sectarian emotions that have been tearing at Northern Ireland for generations'.[17] It was even raised in the Dáil, where the Fine Gael TD Austin Deasy proposed that Bingham should be 'indicted for incitement to national hatred'.[18]

Others saw things differently: the Northern Ireland sports minister Michael Ancram praised the passion of the home crowd while some IFA officials and supporters pointed out that only a minority of the crowd had engaged in sectarian abuse. Offensive as this was, they noted that similar chants (mocking the dead of the Munich or Hillsborough disasters) were regularly heard in football grounds across Britain during grudge matches. Such invective, they argued, was not to be taken literally but was simply part of the ritualised confrontational atmosphere of football grounds. One described it as 'a distorted form of gamesmanship based on a desire to put the opponents off their stride, in which respect it certainly seems to have succeeded' and argued that it was 'unreasonable to expect a substantial and vocal gathering of loyalist football supporters to behave as if at a Sunday school picnic'. It was also pointed out that although the few supporters of the Republic present were subjected to verbal abuse, there were no reported violent incidents and very few arrests.[19]

It was, though, a depressing experience for most Irish soccer supporters and is generally remembered as the nadir in relations between North and South. The intensity of the bigotry expressed on that notorious night in November was very much of its own time and place, stoked by a combustible mix of sporting rivalry, ethno-sectarian animosity and political uncertainty. But even amidst the abuse, nuances could be detected. As the journalist Fintan O'Toole emerged from Windsor Park amidst the home supporters, he overheard: 'It's worked out for the best. England's out. We didn't lose. They're through. I'm not glad they're through, but it would have been a shame if we'd stopped them.'[20] It was also significant that the combative Northern Ireland captain Alan McDonald (1963–2012), who had done his utmost to prevent the Republic from qualifying, came to their dressing room after the match to congratulate them and passionately wish them well in the USA.[21]

It was though an experience that the FAI had no wish to repeat and in January 1994 it lobbied UEFA to keep the teams apart for the qualifiers for Euro 1996. Almost inevitably they were drawn together and met in Windsor Park on 16 November 1994. However, a year on since the previous game the atmosphere had changed markedly. Republican and loyalist paramilitaries had declared ceasefires that year and, although there was still uncertainty about the future, there was also hope that it would not be determined by violence. In football terms, there was much less at stake, with the struggle for qualification yet to take shape. Watched by a relatively subdued crowd, the Republic cruised to an easy 4–0 victory in a stadium that grew quieter with each goal.[22]

* * *

Irish supporters looked to the 1994 World Cup in America with great anticipation. The team would clearly not lack support, with thousands planning to travel and many more already resident in the US. The Republic began where they had left off in 1990, playing Italy in Giants Stadium, New Jersey. Whereas in Rome Irish supporters had been in the minority, this time they filled the stadium. The Republic took an early lead with a goal by Ray Houghton and then defended stoutly to win 1–0. It was to be their highlight of the tournament. In the next game they were beaten 2–1 by Mexico in ferocious heat at the Citrus Bowl in Orlando, Florida. A welcome return to the Giants Stadium saw a flat 0–0 draw against Norway, but this was enough to qualify for the second round and a return to Orlando to play Holland on 4 July. In the first half the Irish conceded two soft goals, after which their weak attack rarely troubled the Dutch and the team exited the tournament with a tameness not seen before.

Many who had had raised expectations now vented their disappointment. Criticisms grew about the predictability and sterility of the team's football (in nine World Cup tournament games it had scored only four goals). Again many international pundits dismissed the Irish style as a travesty of 'the beautiful game'. An Egyptian official suggested that the Irish supporters drank so much to dull the pain of watching their team's football, while the great Pelé told Irish journalists 'I love your fans, but not your football.'[23] Even on a practical level, Charlton's way of playing seemed to have run out of steam. It had initially discomfited more technically gifted opponents, but by now they had learned to cope. The Republic's constant harrying of opponents seemed particularly ill-suited to long tournaments in hot climates as players became progressively more exhausted: Charlton's attritional style now seemed to be wearing down his own players.

The lingering sense of dissatisfaction after USA '94 was accentuated by controversy around the team's homecoming. Disappointed in the failure to match their achievement in 1990, the management and players never expected a celebratory event to be arranged in Dublin. However, the days when the Irish authorities had kept their distance from soccer were long gone, replaced by a somewhat feverish desire to show that they were good sports. At the instigation of the Irish government and Dublin City Council, a reception was arranged in the Phoenix Park in Dublin for the day after the Holland game on 5 July. The venue had been chosen to ensure that there would not be a repeat of 1990's chaotic celebrations, which had almost resulted in serious injuries as young supporters ran around the wheels of the team bus. But the players and management were not informed in time and it had, rather embarrassingly, to be cancelled. In Ireland some were unhappy at being denied their day out, and team and management were cajoled into attending a rearranged reception on 7 July. When they arrived at Dublin airport they were greeted by virtually the entire Irish cabinet and then received at Áras an Uachtaráin by President Mary Robinson, before being presented to the assembled public in the Phoenix Park, where the rather subdued players and manager apologised for not doing better. There was little of the spontaneous outpouring of joy witnessed four years earlier and the reception mirrored the anti-climactic nature of the tournament itself. There were also criticisms that the team had been exploited by Albert Reynolds' Fianna Fáil-led government in an effort to recapture the spirit of Italia '90 and deflect attention away from more pressing political matters.[24]

The Phoenix Park event was billed as a homecoming, although none of the players actually lived in Ireland. It was though instructive in showing that the team's following had broadened beyond the soccer community of the 1980s into a much larger and rather more demanding group. Soccer had become a national sport that was important to the way Irish people saw themselves. A team led by an English manager, half of whose players had been born outside Ireland, had inspired unprecedented levels of communal pride and enthusiasm and given the Republic the most intense and widespread celebrations in the history of the state.

The joy unleashed by the team's performances from 1988 to 1994 is partly explained by the temper of the times. In addition to the shadow cast by the Northern Troubles, the Republic was deeply divided politically and socially: bitterly fought referendums on abortion and divorce in 1983 and 1986 had been defeated, confirming the dominance of conservative Catholic teachings. In some of its laws, norms and attitudes it was a society closer to the 1920s than the 2020s: many young people saw their country as a social backwater and found it difficult to identify with the complacency and conservatism of the established political parties. The economy too was stagnant: after spurts of growth in the 1960s and 1970s, it had lapsed into recession, as foreign investment declined and thousands of jobs were lost. A crushing national debt led to rises in taxation and cuts in social services, and unemployment soared, with emigration reaching levels not seen since the 1950s: 130,000 people (mostly young) left the country (1983–8) and even then unemployment stood at almost 20 per cent in 1987. Overall employment levels in 1993 were lower than the 1920s, a situation unique in contemporary Europe. Both the country and the national football team seemed to have been afflicted by a long history of mismanagement, wretched luck and dashed hopes. Among the thousands who had supported the Republic's team in Germany and Italy were sizeable contingents working on the Continent, in Britain, or further afield. For many, following the Irish team was a way of affirming their national identity and countering the sense of displacement brought on by emigration.

This was given eloquent expression in Dermot Bolger's play *In High Germany* (1990), which features a Dublin-born emigrant to Germany who goes along to the team's games in Euro '88. Reflecting on his personal and national loyalties, he recalls how teachers and authority figures in Ireland had tried to force-feed him with Gaelic nationalism: 'O'Brien drilling us behind that 1798 pike. The teachers who came after him hammering *Peig* into us. The masked men blowing limbs off shoppers in my name. You know, all my life it seemed to me that somebody somewhere was always trying to tell me what Ireland I belonged in. But I only belonged there with those fans. I raised my hands and clapped, having finally ... found the only Ireland whose name I can sing. Given to me by eleven men dressed in green.'[25]

Soccer began to feature more prominently in Irish literature, often as a catalyst that allows characters to relate to their country without the insularity and chauvinism of traditional nationalism.[26] Roddy Doyle's novel *The Van* (1991), set against the backdrop of the 1990 World Cup, features working-class characters who are sceptical of political and religious pieties and contemptuous of overblown nationalist rhetoric, but passionately identify with an Irish football team that provides them with an authentic outlet for national feeling.[27]

Soccer also began to receive more detailed treatment in the media. Before 1988, comment on the fortunes of an Irish soccer team was rarely found outside of sports pages, but during the Charlton era it became a matter for widespread editorialising. During the 1990 World Cup, *The Irish Times* noted that Ireland was now noted not just 'for its literature, its history or indeed for its political intractabilities, but for its capacity to organise and field a world-class team in the world's international game. Jack Charlton and his men have brought us closer to the wider world – including our near neighbours. They have brought about a great boosting of national morale which is not limited by class or creed or politics. They have shown that there is a way to be proud of being Irish, without triumphalism or resentment towards those of other races or traditions. They have done well for Ireland.'[28]

The team's success clearly gained greater recognition and respect for a small country on the periphery of Europe. The Republic was only the fourth team from a country with a population of less than 4 million to reach the quarter-final stage of a World Cup (after Uruguay in 1930 and 1950, and Northern Ireland and Wales in 1958).[29] For many foreigners, it had put Ireland on the map. Liam Brady, who in a distinguished career with top Italian clubs such as Juventus and Inter Milan had himself alerted many in Italy to the fact that soccer was played in Ireland, recalled that it was only in 1990 that most Italians fully appreciated that the Republic of Ireland was an independent state rather than a province of the United Kingdom.[30]

At a time when Ireland was internationally best known for the Troubles, Irish teams had appeared in every World Cup tournament from 1982 to 1994 and shown to the world that there was more to the country than riots and shootings, and more to its people than rancour and sectarianism. There were even claims that the Irish economic boom that began in the mid-1990s owed its origins to the improvement in national morale sparked by footballing success. In truth the boom owed more to the establishment of the European Union single market and the Republic's attractiveness to foreign investment than it did to a Ray Houghton header or David O'Leary penalty, but the pride and confidence inspired by the team's achievements cannot be entirely discounted. Its success coincided with a period when Irish society seemed to be moving in a more progressive direction and shaking off traditional restraints: the liberal campaigner Mary Robinson was elected as Ireland's first woman president in 1990, sexual relations between men were decriminalised in 1993, there were paramilitary ceasefires in 1994, and a referendum on divorce was narrowly passed in 1995. By the mid-90s there was certainly a greater sense of openness and optimism than had been the case a decade earlier. Speaking after he had been awarded the Nobel Prize for literature in 1995, Seamus Heaney noted 'a surge of positive energy going around the country ... in the arts in particular, but then sport got involved ... I don't know how far poetry relates to football or film but there is a sense of cultural self-confidence about.'[31]

The experience of international tournaments for most people was mediated through television, often in pubs and clubs in which there was a strong sense of social and communal solidarity and where songs and chants were loudly aired as if in the stadium itself. Even those who viewed the matches at home usually did so in the company of family and friends, and triumphs and defeats became intense shared experiences.[32] Extensive television coverage was accompanied by considerable analysis from pundits such as John Giles and Eamon Dunphy, whose commentary often departed from events on the pitch to discuss the changing place of soccer in Irish society. When added to the considerable press coverage that also examined the societal implications of these tournaments, soccer was placed at the centre of national discourse as never before. Its growing importance in Irish life was recognised when the government legislated in 1999 and 2003 to designate sporting events that could only be shown on free-to-air terrestrial television: these included the All-Ireland Senior football and hurling finals; Ireland's matches in the Rugby World Cup (although not Six Nations games) and all competitive soccer internationals. Such events were selected because they were considered to have a 'generally recognised distinct cultural importance for the people of Ireland'.[33]

Large numbers of Irish supporters travelled to international tournaments, where they became a visible and audible presence. They supported their team passionately and mixed well with locals and other supporters, without the menacing clannishness (or worse) sometimes exhibited by large groups of fans. The English sportswriter Brian Glanville described them as 'the most genial, good-tempered and sporting of supporters'.[34] It had not always been so. In the past Dalymount Park had often been a rather chaotic international venue, with regular pitch invasions. These were mostly down to over-crowding or over-exuberance, but during the 1970s there had been ugly incidents at some international games: at a European Championship qualifier in October 1975 the Turkish goalkeeper was subjected to a hail of missiles from home supporters, which almost led the referee to abandon the match and resulted in a fine for the FAI. It was also common for visiting teams to be booed as they took to the field and for some home supporters to greet opponents' national anthems with whistles and cat-calls.

There was an improvement in behaviour from 1977, when the team played most of its matches at Lansdowne Road, but it was on the international stage that Irish supporters really excelled themselves. At Euro '88, they were determined to enjoy what many thought might be a once-in-a-lifetime experience. Their behaviour contrasted with that of some England followers, who rampaged through the cities of Stuttgart, Düsseldorf, Cologne and Frankfurt, assaulting bystanders, smashing up bars and engaging in street battles with police. Most English football supporters were appalled by their actions and British Foreign Secretary Douglas Hurd felt compelled to apologise to the German government.[35] Irish supporters were keen to distinguish themselves from English hooligans and their conduct was much admired (not least by themselves). The London Observer's chief sportswriter, Peter Corrigan, noted that the Irish 'were serenading Hanover and Gelsenkirchen with laughter and song and nothing more uncouth than the odd belch ... they took as much pleasure in out-classing the English at behaviour as they did from beating them on the football field.'[36]

Two years later an estimated 50,000 Irish fans travelled to Italy for the 1990 World Cup, making the Republic the best-supported team per head of population among the participating nations. There, they built on the reputation earned in Germany, with one Italian journalist noting that 'They would move you almost to tears, these magnificent Irish supporters. They think only of cheering for their side and not of insulting their opponents', and there were many similar accounts from other European observers.[37] Pride in their conduct became central to Irish supporters' self-image. At the 1994 World Cup, the writer Joseph O'Connor was struck by the fact that 'Irish fans, no matter how drunk they are, are talking about how "ordered" and "disciplined" they are.'[38] This conduct was though not confined to the Irish. Fans from other nations, such as the Dutch and Scandinavians, had long been a friendly and colourful presence at international football tournaments. The thousands of Northern Ireland supporters in Spain in 1982 and Mexico in 1986 were also noted for their passionate support and good humour, as were Scotland's 'Tartan Army', who from the mid-1980s had actively distanced themselves from the xenophobic aggression of English hooligans; the Scots' most ominous threat, sung to their Italian counterparts to the tune of 'Guantanamera', was 'We're gonna deep fry your pizza.'[39]

From 1988 onwards the behaviour of Irish supporters received widespread coverage in the Irish media. The urban working class, which had often featured in bad news stories of unemployment, social disadvantage or crime, now found itself idealised as a repository of national virtue, portraying an image of good humour, friendliness and down-to-earth decency to the world. One journalist credited them with the creation of 'a new benign form of pacific nationalism' and claimed that they had 'done more for the international image of the Republic than any group or individual since the foundation of the State'.[40] At a time when the conflict in Northern Ireland was still ongoing, the Republic's football supporters were lauded for being proud of their country but respectful to others, intent on celebrating life rather than destroying it. One commentator noted that supporting their national team had 'crystallised a yearning amongst Irish people for an uncomplicated sense of pride in the symbols of Irishness which the IRA's abuse of those symbols has denied them. To be able to wave the tricolour ... without conjuring up the demons of sectarian slaughter is an enormous relief. Put bluntly, the team has allowed people in the Republic to celebrate their identity without being encumbered by the dark complications of the North.'[41] The team provided a unifying focus that transcended generations and political, social and geographical differences – all saw themselves as part of 'Jack's Army'. As FAI president Fran Fields welcomed the team home after Euro '88, he noted that 'the players and the technical staff were magnificent in West Germany but the real heroes, the people who brought Ireland to the attention of the sporting world, were the supporters who accompanied the team on its travels'.[42]

***

Many Irish supporters had not been born in Ireland but nonetheless felt genuinely Irish. The FAI team had always drawn support from Irish communities in England and Scotland, and this grew as it began to compete in international tournaments. Green-clad supporters with English or Scottish accents could cause some bemusement to 'Paddier than thou' Irish-born fans, and occasional questioning of their national credentials, but such was their obvious loyalty and commitment to the team that many in Ireland were forced to re-evaluate their conceptions of what it meant to be Irish. This contributed to a greater appreciation of the Irish diaspora as a self-aware ethnic community that took pride in its origins and identified strongly with a football team that itself expressed many of the complexities and contradictions of national belonging.[43]

On becoming manager in 1986, Charlton set about assembling the strongest possible squad and actively sought out new players. Of the fifty-six players he selected as Irish manager, thirty-three were born outside Ireland.[44] This was broadly accepted in Ireland, but sometimes ridiculed abroad: the joke doing the rounds in the English game during the 1980s was that FAI meant 'Find Another Irishman'. Before the Republic faced England at Euro '88, the BBC's *Radio Times* noted that the Republic's squad 'with scarcely an Irish-born player among them ... provide a wealth of self-inflicted comic relief ... Indeed the hardest thing is to find an Irish accent'.[45] Much of this was dressing-room banter, but there was also open hostility. After the Republic beat England in 1988, the criticism became even sharper, with the *Daily Express* dismissing the Irish team as 'a collection of misfits and mercenaries'.[46] When the Republic secured the services of talented players such as Mark Lawrenson, Ray Houghton and Andy Townsend, they were accused of poaching them away from their rightful teams. Some, such as Townsend, John Aldridge and Alan McLoughlin (1967–2021) even received death threats from English far-right groups.[47]

Those who chose to play for Ireland did so for various reasons. In some cases their motivation was professional, even financial, but it could also be personal or even patriotic. Many Irish people who had emigrated to Britain still saw themselves as Irish and kept up links with 'back home' through regular holidays and family gatherings. Catholicism, Gaelic games and Irish music and culture remained central to their lives, and their children often felt a strong sense of kinship with Ireland. One such case was Tony Grealish (1956–2013), born in London to a father from Galway and a mother whose parents were from Limerick; he played hurling in his youth and Gaelic football for London in the All-Ireland minor football championship. Growing up in England during the period of the Troubles, he was regularly confronted with the Irish jokes and negative stereotypes prevalent in the 1970s.[48] Known for his wholehearted commitment and fierce tackling, he represented the Republic with great pride, amassing forty-five caps (1976–85) and captaining the team on seventeen occasions. He lined out several times alongside goalkeeper Seamus McDonagh, born in Rotherham to a father from County Mayo. In his youth McDonagh was fascinated by Irish history and literature, particularly the poetry of W.B. Yeats and the historical novels of Walter Macken. When in 1981 his strong performances for Everton prompted Eoin Hand to approach him to declare for the FAI team, McDonagh began reciting the opening lines of the 1916 Proclamation of the Republic to a dumbfounded

Hand and told him that he 'would swim across the Irish Sea to play for Ireland'. Known as 'Jim' at his club, he had been baptised James Martin Seamus McDonagh, and insisted on being called Seamus when on duty with the Republic (1981–5).[49]

For players like Grealish and McDonagh, representing the Republic allowed them to express an identity they had felt since childhood. The same was true of others capped in the 1980s and 1990s, including Gerry Peyton, Mick McCarthy, Gary Breen, Alan McLoughlin, Terry Phelan and Kevin Kilbane, born in England to an Irish parent or parents who assiduously maintained their links with Ireland. They were often among the team's most committed performers, none more so than McCarthy, who went on to play fifty-seven times for the Republic, twenty-two as captain, and twice managed the team (1996–2002; 2018–20). Some had the option of playing international football for England, but consciously chose to play for Ireland instead. Kilbane, for example, born in Preston to a father from Mayo and a mother from Longford, proudly described himself as a 'son of the Gael'. He had only ever wanted to play for the Republic, and when called up for the England under-18 team he declined, much to the incomprehension of his Preston North End manager Sam Allardyce.[50]

Even players not brought up in a self-consciously Irish environment could feel a strong desire to play for Ireland. The Liverpool-born John Aldridge qualified through an Irish grandmother but, like many Liverpudlians, regarded himself as more Scouse than English, believing that the city had been ignored and neglected by central government, particularly during the prime ministership of Margaret Thatcher (1979–90). He had little difficulty in transferring his allegiance to his grandmother's homeland, recalling that, when Charlton approached him to play for Ireland, 'I didn't have to think for a single second about accepting ... most people in Liverpool consider themselves to be more Irish than English anyway, so the prospect of playing for Ireland [and] possibly even beating England – as we did at the 1988 European Championships – was a massive motivation for me. In fact, the few times we played against England were the games I wanted to win more than any other.'[51]

Not all players were quite so passionate, at least initially. Andy Townsend, who qualified through his County Kerry grandmother, admitted to being an England supporter and opting to play for the Republic primarily for professional reasons: 'the wearing of a green shirt didn't suddenly make me Irish; my affinity towards the team, the nation and its people would be a slowly evolving thing'.[52] Tony Cascarino's parental links with Ireland were even more tenuous, although he recalled growing up in London 'with a strong sense of Irishness' among a large group of Irish relatives. He qualified through his mother Theresa O'Malley, who he believed was born in Westport, County Mayo, but it turned out that she was born in Watford and adopted by Irish parents, and Cascarino played for the Republic for eleven years on a British passport.[53]

Players from all across the UK declared for the Republic: there were several born in Scotland of Irish parents, such as the Glaswegians Ray Houghton and Tommy Coyne; and Kevin Sheedy, born in Wales to a County Clare father; there were also those whose parents had come from Northern Ireland, such as Alan Kernaghan. This ensured that the team fielded by the Republic from the 1980s onwards was considerably more representative of the Irish diaspora than it was of the state's twenty-six counties. Players born outside of Ireland were particularly struck by the mass outpouring of popular joy and political recognition that accompanied the success of 1988–94. When the Yorkshire-born Mick McCarthy first played for Ireland in 1984, it seemed to him that soccer 'was a fourth, fifth or tenth rated sport', but 'the way the team played in Italy changed everything … even the way we looked upon ourselves as a nation … I am always flattered by the attention we receive from politicians and leaders of state. We don't have prime ministers knocking on our doors where I come from.'[54]

In many ways the selection of foreign-born players was a natural development, given Ireland's exceptional levels of emigration and the persistence of a sense of distinct identity in the Irish abroad. Capping players from the diaspora acknowledged that the nation had an ethnic as well as a territorial dimension: national identity was influenced by one's wider cultural community as well as one's place of birth and there was more to being Irish than having an Irish accent. In Bolger's *In High Germany* the main character thinks of his 'uncles and aunts scattered across England and the USA. Of every generation shipped off like beef by the hoof. And at that moment it seemed to me that they had found a voice at last. That all those English-born players were playing for all the Irish mothers and fathers written out of history.'[55] Nuala O'Faolain saw them as 'a wholly unexpected return from the emigration of the 1950s, all we've ever got back from that. That they are playing for us is somehow a reconciliation with all that loss.'[56] When she had received the team at Áras an Uachtaráin, President Mary Robinson observed that the multi-national and multi-racial composition of the team 'was very representative of the modern Ireland'.[57] In the USA in 1994 the sight of three black players (Paul McGrath, Terry Phelan and Phil Babb) in the Irish starting eleven surprised some locals, particularly African-Americans, who previously had not imagined Ireland as a site of racial diversity. Their presence was also important to Irish people of colour, facilitating their identification with a predominantly white nation; the amiable McGrath in particular, the outstanding player during Charlton's tenure, became an inspirational figure for many black Irish people.

Religion too played its part. Most of the players came from a Catholic background and, during these years, Monsignor Liam Boyle from Limerick became an unofficial team chaplain. His pre-match Masses were well-attended and ended with a rousing rendition of 'Hail Glorious St Patrick'.[58] The most striking expression of the team's Catholic faith came during the 1990 World Cup when they were granted an audience in the Vatican with Pope John Paul II, who privately spoke to the manager and some of the players and technical staff. They were the only team in the competition who did so, and several recalled it as one of the most memorable days of their lives. Even Charlton, who was not a Catholic, described 'a sense of occasion I had never previously felt'; however, he was not entirely at ease and was honest enough to admit that 'ninety per cent of what was happening that day was strange to me. I mean, Catholics to me have always been a bit strange.'[59]

Players also bonded over Irish music. After John Giles became manager in 1973, he encouraged his friend Luke Kelly of the Dubliners, a keen football fan and a skilled player with Home Farm in his youth, to socialise with the team after games. Luke and his fellow Dubliner Ronnie Drew led many a singsong in which the players eagerly participated, and these provided one of the most enjoyable aspects of being involved with the team. Music was also part of the team's pre-match ritual during the Charlton years, notably the playing of the martial ballad 'Seán South of Garryowen' on the team coach as it approached the stadium. The song commemorated an IRA officer killed in 1957 leading an attack on an RUC station in County Fermanagh, who was seen as embodying 'physical force republicanism at its most Gaelic, most Catholic, most single-minded and self-sacrificing, its most fanatically pure and uncompromising'.[60] When this was reported by the English press, Charlton received condemnatory letters from the parents of British soldiers and was described in some tabloids as a 'traitor'. Charlton was bemused by the controversy and insisted that 'I never listened closely to the words, but vaguely understood that it was a Republican song which dealt with the Black and Tan period in Ireland in the 1920s. To me, that was unimportant. It had a stirring singalong air, just the kind to fire up the players.'[61] When on one occasion the Furey Brothers' doleful anti-war ballad 'The Green Fields of France' was mistakenly played instead of 'Seán South', Charlton exploded and ordered that it be stopped immediately, fearing its funereal music and melancholy lyrics would undermine his players' fighting spirit.

The Republic's success in harnessing its diaspora prompted other countries to take advantage of FIFA's parentage rules. The qualification of Jamaica and Trinidad and Tobago for the World Cups of 1998 and 2006 respectively was assisted by their recruitment of the children of Caribbean emigrants, many born in Britain and playing in the lower leagues of English professional football, and the option has also been used by European states with large overseas communities, such as Poland, Croatia and Turkey.[62] Northern Ireland too has taken advantage of the regulations, even if initially it did so rather more tentatively than the Republic. The province's smaller population and lower levels of emigration offered a sparser pool of talent, but Billy Bingham was still able to use the rule to strengthen his squad. Two of his most committed players, Chris Nicholl and Iain Dowie, were born in England to Northern Irish parents; the former won fifty-one caps (1974–83) and the latter fifty-nine (1990–2000). Bingham, though, believed that some of those who qualified under the parentage rule were not always fully committed to the team. He recalled that in 1986 he had selected Lawrie Sanchez but quickly reversed his decision when he discovered that 'he had not got that nationalist feeling that you need. When you feel that you're playing for the flag, you're playing for the shirt, you're playing for these people, you want to lay down your life for them. I did that as a player. I felt that. And I just didn't see how he could feel that.'[63]

***

The Republic's achievements in Germany and Italy attracted huge numbers of new supporters and helped popularise soccer throughout the country. Leading figures in the GAA sent messages of goodwill and by 1990 the game's foreign origins were largely irrelevant to most people.[64] Football songs of varying quality crammed the airwaves, houses were draped in the team's colours, shops sold vast amounts of green and white merchandise and the inflatable banana became a national symbol. The team brought joy, excitement and colour into everyday lives and helped create a collective national solidarity that transcended social and geographical differences. In his vivid account of the Charlton years, Declan Lynch noted how the experience created 'a sense that Irish people were generally embarked on a common purpose. In every other significant area of national life, you couldn't go far without encountering this cultural split between the old Ireland and the emerging one ... If he did nothing else, Jack Charlton could claim that he made the Irish feel like they all lived in the same country for a while.'[65]

It helped that Charlton's teams included players from all over Ireland: Cork, Donegal, Drogheda and Dundalk were represented as well as Dublin, and there were players with strong GAA backgrounds, such as Kevin Moran, Niall Quinn, Steve Staunton and Denis Irwin. The team's style of play also appealed to many recent converts: one admitted that he was not a soccer fan before Charlton became Irish team manager, but that his interest grew because of the way in which 'he tapped into the way all of our sport is played; Gaelic football, hurling, rugby are physical, man-to-man sports and you just expect your team to give it a go, no matter how good they are. Jack liked that. A great number of Irish people were not great followers of soccer, myself included when he took over, but they know how they like their sport to be played and I think Jack's "put 'em under pressure" style suited that.'[66]

Charlton became enormously popular, endorsing products, opening new businesses and regularly giving interviews to Irish print and broadcast media. His interest in field sports (especially fishing), down-to-earth manner and direct speech in his distinctive Northumbrian accent made him a genuine folk hero. Although he often insisted that he was simply a professional who was paid to do a job, over time he developed a deep affection for Ireland and its people and loved to spend time in his holiday home near the River Moy in Ballina, County Mayo. The irony that this most popular of figures was an archetypal north of England workingman was not lost on observers. As the journalist Mary Holland put it: 'who's going to shout "Brits Out" now or, more important, continue to believe with quite such certainty that the connection with England is the source of all our difficulties?'[67] The historian Ronan Fanning argued that Charlton had made a crucial contribution to improving Anglo-Irish relations and had 'done much to destroy those dark and twisted roots of anti-English sentiment which have, until now, always poisoned the tree of Irish nationalism'.[68]

Charlton's supporters hailed him as a pragmatist and a winner, whose confidence rubbed off on those around them, invigorating players and supporters. Despite having talented individuals, Irish teams had in the past sometimes looked nervous and rudderless, but under Charlton they had a clear plan and played without fear. Mick Byrne, the long-serving team physiotherapist and a popular and influential figure among the backroom staff, went so far as to compare Charlton's influence with that of the trade unionist Jim Larkin (1874–1947). Byrne, whose father was a Dublin dock-worker, maintained that Charlton, like Larkin, was a tough-minded and charismatic Englishman who had provided Irish soccer with the leadership that Larkin had provided for the labour movement.[69] The comparison is not overly fanciful: in their commanding, abrasive personalities, unwillingness to listen to others, and ruthlessness in dealing with dissidents, while at the same time inspiring great affection and loyalty, 'Big Jim' and 'Big Jack' were not dissimilar. Both vigorously shook up the complacent and dispirited worlds into which they arrived and became deeply influential figures in Irish life. Charlton's achievements were widely acknowledged: in June 1988 Taoiseach Charles Haughey declared him 'an honorary Irishman' and in 1996 he was officially conferred with honorary Irish citizenship, the highest award that can be granted by the state; on 26 May 1994 Dublin Corporation made him a Freeman of the City of Dublin (the three previous recipients were Nelson Mandela, President Patrick Hillery and Mother Teresa). Marvelling at Charlton's popularity, Haughey's successor Albert Reynolds wryly noted, 'I hope he stays out of politics or we'll all be dead.'[70]

However, not everyone thought of Charlton as a messiah, or rejoiced in the team's achievements. Some saw the exuberant public celebrations as a form of mass hysteria, revealing the desperation of a small, insecure country that craved international approval and validation. Such criticisms became more pronounced towards the end of the Charlton era. The playwright Hugh Leonard insisted that he hated 'not only the game itself, but the screeching, the self-praise, the hysteria, the chauvinism, the beeriness and the yobbery'. Where some saw national unity, others saw a social press gang. The poet and arts activist Anthony Cronin, who was simply indifferent to the game, recalled being aggressively confronted at his local pub for not celebrating like everyone else, and was deeply irritated by media reports telling him how proud 'We' should be of what 'We' had achieved.[71]

Some level of distaste from those generally dismissive of sport was inevitable, but there were also sharp criticisms from within Irish soccer. Not everyone found a comfortable place on the bandwagon. Some were put off by Charlton's functional style of football and criticised him as an unimaginative and limited coach whose rigid tactics prevented a talented and committed group of players from achieving even greater

success; his failure to accommodate the highly skilled Liam Brady was
seen as particularly lamentable. A divide opened up between those who
wanted the team to win with style and those who just wanted it to win
(or draw) by any means and prolong the party as long as possible. Some
of Charlton's most trenchant critics came from the League of Ireland.
Robbie Best of Bohemians despaired that 'we are the only nation that
has such a collective inferiority complex that we are prepared to have
anyone as an "honorary Irishman" as long as they can guarantee a bit
of glory. Jack Charlton has given us that bit of glory. In the process of
providing it, however, he has compromised us all.'[72]

Traditional soccer followers rather than Gaelic enthusiasts were
now more likely to question the authenticity of the game played by
the national team: Eamon Dunphy maintained that 'Jack's Route One
football ... was a foreign game to those of us who belonged to the now
ever-diminishing original soccer community ... The mob stole our
game. Now we watched helpless, and largely voiceless, as they paraded
round the world, led by Big Jack.'[73] His fellow pundit and former Leeds
United teammate of Charlton, John Giles, argued that 'in the pursuit
of success something eroded ... There were times I would have liked to
have seen a brand of football that could have been more easily identified
as Irish ... with the kind of flair which the likes of Carey and Brady
brought to the international field.'[74] Giles and others were particularly
concerned that Charlton's style offered a bad example to young players.
Within weeks of his appointment, Charlton's blunt insistence that the
international youth team should play a similar direct game to the senior
team succeeded in alienating the team manager Liam Tuohy, one of
the most popular and respected figures in Irish soccer, and led to his
resignation and those of his assistants Brian Kerr and Noel O'Reilly.[75]

From football's earliest days there have always been tensions between
teamwork and individuality, discipline and flair, physicality and skill,
and arguments between pragmatists and idealists about how the game
should be played. Some styles are regarded as expressive of national
character and have lent themselves to the recurrent stereotyping of
mercurial Latins, cerebral Central Europeans, methodical Germans
and stolid Brits so beloved of many media commentators.[76] The

Brazilian anthropologist Luiz Eduardo Soares maintained that 'when our national team plays, we feel that the identity of our country is being played out on the field. Our values are being shown to the world'.[77] While it is difficult to pinpoint a single Irish style, the Irish climate meant that matches were often played on heavy pitches unsuited to a passing game. Irish teams were renowned for their robust tackling and strong aerial challenges, with courage and commitment valued at least as much as skill and flair, and there were regular complaints that skilful players were kicked out of the game.[78]

It could be argued that some of Charlton's critics were comparing his methods to an idealised version of the Irish game rather than the workmanlike reality. In international matches during the 1950s and 1960s, burly defenders such as Sean Fallon or Noel Cantwell were sometimes selected at centre-forward to rough up opposing goalkeepers. When the Republic won a surprise 3–2 victory over Austria at Dalymount Park in 1963, it was proudly asserted that the team had prevailed not because of its fine football, but rather through 'the breath-taking, pulse-quickening, full-blooded excitement in which the Irish have always gloried'.[79] Attempts by the Irish national team to play a patient passing game (notably under Giles in the 1970s) were often greeted with impatience and slow handclaps from a large section of the crowd, who preferred a more direct approach. Many Irish football fans admitted that Charlton's way was not pretty, but it was effective, and they enjoyed the manner in which the team's physical style unsettled more technically gifted opponents. This was particularly so when it yielded results, but when these began to dry up, demands for a change of direction grew louder.

After the Republic's anti-climactic exit from the 1994 World Cup, there were calls for more adventure and ambition. Some even began to speak of the beginning of the end of the Charlton era, one journalist noting that 'the innocence is seeping out of our involvement in these great football celebrations ... the mind hankers for a freshness that Charlton might not have the flexibility to provide'.[80] Still, the team and supporters went into the qualifying rounds for Euro '96 with strong expectations. The tournament was to be hosted in England and the prospect of playing in the country that was home to the Irish players and easily accessible to Irish supporters were added incentives to qualification. Charlton's team won their first three games, including a 4–0 win over Northern Ireland in Belfast, but stumbled through the latter stages of the campaign, drawing with Northern Ireland and Liechtenstein and suffering home and away defeats to Austria, before being outclassed and eliminated in a play-off match against Holland at Anfield on 13 December 1995.

Afterwards, the FAI board made it clear to Charlton that he no longer had their support and he was left with little choice but to resign. He had raised expectations to a new level which, on this occasion, he failed to satisfy. He was still a popular figure, widely admired for what he had achieved, but this was not enough for him to keep his job. Charlton himself was well aware of the ruthless and fickle nature of professional sport and, keen to maintain his good relationship with the Irish public, thought it better to go before he was pushed. In retrospect it seems a wise decision. The Republic's involvement in the tournaments of 1988–94 stands as a golden age in its history and in the years that followed many people recalled these days as among the happiest in their lives and gleefully seized on opportunities to relive them. When Charlton died in July 2020, a quarter century after managing the Republic, he was widely mourned in Ireland, where there was an outpouring of nostalgia, gratitude and affection on a scale rarely seen for a sporting figure. Tributes were paid to a man who had not just changed the fortunes of the Irish football team, but helped to transform the way people saw themselves, replacing fear of failure and humiliation with confidence and pride.

12

Hibernians and Celts:
The Irish and Scottish Clubs

The history of Irish association football is closely bound up with Scotland. Scots helped to introduce the game to Ireland, Scottish workers dominated some of Belfast's earliest teams and from the mid-1890s many Scottish professionals earned a living in the Irish League. This traffic was not, however, entirely one-way. The Irish contributed significantly to the game in Scotland, founding some of its best-known clubs and doing much to shape its development. While thousands of Scottish workers moved to Ireland in the nineteenth century, the flow in the other direction was far greater. The fast-growing Scottish economy offered abundant employment opportunities in agriculture, manufacturing, mining and construction, which attracted tens of thousands of migrants. Between 1875 and 1921 40 per cent of all Irish emigrants to Britain went to Scotland. Since Scotland's population was far smaller than England's, they had a greater overall effect on their host country. By the early 1890s, 194,087 or 4.8 per cent of the Scottish population was Irish-born, compared with 1.6 per cent for England and Wales.[1]

The Irish settled primarily in Glasgow and the surrounding industrial areas, and there were also significant enclaves in Dundee, Edinburgh and the mining districts of the Lothians. Mostly they took the lowest-paying jobs and attracted the suspicion, contempt and hostility often directed at impoverished immigrants. This was compounded by the fact that most were Catholic, which was considered an alien and dangerous creed by many Scots who prided themselves on their Presbyterian heritage. In response, most Irish Catholics clustered together with those of their own faith and ethnicity, and relied heavily on their Church for temporal as well as spiritual support. Catholic clergy, many born and educated in Ireland, were often important community leaders who took an active role in their parishioners' lives.

Irish immigrants sought diversion as well as employment, and many found it by playing football. However, when they sought to join established clubs, they could find that their nationality, religion and social standing told against them. In response, they founded their own clubs, often on the initiative of local clergy. Most were short-lived but some endured. Edinburgh led the way, with the founding of Hibernian Football Club by the Catholic priest Canon Edward Hannan (born in 1836 in Ballingarry, County Limerick) and the layman Michael Whelahan (born in 1854 in Kilglass, County Roscommon), both of St Patrick's parish in Cowgate, a densely populated area in the city's Old Town known as 'Little Ireland'. On 6 August 1875, during celebrations to mark the centenary of the birth of the Irish statesman Daniel O'Connell, they launched the club to provide a sporting outlet and fund-raiser for the parish's Catholic Young Men's Society (CYMS). Hannan became the club president and Whelahan the captain. The latter suggested Hibernian as the name to mark the recent absorption of the local branch of the Ancient Order of Hibernians into the St Patrick's CYMS, and membership of the club was restricted to members of the CYMS, effectively barring non-Catholics. It was probably the first association football club founded by Irishmen anywhere, and its origins were clearly acknowledged by the adoption of green shirts emblazoned with 'Erin Go Bragh' and a crest that featured an Irish harp.[2]

At first, neither the Edinburgh nor the Scottish Football Associations would admit Hibernian FC to membership, the latter stiffly announcing that 'We are catering for Scotsmen, not Irishmen.'[3] Local teams refused their invitations to play until Heart of Midlothian, founded in the Canongate district of Edinburgh in 1874, lined out against them on Christmas Day 1875. The two soon developed a keen rivalry: Heart of Midlothian, playing in red, white and blue colours, was seen as representing traditional Scottish Presbyterianism, and ethno-religious differences gave their games an additional edge, with their supporters coming to blows during a cup-tie in 1877. This became a regular feature of Hibernian's early matches, prompting the club to form a fearsome 'Hibernian Guard' of Irish navvies and coal-heavers, ready to defend their team against opposing supporters or protest against contentious refereeing decisions.[4]

In 1876 the Edinburgh and Scottish FAs relented and allowed Hibernian to enter their competitions. It soon established itself as one of the city's top clubs, winning the Edinburgh Cup in 1879 and the Edinburgh FA Shield in 1882 and 1885. In 1880 it opened its own playing ground on Easter Road in the east of the city, known to some supporters as 'The Holy Ground'. To draw in as many Irish players as possible, it formed a number of local nursery teams with distinctively Irish names, such as Young Ireland, Emerald (Leith) Harp, Edinburgh Emmet and Loanhead Sarsfield. Its influence also spread to the west of Scotland, with the founding of other 'Hibernians' in Glasgow, Paisley, Cambuslang and Springburn. In Dundee too it inspired the establishment of new Irish clubs, notably Dundee Harp, which gained strong local support and by 1885 was playing charity matches against its parent club before crowds of 8,000 spectators. From its earliest days Hibernian FC saw itself as more than just a sporting venture: in the aftermath of its victory in the Edinburgh Shield in 1885, Michael Whelahan insisted that he and his teammates played 'not for personal glory, but to increase the charity work of the CYMS and to give a real sense of pride to all of Ireland's exiled children in Scotland'.[5]

By the mid-1880s Hibernian was regarded as one of the country's leading teams and in April 1886 two of its Scottish-born players represented Scotland against Wales at Hampden Park, a matter of considerable pride to both Hannan and Whelahan. They were, however, chosen only after a lengthy debate in the Scottish FA on whether the club's players would be genuinely committed to the team, and its players were not selected for matches against Ireland for some years to come.[6] In February 1887 Hibernian managed to reach the final of the Scottish FA Cup, the most valued prize in the Scottish game. Irish supporters

from all over Scotland flocked to the final against Dumbarton FC at
Hampden Park on 12 February 1887, as did large numbers from Ireland,
and Hibernian supporters formed the majority of the 20,000 spectators
present. Many carried the traditional national flag of the golden
harp on a green background and loudly sang 'God Save Ireland' as
Hibernian won 2–1 to claim the trophy. Irish communities throughout
Scotland celebrated the victory and many took up association football,
founding numerous other Hibernians, Harps, Shamrocks, Emeralds
and Emmets.[7] Months later Hibernian further enhanced its reputation
with a prestigious win against Preston North End (who would become
the first champions of the English Football League in 1889) in a match
dubbed the 'Championship of the World', beating the professional
English team 2–1 in Edinburgh on 13 August 1887.[8]

Hibernian's success was seen by many Irish Catholics as a vindication
of their community and a means of expressing their political aspirations.
Before the cup final in 1887 the Irish nationalist politician and agrarian
reformer Michael Davitt, then campaigning in the Scottish Highlands,
had visited Easter Road to present the club with a piece of shamrock-
bedecked turf, which was laid on the centre-spot of the pitch.[9] In
April 1888 Hibernian travelled to Belfast to play two matches against
Distillery and a Belfast XI in aid of the victims of sectarian violence.[10]
Several of Hibernian's committee members and key administrators,
such as John McFadden and Michael Flanagan (also members of the St
Patrick's CYMS), were outspoken advocates for Irish Home Rule, and
the club provided the base for the Edinburgh and Leith branches of the
Irish National League (the Parnellite political organisation that replaced
the suppressed Land League in 1882).[11] The annual report of St Patrick's
CYMS in 1887 noted that the club was 'defending unaided and alone the
cause of Irish nationality on the football field'.[12] However, Hibernian's
close identification with Irish nationalist causes was regarded warily
by some Scottish football administrators, who protested that the club
had become too political and risked entangling Scots in 'the destinies
of unhappy Ireland'.[13]

Hibernian's FA Cup victory had been joyously celebrated in Glasgow,
home to the country's largest Irish Catholic community. After the match

the players attended a reception at St Mary's Hall in the East End of the city, where they were greeted by a large crowd and congratulated on their victory by John Ferguson, a Belfast-born radical and Glasgow publisher who was the effective leader of Scottish-based Irish nationalism. During the celebrations the club secretary, John McFadden, dedicated the victory to the Irish Catholics of Scotland and challenged his Glasgow countrymen to match Hibernian's achievement. Some months later, on 6 November 1887, this led to the founding of the Celtic Football and Athletic Club, which soon began to poach some of Hibernian's best players with large signing-on fees (although the game in Scotland was still amateur). This caused considerable ill-feeling and for some time matches between the two could be distinctly unfriendly affairs.[14]

On the launch of the Scottish Football League in 1890, Hibernian (unlike Celtic) was not one of the ten founder clubs. It briefly ceased to operate because of financial difficulties in 1891–2, before reforming in October 1892 and acquiring a lease on a new playing ground just north of its old stadium, which also became known as Easter Road. A key figure in restoring its fortunes was the Dublin-born priest Fr John J. O'Carroll (1843–1920) of St Mary Star of the Sea Church in Leith, who was chaplain of the local Stella Maris CYMS, which he used as a springboard to revive the club.[15] In 1893 Hibernian was admitted to the Second Division of the Scottish League, topping it in 1894 and 1895 and securing election to the First Division in the latter year. It regained its position as one of Scotland's leading teams, losing 3–1 to Heart of Midlothian in the 1896 Scottish FA Cup final, and in 1902 beat Celtic in the final to win the trophy. The following year it won its first league title, with an entirely Scottish-born team. However, major trophies would subsequently be elusive as Scottish football was dominated by Glasgow's better-resourced clubs.

In the mid-1890s Hibernian dropped its insistence that players had to belong to the CYMS and allowed those of all religions to join. Its commitment to Irish nationalist causes was gradually diluted and it was overtaken by Celtic as the main sporting representative of the Irish in Scotland. Its profile in Ireland was also eclipsed by Celtic: unlike the Glasgow club, Hibernian did not make a particular effort to forge close links with Irish clubs or cultivate support in Ireland. This continued into the early decades of the twentieth century and its Catholic–Irish identification became weaker still after Harry Swan, a noted Freemason and the first Protestant to hold shares in the club, became chairman in 1934. One of Swan's first moves was to rescind the rule that allowed Catholic priests automatic free admission to Hibernian matches; the symbol of the Irish harp was removed during renovations at Easter Road, and there were attempts to change the club's name and colours. Swan insisted that this was business rather than bigotry, and that the club's appeal in a largely Protestant city could only be broadened by emphasising its Scottishness. However, he faced strong opposition from veteran Irish-born directors who had no wish to downplay its Irish Catholic origins, and its players would frequently be referred to as 'the Irishmen' in press reports for many years to come.[16]

While Hibernian retained a strong Catholic following in Edin-burgh, over time it was geography rather than religion or ethnicity that became the prime determinant of its support. After the post-war demo-lition of the 'Little Ireland' ghetto and resettlement of its population in new suburbs, the club drew most of its followers from the north and east of the city, especially from the port of Leith, often regarded as its heartland. Hibernian's rivalry with Hearts remains keen and many of their respective supporters do their best to accentuate the differences between them. Songs and symbols that reflect their respective origins are aired at derby matches, some Hibernian supporters waving the Irish tricolour, while their opponents fly the Union Jack and flag of Northern Ireland. Most maintain that the flags are chosen to wind up the opposi-tion rather than indicate any real political commitment to Orange or Green. Many are also anxious to distance themselves from these 'sec-tarian' displays, seen to be more characteristic of the Celtic–Rangers rivalry, and Edinburgh football supporters often bond together in their opposition to Glasgow.[17]

Attitudes to the Hibernian's Irish origins among present-day followers span a broad spectrum from indifference to pride. However, almost all insist that Hibernian is primarily a Scottish club, and its supporters are among the most committed followers of the Scottish national team.[18] The club, though, still retains significant sentimental and family ties with Ireland. When Hibernian celebrated its centenary in 1975, its captain was the long-serving Pat Stanton, the great-great-great-grand-nephew of Michael Whelahan, its first captain.[19] In recent decades there has been an increased willingness among supporters to acknowledge that Hibernian is 'a Scottish club with a strong Irish history'. By the mid-1990s the ending of the Northern Ireland Troubles made the connection with Ireland less fraught and more supporters were keen to lay claim to a distinct and rooted identity in an increasingly commercialised Scottish Premier League.[20] A redesign of the club's emblem in 2000 brought back the Irish harp, alongside a representation of Edinburgh Castle and a ship that acknowledged the strong connection to Leith. On 17 May 2009 Hibernian provided the opposition for Glasgow Celtic in a match to mark National Famine Memorial Day, despite some Scottish newspapers claiming that such commemorations only served to feed historical grievances and sharpen contemporary tensions.[21] It was also significant that in 2016, the centenary of the Easter Rising, a plaque was erected outside Easter Road to honour the Irish republican socialist James Connolly (1868–1916). Born and reared in St Patrick's parish in Cowgate, Connolly was a lifelong supporter of the club, who would occasionally digress on the club's fortunes in his political speeches and recall carrying the players' kit to Easter Road in return for sixpence and free admission to the ground; even after he emigrated to the United States in 1903 he eagerly followed its fortunes. While many of the working-class republicans who participated in the Easter Rising played or supported soccer, Connolly was probably the only signatory of the 1916 Proclamation who shared their enthusiasm.[22]

The success of Hibernian in the 1880s was an inspiration to the large Catholic community of Dundee, which, per head of population, had more Irish-born residents than any other Scottish city at the time. Many Irish Catholics came to work in the city's expanding jute factories and formed tightly knit communities in which Catholic charities and lay organisations provided an important welfare safety-net. As in Edinburgh, it was members of the local CYMS who founded the city's first Irish club, Dundee Harp, in 1879. It played occasional fund-raising matches against Hibernian, Celtic and other Irish teams, but largely confined itself to local leagues and never achieved a national profile. Sectarian tensions were rather more muted in Dundee than in the west of Scotland: Irish immigration to the city was overwhelmingly Catholic and clashes around religious processions and Orange marches were rare. Partly because the city's Irish community had no great need for a team to assert its position, Dundee Harp was dissolved in 1897. Various Irish clubs sprang up over the next decade, but none lasted, until members of the Irish community founded Dundee Hibernian in 1909 and secured its election to the Scottish League a year later. The club adopted the traditional green and white kit of Irish clubs but soon found that this limited its appeal, and in 1923 it was refounded as Dundee United, playing in neutral black and white colours to attract greater support. This had the desired effect: the club gained promotion from the Second Division of the Scottish League in 1925 and gained followers of all backgrounds until its Irish associations became largely historical. Today, although many supporters are happy to acknowledge the club's Irish origins, they see their club as proudly Scottish and are among the most committed to the Scottish national team.[23]

***

For most nineteenth-century Irish immigrants to Scotland, the main destination was Glasgow, a powerhouse of the Industrial Revolution that acted as a magnet for migrant labour. The Irish formed distinctive communities in the east of the city, as well as in surrounding industrial towns, such as Paisley, Airdrie, Motherwell and Coatbridge.[24] By the late 1880s the Irish Catholic community in Glasgow and its environs was estimated at about 250,000. Many of these celebrated Hibernian's Scottish Cup triumph in 1887 but wondered why Glasgow's far larger Irish–Catholic community had not produced a successful club of its own.[25]

Among them was Brother Walfrid (1840–1915) of the Marist teaching order, born Andrew Kerins in Ballymote, County Sligo. After becoming headmaster of St Andrew's school in Bridgeton in the East

End of Glasgow in the mid-1880s, he was struck by the insidious effects of poverty on education: levels of school attendance were low and many pupils were distracted by hunger. In response, he set up his own charity, the Poor Children's Dinner Table. After attending the reception in honour of the victorious Hibernian team at St Mary's Hall in Calton in February 1887, he arranged a fundraising match for his charity between Hibernian and the Glasgow team Renton to compete for the newly donated Glasgow East End Roman Catholic Charity Cup on 26 May 1887. It attracted a crowd of 12,000 paying spectators and convinced him that a local Catholic football team would be invaluable for his fundraising activities. Accordingly, Brother Walfrid and several prominent Catholic laymen of Irish origins came together at St Mary's Hall on 6 November 1887 and founded the Celtic Football and Athletic Club. Walfrid resisted suggestions for the usual Irish names such as Hibernian and Harp and insisted that the club be called Celtic to acknowledge the shared racial and cultural heritage of Irish immigrants and native Scots.[26]

Celtic played its first game on 28 May 1888. The opposition was a second-string XI of Rangers FC, a club founded in 1872 that had settled in Govan near the Clyde shipyards in the south-west of the city. Celtic got off to an auspicious start, winning 5–2 before 2,000 spectators. Its Irish–Catholic identity was proudly displayed, the team playing in white shirts with green collars and a crest of a large Celtic cross in a red circle, based on the emblem of the Marist order. (The following year they changed to green and white stripes and in 1903 adopted the famous green and white hoops.) Initially most Celtic players were of Irish–Catholic birth or descent: one of its early architects noted that its appeal was such that 'we could depend on the best of our own particular nationality and faith to have aspirations to play for the club'.[27] Scottish newspapers often referred to them as 'The Irishmen' at a time when the terms Irish and Catholic were virtually synonymous in Scotland, and the club's nickname 'The Bhoys' mimicked the Irish pronunciation of its followers. While Celtic's ethnic identification could sharpen competition against local rivals, participation in an increasingly popular sport also provided opportunities for Irish Catholics to interact with native Scots and make new connections and friendships. At first its rivalry with Rangers was an amicable one: the two teams played regular challenge matches and in 1893 were said by the popular newspaper *Scottish Sport* to be 'getting very pally'.[28]

Celtic soon became one of the leading teams in Scotland, finishing as runner-up in their first season in the Scottish FA Cup in 1889 and winning the competition in 1892. It was a founder member of the Scottish League in 1890 and won the league championship in 1893, 1894, 1896 and 1898; there were also Scottish FA Cup wins in 1899 and 1901, and numerous local trophies. The club's sustained success soon made it a standard-bearer for Glasgow's Irish–Catholic immigrants. They were also proud of its charitable activities and thought that it showed the Irish–Catholic community at its best: representing its people with honour on the sports field, but also taking care of the less fortunate.[29] Friend and foe alike saw Celtic as more than just a football club and it attracted important supporters: Archbishop Charles Eyre, the first Catholic prelate of the Glasgow archdiocese (1878–1903) (the Catholic hierarchy was not formally restored in Scotland until 1878), became a patron, and the club's directors reciprocated by making its facilities available for religious parades and festivals.

As with Hibernian FC in its early years, the club did not steer clear of politics: founders, officials, players and supporters were closely involved in the campaign for Irish Home Rule, which intensified from the mid-1880s. Among the most prominent was John Glass (1851–1906), the club's first president and director, who was treasurer of the Glasgow branch of the IPP. Glass, born in Glasgow to Irish parents, was a successful builder and shrewd businessman who assumed a greater role in running the club than Brother Walfrid, who was transferred to London in 1893. Glass led the way in ensuring that Celtic would prosper and was described in 1894 by *Scottish Sport* as 'the father of the club'.[30] Several other founders were also committed Home Rulers, notably William McKillop (1860–1909), a prosperous grocer and publican born in Ayrshire to Irish parents who sat as Nationalist MP for North Sligo (1900–6) and South Armagh (1906–9). When the club's new stadium, Celtic Park, was opened at Parkhead on 19 March 1892, Michael Davitt repeated his earlier gesture and laid a sod of Donegal turf encrusted with shamrocks in the centre circle. He also became a club patron and occasional spectator at Celtic Park and claimed he was often tempted to 'forswear politics for football' so much had the team impressed him.[31]

Celtic's strong religious and ethnic identity was integral to its appeal and the club thrived, particularly after it found an opponent with an equally keen sense of purpose and identity. When Celtic sat at the top of the league in 1896 (with Hibernian in second place), the popular newspaper *Scottish Sport* called on Scottish teams to mount a stronger challenge. Success on the football field mattered to Scots: during the 1880s and 1890s they regularly defeated England in international matches and the belief that Scottish brain had beaten English brawn was a mainstay of national pride. It was, therefore, rather galling to see their domestic league dominated by teams regarded as Irish. The team that responded most effectively to the challenge was Rangers, who in the years immediately afterwards won three FA Cups (1897, 1898 and 1903) and four consecutive league titles (1899–1902). In doing so, they came to be seen as defenders of national reputation and standard-bearers for a singularly Scottish form of muscular Calvinism, drawing support from across Glasgow and surrounding areas. This support did not just include native Scots: a quarter of the Irish immigrants to the west of Scotland in the nineteenth century were Protestant and many adopted Rangers as their team.[32]

As the identification of Celtic and Rangers with their respective communities grew stronger, football and the politics of identity became inextricably linked in Glasgow. This compelling rivalry helped establish Glasgow as the world's pre-eminent football city, which by the early twentieth century had three of the world's largest football stadiums (Celtic Park, Ibrox and Hampden Park). Rangers and Celtic could meet as many as ten times a year in matches for local trophies as well as the Scottish League and Cup, attracting ever-increasing attendances and gate receipts. It was this success in monetising their rivalry that in 1904 prompted a local newspaper to designate the two clubs the 'Old Firm'.[33]

As Celtic prospered, its board saw sharp struggles between idealists and pragmatists.[34] Among the former was the Glasgow-born master cooper James Quillan, who saw the club primarily as a charitable society whose membership should be confined to Catholics of Irish origin and whose profits should be used for their benefit. Others though favoured opening Celtic up to all religions and backgrounds, and prioritised sporting success ahead of charitable works. The latter group prevailed, led by figures such as John H. McLaughlin (1863?–1909), a Scottish-born wine and spirit merchant, who believed that Celtic should stay out of Irish politics and broaden its appeal beyond Irish Catholics. McLaughlin was keen to put the club on a sound business footing and was contemptuous of the 'soup kitchen cranks' who tried to run it as a charity. In 1897 he and other hard-headed businessmen launched Celtic as one of the first limited liability companies in British football. McLaughlin became chairman and ensured that the board was always the dominant shareholder. This brought about accusations that the club had become obsessed by money and abandoned its original charitable principles, sentiments regularly repeated in subsequent years.[35]

McLaughlin was instrumental in appointing Willie Maley (1868–1958) as Celtic's first 'secretary-manager'. Maley was born in Newry, the son of a British Army sergeant who moved to Glasgow in 1869. He became one of Celtic's earliest players in 1888 and secretary-manager in 1897, running the club with a singular thoroughness and ambition. By 1899 Celtic had a fine new stadium with a capacity of over 60,000 (known to its supporters as 'Paradise') and a team to match. While Maley selected his teams on the basis of ability rather than background, the outstanding contributions of Irish-born players such as Patsy Gallacher, originally from Milford, County Donegal (who played from 1911 to 1926), and second-generation Irish Catholics such as Jimmy Quinn (1900–15), and Jimmy McGrory (1922–37) reinforced supporters' identification with the club's roots.

As Celtic tried to reconcile its Irish roots with its Scottish base, it came to mean different things to different people: Maley himself embodied some of its complexities. He strongly emphasised the club's Irish origins but was proud to make his debut for Scotland against Ireland at Celtic Park in March 1893, describing the 6–1 win as his 'greatest football honour'. He spoke in favour of Home Rule for Ireland at a United Irish League rally in Glasgow in 1910 but made a point of distancing himself from physical force nationalism, describing the Fenians as 'foolish fellows, doing only harm to themselves'. Proud of his father's military service during the Crimean War, he encouraged the Scots-Irish to join the British Army in 1914 and made Celtic Park available for recruitment drives. He had unashamed royalist sympathies, recalling with pride being introduced to Princess May of Teck (later Queen Mary) before his second international appearance for Scotland against England at Richmond in April 1893. He was also delighted to meet King George VI during a 1940 visit to Glasgow and was particularly taken by his wife Elizabeth (the future Queen Mother), whom he recalled as 'a real, homely Scots girl with a kindly soft voice'.[36]

Maley managed Celtic until 1940, during which time it won the Scottish League Championship sixteen times, including six titles in a row (1905–10), and fourteen Scottish FA Cups; it was the first Scottish club to win the league and cup double in 1907, and repeated the feat in 1908 and 1914. Celtic's success was replicated by Rangers, which had its own manager heroes, such as William Wilton, who led them from 1899 to 1920 and was succeeded by Bill Struth (1920–54). During the forty-three years of Maley's tenure at Celtic, Rangers won twenty-three Scottish Leagues, dominating the interwar years with fifteen titles (1920–39). From 1905 to 1939 the league was only won once by a team outside the Old Firm (Motherwell in 1932). Seasons without silverware were seen as major disappointments and the destiny of the main trophies was often decided by the Glasgow derbies.

The atmosphere at these matches was often intense, and in 1909 Glasgow experienced its first full-scale football riot during an Old Firm Cup final replay at Hampden Park, which left almost 100 injured. The potential for further violent outbreaks was primed three years later when Harland & Wolff opened a new shipyard at Govan and imported hundreds of Belfast Protestant workers, many of whom became dedicated Rangers supporters.[37] Significant numbers were also Orangemen, whose presence aggravated tensions in Glasgow during the Home Rule crisis of 1912–14. Many signed the Solemn League and Covenant in January 1913 and both Edward Carson and Joe Devlin addressed large meetings of their supporters in the city that year. As the

crisis mounted, Glasgow-based units of the Ulster Volunteers paraded
through the city in March 1914.[38]

* * *

The post-war period saw a marked increase in tensions at Old Firm
derbies, as supporters adopted the symbols and songs of the warring
sides in the Irish conflicts of 1919–22. There was considerable support
among the Irish in Scotland for Irish independence and by 1920 the
country was host to eighty Sinn Féin clubs. In Glasgow alone there were
an estimated 4,000 IRA volunteers, and Scottish sympathisers were
important sources of money, arms and explosives for IRA operations in
Ireland.[39] Although armed political violence was rare in Scotland itself,
in May 1921 a police inspector was killed in Glasgow during an attempt
to free an IRA prisoner. That year some Celtic supporters were arrested
at the club's grounds and accused of running guns to Ireland. There
were claims that the club itself was an IRA front, although in reality
there were more publicans than republicans directing its fortunes.[40]

   With the founding of the Irish Free State in 1922, the question of Irish
self-government appeared settled. Throughout Britain, Irish political
organisations atrophied as many of their members transferred their
energies to trade unionism and local politics. However, in Scotland, a
vocal minority was reluctant to accept them as fellow citizens. In 1923
the influential General Assembly of the Church of Scotland produced
a report entitled *The Menace of the Irish Race to Our Scottish Nationality*
which claimed that the inflow of Catholics had reached levels that
threatened to reverse the Protestant Reformation. Irish Catholics were
accused of afflicting Scottish society with everything from crime and
drunkenness to popery and Bolshevism, and there were calls for stricter
controls on immigration. These demands became even stronger after
the 1929 economic crash which hit Glasgow's staple industries hard. The
anti-Catholic Scottish Protestant League outpolled the Labour Party and
won six seats in elections to Glasgow Corporation, drawing much of its
support from skilled working-class areas devastated by redundancies.
Such sentiments could also be found in Edinburgh, where a new party,

Protestant Action, led by the semi-literate demagogue John Cormack called for the disenfranchisement and deportation of Catholics. More respectable voices also stirred the pot: in 1932 the Scottish Conservative MP for Perth, Lord Scone, asserted that 'there is in the west of Scotland a completely separate race of alien origin, practically homogenous, whose presence there is bitterly resented by tens of thousands of the Scottish working class'.[41] After Orange marches in Glasgow in July 1933 there were outbreaks of street-fighting in Cowcaddens, Calton and Bridgeton, and violent attacks on religious processions and Catholic churches in Glasgow and Edinburgh in 1935.[42]

There were also clashes between supporters of Celtic and Rangers, particularly as large groups made their way to and from matches, displaying flags and banners and singing partisan songs. This was aggravated by the involvement of East End gangs such as the Bridgeton Billy Boys, a 'razor gang' notorious for their anti-Catholic bigotry who identified strongly with Rangers. Their anthem 'The Billy Boys' boasted of being 'up to our necks in Fenian blood' and they had links to the British Union of Fascists through their leader, Billy Fullerton. They also participated in Orange marches and sectarian riots in Belfast, including one in July 1935 in which two people were shot dead and another fifteen wounded.[43] Violence in Scotland was, however, generally isolated and quickly contained. The established political parties distanced themselves from sectarian bigotry, as did the mainstream press, refuting extremist scaremongering with fact-based journalism that showed that immigration from Ireland had never been lower and there was little likelihood of Scots being swamped.[44]

However, Celtic's links with Ireland continued to attract hostility. The club was much admired in Ireland, where it played regularly and built up a strong following. Many of these supporters regarded Celtic as essentially an Irish club: reporting on crowd trouble at an Old Firm match in 1927, the Dublin-based *Football Sports Weekly* noted that 'The Celts and their following are "our people" of course. They are Irish – real Irish – to the backbone. The Rangers and their following are not.'[45] Celtic celebrated its connection with Ireland by flying the Irish tricolour at Celtic Park, and when this was done at a

British Championship match between Scotland and Ireland (IFA) on 16 September 1934, the Scottish FA protested strongly and demanded its removal.[46] The tricolour in question had been presented to the club twelve years earlier by the Irish Free State government to replace the old Irish 'nationalist' flag of a golden harp on a green background that had previously flown over the main stand at Celtic Park.[47] When it was fraying in 1935, the Celtic manager Jimmy McGrory wrote to the Irish government requesting a replacement and was sent one by Éamon de Valera with an accompanying note in which he praised Celtic for its sporting achievements and pride in its Irish origins.[48] Always well-disposed to the club, de Valera attended an Old Firm derby at Ibrox on 16 October 1948, the day before he was due to address an Anti-Partition League meeting at St Andrew's Hall, Glasgow.[49]

The more Celtic cultivated its links with Ireland, the more its loyalty to Scotland was questioned, and this often centred on the flying of the Irish flag. After crowd trouble at an Old Firm match on New Year's Day 1952, the Scottish FA advised that 'the two clubs should avoid displaying flags which might incite feelings among spectators' and specifically instructed that the Irish tricolour should no longer be flown at Celtic Park. The Celtic chairman, Bob Kelly, then president of the Scottish League, refused to comply, arguing that the Union flag and St Andrew's Cross also flew at Celtic Park and that the tricolour simply acknowledged the club's traditions and association with Ireland. Kelly's refusal to accede to the instructions of the FA led some Scottish League clubs to propose Celtic's expulsion from the league. The motion was defeated, but only by sixteen votes to fifteen, with Rangers voting in Celtic's favour.[50]

*** *

After the Second World War there were signs that the sectarian animosities of the interwar years were abating. Scots of all religions and backgrounds had worked, fought and died together in a six-year conflict that put their differences into perspective. Working-class Scots generally benefited from the expansion of the welfare state overseen by the post-war Labour government, particularly from access to universal healthcare and third-level education, which proportionately helped the more disadvantaged Catholic community. During the 1950s the economy expanded and Catholics moved from low-paid employment into public service, the professions, arts and politics to become increasingly integrated into Scottish life.

On the football field, though, the immediate post-war period was a disappointing one for Celtic. Trophies were hard to come by under the management of Jimmy McGrory (1945–65), the club winning only one league title (1954) and two FA Cups (1951, 1954). There was, though, the consolation of the Coronation Cup in 1953, a one-off tournament to celebrate the crowning of Queen Elizabeth II. It featured the four top teams from England and Scotland and was regarded as an unofficial club championship of Britain. Celtic beat Arsenal and Manchester United to reach the final, where they faced Hibernian, who had eliminated Tottenham and Newcastle United. Captained by Jock Stein, Celtic beat Hibernian 2–0 on 20 May 1953 before 117,000 spectators at Hampden Park. Among supporters of Irish descent on both sides, there was considerable pride that the final of such a prestigious trophy was contested by two clubs founded by their forefathers.

While Celtic won on this occasion, Hibernian normally came out on top in these years and for a time was Rangers' main rival, winning three Scottish League titles between 1948 and 1952. Celtic though regained their competitive edge under the management of Jock Stein (1965–78), who led them to ten league championships, including nine in a row (1966–74), eight FA Cups, and their greatest ever triumph when they won the European Cup in 1967. Celtic's victory over Inter Milan in the final on 25 May 1967 takes pride of place in the club's lore. Thousands made the 2,000-mile overland journey from Glasgow to Lisbon and others travelled from Ireland, England and the global Scottish and Irish diasporas. They witnessed Celtic winning in style, playing exciting, attacking football with skilful wingers Jimmy Johnstone and Bobby Lennox running defenders ragged and confounding a team whose defensive 'catenaccio' tactics threatened to stifle the European game. The victory gave a massive boost to the club's support in Ireland: the young Martin O'Neill, then a student in St Columb's in Derry, recalled it as a life-changing event that encouraged him to choose soccer over Gaelic football.[51] Celtic was the first British club to win the trophy, and its supporters were immensely proud of this entirely Scottish team, mostly born within a ten-mile radius of Celtic Park. To many it seemed the ultimate triumph of the underdog: an eminent Scottish historian described the victory as one of the most important milestones in the history of Scotland's Irish–Catholic community, standing alongside the visit of Pope John Paul II in 1982.[52]

Pride in the achievement of Celtic's religiously mixed team was shared by Scots of varying backgrounds. At a meeting of the General Assembly of the Church of Scotland, the Moderator, Rev. W. Roy Sanderson, extended his congratulations to Celtic and was greeted with a sustained burst of applause.[53] Such generosity was not, however, universal. Many Rangers supporters (and some from other clubs) saw little to celebrate in Celtic's victory and highlighted the fact that its supporters in Lisbon had waved Irish tricolours rather than Scottish flags. Some insisted that its close identification with Ireland was incompatible with its status as a Scottish club: according to one Rangers supporter, 'They flew a foreign flag; their directors held their foreign passports; their profits went to a foreign country; yet they took their money from Glasgow, from Glaswegians.'[54]

The main effect of disparagement of Celtic's Irish identity was to reinforce it. The more its colours, emblems, flags, songs and traditions were attacked, the more they appealed to many Celtic supporters as badges of cultural distinctiveness. When the club launched its own newspaper, *Celtic View* in 1964, it regularly advertised recordings of rebel songs such as 'The Merry Ploughboy' and 'James Connolly', and commemorative concerts for republican martyrs such as Kevin Barry and Seán South and the fiftieth anniversary of the Easter Rising, at which Celtic stars made guest appearances.[55] However, after the outbreak of the Northern Ireland Troubles in 1969, many Scots became uneasy with rebel songs that romanticised violence. During an away match against Stirling Albion in August 1972, Jock Stein felt the need to rebuke Celtic supporters for singing IRA songs, arguing that 'surely there are enough Celtic songs without introducing religion or politics or anything else'.[56] In the early 1960s Stein, a Protestant, had introduced 'The Celtic Song', an uncontroversial paean to the club, to be played at Celtic Park before each game. Supporters took to it, although most dropped its breezy assurance that 'We don't care if we win, lose or draw.'[57] Stein was always anxious to defuse the sectarian aspects of the Old Firm rivalry, having experienced them himself at first hand. After he became a Celtic player in 1951, some Protestant friends and family members distanced themselves, and did so even more when he became Celtic's first Protestant manager.[58]

The Northern Ireland Troubles gave a sharper edge to the recurrent controversy over flying the Irish flag at Celtic Park. Conservative Scottish papers such as the *Sunday Mail* and *The Sun* maintained that the club's attachment to a symbol so closely associated with militant Irish republicanism suggested that many Celtic supporters were at best ambivalent about the actions of the IRA and that some secretly approved.[59] As the conflict was reframed in ritualised form on the terraces of Glasgow, the atmosphere at Old Firm games became more aggressively sectarian, alienating some supporters. One lifelong Celtic fan admitted to 'cringing with embarrassment at the defiant and tuneless chanting of Irish and IRA anthems'.[60] While the management of both clubs made some efforts to discourage sectarianism among their followers, the effect was limited as significant numbers accepted or even embraced the increased polarisation brought about by the Troubles.[61]

For some Celtic supporters, the singing of IRA songs was intended not just to provoke other supporters and the Scottish establishment but was also a gesture of defiance to its own board of directors, long seen as a conservative force that held the club back. Since Celtic's foundation there had been considerable continuity in those who owned and ran the club. Chief among them were the Grant, Kelly and White families, who held a majority of club shares and dominated the board and club chairmanship until the 1990s. The best-known was Sir Robert 'Bob' Kelly who joined the board in 1932, served as chairman (1947–71) and was knighted in 1969 for his services to football. The son of James Kelly, Celtic's first captain, Bob Kelly saw himself as a guardian of the club's traditions and, before Stein took up the position in 1965, was often seen as the real team manager. Most of the other directors were more shadowy figures. In the early 1960s many of the Grant family shares were inherited by Felicia Grant, then living in Toomebridge, County Antrim, giving rise to the commonly held belief that an 'old lady in Ireland' had the final say in the running of the club.[62]

The Celtic board had a reputation for being ultra-cautious, particularly in financial matters. It kept a tight rein on players' wages, which were often lower than those at other less-successful Scottish clubs. Even after winning the European Cup, Stein had to struggle to ensure that he and his players were properly paid. The club's financial caution became a matter of particular frustration to supporters from the late 1980s as they watched free-spending Rangers recruit talented international players and win nine successive Scottish League titles (1989–97). Celtic's directors were unmoved and insisted they would continue to run the club as a family trust and were unwilling to price ordinary supporters out of Celtic Park by spending heavily on players or a new stadium.[63]

* * *

The 1990s were a turbulent time for Celtic: after having six managers in its first 100 years, it had seven in that decade alone. The club struggled on and off the pitch, not spending enough to match Rangers, but more than its commercially under-developed operations could sustain. In March 1994 it came close to bankruptcy but was saved at the last minute by the Scottish-Canadian businessman Fergus McCann, a lifelong fan, who bought the club and refinanced it with a share issue that raised £14 million, then the most successful in British football history. McCann believed that Celtic was a sleeping giant, whose cherished traditions had hardened into an introspective conservatism that prevented it from realising its commercial potential as one of Europe's great clubs. He was determined to make it more attractive to Scottish business interests and Scots generally by stressing that Celtic was, first and foremost, a Scottish club. There were many Celtic supporters who believed that such a move was long overdue, but others were suspicious of any airbrushing of its Irish links and insisted that the club's tradition was not for sale to make it more commercially appealing.[64]

The commercial argument provided a new dimension to the long-running debate about the club's identity. Many Celtic supporters admitted to identifying more with Ireland and its diaspora than Scotland. Some insisted that the Scottish FA had a long-standing bias against their club, repeatedly shown by a litany of unfair administrative and refereeing decisions.[65] Such attitudes are often found among those with an ambivalent attachment to the state in which they live: in cities such as Barcelona and Liverpool, for example, highly successful football clubs also act as important focuses for alternative loyalties. In a survey carried out in the early 1990s, 22 per cent of Celtic supporters said they never attended Scotland's games; 43 per cent attended sometimes and a mere 3 per cent always went – by far the lowest among all Scottish clubs. This compared with 80 per cent of Rangers' supporters who sometimes or always attended, and the figure for other Scottish clubs was even higher, with over 90 per cent of supporters from Hibernian and Dundee United sometimes or always attending.[66]

Some Celtic players as well as supporters also claimed to feel more Irish than Scottish. Paddy Crerand, who played for the club in the early 1960s, considered Donegal, the birthplace of his parents, to be his true home. He was capped nineteen times for Scotland (1961–5) but admitted that he would have rather played for the Republic of Ireland.[67] This was the option later taken by his cousin and Celtic teammate Charlie Gallagher, who was born in Glasgow to Donegal parents and considered himself 'Irish at heart, though I was born and brought up in Scotland'. He turned out twice for the Republic in 1967, becoming the first Scottish-born player to represent the team.[68]

When the Republic of Ireland began to qualify for international tournaments from 1988, Celtic supporters (Scottish and Irish) in their club shirts became a conspicuous presence at Irish matches. There were also more Irish internationals playing for the club: before the 1980s, there had been relatively few at Celtic Park, but during the Charlton era players such as Packie Bonner, Mick McCarthy, Tony Cascarino, Chris Morris and Tommy Coyne appeared regularly for both teams. Although born in Scotland, Coyne had chosen to represent the Republic (1992–7), following the example of Glasgow-born Ray Houghton, who, in a distinguished international career, made seventy-three appearances (1986–97). Subsequently other promising young players, such as Aiden McGeady and James McCarthy, followed their example: many in Scotland saw their decision as a betrayal and they were widely slated in the media.[69] This has also happened in the women's game, with the Glasgow-born Ruesha Littlejohn declaring for the Republic in 2012 and going on to win over sixty caps.

Celtic's strong links with Donegal, which traditionally supplied more emigrants to Scotland than any other Irish county, have persisted and been reinforced by the presence of outstanding Donegal players such as Bonner and Shay Given in the Celtic team. Celtic also commands strong support in the neighbouring county of Sligo, birthplace of Brother Walfrid and Sean Fallon (1922–2013), a former Celtic player (1950–8) and assistant manager (1962–75) who was crucial to Jock Stein's success, signing up and mentoring several of the players who won the European Cup in 1967. There are also strong links with Northern Ireland, where three of the club's six managers since 2000 were born: Martin O'Neill (2000–5), Neil Lennon (2010–14; 2019–21) and Brendan Rogers (2016–19). The Irish connection extends to the club's ownership: when Fergus McCann sold his shares in 1999, the Irish billionaire businessman Dermot Desmond bought 2.8 million of them to increase his stake from 13 to 20 per cent and become the club's majority stakeholder.

The club's culture still clearly has a strong Irish dimension. From the mid-1990s, Pete St John's 'The Fields of Athenry', a song of love, resistance and exile set against the backdrop of the Great Famine of the 1840s, was played before matches at Celtic Park and became a great crowd favourite. For many, it struck the right note, acknowledging the trauma of the Famine, but without glorifying violence or martyrdom. It was sung by Irish fans in Germany in 1988 and subsequent tournaments and became a ubiquitous sporting anthem, readily transferring between soccer, rugby and Gaelic games. However, for some in Scotland, the song's sentiments remained unacceptable. In 1994 the Scottish *Sunday*

Mail censured Celtic for airing it before matches, claiming that it only served to feed historical grievances, had no relevance to Scotland and no place in a Scottish football ground.[70] For some Celtic supporters, it seems that full acceptance into Scottish society requires them to turn their backs on their history, particularly its Irish dimension, but there is little likelihood of this. There are few football clubs for whom history means more and past heroes and events are still regularly recalled and acknowledged. When Celtic Park was being rebuilt, Michael Davitt's laying of a sod of Donegal turf in the centre circle in 1892 was re-enacted in the stadium on 10 April 1995.[71] In October 2004, supporters unveiled a memorial to the club's founder Brother Walfrid in Ballymote, and in November the following year, his statue was raised outside Celtic Park.[72]

***

For most of the twentieth century Rangers FC avoided signing Catholic players. However, in July 1989 manager Graeme Souness recruited the former Celtic forward Mo Johnston, the club's first high-profile Catholic. This outraged some traditional supporters: on 23 July 1989 a meeting of Rangers supporters' clubs in Whitehead, County Antrim, announced that they would no longer travel to Ibrox and called for a boycott of club merchandise.[73] However, most other supporters were prepared to live with it, and some even welcomed it as long overdue. In the years that followed, Rangers recruited several continental Catholics and there was little controversy when the Italian Lorenzo Amoruso became Rangers' first Catholic captain in 1999. However, Rangers waited until 2013 to sign an Irish Catholic: the Dubliner Jon O'Neill, who joined from Dundee United and made sixty-seven appearances over the next two seasons. There were occasional subsequent signings of Irish Catholics, but O'Neill remains the only one to make any real impact at Ibrox.

While Rangers supporters often denounce Celtic's Irish connections, Rangers too has close associations with Ireland. More than thirty players born in Ireland have played for the club, most from the six counties of Northern Ireland. In its first 110 years of existence only one non-Scot, the Belfast-born IFA international Bert Manderson

(1893–1946), captained the club (1926–7). Since then other Northern Ireland internationals, such as John McClelland and Steven Davis, have also held the captaincy, and six Northern Ireland internationals have featured in the club's Hall of Fame. Celtic's close relationship with Belfast Celtic was mirrored by that between Rangers and Linfield, and many players have appeared for both clubs. During the Troubles, many Scottish Rangers supporters aligned themselves strongly with the unionist community in Northern Ireland, and some even adopted flags and songs associated with loyalist paramilitaries. Players too have occasionally adopted extreme political positions: Andy Goram (1964– 2022), Rangers' goalkeeper for most of the 1990s, publicly admitted his admiration for loyalist paramilitaries and wore a black armband at the Old Firm game on 2 January 1998, five days after the assassination of Billy Wright, a notorious loyalist responsible for dozens of sectarian killings.[74]

The Glasgow rivalry is heightened by the fact that both clubs command large followings in Northern Ireland, where wearing their colours is often used to declare political allegiance. Rangers have over 100 supporters' clubs in Northern Ireland, while Celtic have about fifty-five in the North and twenty-five in the Republic.[75] Rangers also have a supporters' club in Dublin, 'The Dublin Loyal', made up of Scottish, Irish and Northern Irish members; they insist that they attract little hostility, although they do hold their meetings in private.[76] Thousands of supporters, often among the most committed, regularly cross the Irish Sea to see their teams play, particularly in Old Firm clashes. During the Troubles, these games provided an opportunity to vent commitment in a relatively safe environment: one Rangers supporter from Belfast admitted that 'all the stuff that you've bottled up for months in Ulster, you can let go there in 90 minutes. Things get very intense over there, but you won't get shot.'[77]

The heady mixture of solidarity and anonymity provided by the football stadium can certainly create an extremely tribal atmosphere, but some maintain that this looks rather more serious than it really is. They see the trading of political or sectarian chants and songs as part of the ritual of the Glasgow derby, designed to taunt opposing supporters and express independence from official injunctions, and claim that most of those 'who sing their approval of the IRA and UVF do nothing at all outside football matches to turn those words into reality'.[78] But while offensive songs and chants need not be taken as literal expressions of opinion, they cannot entirely be discounted as the harmless effusions of '90-minute bigots'. Airing such views is a matter of choice and many choose not to do so. Those who do may well be taking the opportunity to give voice to some deep-seated attitudes they would be reluctant to express in other circumstances. The question of whether the Old Firm rivalry is the cause or effect of sectarian bigotry tends to go around in never-ending circles. Some see it as a 'ritual expression of hostility' that allows the release of sectarian impulses that might otherwise fester.[79] However, in his study of football and sectarianism in Glasgow in the interwar period, Andrew Davies maintained that the rivalry itself created occasions for confrontation and added 'another incendiary spark to Glasgow's fraught ethnic and religious division'.[80]

While Old Firm clashes are strictly policed and violent incidents in and around stadiums are rare, they can still provide the occasion for disturbances and assaults in the wider community. These keenly anticipated events encourage heavy consumption of alcohol, and admissions to hospital Accident and Emergency departments in the west of Scotland rise sharply after Glasgow derbies; there have also been several violent fatalities linked to the Old Firm rivalry.[81] Some areas see a marked increase in tension in the lead-up to the games. In February 2001, a proposed visit by Taoiseach Bertie Ahern to dedicate a memorial to victims of the Great Famine at Carfin in Lanarkshire was cancelled after the local Labour MP warned it could spark disturbances because it was scheduled to take place on the evening of a Glasgow derby. (The visit took place uneventfully months later.)[82] Violence can also spill over into Northern Ireland. When Rangers pipped Celtic to the title in 2009, loyalists who were celebrating in Coleraine attacked and beat to death Kevin McDaid, a Catholic volunteer youth worker who had gone to the aid of a neighbour who was being assaulted.[83]

***

Celtic's importance as an expression of Irish–Catholic identity, often in opposition to a more dominant British, Scottish and Protestant culture, has placed the club at the centre of debate about sectarianism in Scottish society.[84] By the 1990s many Scots saw their country as a liberal and secular one in which sectarianism was a thing of the past. The tribalism witnessed at Old Firm matches was regarded as an unpleasant historical hangover, largely confined to a marginalised underclass. In August 1999, this view was publicly challenged by James MacMillan, one of Scotland's most eminent classical music composers, whose expressive and politically engaged work drew heavily on his Catholic faith and Scottish roots. In a lecture entitled 'Scotland's Shame', given at the Edinburgh International Festival, he portrayed Scotland as a land of 'sleep-walking bigotry' that still harboured a 'visceral anti-Catholicism' in the professions, politics and the media. He maintained that the hostility expressed at Old Firm games was not exceptional but rather that 'in football a curtain is lifted upon certain attitudes and mindsets otherwise customarily kept discreetly hidden'.[85]

As changing social mores make overt sectarianism increasingly unacceptable in Scottish society, the Old Firm rivalry provides an outlet for its expression and remains 'the one area in which historic Irish–Catholic and Scottish–Protestant identities retain any salience'.[86] It has survived the sharp fall in religious practice and identification that has occurred in recent decades and is now probably motivated more by political and ethnic considerations than religious ones. While both Rangers and Celtic have intensified their efforts to curb political and sectarian displays in their stadiums, these have been resisted by some supporters who see them as compromising the clubs' traditions. In 2002, the announcement of the death of Elizabeth, the Queen Mother (the same royal who in 1940 had so captivated Willie Maley), was greeted with prolonged booing by significant numbers at Celtic Park. In 2008 and 2010 Celtic's 'Green Brigade', which represents the most partisan elements of the club's support, protested at the presence of the British Legion's poppy symbol on players' shirts in matches before Remembrance Sunday. A banner directed at the British armed services was displayed with the message: 'Your deeds would shame all the devils in Hell. Ireland, Iraq, Afghanistan. No bloodstained poppy on our hoops.'[87] Celtic's board denounced these protests and promised to ban those involved. It also condemned the pro-IRA chants of a minority of supporters, with manager Neil Lennon issuing a strong statement against glorifying paramilitary groups.[88] Some supporters though insist on identifying the club with militant Irish nationalism and in 2012 Celtic was fined by UEFA for its failure to prevent supporters displaying a large banner that featured the image of the IRA hunger-striker Bobby Sands. There is clearly a chasm between supporters such as the Green Brigade and the club, which was again clearly evident after the death of Queen Elizabeth II. While Celtic players wore black armbands at their Champions League match in Warsaw on 14 September 2022, the club thought it better not to have a pre-match minute's silence and some supporters displayed a banner that read 'Fuck the Crown'.

For their part, Rangers' supporters continued to sing sectarian songs and provoked controversy in 2008 with the notoriously anti-Irish and anti-Catholic 'Famine Song', with its refrain of 'The Famine is over, why don't you go home.' The Labour politician John Reid, a former British home secretary and chairman of Celtic, described it as 'vile, racist and sectarian', and the Irish Consulate in Edinburgh submitted a formal complaint to the Scottish government.[89] Aggressive bigotry has in recent years been reinforced by the use of social media, which provides an anonymous platform for abusive extremism and adds an increasingly poisonous element to Old Firm exchanges.[90]

Questions of national identity have taken on a new urgency in Scotland in recent years. The establishment of the devolved Scottish executive and parliament in 1999 created a greater awareness of Scotland as a separate nation and led to growing demands for full independence, narrowly defeated in a referendum in 2014. While supporters and opponents of independence could be found on both sides of the Old Firm, most Rangers supporters prided themselves on their loyalty to the United Kingdom. Identification with the Union and with Northern Ireland has expressed itself at Ibrox in a profusion of Union Jacks, Ulster flags and songs such as 'Rule Britannia'.[91] Before the referendum's polling day, Rangers supporters unveiled a huge 'Vote NO' banner at the stadium, and former Rangers players, such as Sir Alex Ferguson and Ally McCoist, publicly threw their weight behind the 'No' campaign.[92]

In the past most Celtic supporters would have shared their opposition to the prospect of independence. Catholics were traditionally suspicious of the Scottish National Party (SNP), fearing its demands for a devolved government risked creating a Scottish Stormont that would discriminate against them, and in the 1979 referendum they voted overwhelmingly against devolution. However, in the eighteen years of Conservative rule that followed, Scots of all backgrounds became increasingly alienated from Westminster and more anxious to control their own destiny. There were also signs that Catholics in Scotland were growing more comfortable with their Scottish identity: in a 1997 poll 71 per cent of Catholics described themselves as Scottish, compared with 72 per cent of the population as a whole. By 1998 the SNP was receiving greater than proportional support from Catholics, often at the expense of the pro-union Labour Party they had traditionally supported, and Labour's vote in Scotland collapsed in the UK general elections of 2015 and 2019.[93] Before and after the independence referendum, 'Yes' flags proliferated at Celtic Park, even though the notion of the club as a standard-bearer for Scottish independence would have been unthinkable a generation earlier. For some Celtic followers, voting to leave the UK was another way to distance themselves from the traditional unionism of Rangers and the Scottish establishment, but many also saw Scottish nationalism as a progressive movement towards self-determination and the Scottish and Irish dimensions of their identity as complementary rather than conflicting.[94]

Today, Celtic's appeal transcends both Scottish and Irish identities. With more than 160 supporters' clubs in over twenty countries, its worldwide fanbase is estimated at over 10 million people (close to the combined populations of Scotland and Ireland). Its identity defies precise definition, with elements that are Scottish, Irish, Catholic, republican, socialist, pro-underdog and anti-establishment.[95] This has allowed the expression of a broad range of complementary allegiances and identities that have made it the Irish diaspora's most popular, identifiable and enduring institution.

13

Pride and Prejudice:
The Irish and English Clubs

While some Irish immigrants undoubtedly experienced prejudice and discrimination, the story of Irish immigration to England is largely one of successful integration. Association football played its part, becoming central to the lives of many who moved to England's industrial cities. Some played the game at a local level, which often provided a valuable source of friendship and social support, while many others supported their local team, which offered a means of identifying more closely with their new home. Playing and spectating helped Irish immigrants and their children find a place in English society, allowing the expression of local loyalties and communal solidarity that did not compromise previously held allegiances and identities.

For all soccer's popularity with the Irish working class in England, they did not set up identifiably Irish clubs that competed at a national level as they did in Scotland. If this had happened anywhere, it probably would have been in Liverpool, which from the mid-nineteenth century attracted more Irish immigration relative to its size than any other English city; in 1891 over 9 per cent of its population was born in Ireland, double the percentage of Manchester, the city with the second highest rate. The result was that Liverpool had more ethno-sectarian conflict than any other English city, with enmities aggravated by a continuous stream of immigration and competition for work.[1] The city hosted a self-consciously Irish–Catholic community which, as in

Glasgow and Edinburgh, was held together by strong attachments to the Catholic Church and Irish nationalism. Liverpool was the only English city in which the IPP was assured of a seat in parliament, held from 1885 to 1929 by the Athlone-born T.P. O'Connor (1848–1929), a popular journalist and the acknowledged leader of Irish nationalism in England. The Liverpool Irish were also sustained by a range of religious and cultural associations that included confraternities, benevolent societies, charities, temperance societies and local branches of the Ancient Order of Hibernians, the Gaelic League and the GAA. The GAA, though, was never strong in the city, amounting at the end of the nineteenth century to just three hurling clubs, all of whom struggled to field teams.[2] The Irish who wished to play football mostly took up the association code, and from the late 1880s they founded several clubs in the city. At least eleven have been identified, with typically Irish names such as Hibernian or Celtic. Most 'had a relatively short-lived and inauspicious history' and none survived the nineteenth century.[3] Their demise probably helped the Irish integrate into wider Liverpool society, encouraging players and supporters to gravitate to other local clubs.

The clerical intervention central to the establishment of Irish football clubs in Edinburgh and Glasgow was generally lacking in Liverpool and other English cities. Most Liverpool Catholic clergy had been born or ordained in England and few (like the English Catholic hierarchy generally) had any sympathy for Irish Home Rule or cultural nationalism. Lancashire-born Thomas Whiteside, the Catholic bishop (later archbishop) of the city (1894–1921), was an outspoken unionist who encouraged Irish Catholics to assimilate into English society. He generally entrusted the care of Irish districts to continental orders such as the Benedictines, Franciscans and Jesuits, who stressed political and social conservatism and had little interest in Irish nationalism.[4] The political leadership of the city's Catholic Irish was also strongly integrative. While advocating Home Rule for Ireland, T.P. O'Connor regularly championed the interests of the English working class and encouraged the Irish in Britain to play their part in local politics.

While sectarian tensions in parts of Liverpool persisted into the early decades of the twentieth century, they became less open, less violent and largely confined to marginal communities. Religion though was important and had a notable influence on the development of the city's main football clubs. From the late 1870s the game in Liverpool was pioneered by teams formed by Anglican parishes and Nonconformist congregations. The forerunner of Everton FC was St Domingo FC, founded in 1878 by members of the St Domingo New Connexional Methodist chapel in Breckfield Road in north Everton; as Everton FC it became a founder member of the Football League in 1888 and won the league championship in 1891.[5] Merseyside's other most enduring club, Liverpool FC, emerged out of a dispute between Everton players and officials and the club president, John Houlding (1833–1902), a prosperous brewer and businessman who owned Everton's Anfield playing ground. Unhappy with the rent being charged for Anfield, dissatisfied players and officials voted in 1892 to decamp to Goodison Park on the north side of Stanley Park. Houlding, left with a stadium but no team, founded Liverpool FC in June 1892 and it joined the Football League the following year. Its first secretary-manager was John McKenna (1855–1936), a Protestant born in Glaslough, County Monaghan, who helped shape the club's early fortunes, signing a raft of experienced Scottish professionals to augment his new team. He was later club chairman (1906–15) and an important national administrator, who went on to become president of the Football League (1917–36).

Everton's decision to quit Anfield may have had some connection to the religious and political divisions within the city. Both Houlding and McKenna were Tories, Freemasons and Orangemen, while some of the most prominent figures on the Everton side were Liberals or Catholics who supported Irish Home Rule. Among the latter was Dr James Clement Baxter (1857–1928), who served Everton both as club doctor and chairman and provided them with a loan of £1,000 to develop Goodison Park in 1892. Known for his dedication to the welfare of Irish immigrants and the city's poor generally, he sat as a Liberal councillor for St Anne's ward (1906–20). Close allies at Everton included George Mahon (1853–1908), a successful accountant born in Liverpool to Irish parents and reared in Dublin. Mahon was a Methodist, a Liberal councillor and a Home Ruler, who became an Everton director in

1889 and three years later led the breakaway to Goodison. However, despite these political and religious undercurrents, the confessional identification of the city's two main clubs was far weaker than in Glasgow, particularly after Houlding's death in 1902. While Everton was often regarded as the more Catholic of the two, both drew support from across Merseyside's religious divide, a tendency that became more marked as the twentieth century progressed.[6]

***

The situation in Liverpool was roughly replicated in other parts of industrial England. Many Irish immigrants took readily to association football, and some founded their own clubs to play in local and junior leagues. Mostly these were ephemeral, but a few survived and catered for later generations of immigrants and their descendants. None though was ever important enough to join the Football League. The result was that throughout England, Irish football enthusiasts tended to support the same established professional clubs as their co-workers and neighbours.

Having soccer-supporting relatives in England sometimes encouraged family members in Ireland to take an interest in the English game, and the former were often the source of much-prized memorabilia. After the founding of the Football League in 1888, the fortunes of English clubs received considerable coverage in Irish newspapers. Visits to Ireland by Football League clubs were much anticipated and in the 1880s and 1890s attracted large crowds, at first in Belfast and later in Dublin. In April 1900 Derby County became the first English Division One team to play in Dublin when they defeated Bohemian FC 4–0 before a crowd of 2,000 spectators at Sandymount. After moving to Dalymount Park, Bohemians also hosted visits by Preston North End in November 1901, Liverpool and Sheffield United in April 1903 and Aston Villa in April 1906.[7]

Irish interest in cross-channel football was reinforced by the increasing professionalism of the game in England, which began to attract some of Ireland's best players from the 1890s. English professional clubs drew talent from across the UK: the Tottenham team that won the FA Cup in 1901 was made up of five Scots, three Englishmen, two Welshmen and an Irishman (the Wicklow-born Jock Kirwan). By 1902 more than twenty Irish professionals were playing for British clubs.[8] When Ireland won the British Championship in 1914, the core of the team played in England: Mickey Hamill for Manchester United, Val Harris for Everton, Patrick O'Connell for Hull City, Bill Lacey for Liverpool, Billy Gillespie for Sheffield United, and Louis Bookman and Harry Hampton for Bradford City.

Irish supporters often travelled to England to see favourite players or teams or took in a game when work or family visits brought them across the Irish Sea. In April 1926 it was reported that a large contingent of Dublin soccer enthusiasts was taking the Friday night boat to attend the FA Cup Final between Bolton Wanderers and Manchester City at Wembley.[9] There was no strong home-based Irish identification with any particular club until Dublin-born Jackie Carey was appointed captain of Manchester United by manager Matt Busby in 1945. United had spent many of the interwar years in the Second Division, but under Busby and Carey won the FA Cup in 1948 and challenged strongly for the First Division title with four runner-up finishes between 1947 and 1951 before winning the trophy in 1952. Carey retired in May 1953 having played 344 games for his only English club. United had had some notable Irish players in the past, such as Mickey Hamill (1911–14) and Harry Baird (1936–8) of Belfast, Patrick O'Connell (1914–19) of Dublin and Tommy Breen (1936–9) of Drogheda, but none achieved the fame of Carey, whose career was regarded with much pride in Ireland and led to an upsurge in Irish support for the club: the eight-year-old John Giles recalled listening to a radio broadcast of United's 1948 FA Cup final victory, after which United became his favourite team. In the post-war era the club also played regular friendly and benefit matches in Ireland, further boosting its popularity.

Around this time there was also considerable Irish interest in Everton FC, who fielded several Irish internationals, such as the skilful inside-forward Alex Stevenson, who spent fifteen years at the club (1934–49) and helped it to a league title in 1939. Stevenson was joined by other talented Irish players, such as Peter Farrell, Tommy Eglington and Peter Corr. Farrell and Eglington had moved together from Shamrock Rovers to Everton for a combined fee of £10,000 in 1946. Put off by stories of severe food rationing in post-war England, they had moved somewhat reluctantly, but soon settled. Farrell played 453 games for the club over eleven years, the last seven as captain, and was much admired by Everton supporters for his battling midfield performances. The flying winger Eglington was another great favourite and made 394 league appearances for Everton (1946–57). Both men later had suburban streets named after them in Liverpool.

The Irish connection was reinforced in the 1950s with the signing of other international players, such as goalkeeper Jimmy O'Neill and defenders Tommy Clinton, Don Donovan, John Sutherland and Mick Meagan. At one stage there were seven Irish players at Goodison Park, and from 1958 the team was managed by Jackie Carey. The strong Irish presence attracted considerable Irish support, both in England and Ireland, aided by the regular ferry services between Dublin and Liverpool: one Liverpudlian recalled that Everton had 'a great following from Ireland, they used to come over in boats. Everton were the first team I think … that had a big Irish supporters' club.' Many of the Irish-born priests in the city were Everton supporters, and Farrell and Eglington occasionally turned out for a priests' team who would take on (and beat) opposition such as the Bootle police team, contributing to the perception that Everton was the more Catholic of Liverpool's two main teams.[10] The 1950s though was not a particularly successful period for Everton: they struggled in the league and played in the Second Division from 1951 to 1954, their middling fortunes probably acting as a brake on greater Irish support.

Other clubs popular with Irish players and supporters included Aston Villa, the favoured team of many of the Irish in Birmingham and home in the 1950s to Irish internationals such as Con Martin, Davy Walsh and Pat Saward. In London, Woolwich Arsenal had initially drawn support from Irish workers at the Woolwich armaments factory in south-east London, where the club was formed in 1886. The Irish connection grew stronger when it moved in 1913 to Highbury in north

London, an area popular with Irish immigrants. During the 1930s many went to Highbury to see the legendary Jimmy Dunne, who as a Sheffield United player in 1930/1 had racked up fifty goals in league and cup competitions, including a staggering nine hat-tricks; the following season he scored in twelve successive top-flight games, a record that still stands.

After the war most London-bound Irish professionals gravitated to West Ham in the east of the city. These included some of Ireland's leading internationals, such as Tommy Moroney, Frank O'Farrell, Freddie Kearns and Noel Cantwell, all of whom were born in Cork. The city had close economic links with East London through the Ford Motor factory, and after it shed workers in Cork in the 1930s, many took up new jobs in the expanding Ford works in Dagenham. Among these emigrants was the father of the future Irish international Charlie Hurley, who, six months after Charlie's birth in Cork in 1936, moved with his family to Rainham in Essex to work in Dagenham. Charlie made a name for himself with Millwall (1953–7) and Sunderland (1957–69) as a tough and skilful centre-half and made his debut for the Republic of Ireland against England on 19 May 1957, outplaying Tommy Taylor, England's highly-rated centre-forward. This was one of the proudest moments of his father's life, and for weeks afterwards his fellow Irishmen at Ford gladly took on most of his work as he lovingly related the details of his son's performance.[11]

The immediate post-war period saw a marked increase in Irish professional footballers playing in the Football League. Between 1945 and 1949 English clubs paid out the (then) considerable sum of £100,000 for players from the Republic, some of whom became outstanding figures in the English game.[12] These Irishmen played an important ambassadorial role for their country, whose precise constitutional status was often a matter of confusion to many people in England. Jackie Carey, usually known as 'Johnny' in England, led the way. In addition to his achievements with Manchester United, he captained a Rest of Europe team against Great Britain (1947), became the first Irish player to win the English football writers Footballer of Year Award (1949) and was voted Britain's Sportsman of the Year in 1950. Dubbed

'Gentleman Johnny' by the English press, the relaxed, pipe-smoking Carey was widely respected for his skilful play, sporting attitude and genial character. Other notable Irish footballers, such as Peter Farrell, Tommy Eglington, Con Martin, Arthur Fitzsimons and Joe Haverty, were similarly admired for their footballing ability and amiable, unassuming personalities. Many English people who knew and cared little about Irish affairs and would have struggled to recognise a single Irish politician, could reel off the names of Ireland's leading footballers, who made a notable and underrated contribution to improving post-war Anglo-Irish relations. The long-serving Dublin-based Manchester United scout Billy Behan noted with pride 'that emigrant Irish soccer players by their character, sportsmanship and general behaviour in England have done so much towards raising the prestige and standing of Irishmen generally in England'.[13]

Outstanding Northern Irish footballers, such as Peter Doherty, Danny Blanchflower, Jimmy McIlroy, Peter McParland and Harry Gregg, did the same, earning considerable goodwill for 'Ireland'. Blanchflower, twice voted footballer of the year (1958 and 1961), was a singularly articulate figure who wrote columns for several newspapers and the left-wing *New Statesman* magazine, and numbered the Spurs-supporting philosopher A.J. Ayer among his friends.[14] He regularly challenged the game's conventions and values, criticising the maximum wage and restrictive contracts imposed on players, and insisted that football's primary purpose was to entertain. In addition to these well-known personalities, many other Irish professional footballers settled in Britain, raised families there and became respected figures in their localities, making their own unheralded contributions to improving relations between the two islands.

* * *

Partly owing to Carey's influence, there would be a significant Irish presence at Manchester United for the next half century, as it became the club of choice for aspiring Irish professionals. Carey retired in 1953 to make way for a group of talented young players who would later achieve fame as 'the Busby Babes'. Among these was the Dublin-born inside-forward Liam Whelan (known as 'Billy' to his English teammates), who made his first-team debut in 1955 and soon staked a claim to being the most promising Irish player of his generation, winning consecutive League Championship medals in 1956 and 1957 and finishing as the team's top scorer with thirty-three goals in the 1956/7 season. In January 1957 he scored a crucial goal against Athletic Bilbao in the away leg of a European Cup quarter-final, collecting the ball in his own half of the pitch and gliding past five defenders before scoring. When this was shown on a Pathé newsreel in the Savoy Cinema in Dublin, the audience spontaneously leapt to their feet to cheer their local hero. For all his talent, he was a quiet and modest young man, a devout Catholic who tended to fix a look of pained disappointment on teammates who used bad language: Nobby Stiles (a Catholic of Irish descent himself) admitted that he 'would rather be caught swearing by the pope than by Billy Whelan'.[15]

In 1957 Manchester United were drawn against Shamrock Rovers in the first round of the European Cup in the first competitive match between an English and Irish club since the nineteenth century. Like Busby's team, Rovers were a talented, charismatic group of young players who played entertaining attacking football. The first leg on 25 September 1957 attracted over 46,000 spectators to Dalymount Park (despite the fact that the country was gripped by a serious outbreak of the highly contagious Asian 'flu). They witnessed a dazzling display from United, with Whelan, playing only a stone's throw from his family home in Cabra, performing brilliantly and scoring twice in a 6–0 win. Irish supporters had never seen anything quite like it: a glowing newspaper report noted the 'beautiful patterns [and] scintillating brilliance' of United's football. The young Eamon Dunphy recalled that after the game he and his friends 'dispersed in the chill, late evening air to wonder at the spectacle we'd witnessed. We talked of little else for days. We would remember it forever.'[16]

Less than five months later, on 6 February 1958 the aeroplane carrying the Manchester United party back from a European Cup match in Belgrade crashed in Munich. There were twenty-three fatalities, among them eight of the United players, including Whelan. The destruction of this much-loved team was mourned throughout Europe and the death of Ireland's most promising young player compounded the grief of Irish football followers.[17] Other fatalities were also well known to the Irish public, including Frank Swift, the big, genial English goalkeeper who had frustrated home supporters with his superb display at Dalymount in 1946 and had travelled to Belgrade as the football correspondent of the *News of the World*. Oscar Traynor described the crash as 'the greatest tragedy in the history of football in these islands', while Eamon Dunphy (who four years later would join United as an apprentice) recalled that 'the pall of despair that spread across the city touched even those who knew nothing of sport, "foreign" or otherwise'.[18] Whelan's funeral to Glasnevin cemetery on 12 February was the largest seen in Dublin for many years, more akin to that of a revered statesman than a young footballer. The future taoiseach Bertie Ahern remembered hundreds of young Home Farm players forming a guard of honour and, aged six, he decided there and then he 'would always support United'.[19] Busby's team was also much admired in Northern Ireland, which contributed centre-half Jackie Blanchflower and goalkeeper Harry Gregg. The future IRA commander and Sinn Féin politician Martin McGuinness, then seven years old, recalled that the tragedy had a profound effect in Derry and made keen Manchester United supporters of himself and his brothers.[20]

Bobby Charlton's observation that 'before Munich it was Manchester's club, afterwards everyone felt they owned a little bit of it' was particularly apposite for Ireland. The emotional impact of the tragedy multiplied United's appeal. Matt Busby (whose maternal grandfather was Irish) had always felt a strong connection to Ireland and visited regularly. He was a close friend of the Cunningham family who ran Shamrock Rovers and often stayed in their Dublin home. When the pressures of managing Manchester United mounted, he liked to come to Ireland to play golf, attend horse-racing meetings, or hire a car and drive through the Irish countryside, where he was rarely recognised; he also made regular visits to Liam Whelan's grave in Glasnevin.[21] He was often accompanied by the Dubliner Billy Behan, who had been a reserve goalkeeper at Old Trafford for the 1933/4 season before returning to Dublin to resume his career with Shamrock Rovers and winning a second FAI Cup medal in 1936; he also managed the cup-winning Drumcondra team of 1954. Possessed of a detailed knowledge of the domestic game and a keen eye for young talent, he kept up his connection with United, becoming the club's chief scout in Dublin and a key figure in consolidating its links with Ireland. English clubs looked more closely at Ireland after Carey's success at Old Trafford and some outstanding performances by Irish under-age teams: in May 1947 the Irish schoolboys beat England 8–3 at Dalymount Park in their first ever international match, and a year later the FAI Youths beat Liverpool Youths 5–1. Future Irish internationals such as Arthur Fitzsimons and George Cummins came to light in these games, alerting English clubs to a new source of talent. From this time onwards Behan became 'United's man in Dublin' and would direct outstanding players such as Whelan, John Giles, Tony Dunne and many others to Old Trafford.[22]

When recruiting in the Republic, Manchester United probably benefited from the widespread belief that it was a 'Catholic club': Busby was a devout Catholic, as was his Welsh-born assistant Jimmy Murphy, whose parents came from Mullinivat, County Kilkenny. The club drew strong support from Manchester's large Catholic community and Catholic priests were always prominent in the main stand at Old Trafford. The four managers who came after Busby – Wilf McGuinness, Frank O'Farrell (the club's only Irish manager), Tommy Docherty and Dave Sexton – were all Catholics, although this was probably coincidence rather than policy. Busby's assurances to anxious parents that their young sons' spiritual welfare would not be neglected seems to have carried some weight in their decision to allow them to go to Manchester. When signing a player from a Catholic family, the club's devoutly Catholic chief scout Joe Armstrong was known to seal the deal by presenting the parents with one of the many Miraculous Medals he had brought back from Lourdes.[23]

The point though can be pressed too far: people of all religions and none could be found at Old Trafford, and United drew support from across the religious spectrum, including the city's large Jewish population. It was a club with Catholic associations rather than a Catholic club. Renowned United players such as Harry Gregg, Jackie Blanchflower and George Best were Northern Irish Protestants, and were followed by others such as Sammy McIlroy, Jimmy Nicholl, David McCreery and Norman Whiteside. These were usually spotted by Bob Bishop, the club's scout in Northern Ireland (1950–87) who played a similar role to that of Billy Behan in the South.[24] United was by far the best-supported English club in Ireland, with seventy-nine official supporters' branches spread throughout the island. Some saw the club as a genuinely unifying force that brought people of different political and religious outlooks together, and in Northern Ireland it was sometimes regarded as a neutral option for those who wanted to support a club capable of challenging for European trophies without endorsing the tribalism of the Glasgow Old Firm.[25]

After Munich, Irish support for United was consolidated by Busby's use of Irish players, such as John Giles and Joe Carolan of Dublin and Sammy McMillan and Jimmy Nicholson of Belfast, to rebuild the team. In November 1960 he paid West Ham £29,500 (a record fee for a full-back) for Noel Cantwell, who had captained the Republic of Ireland since 1957. Cantwell, an original and incisive theorist of the game, found United stuck in the pre-Munich era, and his leadership qualities led Busby to make him team captain in 1963. This was welcomed by young players like Bobby Charlton, who believed that Cantwell's assurance and authority instilled a new confidence into the team: Charlton recalled 'when he led us out for the 1963 cup final, I thought "This is good – we have a real captain."'[26] United went on to beat Leicester City in that final, with a team that also featured Giles and Tony Dunne (who had joined from Shelbourne in 1960). It was the club's first FA Cup win since Carey had captained the team to victory in 1948, and its first trophy since Munich. Though dogged by injury, Cantwell remained club captain until 1967, and many expected him to succeed Busby.

He was, though, rather eclipsed by another Irishman at Old Trafford. George Best, nurtured at the Cregagh Boys' Club in east Belfast, made his first-team debut aged seventeen in September 1963 and helped the team to win league titles in 1965 and 1967. Best played the game with a unique combination of skill, athleticism and balance that made him one of the all-time greats: he was voted Footballer of the Year in both England and Europe in 1968, before his twenty-second birthday. That year he was outstanding when United won the European Cup against Benfica at Wembley (in a team that also included the Irish internationals Dunne and Shay Brennan). In Ireland Best's popularity knew no border, and he inspired levels of mass adulation never previously seen for a footballer. When United defended the European Cup, they faced League of Ireland champions Waterford in the first round on 18 September 1968. To cater for the unprecedented demand for tickets, the game was played at Lansdowne Road. It drew a crowd of over 48,000, then the largest to attend a soccer match in Ireland, many there simply to see Best. The United midfielder Paddy Crerand's abiding memory of the day was the difficulty in clearing the dressing room of gardaí, so intent were they on getting Best's autograph.[27]

While many had expected the 1968 European Cup win to spark a new golden age, it effectively marked the end of an era. United went into a decline that an increasingly troubled Best could not halt and were relegated from the First Division in 1974. They were promoted the following season but did not win a League Championship again until 1993. During these relatively lean years the club held its support in Ireland, helped by a steady stream of talented Irish players, such as Gerry Daly, Sammy McIlroy, Jimmy Nicholl, Ashley Grimes, Frank Stapleton, Kevin Moran, Paul McGrath, Norman Whiteside and Mal Donaghy, who were among its most impressive performers through the 1970s and 1980s. In the 1978/9 season nine Irishmen played in the first team.[28]

***

There was significant Irish support for other clubs too, including Leeds United, primarily due to the presence of John Giles, who had joined in 1963. Under the management of Don Revie, he became one of the most impressive midfielders in the English game, helping Leeds win League Championships in 1969 and 1974, as well as several cups and a hat-full of runner-up medals. Although the only Irish player at the club, he was such a hero to Irish supporters that many became Leeds' fans and continued their support long after he left. The number of Irish Arsenal supporters also sharply increased during the 1970s, after the club fielded three of the most exciting young Irish talents in years: Liam Brady, David O'Leary and Frank Stapleton. These were complemented by the strong Northern Ireland contingent of Pat Rice, Sammy Nelson and Pat Jennings. When the club appeared in three consecutive FA Cup finals (1978–80), six of their starting eleven in all three games were Irish, and they were managed by the former Arsenal and Northern Ireland captain Terry Neill. The strong Irish presence at Arsenal was further proof of the importance of a discerning scout in alerting a club to talented players: the Dublin-born Bill Darby was Arsenal's chief scout in Ireland from 1968 and was instrumental in the signing of Brady, Stapleton and O'Leary, and later John Devine and Niall Quinn.[29]

Like their predecessors in the immediate post-war period, Irish players such as Cantwell, Best, Giles, Jennings, Neill, Dougan and Brady were among the leading personalities in the English game in the 1960s and 1970s, and among the best-known Irishmen in England. Jennings was voted Footballer of the Year in 1973 and PFA Player of the Year in 1976, while Brady won the latter award in 1979. They were not only skilled sportsmen, but also accomplished media performers. At a time when the Irish were often portrayed in the British media as either violent bigots or perverse idiots, intelligent and articulate footballers did much to refute negative stereotypes. Dougan became one of the key pundits in ITV's pioneering football coverage in the early 1970s and others followed suit. Irishmen were also to the fore in challenging the game's orthodoxies: Best's individuality, Bohemianism and celebrity outraged traditionalists; Cantwell, Neill and Dougan served as successive chairmen of the PFA from 1966 to 1978 and worked assiduously to improve players' contractual position; while Eamon Dunphy's *Only a Game?* (1976) was the first memoir written by a footballer that honestly laid bare the life of the journeyman professional.[30] Of course, Irish players were never universally popular and in the unforgiving atmosphere of the football stadium they could at times be subjected to virulent anti-Irish abuse by opposing players and spectators. And even when the home crowd turned against one, his nationality was rarely an asset. Off the pitch too they received their share of racism and stereotyping: Best's self-destructive behaviour was often attributed to his mercurial Irish temperament and when arrested in London on a drink-driving charge, he was addressed by the police officer as 'You little Irish wanker. You Irish scum. Another piece of Irish dirt.'[31]

From the mid-1970s, the most successful team in England was Liverpool FC, which won ten league titles (1976–90) and four European Champions Cups (1977–84). Despite the strong Irish influence on the city, Irish players had rarely featured at the club. It was only in 1970 that Steve Heighway, born in Dublin to English parents, became the first Liverpool player to represent the FAI team. During the 1980s he was followed by others, such as Ronnie Whelan (who captained the club), Mark Lawrenson, Michael Robinson, Jim Beglin, Ray Houghton, John Aldridge and Steve Staunton. The combination of a strong Irish presence and sustained success in English and European competitions prompted a notable increase in the club's Irish support.

Although English clubs had dominated Europe through the late 1970s and early 1980s, the Heysel Stadium disaster of 1985 marked a sharp downturn. Thirty-nine people were killed and over 300 injured when a wall collapsed after a group of Liverpool supporters charged their Juventus counterparts before a European Cup final. English clubs were subsequently banned from playing in European competitions for five years. Hooliganism remained a serious problem in England, the atmosphere in grounds was often threatening and overt racism was blithely ignored by both clubs and the football authorities. The sport also suffered from a serious lack of investment, with stadiums often rundown and unsafe. This was highlighted by the Hillsborough disaster of 15 April 1989 in which ninety-four Liverpool supporters were killed in a crush against perimeter fencing (another three died later). In response, the government-sponsored Taylor Report (1990) recommended sweeping reforms, including the building of all-seater stadiums to facilitate greater crowd control and safety. Its proposals chimed with the ambitions of the major clubs, who had already taken steps to become more commercialised and maximise revenue. Demanding that television companies pay more for their coverage, in 1992 they led a breakaway from the Football League to form a twenty-team Premier League overseen by the FA.

English football changed dramatically. Television deals, commercial sponsorship, intensive marketing of club merchandise and increased ticket prices generated ever greater levels of income for the leading clubs, which began to recruit the best players from across the globe. There were fewer places for Irish players at top clubs, with the exception of Manchester United, which still maintained a strong Irish presence during the 1990s and early 2000s. The most notable of these was Roy Keane, who became the club's most successful ever captain (1997–2005), leading them to four league titles, two FA Cups and a unique treble that included the European Champions League in 1999; he became the first FAI international to be inducted into the English Football Hall of Fame in 2004. Other Irishmen, such as Denis Irwin, John O'Shea and Jonny Evans, also had successful careers at Old Trafford, but most Irish players struggled to hold down first-team places in an increasingly competitive environment. More and more Irish professionals found themselves joining the Premier League's less fashionable teams or dropping down into the lower tiers of the Football League. In recent years Republic of Ireland internationals have clustered in clubs such as Burnley, Sheffield United and Sunderland (taken over in 2006 by the Drumaville consortium of Irish businessmen led by Niall Quinn), although this does not appear to have resulted in any significant increase in their Irish support. Commitment to English clubs is clearly not solely dependent on the presence of Irish players.

Manchester United, Liverpool and Arsenal continue to draw most Irish support, with Everton, Leeds, Aston Villa and Chelsea accounting for most of the rest.[32] In 2014 it was calculated that 121,000 Irish fans travelled to watch football in England, topping the list of foreign visitors ahead of Norway (93,000), Sweden (58,000) and the United States (53,000). This usually amounts to over 3,000 travelling supporters a week, most of whom attend the grounds of the 'Big Three'.[33] While there are some in Ireland who support both a local and a cross-channel club, some domestic supporters dismiss followers of English clubs as either sports tourists or armchair fans in thrall to the aggressive marketing of the Premier League and their broadcasting paymasters. In response, followers of English clubs point to the poor standard of football and facilities in Ireland and insist that to see the best Irish players in action they have no choice but to watch them on television or travel to games in England. They maintain their commitment is no less sincere or genuine than that of domestic supporters, and often point to their clubs' strong historical links with Ireland. Such support has generally proved to be steadfast, with the emotional bond between club and supporters reinforced by adversity as well as success, disappointment often producing a dogged solidarity and the irrepressible hope that next season will be better.

Irish tricolours emblazoned with the names of English clubs are often seen in cross-channel stadiums. They illustrate the complex and complementary nature of identities, which are not entirely defined by national origins but also have important personal, familial, local, civic, regional and trans-national dimensions. For most Irish supporters national and club loyalties present no contradiction, but seamlessly overlap. Major football clubs, just like nations, cherish their anthems and emblems; attract fervent and enduring allegiance; detail their trials and triumphs in elaborate (if not always impartial) histories; define themselves in opposition to their rivals and enemies; celebrate their victories with mass public events, and commemorate their heroes with statues and buildings. Irish followers no more regard the cross-channel clubs they support as foreign entities than they regard the game they watch as a foreign game. (It is noteworthy that their support is rarely transferred to the English national team, even when that team features players from a favoured club.) Many committed Irish nationalists have no difficulty in combining their politics with keen support for an English club. During the 1970s Paddy Crerand met republican paramilitaries in Northern Ireland in an effort to persuade them to renounce violence; he was particularly struck by the fact that so many were keen Manchester United supporters. Eventually recognising that many working-class republicans were eager supporters of English clubs, in the 1990s the

Sinn Féin newspaper *An Phoblacht* began to give English soccer wider and more sympathetic coverage.[34]

Irish soccer supporters have long stressed the game's international rather than English character, something which has become increasingly evident as it has become ever more globalised. Today support for the leading English clubs extends far beyond the community that originally nurtured them, and a Manchester United or Liverpool replica shirt is as likely to be seen in Bangkok or Durban as it is in Belfast or Dublin. It can be argued that in the twenty-first century, major football clubs are the purest form of imagined community. After all, nations are not simply products of the imagination, but are also usually based on genuine geographical, historical, linguistic, ethnic, political, religious and cultural foundations. In contrast, the internationally supported football club attracts followers across all such boundaries, linked together by a shared bond of support that is freely chosen and open to all. This is fed by a lifelong store of experiences and memories that readily emerge in conversation, argument and reminiscences, and supporters, regardless of where they live, see themselves as part of the club's history and traditions.

14

Struggle and Survival: Domestic Football Since 1972

The 1970s were the bleakest decade yet for Irish domestic football, North and South. Attendances continued to fall, along with the general level of excitement at grounds, the one compounding the other. To make matters worse, in imitation of what was happening in English football, small-scale hooliganism and offensive chanting had crept into some stadiums by the 1970s, making attendance even less attractive. As they had done in earlier decades, clubs tried to spark public interest by recruiting famous players from abroad, such as England World Cup winners: Bobby Charlton played three times for Waterford in 1976, while Geoff Hurst managed three goals in three appearances with Cork Celtic, and goalkeeper Gordon Banks played once for St Patrick's Athletic in 1977. The Glasgow Celtic legend Jimmy Johnstone played nine times for Shelbourne (1977–8) and the great German striker Uwe Seeler scored twice in a single game with Cork Celtic (1978), for whom George Best also made three appearances (1975–6). Although these well-known figures attracted large crowds at first, they were usually past their prime; particularly so in the case of Best, who clearly lacked both fitness and motivation. Such temporary signings smacked of desperation and led to accusations that the league had become a circus, preferring to pay inflated salaries to ageing celebrities rather than nurture its own talent. They probably did more to alienate existing supporters than attract new ones, and the overall effect was to weaken the league further.

Some clubs seriously overstretched themselves by paying wages they could not afford. After signing the former England international Rodney Marsh in February 1976, Cork Hibernians ran up unsustainable debts and withdrew from the league the following August. Hibs had been one of the most successful clubs of the early 1970s, winning the league title in 1971 and the FAI Cup in 1972 and 1973. Although there was strong support for the game in Cork, an unsettled period ensued for League of Ireland soccer in the city, which until then had hosted two clubs: Cork Celtic and Cork Hibernians. Albert Rovers replaced Hibs in 1976, playing as Cork Alberts and later as Cork United. The club, though, enjoyed little success and the division of playing talent and support among Cork's two league clubs proved unsustainable: Celtic failed to gain re-election to the league in 1979 and went out of business. Flower Lodge, their home ground, was sold to the Cork County GAA Board and redeveloped as Páirc Uí Rinn. Cork United also found itself in serious financial trouble and was expelled from the league in 1982, leaving the city without a league club until Cork City FC was elected in 1984.[1]

Life was particularly difficult for newly elected clubs such as Thurles Town FC, who were admitted to the League of Ireland in 1977. Although they brought league football to Tipperary for the first time, they relied strongly on Dublin-based players and failed to attract much local support. Unable to pay players' wages, Thurles withdrew from the league in 1982. Regional clubs often found it difficult to survive long enough to build up a strong local identity and support-base, and regularly went out of business and reformed, often under a new name. Galway Rovers became Galway United, Waterford AFC became Waterford United, and Limerick AFC became Limerick United; some members of Limerick United then broke away to form Limerick City, which led to a High Court case in 1983 in which City were elected to the league in place of United. None of this did anything for the league's reputation as a sustainable competition.[2]

During the 1970s the League of Ireland found itself in a state of almost permanent crisis. Televised English football, which had already eaten into attendances, became more extensive and sophisticated and proved more attractive to most supporters than the domestic game. Critics dismissed the league as a backwater that had forfeited public support by serving up mediocre football in shabby surroundings and maintained that falling attendances showed discernment rather than disloyalty. In the early 1980s the sponsorship of the league by a fast-food entrepreneur under the unwieldy title of the 'Pat Grace Kentucky Fried Chicken League of Ireland' was gleefully seized upon by detractors, and the failings of the 'Chicken League' provided ample scope for ridicule.[3]

While the popularity of domestic association football was declining sharply in Dublin during the 1970s, Gaelic football was on the rise. In 1973 Kevin Heffernan, who had captained Dublin to an All-Ireland title in 1958, took over a struggling team that had been playing to dwindling crowds for the last decade. He transformed its fortunes, guiding it to All-Ireland senior titles in 1974, 1976 and 1977. Attendances at Dublin's games exploded, dwarfing those of domestic (and even international) soccer matches. Many of Dublin's new supporters were soccer fans, who brought with them soccer songs and chants, much to the chagrin of GAA traditionalists. Offending Gaelic sensibilities mattered little to most Dublin supporters, one of whom, Fran Gavin, later head of the PFA of Ireland and the FAI's League of Ireland director, recalled that for 'soccer fans who didn't like the GAA, and personally I didn't ... it gave me an excuse to say ... it's not really the GAA, it's the Dubs'.[4]

Most of the Dublin team and management were well disposed to soccer; Heffernan was a keen supporter, the team regularly played soccer matches for charity, and one of its key players, Kevin Moran, joined Manchester United in 1978. This helped blur the lines between the two codes, with many sports fans taking a strong interest in both. The intense rivalry between Dublin and Kerry was particularly compelling: played in front of crowds of over 70,000, these epic clashes offered a level of spectacle and excitement far greater than anything in domestic soccer. Although Dublin struggled to sustain its success, winning only two All-Ireland Championships between 1978 and 2010, support for the team remained strong and was sealed with an unprecedented six All-Ireland senior titles in a row in 2020. It provided something that had always been lacking in the fragmented world of Dublin soccer – a team that represented the entire city and gave enthusiastic expression to its civic identity.

From the early 1970s there was a widespread recognition that drastic action was required to reinvigorate Irish domestic soccer. In August 1973 'the biggest coaching scheme ever attempted in Ireland' was launched by the National Commission for Amateur Football, a body set up with government assistance. Chaired by the FAI patron David Andrews TD, whose family had a long-standing association with the game, it published an ambitious report in May 1973 that sought to promote soccer intensively and broaden its nationwide appeal. It aspired to create improved facilities in local clubs, schools and workplaces to develop the game at grass-roots level and provide a stream of players and support for the League of Ireland. Funding for the new coaching scheme was to be provided by a grant from COSAC (the National Council for Sport and Recreation) and a private sweepstake, the FAI Development Fund Members Draw. John Jarman (formerly the English FA's amateur midland regional coach) was appointed FAI national coach in 1974, the first time the position was filled since it had been briefly occupied by Alex Stevenson in 1953. Jarman, though, soon found himself hampered by poor funding and administrative structures that handicapped his efforts and quit after eighteen months, leaving the report's ambitious aspirations unfulfilled.[5]

The decline in the League of Ireland's popularity affected all clubs, including the once glamorous Shamrock Rovers, who failed to win a league title from 1965 to 1984. Their attendances fell drastically and rivalries with other clubs lost their intensity; in 1976 the club was even forced to apply for re-election to the league for the first time in its history. This prompted the Kilcoyne brothers, who had taken over Shamrock Rovers from the Cunningham family in 1972, to embark on a bold experiment by appointing John Giles as team manager in 1977. Giles immediately took steps to improve the club's pitch and facilities at Glenmalure Park and brought in Irish internationals such as Eamon Dunphy, Ray Treacy and Paddy Mulligan. His plan was to transform Rovers into a high-quality professional club that would attract the best local young players who might otherwise go to England. He hoped that its example would encourage other clubs to improve standards and raise the overall quality of the league; there was even talk of Rovers challenging for European trophies.[6]

However, some other clubs and supporters looked on Giles's efforts with suspicion, fearing that Rovers would monopolise young talent and dominate the league. In the event, Giles led Rovers to an FAI Cup victory in 1978 but failed to win any other major trophies. Crowds at Glenmalure Park remained modest and investment in players and facilities caused the club's debts to mount. Disappointed by the lack of progress, Giles quit in 1983. He was succeeded by Jim McLaughlin, a Derry-born former Northern Ireland international who had led Dundalk to three League Championships and three FAI Cups in the 1970s. McLaughlin built on the foundations laid by Giles and managed Rovers to the most successful period in its history, with four consecutive league titles (1984–7) and three FAI Cups (1985–7). The league, though, was in such a depressed state by this time that even the sustained success of a club with Rovers' history and crowd-pulling potential had little effect on its fortunes.

Despite McLaughlin's achievements, the Kilcoynes decided that the club's growing debts could only be cleared by selling Glenmalure Park to property developers. Their plans provoked fierce opposition from supporters, who organised themselves into the lobby group KRAM ('Keep Rovers at Milltown'). The campaign mobilised many followers who no longer regularly attended games but still had a strong sentimental attachment to the club. Their frequent and vocal protests were ignored by the Kilcoynes, who sold the stadium in 1988. Within a couple of years Glenmalure Park was obliterated by a suburban housing estate; a memorial erected by supporters in 1998 is all that recalls its former use. The loss of Glenmalure Park was lamented not just by followers of Shamrock Rovers but by supporters generally, who remembered it as one of the league's better stadiums and the scene of many memorable matches. That this could happen to the most successful club in the league's history showed the sorry state to which Irish domestic football had fallen; that it was done by a family deeply involved in Irish soccer for decades seemed like a particularly bitter betrayal. It highlighted the fact that a football club could mean very different things to different people: to some, it was a home from home, an institution that added excitement and community to their lives, whose heritage and traditions were not for sale; to others, it was primarily a business that had to pay its way.

Supporting a domestic club in preference to one of the top English teams was by this time often seen as a form of eccentricity or perverseness. In 1992 pressure on Ireland's domestic game intensified with the founding of the Premier League in England, which became the most popular sports league in the world with a global audience of over four billion viewers. Live televised games, often featuring teams with strong Irish support, became ever more common and sometimes clashed with domestic fixtures. In terms of finance, facilities and football the gap between the Premier League and the Irish domestic leagues became even more glaring. This formed the backdrop for proposals in 1996 for Wimbledon FC to relocate to Dublin. Wimbledon, a modestly supported Premier League club managed by the former Irish international Joe Kinnear, had no stadium of its own after leaving its Plough Lane ground in south-west London in 1991. It was proposed therefore that a consortium of Irish businessmen should buy a majority stake in the club, which would then move to a new purpose-built stadium in Dublin but still play in the Premier League. Advocates of the scheme argued that it would bring regular top-class club soccer to Dublin and that Wimbledon would evolve into an Irish club, attracting the best young Irish players and growing Irish support. The proposal, though, foundered on the steadfast opposition of Wimbledon's supporters, the FAI, and League of Ireland supporters and clubs, all twenty-two of which voted against it, claiming that an Irish-based club playing in the English Premier League would do irreparable harm to the domestic league.[7]

Since the mid-1980s the League of Ireland had tried various ways to revive its fortunes. In 1985 it split into a Premier Division and a second tier (First Division) that included several new clubs to broaden its nationwide appeal and add the excitement of promotion and relegation battles. Live television screenings began in 1996 with the showing of Derry City against Shelbourne at Tolka Park on RTÉ's Network 2. Matches were often played on Friday evenings to avoid clashing with televised English games, and in 2003 there was a break with over a century of tradition as 'summer football' was introduced: the new league season ran from March to October rather than August to April to spare crowds and pitches from the worst of the Irish winter. None of these measures caused any great upsurge in attendances, but they probably contributed to the league's survival. Most Irish clubs retained a dedicated hard-core support, who saw themselves as holders of a more authentic faith than those in thrall to the corporate excesses of a foreign league.

The unprecedented success enjoyed by the Republic's national team from 1988 had little effect on domestic soccer. Jack Charlton saw himself as responsible for the results of the national team rather than the development of Irish football. He made it clear that he had no interest in a struggling semi-professional league, never selecting even a token home-based player in his squads. After the appearance of Pat Byrne of Shamrock Rovers against Denmark on 13 November 1985, no League of Ireland footballer played for the Republic in a competitive international until Jack Byrne of Rovers was capped against Wales on 11 October 2020. In the middle of this period even former League of Ireland players rarely featured: of the 2002 World Cup squad, only one had ever played in the league (Roy Keane for Cobh Ramblers (1989–90)). As for supporters, most of those who scrambled for tickets for international matches and were prepared to spend large sums of money following the Republic abroad regarded the League of Ireland with indifference or contempt, although many keenly supported British clubs such as Manchester United, Liverpool and Celtic. This led some followers of domestic soccer to dismiss the Republic's 'International Brigade' as glory-hunters without any real commitment to the Irish game. There was clearly more than just one soccer community in Ireland and while international football had moved into the mainstream, the domestic game remained on the margins.[8]

There were, though, occasional success stories. After withdrawal from the Irish League in 1972, Derry City FC continued as a junior club. Applications to the IFA to rejoin the Irish League were repeatedly refused so long as the club insisted on playing at the Brandywell. In 1973 Derry had applied to be admitted to FAI competitions but was told that this was not possible under FIFA regulations.[9] Eventually, however, after much lobbying, the club was granted a special dispensation from FIFA and the IFA in 1985 to play in the League of Ireland. Derry's admission invigorated the league: it regularly drew home crowds of up to 8,000 and brought a huge travelling support wherever it went. This provided the resources to build up a strong team that had considerable success, winning the treble of League Championship, League Cup and FAI Cup in 1989, an achievement that gave an enormous boost to a city that had endured twenty years of conflict. Many saw the club's revival as the single most hopeful development in the city over the course of the Troubles, providing much needed entertainment, escapism and solidarity. There were also claims that it brought the city together, but in reality its support was almost entirely confined to the nationalist community.[10]

For Derry, playing in the League of Ireland affirmed the belief held by most of its supporters that the Republic was its natural home. The republican, and long-time Derry City supporter, Martin McGuinness (whose younger brother Paul played for the club) maintained that its followers 'were loyal soccer fans but they were also making a political statement by telling the football authorities in Belfast that they could keep their northern league with all the bigotry, prejudice and sectarianism associated with it'.[11] Derry City acted as an important unifying force for nationalists of all descriptions: the SDLP leader John Hume was a passionate supporter and club president until his death in August 2020. Hume paid tribute to the club as 'the linchpin in the life of the community ... The pride people have in this club reflects the pride we hold in our city. ... Derry City would be nothing without the people of the city'.[12] While football helped take people's minds off the Troubles, these were never too far away, such as when a large explosive device was found in the cemetery near the Brandywell before a European Cup tie against Benfica on 13 September 1989. Club officials, realising that notifying the security forces risked a lengthy bomb disposal operation and cancellation of the fixture, decided instead to contact McGuinness, who managed to disarm the device himself while the officials sheltered behind gravestones. This allowed the match to go ahead as planned, watched by a sell-out attendance of 12,500.[13] However, as the novelty of playing in the League of Ireland wore off and the team's performances became more erratic, Derry City too struggled to hold its support and fell into financial difficulties. By 2000 it was facing bankruptcy owing to an accumulation of unpaid taxes. Extensive fund-raising by local supporters and a series of friendly matches against Manchester United, Celtic, Real Madrid and Barcelona eventually helped keep it afloat, and it continues to make a vital contribution to Derry's sporting and civic life.

Between Shamrock Rovers' four successive titles (1984–7) and Dundalk's five triumphs (2014–16; 2018–19), no single club dominated the league. Established Dublin clubs such as Shelbourne (6), St Patrick's Athletic (5), Bohemians (4) and Shamrock Rovers (3) took eighteen of the twenty-seven titles (1988–2013). The remainder went to Dundalk (3), Cork City (2), Derry City (2) and one apiece for Drogheda and Sligo Rovers. From 2014 Dundalk were the dominant team, with Cork City (who won a league and cup double in 2017) and Shamrock Rovers their main challengers. Rovers went on to dominate the early 2020s, winning three consecutive titles (2020–2). In a survey carried out in 2019 to determine the best-supported teams in Ireland, the only domestic clubs to make the top ten were Cork City in sixth place (with 7 per cent of respondents) and Dundalk in eighth (with 4 per cent).[14]

These years saw considerable turmoil for many clubs. The feverish overspending characteristic of the Irish economy in the early 2000s found its way into the League of Ireland, where clubs have often been prone to their own form of boom-and-bust economics. Some, such as Bohemians and Shelbourne, spent nearly €2 million a year on wages for full-time professional players. Gate receipts brought in less than a quarter of this amount; clubs scrambled to make up the remainder from general fundraising, payments from television networks and UEFA prize money.[15] The 2005 Genesis report described the league as 'trapped in a downward spiral. A poor product with unattractive facilities leads to a lack of support, minimal sponsorship and low levels of income.' It further noted that the league 'is near to being economically bankrupt and is unsustainable in its current format and incapable of sustaining itself into the future'. Among the failings listed were the poor stadium facilities, excessive spending on players' wages, failure to secure adequate funding from the FAI and local and central government, failure to develop strong links with local communities and under-age football clubs, and poor promotion and marketing.[16] In line with the report's recommendations, the league merged into the FAI in 2006 and the following year introduced a salary cap. Even before the financial crash of 2008–9, most league clubs were under severe pressure, and in the recession that followed, long-established members such as Shamrock Rovers, Bohemians, Shelbourne, Cork City, Drogheda United and Derry City went into examinership and came near to extinction, only to be saved by the efforts of dedicated supporters. Others were not so lucky and during 2010–12 Cobh Ramblers, Sporting Fingal, Galway United and Monaghan Town were forced to withdraw from the league.

The fortunes of Shamrock Rovers perhaps most accurately reflect the general fortunes of the league. After the sale of Glenmalure Park, the club moved around Dublin, playing at Dalymount Park, Tolka Park, Richmond Park, Morton Stadium, the RDS, and even had a 'home' game in Cork in 2003. For many followers, it seemed to have lost its identity and support fell away. However, from the late 1990s, in conjunction with South Dublin County Council, plans were set in train to give Rovers a permanent home in a new stadium in the sprawling south-western suburb of Tallaght. In 2000 the first sod was turned on the site by Taoiseach Bertie Ahern, but there followed a series of delays and legal wranglings, including a bitter dispute with the local GAA club, Thomas Davis. In the meantime, the club's debts mounted and in 2005 it went into receivership but was saved by a supporters' group who assumed ownership. Legal battles eventually went its way, allowing development to resume. The new ground, a compact modern stadium with an all-seated capacity of 6,000 (later increased to 8,000), finally opened in March 2009. It brought league football to one of Ireland's most populous suburbs and helped gain new supporters and forge links with local schools and under-age clubs. Buoyed up by the backing of the local community and the return of disenchanted supporters, Rovers recorded the highest attendances in the league, regularly filling the ground, and its fortunes improved. It won five league titles from 2010 to 2022, and in 2011 became the first Irish club to qualify for the group stages of the Europa League.[17]

**

From the mid-1970s Linfield resumed its dominance of the Irish League. Under the management of Roy Coyle (1975–90) the club won ten league titles and three IFA Cups, including six consecutive titles (1982–7). The league, though, struggled to attract support. Football in the North faced many of the same problems apparent in the South, with the added danger of sectarian violence. In the absence of any other club to support, growing numbers of nationalists in Belfast began to gravitate towards Cliftonville FC. This was partly because of the proximity of the club's ground Solitude (named after a nearby stately home) to Catholic areas of north Belfast. Before the Troubles, the streets around Solitude had been a largely lower middle-class Protestant district, as well as home to Belfast's Jewish community, but from the late 1960s there was a large influx of Catholics.[18] Throughout its history Cliftonville's amateur status and modest support often curbed its ambitions and, after winning the Irish League in 1910, the club waited another eighty-eight years to regain the trophy. On turning professional in 1974, its prospects improved, and it began to attract Catholic supporters from north and west Belfast. This provided a boost for an ailing league, but at the price of increased crowd trouble. Cliftonville's 'Red Army' of supporters included a hooligan element that frequently clashed with loyalist opponents.[19] On 21 August 1979 there were more than 1,900 police officers on duty for a match between Cliftonville and their north Belfast rivals Crusaders, the largest ever recorded at a football match in the UK, and in December 1980 rioting broke out when Cliftonville played Linfield at Windsor Park.[20] While a strong police presence (often out-numbering spectators) usually prevented violence, games between Cliftonville and its Belfast rivals were highly charged and Irish League grounds became one of the main arenas for the public expression of political and sectarian antagonisms.[21] One observer summed up domestic encounters as 'uninspired thump-it-Sammy performances in the company of racist and sectarian thugs', and was not surprised that thousands of local fans 'opt to travel to Manchester, Liverpool, London or Glasgow rather than stare into the cesspit of local soccer at close range'.[22]

The founding of the English Premier League in 1992 made the struggle to attract crowds, media attention and sponsorship even more difficult. To make the Irish League more competitive and stimulate public interest, in 1995 it was split into premier and first divisions. This though had a minimal effect and in 2003 the IFA took direct charge of top-tier football with the creation of the Irish Premier League (IPL) (renamed the Northern Ireland Football League (NIFL) in 2013). In 2004 the IFA also took over the lower two Irish League divisions, which became the Irish Intermediate League. Attendances remained low: a survey carried out in January 2004 found that 62 per cent of respondents had no interest in Irish League soccer; 35 per cent were armchair fans who rarely went to games, while only 3 per cent attended domestic matches regularly. With such a narrow support base, even established clubs struggled, and some, such as Glentoran, Ards and Coleraine, came close to collapse.[23]

Belfast remained the heartland of soccer in Northern Ireland. The dominance of the city's clubs that began in the 1880s persisted into the twenty-first century: of the 116 Irish League championships completed between 1890 and 2022, 106 were won by Belfast clubs (56 by Linfield). Despite regular predictions that the league is about to implode, it manages to survive, with its long-established clubs firmly rooted in their local communities. The traditional identification of soccer with the working class persists and has been reinforced by a highly selective education system. Catholics generally attend schools that favour Gaelic games, while among Protestants, school soccer teams are more likely to be found in working-class areas, with middle-class students mostly playing rugby, hockey and cricket. The Northern Ireland international Gareth McAuley, who won eighty caps for his country (2005–19), recalled being told at his rugby-playing school that he should give up any ambitions to play professional football and concentrate on rugby where he would meet better-connected people who could help him get on in life. Soccer's working-class character was reinforced by the Troubles: as clubs shed supporters, those most likely to remain have generally been from working-class communities.[24]

***

Since the split of 1921, inter-league fixtures kept open lines of communication between North and South, but the violence of the 1970s largely brought these matches to an end. During that decade just one game between the League of Ireland and Irish League was held (at Dalymount Park on 18 March 1974), watched by 2,000 spectators. Instead, League of Ireland selections began to arrange matches against other leagues (notably the Italian B-League), club sides and even full international teams. The league was often outclassed but battled bravely in most of these encounters: among the most notable was a 3–1 defeat in Buenos Aires on 19 April 1978 to an Argentinian team featuring ten players who would help it to win the World Cup three months later. The teams met again on 30 April 1980 at the Estadio Monumental, when a young Diego Maradona scored to give Argentina a 1–0 win. In another notable game a League of Ireland XI became the first representative team to play the Basque Country on 16 August 1979 in Bilbao, going down to a 4–1 defeat. On other occasions, League of Ireland selections, invariably managed by Brian Kerr, brought Irish soccer to places it had never been before, such as the Al-Shaab Stadium in Baghdad against Iraq on 28 April 1986 (during the war with Iran); there were also games against Saudi Arabia in Singapore in August 1986 and against the Libyan club Al Ahly Benghazi in February 1989, the last watched by a 50,000 crowd that included President Muammar Gaddafi. For such games, their hosts were usually oblivious to the intricacies of Irish soccer and tended to bill league XIs as the full Irish international side.

Teams composed of amateur League of Ireland players represented Ireland in the qualifying rounds of the 1960, 1972, 1976 and 1980 Olympic Games. Usually, Olympic football was dominated by ostensibly amateur teams from East European communist states and the league's genuine amateurs failed to progress. New rules allowed semi-professional players to represent their country in the qualifying stages of the 1988 Olympic Football Tournament, and this considerably strengthened the Irish team, which was essentially a League of Ireland XI. They were, however, drawn in a difficult group that included Spain, Sweden, Hungary and France, and failed to qualify, despite away draws in Spain and France and a memorable 3–0 win over France (the 1984 Olympic champions) at Dalymount Park on 18 November 1987, watched by a crowd of 4,000 supporters.

Games between the Irish League and League of Ireland were resumed in the 1980s and 1990s but sparked little interest. One held on 17 May 1989 at Oriel Park, Dundalk, was watched by a mere 500 spectators, and crowds at other matches in Dublin and Belfast were little better. The last encounter between the two was played before 350 spectators at Terryland Park, Galway, on 1 November 2000, and was won 2–0 by the Irish League. Afterwards inter-league contests were allowed to slip into oblivion. Since their first meeting in 1926 the two leagues played each other sixty times: the Irish League won twenty-five of these games; the League of Ireland twenty-two, and thirteen were drawn. While never rousing the level of interest or passion of full internationals, they managed to bring together players, officials and supporters from North and South, and made some contribution to easing the divide in Irish soccer.

After a decade or so of inaction, in recent years league selections (North and South) have hosted pre-season matches against English or Scottish club sides. A League of Ireland XI played the first ever soccer match at the newly built Aviva Stadium on 4 August 2010, losing 7–1 to Manchester United. The League of Ireland also provided the opposition to Manchester City and Glasgow Celtic when the Aviva hosted the Dublin Super Cup in 2011, and was well-beaten in both games, while Manchester United beat the Irish League 4–1 at Windsor Park on 15 May 2012. Perhaps the most notable feature of these games is that the visitors receive far more support than the home teams, highlighting the marginal status of domestic league football in both jurisdictions.

Since both northern and southern leagues have struggled over the last half-century, there have been regular proposals for cross-border competitions to add interest and variety to the domestic game. From 1924 club matches that pitted North against South in the Condor Cup (1924–32; 1938–44) and Intercity Cup (1941–9) were played intermittently, with varying degrees of success. There were few games after the deterioration in North–South relations in 1949–50, but matters improved sufficiently in the early 1960s to allow for a new North–South Cup, won by Linfield in 1962 and Glenavon in 1963. It was followed by the Blaxnit Cup (1968–74) (sponsored by a Newtownards hosiery manufacturer), an eight-team competition played through the deadliest days of the Troubles. Security concerns led some games to be cancelled and crowds were generally disappointing, with southerners reluctant to travel north. There were also some serious crowd disturbances, notably in the 1971 final between Cork Hibernians and Linfield at Dalymount Park. Northern teams won the trophy on five occasions: Coleraine (1969, 1970), Linfield (1971), Glentoran (1973) and Ards (1974), with Shamrock Rovers (1968) and Cork Hibernians (1972) claiming the remaining two.

Teams from both jurisdictions competed in the Texaco Cup (1970–2), which also involved English and Scottish clubs; the latter, however, refused to travel to Ireland in the early 1970s and Irish clubs took part in a separate Texaco All-Ireland Cup (1973–5). Like the Tyler Cup (1977–81) that followed, it roused little interest and it was over twenty years before another cross-border competition was launched. This was the Setanta Cup (2005–14) (sponsored by an Irish television subscription sports network), which in various iterations was open to between three and six clubs from each league. There were some worrying signs with disturbances in Dublin at the inaugural final between Linfield and Shelbourne in May 2005 (and violent incidents in Dublin involving Glentoran fans in 2008 and 2010), but most games were largely trouble-free and attracted solid crowds by domestic standards. In 2013, however, Linfield declined entry, citing inconvenient fixture scheduling, reduced prize money and the hostility faced by its supporters in attending away games. The 2013 Irish League champions Cliftonville also withdrew, dealing another blow to the competition's prestige, and in 2015 it was postponed and ultimately cancelled. It had, though, been the most successful cross-border competition since the 1940s, lasting nine years, during which it was won seven times by southern teams (Drogheda United (2), Shamrock Rovers (2), Cork City, Bohemians and Sligo Rovers) and twice by northern teams (Linfield and Crusaders).

In November 2019, competitive North–South football resumed with the Unite the Union Champions Cup, contested by the winners of the two leagues in home and away legs. Sponsored by the UNITE trade union, it adopted the slogan 'Celebrate the Difference'. The first leg between Dundalk and Linfield at Windsor Park on 8 November 2019 drew a crowd of almost 3,000 spectators, including several hundred from Dundalk. Some spectators on both sides celebrated the difference by trading sectarian chants. After a 1–1 draw at Windsor, Dundalk won the second leg 6–0 at Oriel Park on 11 November to become inaugural champions.

The stop-start nature of cross-border competitions suggests limited interest from football supporters in both parts of the island. They generally begin with some level of expectation and curiosity to see how teams from the two leagues will compare against each other, but attendances soon fall away. A full all-Ireland league has sometimes been suggested as a way of improving standards and generating greater interest in the domestic game, but no serious steps have been taken to bring this about. Administrators on both sides of the border cite a host of intractable logistical problems and the narrowing of options in European competitions, which today provide the only real opportunity to make significant revenue. In recent years the idea has been vigorously championed by the Kerry businessman Kieran Lucid, who has proposed a league-style cross-border competition that would complement the two existing leagues. In 2019 ten of the twelve clubs in the Northern Ireland Premiership wrote to the IFA expressing an interest but received little support from the organisation, which, in May 2020, stated its preference for an expanded version of the Unite the Union Champions Cup. The FAI has shown signs of being more sympathetic, and in July 2020 the ten clubs of the League of Ireland Premier Division wrote to the association to suggest beginning discussions with the IFA and UEFA to explore the possibility of creating an all-island league.[25]

***

For Irish clubs the prospect of playing against top-quality British or continental opposition in European competition is decidedly more attractive than facing fellow part-timers from across the border. While usually outclassed in Europe, they have achieved enough creditable results (particularly in home games) to salvage some pride and whet the appetite of ever optimistic supporters for future fixtures. Among these were Glentoran's 4–2 aggregate victory over Brann of Norway in November 1973 that qualified them for the quarter-finals of the European Cup; Athlone Town's 0–0 draw at home against AC Milan in the 1975 UEFA Cup; Dundalk's 1–1 draw in the European Cup in 1976 with the Dutch side PSV (who won the competition in the following season); Cork City's 1–1 draw with Bayern Munich in the 1991 UEFA Cup; Bohemians 3–2 home win over Glasgow Rangers in the 1984/5 UEFA Cup, and their elimination of Aberdeen in the 2000 UEFA Cup followed by a 1–0 away victory against Kaiserslautern of the Bundesliga. These matches are ranked among the most memorable events in club histories and are regularly recalled and celebrated by supporters.

However, by the 1990s changes in European competitions made it far more difficult for Irish clubs to secure attractive ties. In 1992 the UEFA Champions League replaced the European Cup and in 1999 the UEFA Cup absorbed the Cup Winners' Cup, eventually becoming the UEFA Europa League in 2009. The new competitions were designed primarily to allow Europe's top clubs to play each other more frequently and consigned lowly ranked teams to preliminary rounds. Teams drawn in these rounds were generally little-known in Ireland and such ties combined limited crowd-pulling potential with high travel costs. Some clubs did, however, negotiate their way through the preliminaries to meet attractive opposition or even qualify for the Europa League's group stages, opening the way to lucrative prize money and television deals. In a 2004 Champions League qualifier, Shelbourne met Deportivo La Coruña (the previous year's semi-finalists) and achieved a creditable 0–0 draw before a crowd of 25,000 at Lansdowne Road. In a Europa League qualifier in 2011, Shamrock Rovers defeated Partizan Belgrade 3–2 on aggregate, including a 2–1 victory in Belgrade, to reach the group stages. However, they proceeded to lose all six group games, highlighting the significant gap between the League of Ireland and professional European teams. In 2016/17 Dundalk qualified for the group stages and took points from AZ Alkmaar and Maccabi Tel Aviv; they qualified again in 2020/1 but lost all six matches.

Playing at this level gave a tremendous boost to Irish clubs, whose achievements were seen by most supporters as vindication for the entire league. Some admitted to getting more satisfaction from seeing an Irish club do well in European competition than from the successes of the Irish national team.[26] However, playing in Europe highlighted the poor facilities of most Irish clubs: Dundalk, the outstanding domestic team of the 2010s, were unable to play their games at their home ground of Oriel Park, which was deemed unsuitable by UEFA. Instead they had to use Shamrock Rovers' Tallaght Stadium, leading to calls for the FAI and national and local government to invest in Oriel Park and provide the town with a stadium worthy of its football team.

While European matches have often been highlights for clubs, they have on occasion sparked serious crowd violence, especially when North meets South. On 29 August 1979 Linfield played Dundalk at Oriel Park in a first-leg European Cup preliminary match only two days after one of the bloodiest days in the Troubles, when IRA bombs killed Lord Mountbatten and three others on a boat off Mullaghmore, County Sligo, and eighteen British soldiers at Warrenpoint, County Down. Linfield supporters rioted, injuring dozens of spectators and battling hundreds of gardaí. It was claimed that any hopes for an all-island league were 'killed stone dead' after 'two hours of raw, naked tribalism on the terraces' confirmed that 'the dark gospel of the paramilitaries has permeated Irish sport to the point where all attempts at reconciliation are futile'.[27] UEFA moved the second leg from Windsor Park to the Haarlem Stadion in Holland. Games involving the Glasgow Old Firm were also flashpoints. On 18 September 1984 Bohemians played

Rangers at Dalymount, the latter drawing thousands of supporters from Northern Ireland, whose presence attracted some intent on confrontation. Before the kick-off there were disturbances in the ground, with incessant sectarian taunts and the burning of opponents' national flags. After the game the trouble spilled over into the streets of Phibsborough and homes and businesses were damaged as gardaí had to draft in hundreds of riot police to restore order.

***

The difficulties that stem from proximity to one of the strongest leagues in the world have become progressively greater for the Irish domestic game. English football has continued to attract players, supporters and significant investment from Ireland, often at the expense of the home game. Many have regularly predicted the demise of domestic league football, and the Covid-19 public health emergency of 2020–1 seriously threatened the existence of clubs who rely heavily on gate receipts to stay afloat. The difficulties of running a largely semi-professional league dependent on a small support base are immense. Part-time professionalism can often seem to offer the worst of all worlds, creating the pressures and resentments that come with introducing money into the game, but rarely paying players enough to allow them to dedicate themselves fully to their sport or earn a good living from it. Most domestic clubs live hand-to-mouth, scraping by from year to year. Fundraising to pay players' wages has usually been the main priority, to the detriment of long-term planning.

This has been particularly evident in two areas: the nurturing of young players and the development of facilities. Until recently, few clubs had clear, structured links with local junior and schoolboy clubs or the foresight and resources to develop their own young talent; most promising youngsters went to English clubs, where many did not make the grade and drifted out of the game. There have though been some improvements lately, with both the FAI and IFA working with league clubs to create academies for the development of young players and open up pathways of progression from youth and junior clubs to the senior game. The League of Ireland now consists of four under-age divisions ranging from under-13s to under-19s, as well as its senior Premier and First Divisions. Such initiatives not only provide greater opportunities for young players, but also help root clubs more deeply in local communities and broaden their potential support base.

The importance of clubs having a permanent and suitable home ground has also become increasingly evident. Periods of homelessness did considerable damage not just to Shamrock Rovers, but also to clubs such as Shelbourne and St Patrick's Athletic, eroding connections with their home base. The improvement in Rovers' fortunes since their move to Tallaght Stadium in 2009 points the way forward to other clubs scraping by with inadequate or decrepit stadiums. Such developments though are rarely straightforward, tied up as they are with questions of tradition and identity. Bohemians and Shelbourne, both playing in grounds that had seen better days, agreed with Dublin County Council to share a new purpose-built 6,000-seat stadium on the site of Dalymount Park. Funding was to come primarily from the sale of Shelbourne's Tolka Park for residential use, but the prospect of the obliteration of the Drumcondra venue met with strong opposition from Shelbourne supporters and local residents. During 2021 a 'Save Tolka Park' campaign took off and in February 2022 Shelbourne announced its intention to remain at the ground. This decision and spiralling construction costs which had raised the estimated cost of the Dalymount redevelopment from €36 million to €52 million led Dublin City Council in July 2022 to propose a more modest redevelopment that would include a combination of refurbishment and new construction.

For all the problems of the domestic game, there are some grounds for optimism. The playing of the FAI Cup final in the Aviva Stadium since 2010 has been a major success, attracting large crowds which at times have exceeded 30,000. After many years of disappointing attendances at finals, such crowds recall the league's golden age in the 1950s and 1960s. Despite being shown live on terrestrial television and taking place during the Covid-19 pandemic, the 2021 FAI Cup final between Bohemians and St Patrick's Athletic drew 37,000 spectators, the largest crowd at a final in over fifty years. While most of those at cup finals are not regular attenders of matches, they show that a large reservoir of potential support exists. For those who do attend regularly, the down-to-earth nature of domestic football is one of its attractions, setting it apart from the multi-millionaire players and aggressive marketing of the English Premier League and other elite competitions in which clubs are often owned by shadowy investment groups, dubious oligarchs or the agents of oppressive states, intent on exploiting the traditions of long-established clubs to project a more benign image. The abortive attempt in April 2021 by twelve of Europe's leading clubs (including six from the English Premier League) to form a Super League showed the sharply differing priorities of their owners and supporters.

In contrast, most League of Ireland clubs are now owned by their fans, who generally take an active interest in their running. Supporter-owned clubs are more likely to attract financial support from central and local government, and serve the interests of local communities rather than owners or shareholders. For some, supporting a domestic club is a form of engagement rather than escapism, with the club's stance on social issues being seen as an important part of its identity. Bohemian FC, for example, has tried to champion progressive social causes, aligning itself with groups such as Amnesty International and flying the rainbow flag at Dalymount Park in support of LGBT rights. In 2013 it hosted a 'Homeless World Cup', which led to the setting up of a Bohemian Foundation that provides opportunities for sport and education for prisoners in Mountjoy, mounts anti-racism campaigns and welcomes refugees and those in direct provision to its home games. Clubs such as Galway United and Drogheda United have also established close links with local asylum seekers, seeking to involve them as much as possible as players and spectators, while St Patrick's Athletic has appointed a community officer to liaise with Dublin's large Polish community.[28] To improve the atmosphere in grounds some supporters have developed continental-style 'ultra' groups, which have made the Dublin derby between Bohemians and Shamrock Rovers into a particularly passionate event. The domestic league also rejoices in some high-profile followers, none more so than the Republic's first citizen, President Michael D. Higgins, who formerly served as president of Galway United FC. An informed and committed supporter, he regularly attends domestic matches in an official capacity but also does so out of love for the game and has often praised soccer's important contribution to Irish society.[29]

Despite the merger of 2006, the FAI has at times seemed to have scant interest in the league, making little effort to promote it and has even appeared to stand in its way. In 2010 it refused to sanction a friendly match between Limerick FC and Barcelona in Thomond Park, primarily because it had not been involved in organising it. That same year it also announced that the first match to take place in the new Aviva Stadium would be between Manchester United and a League of Ireland XI on 4 August, even though there was a possibility that this could clash with a Bohemians' Champions League qualifier. Supporters of the domestic league accused the association of treating it with contempt.[30] When the FAI took over responsibility for the League of Ireland, it was placed thirty-eighth of fifty-one leagues in the UEFA coefficient table; by 2019 it had regressed to forty-second of fifty-five leagues (the Northern Ireland Football League was in forty-eighth place). Since the FAI's stewardship has clearly not been a success, it is possible that its administrative crisis of 2019–20 may work to the league's advantage. The crisis prompted a 'Visionary Group' of reformers headed by the businessmen Roy Barrett and Gary Owens, and former international player Niall Quinn, to produce a blueprint for the restructuring of the league, which proposed that it should be run by a commercial third party rather than the FAI. During his brief tenure as chief executive of the association in 2020, Owens made clear that once the internal financial management processes of the FAI had been addressed, his priority would shift to the league. He described its current state as 'embarrassing' and insisted that the association has to take responsibility for its renewal.[31] The League of Ireland celebrated its centenary in 2021. During that century it has weathered many crises and still survives, primarily because of the enduring connection between clubs and supporters.

15

Administration and Its Discontents

The transformation of football from an informal activity played under ad hoc rules to a codified sport with regulated competitions required the establishment of associations to organise games and adjudicate on disagreements. The creation of these bodies was a crucial part of the sporting revolution of the late nineteenth century. Some developed into permanent, broad-based organisations that represented hundreds or even thousands of separate clubs and did much to create a more inclusive and vigorous civil society, while those organised on a national basis helped reinforce the connection between the nation and sport that has proved to be so enduring.

In the early days of codified sport there was often considerable overlap between those who played and administered the game. The pioneering organiser, player and founder of Cliftonville FC, J.M. McAlery, was appointed secretary of the IFA on its creation in November 1880 and captained Ireland in its first international match fifteen months later. However, as the sport developed and the demands on both players and administrators grew, there was an increased divergence in their roles. Most players had been attracted to the game for the vigorous out-of-doors exercise it offered and had little desire to spend their spare time tabling motions and making points of order in cramped rooms. One of the most common reasons for the collapse of clubs was the reluctance of members to take on the necessary administrative tasks. Capable administrators were crucial to clubs' survival, but there were often tensions: administrators could regard players as unruly schoolboys who needed to be directed and disciplined, while players could chaff at official interference and bureaucracy. It was, though, mostly administrators who held sway and, as they became more powerful, their positions were keenly contested.

While sporting associations habitually denounced the mixing of politics and sport, they themselves were often intensely political bodies, given to keen factionalism, insidious intrigue and ruthless self-promotion. Both internal and external politics helped bring about the IFA split in 1921, which allowed the two national associations to follow their own paths and assert separate identities. The IFA administered football in an 'Ireland' that was still seen as an integral part of the UK; it participated enthusiastically in the annual British Championship and was proud of its membership of the International Board, which allowed it to enjoy the status of an original founder of the game. The situation for the FAI was rather different. Although provisionally admitted into FIFA in 1923, its peripheral status and location seriously limited its international engagement during its early years.

With many of the top Irish professionals playing in the English League, the two Irish associations often selected international teams composed predominantly of players based outside their respective jurisdictions. Neither was used to dealing with full-time professionals and both faced accusations of incompetence when preparing teams for international football. Such criticism was directed more frequently at the FAI, but the IFA was not spared either: some ex-players maintained that its officials lacked foresight and ambition and did little to assist the international team. Several complained that the logistical arrangements for the Northern Ireland team during the 1958 World Cup were grossly inadequate; Billy Bingham later described them as 'diabolical'.[1] Looking at the sad state of domestic football in Northern Ireland at the turn of the millennium, one observer attributed it mainly to 'the twin peaks of ineptitude', the Irish League and the IFA.[2]

The IFA, though, had significant advantages over the FAI: it not only benefited from its ties to the other UK associations, but from 1960 was also closer to the inner councils of FIFA. This was through the agency of Harry Cavan (1916–2000), the most influential Irish football administrator of the twentieth century. Cavan, a trade union official who represented Ards FC on the IFA council, became IFA president in 1958, and two years later secured the vice-presidency reserved for the IFAB on FIFA's executive committee. (At the time the UK associations attached little value to the position.) He held this job without interruption until 1990, making him one of FIFA's longest-serving officials. From the start he established a good working relationship with Sir Stanley Rous, FIFA president (1961–74), and an even better one with his successor, João Havelange (1974–98). Cavan chaired the FIFA congress in Frankfurt in 1974 when Havelange ousted Rous, and thereafter was a staunch supporter of his presidency. In return Havelange appointed him to several important FIFA positions, including the organising committees for all World Cup tournaments from 1970 to 1986. Cavan also chaired the important rule-making technical committee, the World Youth Tournament committee and the referees' committee, regularly using his influence to have referees from Northern Ireland nominated for important international fixtures. For six months in 1984 Cavan acted as FIFA's caretaker secretary general until the appointment of the Swiss administrator Sepp Blatter (Havelange's chosen candidate). Cavan had known Blatter since the mid-1970s and the two men became close, with Cavan often describing him as his protégé; Blatter would later serve as FIFA's president (1998–2015). When world soccer began to generate ever-increasing amounts of money in the 1970s, some of which found its way to administrators, Cavan was cited as one of those who had facilitated the take-over of FIFA by officials whose personal pursuit of wealth and prestige took precedence over the interests of the game.[3] In the IFA, however, he was much respected and admired for using his influence to raise Northern Ireland's international profile. On his retirement as FIFA vice-president in 1990, he received numerous accolades and was awarded the CBE.[4]

Without the springboard of the International Board, no FAI official ever reached the heights attained by Cavan. Its longest-serving and most influential official was Joe Wickham, who was general secretary from 1936 to his death in October 1968, when he suffered a heart attack at an international game in Poland. A genial but determined administrator,

Wickham strongly argued the case for the FAI at international conferences, particularly in relation to jurisdictional matters, such as the
IFA's insistence on selecting players born outside Northern Ireland and
describing its national team as 'Ireland'. He was a respected figure in
the Irish game, which he represented with dignity, often in difficult
circumstances. As the general secretary of an association that generated little income, his remuneration was relatively modest: in 1946 he
earned £484 a year, which was less than his predecessor had earned
twelve years earlier, and the association agreed to increase it to £500.[5]
Helpful and courteous to the press, he was awarded the Irish Soccer
Writers' Association Personality of the Year award in 1964 – the first
(and only) time it was given to an administrator. He was also well-
regarded by many outside the game, particularly for his efforts to raise
his country's international profile: his funeral attracted a broad sweep
of figures from Irish sporting and political life, including President
Éamon de Valera. Wickham was even popular with most players,
although some thought that his conservatism inhibited the progress of
the international team. It was only after Wickham's death that the FAI
abandoned its policy of selecting the team by a committee of officials
and entrusted it to a professional team manager. Even then officials
rarely missed an opportunity to assert their authority. One Irish team
manager believed that the second-rate travel and accommodation
arrangements provided for players were a reminder to them to know
their place.[6]

The international team's failure to qualify for a major tournament
for over fifty years was frequently laid at the door of the FAI, by both
players and spectators.[7] Many developed an antipathy for the national
association, which they believed hindered rather than helped Irish
soccer. Liam Tuohy, who had experienced these frustrations when
representing his country (1955–65), did his best to challenge the
association's hidebound ways when he became manager in 1971 but
faced stubborn opposition. He later recalled the 'great mutual respect'
between himself and officials: 'I hate them and they hate me.'[8] Eoin
Hand, who managed the team from 1980 to 1985, found dealing with
the association the most exasperating part of the job. In 1982, after the

Republic missed out on World Cup qualification by goal difference, he asked for the association's help to attend the tournament in Spain but was greeted with 'a mixture of bafflement and resistance' and the all-powerful argument that no previous manager had ever made such a request. He went in the end but had to use contacts in the media and other national teams to gain admittance to games.[9]

Hand found the FAI's structures confusing, convoluted and ill-suited to administering the modern game. Its governing body was an executive committee of nineteen to twenty-three members, elected by a fifty-two-member council that represented various bodies, such as League of Ireland clubs, regional associations and junior and schoolboy associations. This was chaired by a president who was elected every two years and was assisted by a number of elected officers: a vice president, honorary secretary, honorary treasurer, assistant honorary treasurer and the outgoing president, all also elected by the council. The real power was held by the elected officers, who were often re-elected (or sometimes just re-appointed) and could hold office for several terms. Decision-making was unwieldy, with elected officers and council members often putting local and sectional interests ahead of national objectives. The accession to the FAI presidency in 1996 of Pat Quigley, whose background was in junior football, brought about a prolonged power struggle between the junior game, which was growing in strength, and the League of Ireland, which was in decline.[10] Their failure to work together held back Irish soccer at all levels and prevented the undertaking of any far-reaching initiatives. The squandering of so much of the association's effort on internal politics led Brendan Menton, general secretary from 2001 to 2003, to admit that 'Irish football thrives despite the FAI.'[11]

The association was badly resourced, with only a handful of paid staff, the most important of whom was the general secretary, who acted as secretary to the executive committee and looked after day-to-day matters. It was, therefore, a rather threadbare operation that, even when it put factional disputes aside, often struggled to cope with the increasing demands of international football.[12] Disquiet about logistical arrangements persisted into the 1990s: there were complaints about the qualities of hotels and training facilities used by the international team in the 1990 and 1994 World Cup tournaments and, until the mid-1990s, it was officials rather than players who occupied the roomier first-class seats on flights to away matches.[13]

During the mid-1980s the FAI found itself in serious financial trouble. Although often criticised for its penny-pinching ways, it had managed to live within its modest means until then (the avoidance of excessive expenditure is a recurrent concern in its records). It was highly dependent on gate receipts from international games for its income and, as public interest began to wane after a woeful qualifying campaign in 1985, it came close to insolvency. With a debt of over £30,000, it was forced to borrow from the FAI Junior Council to pay the salaries of its four full-time employees. Financial meltdown was prevented only by the timely signing of a sponsorship deal with Opel Ireland worth £400,000.[14] Another important development was the appointment in 1988 of Dr Tony O'Neill as general secretary to succeed Peadar O'Driscoll, who had held the position since 1968. O'Neill was a shrewd and imaginative administrator who had transformed UCD Football Club. Together with the new commercial manager, Donie Butler, he brought a dynamism and professionalism to the FAI that complemented the team's qualification for Euro '88. The tournament significantly improved the association's finances: it made a profit of £1.3 million, and the team attracted additional sponsors.[15] However, success also served to throw up new challenges and between the tournaments of 1988 and 2002, the FAI lurched from one crisis to another, sacrificing more and more public confidence along the way.

At both the 1990 and 1994 World Cups, FAI officials had sought to acquire extra tickets for Ireland's matches by exchanging tickets allocated for other games. Mostly this was done with other football associations, but sometimes ticket agencies or even unofficial sellers were involved. In 1990 the lack of central control and irregular procedures resulted in serious financial losses for the association and the embarrassment of its vice-president, Louis Kilcoyne, being detained by Italian police for selling tickets outside a stadium without authorisation. Four years later in the USA, things were no better. When the FAI treasurer, Joe

Delaney, lost money in transactions with touts to secure tickets for Irish matches, he made up the shortfall by transferring money from his own account to the FAI's. When some months later this came to light, an independent financial investigation revealed a general financial and administrative mess. The general secretary, Sean Connolly (whose performance in office had otherwise attracted praise), and accountant Michael Morris resigned, as did officers Pat Quigley, Michael Hyland, Des Casey and Joe Delaney (Quigley, Hyland and Casey were later restored). Kilcoyne was another casualty: he had been elected president of the FAI in July 1994 but was forced to resign after receiving a vote of no confidence from the FAI Council on 8 March 1996.

A report into the FAI's procedures published in May 1996 by Ray Cass Consultancy criticised the association for its 'lack of vision, direction and planning, its fragmented and indecisive structures and its marked reluctance to consider necessary change'. It maintained that the association's decision-making bodies were unwieldy and inefficient, and recommended handing over the powers of the fifty-two-strong council to a smaller board of management elected from within the council.[16] A new twenty-member board was elected at the association's AGM in June 1997, while the original council became a largely advisory body. This, though, did not resolve the FAI's deep-seated weaknesses and it subsequently became a regular customer of the business consultancy sector, commissioning reports on its structures and functions every couple of years. While publicly accepting recommendations for improved governance, these were often ignored or only partly implemented, and the association's structural flaws persisted.

The workings of the FAI received additional scrutiny in the aftermath of the Saipan controversy of 2002, after which it commissioned a report from the Genesis consultancy firm. The complete report was never published for legal reasons, but even the summarised version that appeared on 11 November 2002 was scathing about the association's outdated management structures and its general lack of efficiency, foresight and professionalism. The FAI subsequently implemented a number of the Genesis recommendations to streamline its administrative structures and better discharge its commercial and social responsibilities. This involved the creation of a number of new management roles, including a chief executive who replaced the general secretary and became a director on a newly constituted Board of Management, which also included the five main elected officers and the chairs of new committees on domestic affairs, development, legal and corporate affairs, finance and international. Genesis had also suggested the appointment of two non-executive directors from outside football to oversee the board's work, but this did not happen.

In the period that followed, John Treacy, the chief executive of the Irish Sports Council, expressed his unhappiness at the slow pace of reform. After the departure in November 2004 of the new FAI chief executive, Fran Rooney, who had served only eighteen months, the government announced that it was suspending €500,000 of the association's funding. Minister for Sport John O'Donoghue maintained that the 'general public has lost confidence in the FAI and formed the view it is in disarray'.[17]

The association's ability to frustrate and antagonise Irish football followers continued. In 2002 it announced a deal with British Sky Broadcasting to televise all the Republic's international matches on its satellite subscription service. This caused a public outcry from supporters who maintained that the proper place for national sporting events was on RTÉ's terrestrial public service channels. Government figures also spoke out against the Sky deal and, faced with the prospect of legislation to prevent it going ahead, the FAI accepted an improved offer from RTÉ to cover the games. The FAI's action did little to assure the government, which in 2003 passed the Broadcasting (Major Events Television Coverage) (Amendment) Act to protect the national team's most important fixtures from future attempts to restrict them to satellite broadcasters.[18]

***

One of Irish soccer supporters' most frequents complaints was the FAI's failure to develop a modern national stadium. Dalymount Park was clearly inadequate for major international matches and on 5

February 1985 a disaster was only narrowly averted when an over-capacity crowd converged on the stadium for a non-ticket friendly against world champions Italy. The FAI responded by imposing a limit of 22,000 on attendances at Dalymount and it was no longer used for competitive matches. After the Republic's strong showing in the European Championship in 1988, the team captain Frank Stapleton called on the association to build a new stadium that would be a worthy home for Irish soccer. This though received a rather cool response from FAI treasurer Joe Delaney, who maintained that building a new venue was beyond the association's means and that it was happy to use the 'fine stadium' of Lansdowne Road while progressively developing Dalymount Park to international standard.[19]

However, while the national team went from strength to strength after 1988, qualifying for consecutive World Cups, drawing strong crowds and boosting the finances of the FAI, there was no serious attempt to develop Dalymount and most international matches were played at Lansdowne Road. The association's complacency was probably reinforced by the fact that team manager Jack Charlton never expressed any dissatisfaction at playing at Lansdowne, and actually rather liked a playing surface more suited to rugby than soccer.

There were though many soccer supporters who were never really at home at the IRFU's stadium, where the atmosphere was rarely as intense as Dalymount, and they called for the building of a dedicated home for Irish soccer. Eventually, in 1998 the FAI set up a stadium committee that suggested possible sites and sources of finance. At a grand launch event in January 1999 it was announced that Ireland's leading telecommunications company would help to finance the building of 'Eircom Park', a 45,000-seater stadium costing £60 million on a greenfield site in City West on the outskirts of Dublin.[20] The announcement though did not meet with universal approval. The FAI general secretary, Brendan Menton, dissented, believing that it would bankrupt the association. League of Ireland clubs were also generally opposed, arguing that any available funds should be used to improve existing stadiums; junior clubs, represented by Bernard O'Byrne and Pat Quigley, were mostly in favour.[21] At the same time, other plans were being advanced. In 2000, with the economy booming and the public finances healthy, Taoiseach Bertie Ahern, the first genuine soccer fan to hold the office, advocated the building of 'Stadium Ireland' in Abbotstown, County Dublin, to serve as the centrepiece of a large multi-sports complex that would be available to all sports and have a capacity significantly above that planned for 'Eircom Park'. Since 'Stadium Ireland' would be financed by the state, choosing it over 'Eircom Park' would, he insisted, allow the FAI to invest in the development of the under-resourced domestic game while still having a state-of-the-art facility for international matches.[22]

The FAI was not prepared to abandon its own initiative but stated its willingness to avail of 'Stadium Ireland' when 'Eircom Park' did not meet capacity requirements. Emboldened by the prospect of its own stadium and the possible use of another, in summer 2000 the FAI opened discussions with the associations of Scotland, Wales and Northern Ireland for a joint bid to UEFA to host the 2008 European Championships. Wales and Northern Ireland declined, but Scotland expressed an interest. At the time though the FAI did not have a single stadium suitable to host international football and was compelled to approach the GAA to seek the use of the redeveloped Croke Park. They were assisted in their lobbying by Bertie Ahern and Paidí Ó Sé, the renowned Gaelic footballer and manager of the Kerry county team, who argued that 'the GAA should give the people of Ireland a dig-out to help the FAI get this tournament ... If we do this now, we would help put our country on the map.'[23]

Such goodwill was widely voiced in the GAA but proved insufficient to secure the use of the stadium. In October 2002, with UEFA's final deadline approaching, the GAA's Special Congress refused to discuss the playing of soccer in Croke Park. (The previous year, a motion to repeal Rule 42, banning non-Gaelic games from GAA grounds, was narrowly defeated at Annual Congress.) The absurdity of all this was highlighted in the Dáil, when the Labour Party TD Brendan Howlin reported that a UEFA inspection team evaluating the bids to host the 2008 tournament had recently visited Dublin to inspect the undeveloped site of one stadium and another that did not permit the playing of soccer.[24] The

FAI's inability to provide even one suitable venue undermined the overall proposal, which was placed fourth in the UEFA vote, and the episode did little to enhance the association's reputation, at home or abroad.[25]

In the end neither of the two proposed stadiums was built. Plans to proceed with 'Eircom Park' were abandoned after surveys revealed a serious infrastructural deficit at the site. 'Stadium Ireland', so closely associated with the taoiseach that it was popularly known as the 'Bertie Bowl', became tangled up in politics and fell victim in 2003 to spending cuts implemented by the Fianna Fáil–Progressive Democrats coalition government.[26] The government though made it clear that it would be prepared to assist upgrading Lansdowne Road if the FAI were given a major stake in the redeveloped stadium. In January 2004 the FAI and the IRFU announced plans for a €250 million redevelopment to cater for both soccer and rugby, with subsequent upgrades raising the cost to €410 million. The government agreed to provide €191 million over five years, with the IRFU and FAI making up the remainder.[27] However, the tortuous nature of the process once again showed the FAI in a poor light, as a divided, inept organisation unable to take straightforward decisions in the best interests of Irish soccer.

The decision left the FAI and IRFU without a stadium while Lansdowne Road was being redeveloped. With the possibility looming of the Irish teams having to play their home matches abroad, another approach was made to the GAA for the use of Croke Park. In April 2005, after lengthy debates, a GAA Congress voted overwhelmingly to make the stadium temporarily available for soccer and rugby internationals. Thirteen international soccer matches were played at Croke Park between March 2007 and November 2009, the first against Wales on 24 March 2007 attracting a record crowd for an Irish home international of over 72,500. In the meantime, the old Lansdowne Road was transformed into the modern Aviva Stadium, capable of holding over 50,000 seated spectators, and hosted its first international soccer match on 11 August 2010 (a 1–0 defeat to Argentina).

* * *

While the completion of the new Aviva Stadium enhanced the FAI's standing, it also left it with a debt of €38 million. The association planned to clear this with a 'Vantage Club' scheme that offered 10,000 ten-year tickets to high-income and corporate supporters and was projected to raise €185 million. The scheme was launched on 18 September 2008, just three days after the collapse of the American investment bank Lehman Brothers, which triggered a global financial crisis. In these circumstances it was worrying that the most expensive tickets were priced at €32,000, over twice the amount of the equivalent rugby tickets, and almost three times the cost of ten-year premium seats in Croke Park. Despite this the FAI chief executive John Delaney was bullish about 'Vantage Club', insisting that it would sell out quickly. Previously a director of Waterford United, Delaney represented the club on the FAI senior council and became FAI treasurer in 2001. Having emerged as one of the association's more confident and capable officials during the Saipan crisis, he was appointed chief executive in December 2004. However, his optimism about 'Vantage Club' proved misplaced and over half of the premium tickets were left unsold.[28] The FAI then offered these to clubs throughout the country, with FAI development officers such as Packie Bonner encouraged to promote their sale on visits to local leagues. Some were sold, but the high price was beyond most clubs and it would be three years before this was reduced. Many of the FAI's subsequent problems could be traced to the failure of 'Vantage Club' to realise its projections: according to one FAI source, this meant that the association was effectively insolvent from 2010.[29]

This though was not the image portrayed by the FAI's chief executive. Delaney was a more populist and flamboyant figure than any of his predecessors, happy to join the celebrations of Irish supporters and treat them to rounds of drinks. On occasion, when the team achieved a notable result, he would parade before spectators with arms aloft, milking the applause as if he were a player and even throwing his FAI tie into the crowd. After he had served ten years as chief executive, he was the subject of an FAI-commissioned documentary film, *John the Baptist* (2014), that celebrated his contribution to Irish football.[30] In April 2017 he was elected to the UEFA executive committee, becoming one of the most influential officials in European football. Delaney divided opinion sharply. Some saw him as a dynamic and ambitious administrator who brought much-needed energy and imagination to Irish soccer. He had strong support among regional administrators, who appreciated his efforts to promote and finance the game outside Dublin. In 2019 a joint statement from the four provincial associations praised him for visiting 'almost 2,000 grassroots clubs all over the country from Wexford to Donegal and Kerry to Louth'. Many regional officials had long believed that the FAI was a Dublin-centric body and that Delaney deserved credit for his attempts to redress the balance.[31] Others, however, saw him as a self-serving careerist, whose brash confidence covered his administrative limitations and poor judgement. An example of the latter was his singing in November 2014 in a Dublin pub of 'Joe McDonnell', a ballad about an IRA prisoner who died on hunger strike in 1981. At first Delaney denied doing so but, when confronted with recorded video evidence, defended himself by citing his nationalist background, noting that his 'grandfather fought in the civil war, war of independence ... To sing a song like that, you don't believe in every word. I sing a large number of songs.'[32]

The recommendation in the Genesis Report of 2002 that the FAI chief executive should be a voting member of the Board of Management was unusual in European football associations and contradicted FIFA guidelines. The arrangement rather blurred the distinction between executive and administrative responsibility and helped create a situation in which a strong chief executive could dominate a supine board. FAI administrators had in the past been criticised for their caution and parsimony. This could not be said of Delaney: both as treasurer and chief executive, he had no compunctions about loosening the association's purse-strings, particularly when it came to his own remuneration. His annual salary averaged about €430,000, a multiple of that earned by his equivalents in the GAA and IRFU, and usually twice the sum received in prize money by the League of Ireland champions. Delaney regarded the domestic league as a troublesome backwater and accorded it a low priority, preferring to cultivate contacts in Irish junior football or deal with the power brokers of FIFA and UEFA. For all his extravagance, he could be ruthless in cutting the association's costs, and unceremoniously dismissed former players and managers such as Eoin Hand, Packie Bonner and Brian Kerr from their FAI development roles.

In March 2019 the *Sunday Times* journalist Mark Tighe revealed that Delaney had loaned €100,000 of his own money to the FAI in April 2017. Always ready to resort to legal action, Delaney took an injunction against the newspaper to prevent details emerging, but the court ruled against him. Delaney claimed that he had simply made a 'bridging loan' to fund the association through a temporary cash-flow problem. The transaction though raised troubling questions about the association's procedures and finances and undermined his position as chief executive, leading to his resignation on 25 March. He was, however, to assume the newly created position of executive vice-president, reporting directly to the FAI board, and to keep his paid position on the UEFA executive committee.

The matter did not end there. Delaney's transaction led to increased scrutiny of his own remuneration and it emerged that in addition to his large salary, he had received hundreds of thousands of euros in various expenses and had renegotiated his contract in 2013–14 to secure an extra €3 million in bonus payments if he remained as chief executive until the end of 2020.[33] On 10 April 2019 Delaney was part of an FAI delegation that appeared before the Oireachtas Committee on Sport in Leinster House; he read a bland prepared statement and repeatedly refused to answer any questions. His action received widespread political and public criticism, even from some erstwhile supporters, and prompted a chastened FAI board to confront him with his failure to manage the association's finances and control his personal expenses. On 28 September 2019 the FAI announced his resignation as executive vice-president, and he resigned from UEFA's executive committee in January 2020.[34]

Some months earlier a thorough review of the FAI's governance structures was carried out by a group of five: two FAI appointees and three from Sport Ireland. Published on 21 June 2019, it made seventy-eight recommendations, notably the reconfiguration of the Board of Management to include four independent directors, one of whom would be the chair. The new chief executive would not be a board member, and the FAI council would be expanded to seventy-nine members, to include representatives from the Professional Footballers' Association of Ireland and supporters' groups for the first time.[35]

This pointed the way forward, but the association's financial position remained disastrous. Its accounts were published on 7 December 2019 and revealed current debts of over €50 million and long-term debts of about €30 million. According to the journalist who broke the story, the FAI needed Delaney's €100,000 in 2017 'because it was so financially stretched that it feared being unable to meet its payroll bill that month'.[36] The association's massive debts had been hidden in previous statements of accounts, with those for 2016 and 2017 showing profits rather than the actual losses incurred. An independent audit into the FAI found it unfit to handle public funds, and its report was handed over to the gardaí. All of this did immense harm to the image and standing of Irish soccer and was a matter of deep embarrassment and resentment to those involved in the grass-roots game. John McCarthy of University College Cork (UCC), a delegate at the association's AGM on 29 December 2019, argued that recent disclosures had made it even more difficult to compete for players against rival sports such as rugby and the GAA, and noted that 'It was bad when they were laughing at us, but it's worse now because they're saying they actually feel sorry for us.' Recognising the serious damage that had been done to Irish football over the last couple of decades, the FAI board formally apologised to the Irish football community and its own staff for 'the mistakes of the past'.[37]

Even by the FAI's standards, the level of administrative turmoil in 2019–20 was exceptional. After Delaney's resignation in March 2019, the position of chief executive changed five times until the appointment in November 2020 of Jonathan Hill, the former commercial director of the English FA. The association faced not only bankruptcy, but even the national team's continued participation in the 2020 European Championship qualifiers was in doubt. For an association that had known its share of embarrassments, this was probably the greatest in its history. In January 2020 a troika of the Irish government, UEFA and the Bank of Ireland agreed a bail-out package that saved the association from immediate bankruptcy, allowed the national team to fulfil its fixtures for 2020, and committed the FAI to continue its programme of reform.

***

Throughout its history the FAI was widely blamed for the under-development of the domestic game and the poor performance of the national team. Its achievements were usually overlooked. Born in difficult circumstances in 1921, it overcame major political, cultural and economic obstacles to run successful league and cup competitions. Despite operating on a financial shoestring and receiving minimal recognition from the established UK football associations, it managed to become a member of FIFA in 1923, and during the interwar period gained important international recognition for the emerging Free State. It consolidated its international profile after the war, and in 1955 showed considerable courage to play against a team from communist Yugoslavia in defiance of pressure from both Church and state. While often criticised for its financial caution, this usually owed more to prudence than parsimony, and its largely unpaid officials were often conscientious and hard-working figures who managed to keep the association solvent through difficult times. The nationwide development of the game in the 1990s was often driven by FAI coaches and programmes, and had considerable success. At under-age level, Brian Kerr, who as FAI technical director (1996–2003) led its youth teams to win two major international tournaments in 1997–8, acknowledged the support he received from the association's officers and administrative staff, and credited this as an important contribution to the achievements of his teams.

However, for most of the last thirty years, Irish soccer followers have been regularly dismayed by the actions of the FAI. The qualifications of 1988–94 opened up commercial opportunities and challenges that were beyond its rudimentary financial and accounting structures. Run in an ad hoc manner, with little oversight or accountability, the FAI found itself unable to adapt. The reforms required to operate effectively in the twentieth-first century were usually stymied by factionalism and self-interest, and the association's mismanagement and endemic weaknesses culminated in the existential crisis of 2019–20. Rather than co-ordinating the efforts of all those involved in the game, the FAI seemed primarily to create division, providing a forum for dissension, obstruction and feuds. Disagreements in national sporting organisations are common, but most seem to manage them rather better than the FAI. The IFA, for example, has attracted criticism for its own blinkered conservatism and failure to appeal to nationalists in Northern Ireland, but it has generally managed to run its administrative and commercial activities competently. The IRFU, which administers its sport in two separate political jurisdictions, does so rather more harmoniously than the FAI in a single state. The democratic structures of the GAA allow for vigorous debate and disagreement, but this does not prevent the association from promoting its games effectively and properly discharging its corporate responsibilities without repeated administrative crises.

Any sport is about much more than its national association and at a local level, soccer has often been run effectively, mainly through voluntary efforts. But for Irish soccer to realise its full potential for all those who play, coach, organise and watch the game, it needs national administrative structures that help rather than hinder its development. For most of the FAI's century-long history, these have been lacking. The crisis of 2019–20 did at least reveal the deep concern for soccer that exists throughout the country. Even critics of the FAI realised that its collapse would leave Irish society in a poorer state and there was no shortage of volunteers ready to offer their services to repair the damage and put Irish soccer on a sustainable path to recovery. Out of the chaos there emerged a hope that this time the reforms would be genuine and lasting and would effectively harness the immense goodwill that exists towards Irish soccer and begin to do justice to those who love the game.

16

Football for All?:
Northern Ireland since 1986

After qualifying for the 1986 World Cup, Northern Ireland did not reach the final stages of another international tournament for thirty years. There were few successors to the talented players of the early 1980s and the team struggled. Things also took a turn for the worse off the pitch. The prominence of players from a nationalist background such as Pat Jennings, Martin O'Neill and Gerry Armstrong had helped blunt the partisan leanings of elements of the Windsor Park crowd but, with the decline of that team, latent sectarianism became more overt. In the late 1980s some supporters began to direct abuse at nationalist players such as Anton Rogan, a Catholic from west Belfast who played for Glasgow Celtic. While the team's achievements had significantly raised its profile and popularity in the province, nationalist support remained low. Even after the paramilitary ceasefires of 1994, most nationalists stayed away from Windsor Park, deterred by the ground's reputation as a loyalist stronghold and the display of banners such as 'No Ceasefire at Windsor Park'. Many Protestant supporters were also alienated by sectarian songs and chants and the sullenly clannish atmosphere. Attendances fell to 3,000–4,000 for some international matches. The dilapidated surroundings of Windsor Park added to the general sense of grimness. Running out into the ground to play a friendly international in May 1996, the German international Jürgen Klinsmann exclaimed, 'Ah, East Germany 1983!'[1] In August 1999, when

Northern Ireland played the world champions France in a friendly match – a major coup for the IFA – the stadium was far from full and, as they ran on the pitch, the French team were greeted with sectarian and racial abuse from a section of the crowd.[2]

A quarter-century of violence in Northern Ireland had done much to reinforce sectarian polarisation. While the 1998 Belfast Agreement sought to provide a basis for political co-operation, it reflected the uneasy compromises and entrenched differences of northern society rather than any new-found unity. Trust between political opponents remained fragile and co-operation was fitful and easily derailed. As arguments over IRA decommissioning dragged on and sectarian riots erupted in Belfast in summer 2001, many thought that the gulf between the two communities was wider than ever. The agreement's efforts to accommodate a range of identities was perceived as a threat by many unionists; working-class Protestants in particular believed they were steadily losing ground to nationalists and felt increasingly alienated. In an uncertain political landscape, supporting a Northern Ireland football team whose symbols and culture reflected a solely British identity became even more important to much of the Windsor Park crowd, who regularly voiced political and sectarian chants.[3] This was accepted by both football and civil authorities as 'simply part of the social fabric of Northern Ireland' and, once it did not result in violence, no action was taken.[4]

The question of sectarianism among the team's supporters crystallised around Neil Lennon, who unlike most other players was open about his political leanings. From a nationalist background in Lurgan, he played for Glasgow Celtic (2000–7) and admitted that he would like to see a united Ireland and play for an all-Ireland team. This resulted in him being targeted for sectarian abuse while playing for Northern Ireland at Windsor Park, notably against Norway in March 2001, when some of the crowd booed his every touch of the ball and chanted, 'We've got a Provo on our team.'[5] After being selected to captain Northern Ireland against Cyprus on 20 August 2002, Lennon received a death threat, allegedly from the small and unpredictable loyalist paramilitary group the Loyalist Volunteer Force, which led him to withdraw from the team and end his international career. His alienation from the Northern Ireland team had, though, been some time in the making: when subjected to earlier abuse, he had been disappointed by the reluctance of the team manager Sammy McIlroy and the IFA to acknowledge and confront sectarian bigotry. Throughout his career Lennon continued to receive abuse and threats and was the victim of a serious physical assault in Glasgow in 2008.[6]

The Northern Ireland team's poor public image was reinforced by dismal performances on the pitch. After Bingham's retirement in 1993 successive managers Bryan Hamilton (1994–7), Lawrie McMenemy (1998–9) and Sammy McIlroy (2000–3) failed to improve its fortunes. Between March 2002 and February 2004 Northern Ireland went thirteen games without scoring a single goal (then a European record for an international team); this eventually came on 18 February 2004 in a 4–1 home defeat to Norway.

By the early 2000s some leading IFA figures, including Jim Boyce, who was the association's president (1995–2007) and a FIFA vice-president, recognised that the atmosphere at Windsor Park was damaging their national team. Not only had supporters drifted away, but it was also becoming increasingly difficult to attract sponsors or find dignitaries willing to attend games. The IFA discussed the matter with Northern Ireland supporters' clubs and made clear its belief that the loyalist flags and sectarian songs in evidence at Windsor Park were 'reflecting badly on our culture and national game' and that it was essential to try to broaden the team's appeal.[7] In 1998 the IFA had appointed a community representative officer, a position assumed in 2000 by Michael Boyd, who strongly pressed the 'Football for All' initiative to create a more inclusive atmosphere at international games. This encouraged supporters to wear the Northern Ireland team colours rather than those of Linfield or Rangers, and to drown out sectarian chants with inoffensive songs, such as 'Stand up for the Ulstermen' or 'We're not Brazil, We're Northern Ireland'.[8] The improvement was gradual but cumulative and, over time, the atmosphere at Windsor Park became less partisan and threatening. Neil Lennon was among those who praised the 'Football for All' initiative, and in 2005 the IFA's campaign was commended by the Belfast-based Institute for Conflict Research as 'remarkably effective in transforming the atmosphere at international games'. This transformation was further recognised in 2006 when Northern Ireland's supporters won the Brussels International Supporters Award for their sporting behaviour.[9]

In August 2011 the Minister of Culture, Arts and Leisure Carál Ní Chuilín became the first Sinn Féin representative to attend an international match at Windsor Park, and she praised the IFA for its efforts to broaden the team's support. Football matches would subsequently become important symbolic opportunities for Sinn Féin ministers to show goodwill to the unionist community: Deputy First Minister Martin McGuinness was present at a Setanta Cup match between Derry City and Linfield at Windsor Park in March 2012 and also attended Northern Ireland's Euro 2016 matches in France. After the renovation of Windsor Park and its renaming as the National Football Stadium at Windsor Park, McGuinness sat alongside DUP First Minister Arlene Foster at the first match held in the stadium, a World Cup qualifier against San Marino on 8 October 2016.[10]

The team's form also began to improve. After finishing bottom of the group in the 2004 European Championship qualifiers, there was progress under the management of Lawrie Sanchez (2004–7) as the team won three and drew three of the six friendlies played in 2004. It failed to qualify for the 2006 World Cup, but had some encouraging results in the group matches, notably a 1–0 victory over England in Belfast on 7 September 2005, the first win against England since 1972. The team also found a new hero: David Healy, who scored the winning goal against England and a record thirty-six goals in ninety-five appearances for Northern Ireland (2000–13). The improvement continued into the 2008 European Championship qualifying campaign (in which Healy scored a record thirteen goals), with impressive wins in Belfast over Spain, Sweden and Denmark; Northern Ireland finished third in a seven-team group, narrowly missing out on qualification. In the qualifiers for the 2010 and 2014 World Cups and the 2012 European Championship, the team had some notable home wins but lacked consistency in away matches and finished in the lower half of all three groups. On 28 December 2011, Michael O'Neill, who was capped thirty-one times for Northern Ireland (1988–96), was appointed team manager. O'Neill, a Catholic who had played Gaelic football at minor level for Antrim, had previously managed Shamrock Rovers to win League of Ireland titles in 2010 and 2011. He went ten games with Northern Ireland before recording his first victory, a 1–0 win over Russia in Belfast on 14 August 2013, but his careful planning and organisation gradually bore fruit and he went on to become one of the team's most respected and successful managers. In the qualifying rounds for the 2016 European Championship Northern Ireland managed away wins over Hungary and Greece, and qualified for the finals in France for the first time.

The team performed solidly, losing 1–0 to both Poland and Germany before beating Ukraine 2–0 in Lyon to progress to the second round, where it was eliminated by Wales on 25 June. The players had, however, given their large following something to cheer about and were widely praised for their courage and endeavour. The 2016 European Championship was the only major tournament for which both Northern Ireland and the Republic qualified, and their fans mingled together without incident. Northern Ireland's supporters were awarded the Medal of the City of Paris and the city's deputy mayor, Jean-François Martins, described them as 'a model for all the supporters of the world'. They also received a special award from UEFA's Executive Committee, as did the followers of Iceland, Wales and the Republic of Ireland.[11] Thousands of supporters at home had watched the competition at fanzones throughout Northern Ireland, and 40,000 attended the team's homecoming at the Titanic Centre in Belfast on 27 June 2016.

The Northern Ireland football team is one of the few sports teams that represents the province itself rather than being subsumed into Ireland or Great Britain. When the English FA floated the idea of fielding a Great Britain football team at London 2012 Olympic Games, the IFA was wary (as were the Scottish and Welsh associations), seeing it as a possible step to losing its separate international status altogether.[12] The team has become increasingly important for those who seek to maintain Northern Ireland's autonomy, and celebration of the achievements of 'Our Wee Country' features widely on murals and in other representations of Protestant unionist culture. This culture continues to exercise a strong influence and until recently the IFA was the only member of UEFA that maintained a ban on Sunday football. In 2000 Newry Town FC proposed allowing Irish League and cup matches to be played on Sunday, but this was rejected by the IFA, as was a similar proposal by Cliftonville in 2003. In subsequent years the ban came to the attention of the Equality Commission, which, in 2006, supported a legal challenge on the grounds of religious discrimination. The following year, despite opposition from the DUP, the IFA voted overwhelmingly to overturn the ban and allow teams to play on Sundays.

On 1 June 2008 Glentoran and Bangor played the first Irish League match on Sunday at The Oval. Some individual clubs, such as Linfield, however, still retained rules that banned Sunday play. Since the controversy that preceded the 1958 World Cup, the IFA generally tried to avoid scheduling international matches for Sunday. However, in 2014 UEFA changed from a system of allocating fixture dates by the mutual agreement of associations to one where they were selected by computer. Although this raised the possibility of Northern Ireland playing on Sunday in the 2016 European Championship qualifiers, the IFA was left with no choice but to agree if it wanted to take part. On 29 March 2015 Windsor Park hosted its first international match on Sunday, a European Championship qualifier against Finland. There were some protests, but they were small and muted and progressively weaker for subsequent Sunday internationals.

The more the Northern Ireland team expressed the identity of the unionist community, the less attractive it became to nationalists. While the progress made by the IFA to counter sectarianism was widely acknowledged and often appreciated, many remained wary. Since partition, most nationalists had kept their distance from the IFA team, which they believed had made no attempt to accommodate their culture or identity. They pointed to sectarian chanting and the abuse of Catholic players, the fact that the team played all their home matches at Windsor Park and employed symbols such as the Union flag and 'God Save the Queen' that represented only one of the province's traditions. This was in contrast to Scotland and Wales, who by the 1990s had their own flags and anthems that highlighted their separateness from England. This stasis is notable in a province in which definitions of identity have been changing. Increasing numbers of people in Northern Ireland, particularly the young, are rejecting the binary labels of unionist and nationalist, and see themselves as having a hybrid identity that combines elements of Britishness, Irishness and Northern Irishness: in the 2021 census 598,800 people (31.5 per cent of the population) identified solely or with other national identities as 'Northern Irish', up from 533,100 people (29.4 per cent) in 2011. Tapping into this group could perhaps broaden the support base for the Northern Ireland team, but this would probably require the IFA to adopt more inclusive symbols, which would be strongly resisted by much of the team's current core support.[13]

Nationalists who wanted to support an international team mostly backed the Republic of Ireland. They often insisted that they did this on their own terms, as an expression of their aspiration for Irish unity, and as a separate element of the Republic's following that did not necessarily endorse the southern state.[14] In a survey carried out in 1991 among 100 nationalist and 100 unionist football supporters in Northern Ireland, participants were asked to rank which teams they would support in an international competition: 91 per cent of nationalists chose the Republic of Ireland first; 8 per cent went for Northern Ireland; while 64 per cent put England in last place. In contrast 88 per cent of unionists chose Northern Ireland first; 41 per cent for Scotland second; 39 per cent England second; 60 per cent for Republic of Ireland last; and 24 per cent for England last. If the Northern Ireland team were to be disbanded, 85 per cent of nationalists favoured an all-Ireland team; while 43 per cent of unionists favoured a UK team and 42 per cent an all-Ireland team.[15]

***

The priorities of professionals are usually rather different from those of supporters and, for most players from nationalist backgrounds, the ambition to play international football has generally outweighed reservations about the team's partisan support or British symbolism. (There are clear parallels with the national minorities who played for Yugoslavia before its break-up, or the position of Basque and Catalan players in Spain.) However, some players admitted they had not always felt at home playing for Northern Ireland. The Newry-born Pat Jennings was proud to be selected for Northern Ireland, but was taken aback by the hostility directed at him when he made his debut at Windsor Park in 1964; he recalled that 'being a Catholic was no popularity boost ... I was appalled by some of the remarks shouted at me', among the milder of which was the rather puzzling 'Go back where you belong.' After his retirement from international football in 1986, he expressed his regret at never having the opportunity to play for an official thirty-two-county team.[16] Representing the IFA team often involved a process of regular negotiation and adjustment: when Martin O'Neill was awarded an MBE after captaining Northern Ireland in the 1982 World Cup, he accepted only after considerable reflection and discussion with family members living in the province.[17]

The option of playing for the FAI national team had been taken up in the 1930s and 1940s by a few Catholic players already capped by the IFA. From 1950, however, the two Irish associations confined their choice to players born within their own jurisdictions or who qualified through parentage rules. This effectively remained the situation until the 1998 Belfast Agreement stressed that citizenship in Northern Ireland was a matter of choice rather than birth: since all those born in the province were entitled to hold dual citizenship, this explicitly meant they could choose to play for either the IFA or FAI international team. From this time, an increasing number of Catholic players born in Northern Ireland began to declare for the Republic. In 2001 Brian Kerr, the FAI's technical director with responsibility for youth football, noted that he was getting an 'embarrassing' number of calls from young northern players inquiring about playing for the Republic.[18] In 2007 Darron Gibson became the first player born in Northern Ireland to play for the Republic since 1946 and subsequently others from nationalist backgrounds, including Marc Wilson, James McClean and Shane Duffy, all declared for the Republic. Their decision caused friction between the FAI and the IFA, with the latter accusing the former of poaching players it had helped to develop (Gibson and McClean had previously represented Northern Ireland at youth level). Moreover, during his tenure as manager of Northern Ireland (2011–20), Michael O'Neill complained that the FAI confined its approaches to players from nationalist backgrounds, aggravating the tensions around questions of identity in Irish soccer.[19]

There were a number of players who had decided to play for the Republic after unhappy experiences while representing Northern Ireland youth teams. Some claimed that those from a Protestant-unionist background at underage level were favoured in terms of selection and attention from coaches; others reported receiving tongue-lashings for failing to hold their heads high during the playing of 'God Save the Queen'.[20] As late as 2007, the IFA was insisting that all who played for Northern Ireland should travel to international games on British passports, despite the fact that several held Irish passports.[21] Such incidents led more young players to declare for FAI teams. The Derry-born Shane McEleney, for example, who opted to represent the Republic at under-19 and under-21 levels, claimed that his decision 'has given me something new and to be honest, it gets me away from all the political problems you have up here [in Northern Ireland]. The thought of now being able to represent "my country" makes me feel great ... I do see the Republic of Ireland as my country.'[22] When Michael O'Neill stressed at his team's homecoming after Euro 2016 that he 'want[ed] every young boy, wherever they're from in Northern Ireland, to play for Northern Ireland', the Sinn Féin MLA for Foyle Raymond McCartney tweeted, 'He might, but they won't.'[23]

Of all the northern-born players who have played for the Republic, the one who has attracted most attention has been James McClean. McClean was born in the nationalist Creggan area of Derry and played in the League of Ireland with Derry City (2008–11). Capped for various IFA youth teams up to under-21 level, he was called up for the senior team to play against the Faroe Islands in August 2011 but declined, claiming that he had never felt fully at home playing for Northern

Ireland. He then declared for the Republic, and made his debut in February 2012, going on to win over ninety caps. McClean, who signed for Sunderland FC in 2011, made the news in Britain in November 2012 for his refusal to wear a team shirt with the symbol of the British Legion poppy in matches before Remembrance Sunday. In a country in which wearing a poppy was practically compulsory for those in the public eye, his decision attracted widespread incomprehension and denunciation. However, McClean insisted that having grown up in the Creggan, home to six of those shot dead by the British Army on Bloody Sunday (30 January 1972), he could not wear the poppy in good conscience. He maintained this position after moves to Wigan Athletic, West Bromwich Albion and Stoke City, for which he has continued to receive regular criticism. McClean has made no secret of his republican views and desire to see a united Ireland, and in November 2019 was one of over a thousand public figures who signed an open letter to Taoiseach Leo Varadkar calling for a Citizens' Assembly to consider the constitutional future of Ireland after Britain's departure from the European Union.[24] Virulent abuse of McClean and his family persisted, including death threats, and reached such a level that in February 2021 it was publicly condemned by both Northern Ireland First Minister Arlene Foster and Taoiseach Micheál Martin.

There were, though, other northern nationalists who aspired to a united Ireland but were still happy to play for Northern Ireland. The Derry-born Paddy McCourt for example, admitted that while he identified more with the Republic politically, he was still pleased to receive an offer to play for Northern Ireland at under-age level and, having committed himself to the IFA, preferred to stay with them; he went on to win eighteen caps for Northern Ireland (2002–15).[25] Other players readily admitted to ambivalent attitudes. When the Celtic winger Niall McGinn played on a Northern Ireland team beaten 5–0 by the Republic of Ireland in Dublin on 24 May 2011, he tweeted afterwards that he was actually a fan of the Republic's team and that 'the only good thing to come out of tonight is that I got Robbie Keane's jersey'; this did not stop McGinn becoming one of Northern Ireland's most effective and reliable players, winning over seventy caps for the team.[26] When on international duty, players of all backgrounds seem to have mixed well together. Keith Gillespie, who made eighty-six appearances for Northern Ireland (1994–2008), insisted that 'there were no cliques based on religion', but rather religious difference was treated as 'part of the banter' common to all football dressing rooms. Far more important than religion, he maintained, was the shared experience of both Catholics and Protestants who grew up in a province regarded by outsiders as a dangerous sectarian warzone. According to Gillespie, their common awareness of the nuances and complexities of life in Northern Ireland had a powerful bonding effect on the team and 'made us tighter'.[27]

In recent years the challenge of 'Football for All' has also been applied to gender. Spurred on by the worldwide upsurge in women's football in the early 1970s, the Northern Ireland women's team began playing international matches in 1973. Results were uneven and qualification for a major international tournament proved elusive: between 1989 and 2005 the team rarely even participated in European Championship or World Cup qualifiers and was actually disbanded between 2000 and 2004. Under-achievement was largely attributable to the low priority accorded to the women's game by the IFA, which entrusted the running of league and cup competitions and the national team to the poorly resourced Northern Ireland Women's Football Association (NIWFA), founded in 1976. In April 2014 Carál Ní Chuilín warned that the IFA's funding would be cut if it did not begin to treat women's football more seriously.[28] This provided the necessary jolt, and the team has become increasingly competitive, drawing players from strong Northern Ireland Women's Premiership teams such as Linfield, Glentoran, Cliftonville, Crusaders Strikers and Sion Swifts, as well as clubs in England and Scotland. This was clearly demonstrated when in April 2021 it became the first Irish international women's team to reach a major international tournament after beating Ukraine home and away to qualify for the 2022 European Championship in England.

∗∗∗

Just as the Northern Ireland men's national team is closely associated with the Protestant-unionist community, so too is the men's domestic game. Most clubs who play in the Irish League were formed more than a century ago in towns or urban areas that had largely Protestant populations. Linfield FC in particular has provided a focus for an uncompromising unionist and Protestant identity to a greater extent than any other club in the Irish League.[29] It attracts support far beyond its original Belfast heartland, with significant followings and supporters' clubs in towns such as Bangor, Newtownards, Lisburn, Carrickfergus, Ballyclare, Larne, Coleraine and Ballymena (which also host their own local Irish League clubs). Linfield's dominance of the Irish League and its ultra-Protestant heritage has often been resented by other clubs, irrespective of their religious composition.[30] These are often critical of the close links between Linfield and the IFA, particularly the playing of home internationals at Linfield's Windsor Park until 2085, which gives the club a major financial advantage. Linfield's rivalry with its Belfast neighbour Glentoran has often been vexed and on occasion has spilled over into violence: some of the most serious crowd trouble of the 1980s took place when the two clubs met in the IFA Cup final on 30 April 1983.[31] Their Boxing Day derby has long been an established highlight of the season and usually attracts the largest league attendance. However, partisan passions appear to have cooled in recent years and the occasional hooliganism that sometimes marred derby matches into the early 2000s has since declined, without entirely disappearing.

During the Troubles, Linfield's image and values came under increased scrutiny: in particular, the absence of Catholic players on the team, which was regarded as a core part of the club's identity by at least some supporters. Pressure mounted from 1989 when its sister club, Glasgow Rangers, with whom it shares considerable support, reversed its long-standing policy and began to sign Catholics. Although Linfield repeatedly claimed that it did not discriminate against Catholics, throughout the 1970s and 1980s its playing staff was almost entirely Protestant. In an attempt to refute claims of discrimination, in 1992 it listed the names of seventy Catholics who had played for the club since its foundation in 1886. However, almost all of them had played before the Troubles, and the few who appeared from the 1970s onwards were recruited from outside Northern Ireland. The club's failure to sign local Catholics had important symbolism in a province in which religious discrimination in employment had long been a major grievance. During the 1990s Linfield began to take steps to reverse its traditional policy, signing several Catholic players from both the Republic and Northern Ireland. Initially at least, this was rarely a straightforward decision for such players: when the Dublin Catholic Pat Fenlon signed for the club in 1994, he found himself warmly welcomed at Windsor Park and was impressed by the club's professional approach but was denounced as 'an Orange bastard' by some supporters in the South. As most Linfield supporters acclimatised themselves to a changing world, Catholics gradually formed a larger element within the club and regularly made up half the team by the 2010s.[32]

Linfield sought to improve its image on other ways. In 2005 it supported the IFA's 'Give Sectarianism the Boot' campaign, an attempt to make attending football games in Northern Ireland more appealing to people of all backgrounds. The club made efforts to nurture links with the GAA and provided a place to train for a local Belfast camogie team. To show that times had changed, Linfield played a friendly match against Derry City on 22 February 2005 at the Brandywell, the first time Linfield had played there since 25 January 1969, when their appearance had sparked serious crowd trouble. The club also tried to come to terms with the legacy of sectarianism. A play by Padraig Coyle, *Lish and Gerry at the Shrine*, that examined conflict and contradictions in Irish football through the characters of the Protestant Elisha Scott, who managed Belfast Celtic for fifteen years (1934–49), and the Catholic Gerry Morgan, who played with Linfield (1921–3) and later worked as team trainer and physiotherapist for over twenty years, was staged by the IFA with the co-operation of the Linfield management at Windsor Park in October 2010.[33]

In a society in which allegiances are so sharply divided, many issues remain to be resolved. In domestic as in international football the use of the English national anthem as the anthem of Northern Ireland can create difficulties for players from nationalist backgrounds. In

2013 the IFA decided against playing 'God Save the Queen' before that year's Irish Cup final between Cliftonville and Glentoran in an effort to create a politically neutral environment. However, when Cliftonville met Coleraine in the 2018 final, the IFA decided that the anthem should be played. In protest, Cliftonville players stood with their heads bowed during its playing. Months later this led some players from Linfield to avoid shaking hands with their Cliftonville counterparts when the two sides met in a league game at Solitude, and Cliftonville players did the same when the two sides played at Windsor Park in November 2018.[34] The Northern Ireland Football League mirrors wider society, as nationalist and unionist communities make occasional progress in community relations, but also suffer setbacks in what is still a fragile environment. The overt expression of sectarianism is much rarer than before, but it remains beneath the surface and can be stirred up by controversies over the contested symbolism still entrenched in the life of the province.

17

Association Football in Modern Ireland

With the success of the Republic's team from 1988, soccer grew steadily in popularity. Across the country, thousands of young players took up the game. FAI programmes for development at grass-roots and schoolboy level were complemented by local initiatives: a South Donegal Schoolboys League was founded in 1988, a Kildare and District League in 1994 and a Midlands Schoolboys and Schoolgirls League in 1996.[1] The FAI's first comprehensive survey of its 110 affiliated leagues recorded 80,000 players in 1986; there were 140,000 in 1991, and 161,000 in December 1993 (just 20,000 fewer than the number playing Gaelic football). The trend continued and by 1996 there were 175,000 registered soccer players and 10,000 teams in the twenty-six counties.[2] Counties where soccer had been a minority sport, such as Mayo, Clare, Tipperary and Kerry, saw particularly notable increases; its progress in the last of these was shown strikingly in May 1998 when Tralee Dynamos beat the long-established Dublin club Stella Maris in the final of the FAI Youths Cup.[3]

Since then, the game has continued to grow nationally and in 2015 the FAI published its 'Player Development Plan', designed to develop talented players from every part of the country. To counter the dominance of the Dublin and District Schoolboys League, it introduced a system of under-age National Development Leagues to improve standards for all young players and provide a pathway into the international youth teams. These measures have had some success and in recent years it is noticeable that the senior team has drawn players from a wider range of counties: to date, twenty-one of the Republic's twenty-six counties have had players capped at senior level (the only exceptions being Carlow, Clare, Offaly, Leitrim and Roscommon).[4]

There was also a significant growth in school teams across the country, with the FAI's 1993 census recording an increase from 519 to 842 schools playing soccer nationally, an increase of 9,000 first- and second-level students.[5] By the early 2000s soccer was the most popular sport played in schools by second-level Irish schoolchildren (72 per cent) with Gaelic football in second place (69 per cent). However, judged by the number of schools who played in inter-school competition, it was only in fifth place (58 per cent), with Gaelic football in first (75 per cent), hurling in sixth (45 per cent) and rugby in tenth (28 per cent).[6]

Soccer's growing popularity provided a broader pool of talent for the FAI's international youth teams. During the Charlton years, many believed that these had been neglected and that there had been a general failure to nurture young players. Youth teams were the responsibility of Charlton's assistant Maurice Setters, but he accorded them a relatively low priority and they made little progress. This changed when Brian Kerr, who had previously led St Patrick's Athletic to two League of Ireland titles (1990 and 1996), became technical director of the FAI in 1996, a position that carried with it responsibility for the international youth teams. Kerr and his assistant, Noel O'Reilly (1948–2008), were steeped in the game, with a vast knowledge of under-age football and a passion to see teams play skilfully. Both had worked with Liam Tuohy when he was the Republic's youth team manager (1981–6) and brought the team to the final stages of the UEFA European Under-18s Football Championships on three occasions (1982–4). In the last of these, held in the Soviet Union, the Irish were beaten by the hosts in the semi-final. This qualified them for the 1985 FIFA World Youth Championship, also held in the Soviet Union, the first time an Irish team had managed to qualify for a world tournament. Having benefited from Tuohy's tutelage, Kerr and O'Reilly brought meticulous preparation, tactical shrewdness and original motivational skills to youth football, and were helped by the emergence of a group of talented players.

The combination of skilled management and players soon yielded dividends when the Republic's under-20s finished third in the 1997 World Youth Championship in Malaysia. Better was to come: in 1998 Kerr and O'Reilly led both the under-16 and under-18 teams to European Championship titles. In the first of these, in Scotland, the under-16s beat Spain, Portugal and Italy to win the tournament, while in the second the under-18s beat Germany in the final in Cyprus after a penalty shoot-out. The latter stages of the tournaments were televised on RTÉ and attracted strong public interest and admiration for the teams' skilful attacking football, which helped develop players who had distinguished senior careers, such as Damien Duff, John O'Shea, Richard Dunne and Robbie Keane, with Keane going on to become the team's most-capped player (146 caps) and highest scorer (68 goals).

* * *

The Republic's under-age success coincided with a dip in the form of the senior team. In February 1996 Jack Charlton was succeeded as the Republic's manager by his former captain Mick McCarthy. The team narrowly missed out on qualification for the 1998 World Cup and the 2000 European Championship, after losing play-off ties to Belgium and Turkey, but managed to win a play-off against Iran to reach the final stages of the 2002 World Cup in Japan and Korea. In Ireland the tournament would be most remembered for the clash between McCarthy and team captain Roy Keane. There had already been tensions between the two during the qualifying campaign, which grew once the squad began its preparations. As captain of Manchester United, Keane had led his club to multiple trophies and was renowned as one of the most competitive and intensely driven players in world football who demanded the best from all around him. He had never been impressed with the Republic's preparation for matches and believed that both Charlton and McCarthy had put the team at a disadvantage by their complacent acceptance of shoddy FAI arrangements. Soon after arriving at the team base on the island of Saipan on 18 May, he complained of poor training facilities and, after arguments with some of the coaching staff, announced his intention to quit the squad. He was persuaded to remain but in subsequent newspaper interviews voiced his frustration at the management and preparation of the team.[7] When confronted by McCarthy at a meeting of the players on 22 May, years of accumulated resentment boiled over and Keane rounded sharply on the manager in a manner that shocked even hardened professionals. Senior players took the manager's side and Keane returned home before the tournament had even begun.

The dispute became a soap opera that transfixed the nation: even those with no interest in football found the human drama compelling. It was given saturation media coverage, dominating the front pages of both broadsheets and tabloids, and was discussed in depth on radio and television current affairs programmes. An RTÉ television interview with Keane after he had left the Irish camp was one of the most watched programmes of the year. Hits on Keane-related stories on the *Irish Times* website shattered all previous records, including those of the terrorist attacks on the World Trade towers of 11 September 2001. Editorials and opinion pieces drew moral lessons for the Ireland of today. The director of the Irish Society for the Prevention of Cruelty to Children (ISPCC) noted that large numbers of children were 'understandably traumatised' and urged parents to use the dispute as an 'opportunity to talk to kids about the nature of conflict'.[8] People were quick to take sides, and for weeks 'Saipan' was the most hotly debated issue in Irish life, as arguments raged in homes and workplaces across the land. Frantic attempts to broker a reconciliation even drew in Taoiseach Bertie Ahern (in the midst of a general election campaign), but came to nothing.

Keane became a polarising figure, reviled by some and lauded by others. Detractors condemned him for walking out on his country, while supporters saw him as a courageous leader prepared to take a stand against the traditional Irish acceptance of mediocrity. Perhaps one of the reasons for the bitterness of the dispute was that it rested on differing conceptions of patriotism: for the McCarthyites, one that stressed loyalty; for the Keanites, one that stressed ambition. Some saw Keane as representative of the new impatience and ruthlessness characteristic of Ireland's booming 'Celtic Tiger' economy. Keane himself linked his actions to the condescending attitudes and Irish jokes he had endured in English dressing rooms throughout his career; he noted that these had 'long since ceased to amuse me' and he was determined to refute them.[9] Over the years many players had been frustrated by the inadequate preparation and limited ambition of Irish international teams, but they generally put up and shut up for fear that any public protest would end their international careers. However, as club football became a multi-million-pound industry, top-level players became rather less deferential, and when the row came, it was no surprise that one of the world's most successful club captains was at its centre.

The dispute though seemed to galvanise Keane's teammates. Perhaps stung by accusations that they were a one-man team, they achieved hard-fought draws against Cameroon and Germany in their first two games and then beat Saudi Arabia to qualify for the second round. Their match against Spain in Suwon on 16 June went to a penalty shoot-out, but there was to be no repeat of Genoa and this time the Republic lost out. Players and supporters were bitterly disappointed, but, once this had faded, the consensus was that the Republic had performed well, with Robbie Keane's last-minute equaliser against Germany on 5 June providing a particularly memorable moment. World Cup games were by this time national events watched by most of the population. The national bonding observed in the 1990s was still evident: one newspaper noting that 'No one who has observed the effect of Ireland's participation in this World Cup can deny the unique place football occupies in our lives today ... football levels and unites in a display of uplifting nationalism.'[10] When the team returned home they were congratulated by both the taoiseach and Northern Ireland's deputy first minister, Mark Durkan, and received by President Mary McAleese in Áras an Uachtaráin. There was also a homecoming in the Phoenix Park on 18 June, attended by about 100,000 people, who loudly showed their appreciation for the team's achievement.

***

The 2002 World Cup confirmed soccer as the most popular international team sport in the country. While the Irish soccer team had enjoyed considerable success in the previous fourteen years, the same could not be said for rugby. Since winning the Five Nations Championship in 1985, the Irish rugby team had generally underperformed and made little impact in successive Rugby World Cups, held every four years from 1987, struggling to compete with better-prepared teams who stretched the definition of amateur. Bowing to the inevitable, the International Rugby Board decided in 1995 to remove restrictions on payments to players. Irish rugby soon adjusted itself to professionalism and began to enjoy some success, particularly in international club competitions where it was represented by provincial teams. Ulster was the first Irish team to win the European Champions Cup in 1999, followed by Munster (2006 and 2008), and Leinster (2009, 2011, 2012 and 2018). Support and sponsorship for the provinces grew rapidly, interprovincial rivalries intensified and matches between Munster and Leinster regularly filled the Aviva Stadium.

The success of the provinces boosted rugby's popularity and profile, and revitalised the international team. During the 2000s Ireland regularly challenged for the Six Nations Championship before winning it outright with a Grand Slam in 2009, claiming further titles in 2014 and 2015, and winning Grand Slams in 2018 and 2023. This success put the inconsistent soccer team in the shade, and in recent years major rugby matches have often drawn the largest television audiences of all sports events, with important Six Nations games and World Cup ties regularly attracting over 900,000 viewers.[11] Rugby's rising popularity did not encroach directly on domestic soccer, but it did serve as another reminder of its Cinderella status. Within a decade of going professional, domestic rugby had gone from modest beginnings to become an immensely popular spectator sport played by Irish teams that were among the most competitive and successful in Europe. It stood in sharp contrast to domestic soccer which, despite a century of professionalism, struggled to attract crowds and investment.

At an international level, there were some instructive contrasts between soccer and rugby. The IFA–FAI split of 1921 had created two distinct associations, each largely representative of the political beliefs of the game's followers in North and South. Political tensions were less obvious in rugby, although the IRFU still had to try to accommodate differences. When Ireland played Wales at Ravenhill in Belfast in March 1950, supporters from the South were forbidden to display tricolour flags, which were confiscated by the RUC. At a later international against France on 24 January 1953 at Ravenhill, in keeping with the IRFU's protocol for matches in Belfast 'God Save the Queen' was played as the Irish anthem and the Union Jack flew as Ireland's national flag. This led to sharp criticism of the IRFU in the South and some Munster and Connacht players threatened to withdraw from the Irish team should it happen again.[12] Eventually the IRFU defused the situation by deciding to host all home internationals in Dublin, where 'Amhrán na bhFiann' was sung and the tricolour flown (alongside the IRFU and nine-county Ulster flags). At away games, the IRFU flag was used and no anthem was played. This resulted in some farcical situations, such as Ireland's opening game at the 1987 World Cup, when players settled on 'The Rose of Tralee' as their pre-match anthem, sung along to an instrumental version by James Last broadcast on the public address system. Eventually the IRFU commissioned the renowned songwriter Phil Coulter to write 'Ireland's Call', a new official anthem for the 1995 World Cup that stressed the united, all-island nature of the team and offended nobody except music lovers. Played after 'Amhrán na bhFiann' at home, and instead of it at away matches, it often elicited a rather half-hearted response from the crowd. The Irish rugby team, though, had generally fared well with the difficulties of representing two separate political jurisdictions, usually managing to accommodate difference rather than accentuate division.

Soccer's relations with the GAA were generally more fraught than those with the IRFU, but these too had their complexities. The GAA ban on soccer until 1971 was of considerable symbolic importance, but it was also widely ignored and defied. When the former Irish team manager Eoin Hand met the legendary Kerry Gaelic footballer Mick O'Connell on Valentia Island in the 1980s, Hand recalled that 'he invited me to his home and proceeded to amaze me with his in-depth knowledge of soccer'. Mick O'Dwyer was another Kerry legend who was also a keen soccer fan.[13] Such figures largely kept their enthusiasm for soccer to themselves, but this began to change in the late 1980s as the Republic's international soccer team received nationwide support, including that of many committed GAA supporters. Most soccer clubs co-existed harmoniously with their GAA counterparts and Irish team managers such as Charlton and McCarthy were regularly invited to games in Croke Park.[14] Before the Irish squad departed for the 2002 World Cup, the GAA sent them a goodwill message which McCarthy noted meant 'a lot to me and to the lads. Many of them are staunch GAA fans.'[15]

Some of the GAA's wariness towards soccer was understandable. The different codes were often in competition for the same young players and it seemed that soccer, with its greater international profile, had significant advantages. By the early 2000s, however, it was clear that soccer's growth in popularity in Ireland had done little to damage Gaelic games, which were still attracting large numbers of players and spectators. Support for the various codes of football seemed complementary, and for many it was perfectly natural to support their GAA county team, while also supporting the Irish national soccer team and an English Premier League club as well. Outstanding Kerry Gaelic footballers such as Colm Cooper and Dara Ó Cinnéide admitted to being fanatical Liverpool supporters. Cooper, who played soccer with Killarney Celtic until he was seventeen, suggested (half-jokingly) that he would swap one of his All-Ireland medals to play in a Champions League final for Liverpool. The Mayo footballer Conor Mortimer is also a dedicated Liverpool fan and regularly travels to games in Anfield, admitting that he prefers watching soccer ahead of Gaelic football.[16] There was a time when such admissions by leading inter-county Gaelic footballers would have attracted censure, but today they elicit little notice.

***

Although organised women's football did not entirely disappear after the mid-1930s, it became a more informal activity, with women playing in loosely organised groups, often in makeshift venues. During the ballroom boom in Ireland, female footballers showed particular resourcefulness by using these venues to form the Abbey Ballroom Indoor Football League in Drogheda in 1966.[17] Such competitions helped revive interest in women's football and led in 1968 to the founding of clubs such as Dundalk Ladies, who played in an unofficial national league of women's teams mostly linked to League of Ireland clubs. As regular winners of the league, in 1970 Dundalk were invited to play one of the best teams in England, Corinthian Nomads of Manchester. The match, which was billed as 'Ireland against England', took place on 10 May at Prestatyn Raceway in north Wales (the English FA's ban was still in force) and was watched by a crowd of 4,000, who saw the more experienced English XI win 7–1.[18] The match received little publicity but did reintroduce an element of international competition into the Irish women's game for the first time since the 1930s.

Until the 1960s, the worldwide growth of women's football was sporadic, with brief advances usually rolled back quickly by the established authorities. However, the growth of feminism encouraged women to challenge gender stereotypes in all areas and by the latter part of the decade women's football began to gather real momentum, especially in western Europe and North America. An independent International Women's Football Federation was founded in 1967 and international competitions were held in Italy in 1967 and 1970 and Mexico in 1971 that drew growing numbers of national teams. This prompted FIFA and UEFA to act: the latter officially recognised the women's game in 1971 and instructed affiliated associations to assist its development. In 1971 a match between France and the Netherlands was the first between women's teams to be recognised by FIFA as a full international. The following year saw official international debuts for teams from England and Scotland, joined by the Republic of Ireland and Northern Ireland in 1973. In 1982 UEFA launched its first official European championship for women's football, with Sweden beating England in the final on 12 May 1984.

The inaugural women's World Cup was held in China in 1991 and was won by the United States. Subsequently held every four years, it has attracted increasing numbers of teams, and greater levels of public interest and media attention. A major step in its development came in 1999 when it was hosted by the US, the recognised global leader in the women's game, which was well-funded and strongly promoted at school and college level. Matches were played before capacity crowds and the final, again won by the USA, attracted over 90,000 spectators. Women's football became a full Olympic sport at Atlanta in 1996; without restrictions on professionalism or age, the competition attracted the world's best teams such as China, Germany, England, the Nordic countries and the USA. The most recent World Cup in France in 2019 was watched by over 1 million spectators in nine host cities and by a worldwide television audience of 1.12 billion. The Euro 2022 competition hosted by England was also a resounding success, attracting strong attendances and unprecedented media coverage, and confirming the game's move into the sporting mainstream. When England and Germany met in the 2009 Euro final in Helsinki they were watched by 15,000 spectators; when they met again in the final on 31 July 2022 a sell-out crowd of 87,000 witnessed England's 2–1 victory in Wembley Stadium; there were also 17.4 million television viewers. At grass-roots level, the numbers playing the game also rose rapidly. In 2014, a FIFA survey recorded 88,262 coaches and 4,801,360 players. By 2019 there were an estimated 13.36 million females playing organised football worldwide, with 176 international women's teams affiliated to FIFA.[19]

In Ireland, the women's game saw steady rather than spectacular growth. In the early 1970s the country's two associations acceded to UEFA instructions without enthusiasm and did little to encourage women to play. Those who did often faced condescension, ridicule and even hostility from some male administrators, players and followers. As newcomers to the international game, the two Irish teams took time to adjust: the Republic's international debut in 1973 was a 10–1 defeat to Scotland, while Northern Ireland lost 5–1 to England. In 1973 a Ladies Football Association of Ireland was founded. This was at first independent of the FAI but affiliated to it in 1991, and in 2001 it became the Women's Football Association of Ireland.

In these years Ireland produced some fine players, such as the Inchicore-born Anne O'Brien (1956–2016), a skilled midfielder who played professionally for top European clubs including Stade de Reims (1973–5) and Lazio (1976–83; 1984–6). She won three league titles in France and another six in Italy and became one of the most admired figures in the Italian game. However, she played only four times for the Republic (between 1973 and 1990), simply because the team did not have the funds to fly her to games.[20] Hampered by poor logistical support, the Republic had to wait until 2 October 1982 for its first official competitive win, a 2–1 victory over Northern Ireland in a qualifier for the 1984 UEFA Championship. For the most part, the southern team's form throughout the 1980s and 1990s was patchy, with some heavy defeats. However, the broadening of support for soccer in the 1990s drew in more women and laid foundations for significant increases in the numbers playing: in 1991 the FAI had 2,208 registered women players; two years later this had grown to 3,769, and by 2006 it was 12,000. In 2001, the association finally appointed a development officer for women's football, and in 2006 it issued a comprehensive *Women's Development Plan* to encourage the growth of the game at all levels and develop coaches, referees and administrators as well as players.[21]

The international team's form began to improve as it came close to qualifying for the 2005 UEFA Championship and performed well at several invitational tournaments. Many players have represented the team with pride, and several have had distinguished international careers. Four have made over 100 appearances: goalkeeper Emma Byrne (1996–2017: 134 caps); forward Olivia O'Toole (1991–2009: 130 caps); midfielder Ciara Grant (1995–2012: 105 caps) and winger Áine O'Gorman (2006– 114 caps to 2022). O'Toole is top scorer with fifty-four goals. The team has played at various venues throughout their history, but since 2013 have played their homes games at Tallaght Stadium and of late have regularly filled the venue. In 2019, the experienced Dutch coach Vera Pauw became the team manager and in the qualifying campaign for the 2022 European Championship the Republic scored home victories over Montenegro, Greece and Ukraine, but narrowly missed out on qualification. In October 2022, they went one better, beating

Scotland 1–0 in a play-off at Hampden Park to win a place in the 2023 World Cup. The Republic have also enjoyed some success at underage level, finishing runner-up in the 2010 UEFA Under-17 Championship, beating Germany in the semi-final, and making the quarter-final of the 2010 FIFA Under-17 World Cup. They also qualified for the semi-final of the 2014 UEFA Under-19 Championship.

Official women's national domestic leagues have existed since 1973, starting with the Ladies League of Ireland. These, though, tended to falter after a few years and had to be regularly relaunched. In 2011, a Women's National League was founded consisting of six clubs: Castlebar Celtic, Cork Women's FC, Peamount United (based in Newcastle, County Dublin), Raheny United, Shamrock Rovers and Wexford Youths. The league achieved worldwide publicity in the 2013/14 season when Stephanie Roche of Peamount United was filmed scoring a superb volley that became a contender for the 2014 FIFA Puskas Goal of the Year competition. Roche had earlier helped Peamount win the inaugural 2011/12 Women's National League by scoring twenty-six goals, which earned her that season's Golden Boot (a feat she repeated in 2013/14). Peamount also won the league title in 2019 and 2020, finishing ahead of Shelbourne (who joined the league in 2015) in second place and Wexford Youths in third in both seasons. Wexford though are the league's most successful team, winning four titles (2015–18), and four FAI Cups (2015, 2018–19 and 2021). In 2020 the league was expanded to nine teams, with Athlone Town, Bohemian FC and Treaty United of Limerick participating for the first time. In recent years Shelbourne have been dominant, winning the League Championship in 2021 and 2022.

The slow and uneven development of the women's game in Ireland has often compelled female footballers to move abroad to earn a living or play at a higher level. Most have gone to leading English clubs, but several have travelled further afield. Between 2014 and 2020 Stephanie Roche played in France, the US, England and Italy before returning to play with Peamount in 2020. Several other Irish-born internationals have also had successful careers abroad. Louise Quinn has played in Sweden (2013–16), England (2017–20; 2021–) and Italy (2020–1) and Diane Caldwell in the US (2010–11; 2021–), Iceland (2011), Norway

(2012–15) and Germany (2016–20). Denise O'Sullivan made her mark in Scotland (2013–16), the US (2016–17) and Australia (2018–20), before signing for Brighton & Hove Albion in the Women's Super League. Claire O'Riordan joined MSV Duisburg in the Frauen-Bundesliga in 2018, while Amber Barrett, who was top scorer in the Women's National League with Peamount in three successive seasons (2016–18), has played in Germany for 1. FC Köln since 2019. Just like Anne O'Brien before them, all made significant contributions to raising the international profile of the Irish women's game.[22]

While only about 20 per cent of the coaches in the women's game are female, that number has been increasing and some have even begun to break into the men's game. Dubliner Lisa Fallon, who had spells playing for Southampton and Gillingham in England, took up coaching at an early age and was involved with several men's under-age and amateur teams. In 2017, she became a first-team coach with Cork City in the League of Ireland and has also worked in the management teams of Shamrock Rovers, Bohemians, Northern Ireland, Chelsea, the Dublin Gaelic football team and London City Lionesses, as well as being a regular media pundit. In January 2021, she was appointed first-team head coach of Galway United of the League of Ireland First Division. An informed and astute commentator on the game, she wryly observed that 'if I got a euro every time I was asked if I was the physio I could retire', but also noted that as she has worked hard, 'the opportunities have come, and I believe that they will continue to come'.[23]

In 2015, the Women's Football Association of Ireland adopted a strategic plan whereby it became fully integrated into the FAI, which formed a national Women's Football Committee to oversee the development of the women's game. Eight Women's Regional Football Committees were also created to encourage development at local level. By 2019 there were 24,800 female players registered with the FAI, with the game spreading throughout the country: when the Republic played Germany in a European Championship qualifier in November 2020, there were representatives from thirteen different Irish counties in the squad, with players from all four provinces. However, in trying to compete at the international level, the women's senior team has often been frustrated by the lack of support from the FAI. Until recently, international players were not even provided with their own tracksuits and sometimes had to change in airport toilets. In April 2017, players had to threaten to boycott a home match against Slovakia to improve their conditions. During the FAI's 2019–20 administrative crisis, its neglect of the women's game received particular censure, and future government funding of the association was linked to a commitment to give greater administrative representation and financial support to women's football.[24] At the end of August 2021, the FAI announced that henceforth the women's national team would receive the same match fee as the men's, following the example of other associations in Norway, England, Brazil, Australia and New Zealand.

While much remains to be done, women's national sports teams are beginning to receive greater recognition. The achievement of the Irish women's hockey team in reaching the World Cup final in 2018 generated considerable admiration and support, and significantly raised their public profile. As the history of men's football has shown, playing in major tournaments is the key to broadening interest in the game from committed supporters to the nation at large and the Republic's victory over Scotland on 11 October 2022 to qualify for the 2023 World Cup was watched by 593,000 television viewers, the largest ever audience for a women's match in Ireland. Football is however about far more than the success of national teams. In recent decades the growth in female football at local, school and junior levels has allowed tens of thousands of women and girls to enjoy the excitement of playing and the satisfaction of belonging to a team, to savour the joy of winning and overcome the disappointment of defeat. It has also provided a highly visible means to challenge and overcome traditional restrictions and prejudices, and played its part in the ongoing story of universal female emancipation.

***

In the men's game the fallout from the Saipan controversy took time to clear. An independent inquiry into the FAI's handling of the squad's preparation produced a damning report, prompting General Secretary Brendan Menton to tender his resignation. The controversy also undermined McCarthy's position and, after defeats to Russia and Switzerland in autumn 2002, he resigned. In January 2003, he was succeeded by Brian Kerr, whose work as international youth team manager since 1996 had earned him widespread admiration. The appointment was broadly welcomed within the Irish soccer community, which hoped that the chasm between the domestic and international games could be bridged. However, Kerr's reign was relatively short, and after the team's failure to qualify for the 2004 European Championship and 2006 World Cup, he was replaced in January 2006 by Steve Staunton, who had made 102 international appearances for the Republic (1988–2002) in a distinguished playing career but had little management experience. Staunton lasted only twenty months during which the Republic suffered some embarrassing defeats and failed to qualify for the 2008 European Championship. The FAI then sought a seasoned international manager and in February 2008 appointed Giovanni Trapattoni, who had successfully managed clubs such as AC Milan, Juventus, Inter Milan and Bayern Munich, as well as the Italian national team. Trapattoni (whose salary was partly funded by the wealthy businessman Denis O'Brien) restored solidity and discipline to the team who went through the qualifying group for the 2010 World Cup unbeaten to reach a play-off tie against France in November 2009. The Irish lost the home leg 1–0 in Croke Park and, with nothing to lose in the return in Paris on 18 November, shed their usual caution and attacked from the start, taking the lead in the first half to level the aggregate score. However, Irish hopes were dashed when the French forward Thierry Henry set up the decisive goal to give France a 2–1 aggregate win. In doing so Henry twice handled the ball, but this was missed by the referee and the goal stood, sending France to the World Cup in South Africa. Irish supporters were outraged and the FAI called for the game to be declared void and replayed. As it had once united in celebration, the country now united in indignation; public figures queued up to denounce the injustice done to Ireland by the 'Hand of Gaul', but FIFA held firmly to its position that a result could not be overturned because of a refereeing mistake. (It did though offer the FAI a secret payment of €5 million to forestall a possible appeal to the Court of Arbitration for Sport, and this was accepted.)

Trapattoni though did manage to secure qualification for the 2012 European Championship in Poland and Ukraine. In the aftermath of a severe banking crisis and recession that had compelled the Irish government to call in the International Monetary Fund to forestall national bankruptcy, the country needed a lift and, despite the ravages of austerity, the team brought a huge travelling support. It faced a difficult task, drawn in a group with three of Europe's strongest sides: Spain, Italy and Croatia. The team's defensive tactics and workmanlike play rarely troubled opponents, and it was outclassed in all three games. This was its poorest ever performance in an international tournament, and although Irish supporters sang in defeat, they did so with as much resignation as defiance. No one seriously suggested a celebratory homecoming.

The team limped through the next World Cup qualifying campaign, suffering a humiliating 6–1 defeat to Germany at home on 29 May 2013. Discontent with Trapattoni's management began to mount, as did a general apathy towards the team. Most international matches were laboured affairs that provided little excitement. The hard-won confidence and fearlessness that had marked the Charlton era now seemed replaced by caution and doubt. The Republic failed to win all but one of their remaining qualifying matches, eventually finishing fourth in their group. Trapattoni, with his keen knowledge of the game and idiosyncratic English, had been a popular figure for most of his tenure but his retirement announcement in September 2013 was generally greeted with relief.

He was succeeded in November 2013 by Martin O'Neill (the Republic's first manager from Northern Ireland) assisted by Roy Keane, who had managed Sunderland and Ipswich after his retirement from playing. The team secured qualification for the 2016 European Championship in France, where it performed well, beating Italy and qualifying for the second round of the tournament, before going out 2–1 to the hosts. Again it was accompanied by tens of thousands of travelling supporters, who, as ever, earned considerable praise for their good-humoured conduct. A new development was their extensive use of social media to publicise their good deeds, demonstrating how central a reputation for good behaviour had become to the self-image of Irish supporters.[25]

France 2016 was the high point of O'Neill's tenure. The Republic managed to qualify for a play-off for the 2018 World Cup but were resoundingly beaten 5–1 by Denmark at home on 14 November 2017. Public support waned and O'Neill was replaced in November 2018 by Mick McCarthy, who took the job on a transitional basis and in March 2020 handed over to Stephen Kenny. Kenny had achieved considerable success as manager of Dundalk, winning five League of Ireland titles in six years (2014–19), and had also managed the Republic of Ireland under-21s (2018–20). His appointment was widely welcomed. As a young coach who encouraged his teams to play attractive football, it was hoped that he might infuse the international game with greater excitement and entertainment. There were tentative signs of this in his first game in charge, a 1–1 draw against Bulgaria in Sofia on 3 September 2020 in the UEFA Nations League (a biennial competition founded in 2018 to give teams more competitive games against opponents of similar standing). However, Kenny's preparations for subsequent matches were disrupted by the Covid-19 pandemic and he could rarely play a settled team. It took thirteen attempts for the team to gain its first competitive win, in a World Cup qualifier against Azerbaijan on 9 October 2021. It failed to make the Euro 2020 finals or the 2022 World Cup, but criticism was muted by Kenny's readiness to look to the future by blooding young players and encouraging them to play constructive football, and the team continued to enjoy strong public support.

During this period the team suffered its first defeat to England in thirty-five years, beaten 3–0 at Wembley in a friendly international on 12 November 2020. The preparations for the match gave rise to some controversy when claims emerged that some within the Irish camp had taken exception to a short motivational video said to have featured Irish goals from previous games with England intercut with footage of the 1916 Rising. An FAI investigation cleared Kenny of any wrongdoing, but the episode served as a reminder that different members of the Irish squad and staff related to their country's past in different ways and that not everyone was comfortable with attempts to link sport and past political quarrels. This was even more starkly evident in October 2022 after the Republic's women's team celebrated qualification for the World Cup by singing a pro-IRA chant in their Hampden Park dressing-room. Their action was widely criticised, including by victims of IRA violence, and the FAI, team manager and players were quick to apologise. Manager Vera Pauw regretted that the incident was at odds with the respectful values she had worked hard to inculcate in the team and admitted that it had tarnished their achievement.[26]

The FAI was well aware that mixing sport and politics could have repercussions. Some years earlier it had sought to acknowledge the centenary of the Easter Rising before a friendly match against Switzerland at the Aviva Stadium on Good Friday, 25 March 2016. The 1916 veteran Oscar Traynor featured heavily in the match programme and some 250 descendants of participants in the Rising were invited to the game. The teams were led out by an Irish Army colour party and re-enactors in Irish Volunteer uniforms, the 1916 Proclamation was read and the Irish team shirts featured a special commemorative logo. The last of these breached FIFA's rules on the display of political symbols and was punished with a fine of 5,000 Swiss francs. The FAI were not the only ones to face such sanctions: when the four UK countries played on 11 November 2016 in shirts displaying poppies in remembrance of the dead of the Battle of the Somme, FIFA imposed fines ranging from 45,000 to 15,000 Swiss francs on their four associations.[27]

Kenny was the Republic's sixth manager in eighteen years. Many had hoped that the solid showing in the 2002 World Cup would provide the Republic with a springboard to greater success, but the team failed to qualify for the next five World Cup tournaments. Few outstanding players emerged and the team became less attractive to those eligible under the parentage rule; talented English-born players such as Jack Grealish and Declan Rice were courted at length by the Irish management, but eventually declared for England. Memorable international matches were rare, and the atmosphere at the new Aviva

Stadium was sometimes flat. Television audiences for routine qualifiers were often below 500,000, considerably less than those for major international rugby matches and GAA finals, which usually attracted between 900,000 and a million viewers. However, levels of interest rose significantly when the Republic qualified for major tournaments: audiences for individual matches at the European Championships in 2012 and 2016 generally exceeded a million. This suggests that, despite the team's uneven form in recent years, soccer has strongly established itself in Irish life and remains important to much of the population.[28]

**

From the mid-1990s that population was growing as Ireland's economy boomed, with large multinational firms investing heavily in areas such as pharmaceuticals, medical devices, electronics and information technology. Unemployment fell from 16 per cent in 1993 to 4 per cent in 2000. Many emigrants returned and there was strong immigration from continental Europe and further afield. The numbers seeking political asylum also increased significantly. Migrants from southern and eastern Europe, Africa and Asia changed the Republic from a homogenous society to a multi-cultural and multi-racial one. The 2016 census recorded people from over 180 countries living in the Republic, with 17 per cent of the total born outside the state.

This presented Ireland with some of the challenges that other countries had faced for decades. The experience in many of these was that sport was particularly effective in helping new immigrants to integrate. To encourage this process, in 2003 the Irish government developed *A Charter Against Racism in Sport*, which was ratified by the FAI and other sporting bodies. Many migrants became involved in football of their own accord, in schools, workplaces and clubs, but there were also more formal attempts to bring people together. Acknowledging that it had an important social as well as sporting role, the FAI in 2002 launched its own 'Football for All' programme to allow players of all abilities to play the game, whether for recreation or more serious competition. This led to significant growth in the numbers of those with physical and intellectual disabilities taking up the game and by 2017 the FAI was supporting eight international disability teams.[29] Packie Bonner, who became a technical director in February 2003, acknowledged that the association was 'charged with looking after football as a whole, not just the best players' and that football could play an important role in improving the lives of the marginalised or socially disadvantaged.[30] In 2006, the FAI came together with the Department of Justice, Equality, and Law Reform, the National Consultative Committee on Racism and Interculturalism, Sport Against Racism in Ireland (SARI) and Show Racism the Red Card to create a Football Intercultural Advisory Group to assist the association to develop a comprehensive intercultural football plan and programme.

There were also several grass-roots initiatives such as the Ireland League of Nations founded by the Israeli immigrant Gil Berkovich, which was officially relaunched as the Brian Kerr Intercontinental League in 2006 and brought together over twenty teams of players from some fifty nationalities.[31] (Kerr was a director of SARI and a high-profile champion of using soccer as a means of integration.) In 2006, the FAI established its own intercultural programme to promote increased participation from people of diverse ethnic, cultural and national backgrounds, and in *Intercultural Football Plan: Many Voices One Goal* (2007) outlined its intentions to combat racism in football, promote participation among minority ethnic communities and contribute to their integration into Irish society. The report argued that soccer, a sport already familiar to many immigrants, could play a central role in promoting increased contact and social interaction among migrants and between migrants and the wider community. Regularly playing soccer was found to be particularly helpful for asylum seekers living in direct provision who were at risk of social isolation, helping with language competency and providing opportunities to engage with local communities.

In all of this, there are also benefits for Irish football, with increased cultural diversity having enormous potential to enrich the game at local and national level. In recent years the children of migrants who came to Ireland in the last few decades have played in the League of Ireland

and represented the Republic at under-age level, developments that contribute to the wider process of intercultural integration.[32] Some have also graduated to the Republic's senior national team. In a friendly match against Hungary in Budapest on 8 June 2021, the team, drawn from a squad that included four players of Nigerian descent (Gavin Bazunu, Andrew Omobamidele, Adam Idah and Chiedozie Ogbene – the first three born in Ireland), showed their opposition to racism by dropping to one knee before kick-off. Their action was all the more significant because of the nativist, anti-immigration policies of the Hungarian prime minister, Viktor Orbán, always ready to use football to promote his brand of nationalist populism, who afterwards defended supporters who booed the players' gesture, which he described as 'a provocation' to the home crowd.[33]

Such episodes continue to highlight the fact that in the near 150 years in which association football has been played by Irish teams, it has often been more than just a game for many players and followers. In its early days, those who wished to keep football free of wider political and cultural influences were mostly well-intentioned, but the game's constant interaction with wider societal developments tended to defeat their best efforts, particularly as it grew in national and international popularity. The game's capacity to draw in massive numbers of followers as well as participants has always multiplied its influence. The football stadium can provide an arena in which questions of identity are laid bare, sometimes fiercely so, and many have seen their share of tribalism and violence. In the past and present, the readiness of authoritarian regimes to associate themselves with top-flight club and international football provides clear evidence of its potential to be used for dubious ends, whether that be whipping up partisan passions or acting as a compelling distraction from brutal realities.

But that of course is not the whole story: football can be a catalyst for unity as well as division and can energise as well as tranquillise. It has enriched lives with colour and excitement and regularly unleashed joy and celebration, and at its best has encouraged universal values of diversity, tolerance and solidarity. As society evolves, football evolves with it, and in doing so provides opportunities for self-expression to ever wider groups. In recent years this has been particularly striking in the case of women's football. After a long struggle for greater recognition and acceptance, the women's game has moved from the margins to the mainstream and continues to go from strength to strength, making its own important contribution to creating a fairer and more open society. While football's integrative potential is usually most noticeable on the national stage, it also operates effectively at regional, civic, local and youth levels, contributing to people's sense of community and adding to the complex and complementary layers of belonging that make up all individuals. Ultimately, football, culture and politics cannot easily be separated because they all express identities that set us apart and help us define who we are.

Endnotes

INTRODUCTION

1   Benedict Anderson, *Imagined Communities: Reflections on the Origins and Spread of Nationalism* (1983; revised ed., London, 2006), pp. 36, 48–50; Eric Hobsbawm, *Nations and Nationalism since 1780* (Cambridge, 1990), p. 143.

1. SCUFFLES, SCHOOLS AND SCOTS

1   Malcolm Brodie, *100 Years of Irish Football* (Belfast, 1980), pp. 1–2; Peter Byrne, *Football Association of Ireland: 75 Years* (Dublin, 1996), p. 15.
2   This more complex and detailed account is given in Martin Moore, 'The origins of association football in Ireland, 1875–1880: a reappraisal', *Sport in History*, 37:4 (2017), pp. 505–28.
3   *The Northern Whig*, 12 Dec. 1875.
4   *Sport*, 9 May 1885; Colm Kerrigan, 'Ireland's greatest football team?', *History Ireland*, 13:3 (July 2005), p. 26.
5   Tom Hunt, *Sport and Society in Victorian Ireland: The Case of Westmeath* (Dublin, 2007), p. 181.
6   *Cork Constitution*, 29 Nov. 1877; David Toms, *Soccer in Munster: A Social History 1877–1937* (Cork, 2015), p. 1.
7   *The Freeman's Journal*, 24 Oct. 1879.
8   *Sport*, 12 Mar., 12 Nov. 1881; *The Freeman's Journal*, 2 Apr. 1881.
9   *Belfast News Letter*, 24, 25 Oct. 1878.
10 *The Northern Whig*, 30 Oct. 1878.
11 See the reply to a letter from J.M. Calder of the 'Old Windsor Club' in *Sport*, 9 May 1885, in which McAlery plays down earlier attempts to introduce the game and claims 'Alone I did it' (*Sport*, 16 May 1885).

12 *Sport*, 26 Feb. 1881.
13 See especially Fergus A. D'Arcy, *Horses, Lords and Racing Men: The Turf Club 1790–1990* (The Curragh, Co. Kildare, 1991), p. 12.
14 Arthur Samuels, *Early Cricket in Ireland* (Dublin, 1888), pp. 7–9.
15 John Stubbs, *Anatomie of Abuses in the Realm of England* (1583?) cited in Montague Shearman, *Football: History: The Association Game by W.J. Oakley and G.O. Smith* (London, 1904), p. 10.
16 Robert Malcolmson, *Popular Recreations in English Society, 1700–1850* (Cambridge, 1973), p. 34.
17 H.J. Lawlor, 'Calendar of the Liber Ruber of the diocese of Ossory', *Proceedings of the Royal Irish Academy*, XXVII, Sect. C, No. 2 (July 1908), p. 165.
18 James Kelly, *Sport in Ireland 1600–1840* (Dublin, 2014), pp. 238, 273.
19 Patrick Fagan, 'A football match at Swords in the early 18th century', *Dublin Historical Record*, 57:2 (Autumn, 2004), pp. 223–7; Liam P. Ó Caithnia, *Báirí Cos in Éirinn* (Baile Átha Cliath, 1984), pp. 30–42.
20 *Faulkner's Dublin Journal*, 15 Apr. 1765; *Dublin Gazette*, 28 Apr. 1765; *The Freeman's Journal*, 4 May 1765, 17 Apr. 1793, 5 May 1799; *Hibernian Journal*, 23 May 1774. See also the newspaper clippings referencing the *Universal Advertiser*, 19 Mar. 1754; *Faulkner's Dublin Journal*, 1 July 1758, 15 Apr. 1766, 12 Feb. 1789; *Sleater's Public Gazetteer*, 21 Apr. 1759; *Hibernian Journal*, 20 Apr. 1774, 10 Apr. 1780; and also the *Irish Independent*, 29 Mar. 1934 in NLI MS 8723(3), P.D. Mehigan papers.

21 Kelly, *Sport in Ireland 1600–1840*, pp. 262–3, 328–9.

22 James Walvin, *The People's Game: The History of Football Revisited* (Edinburgh, 2000), p. 34.

23 Shearman, *Football: History*, pp. 85–96.

24 David Goldblatt, *The Ball is Round: A Global History of Football* (London, 2006), p. 32. In most countries the game is simply known as football. Where there are other popular indigenous football codes such as in America, Australia and Ireland, the term 'soccer' is commonly used. In Britain the association game is usually described as 'football', although devotees of other games sometimes refer to it as soccer. Throughout this work, I use the terms association football, football and soccer interchangeably.

25 See for example Tony Collins, 'Early football and the emergence of modern soccer, c.1840–1880', *International Journal of the History of Sport*, 32:9 (2015), pp. 1127–42; John Goulstone, 'The working-class origins of modern football', *International Journal of the History of Sport*, 17:1 (2000), pp. 135–43; Peter Swain, 'The origins of football debate: football and cultural continuity, 1857–1859', *International Journal of the History of Sport*, 32:5 (2015), pp. 631–49; Peter Swain, 'Early football and the emergence of modern soccer: a reply to Tony Collins', *International Journal of the History of Sport*, 33:3 (2016), pp. 251–71.

26 Swain, 'The origins of football debate', p. 641; *Belfast News Letter*, 11 Aug. 1860, cited in Swain, 'Early football ... reply to Tony Collins', pp. 262–3.

27 Adrian Harvey, '"An epoch in the annals of national sport": football in Sheffield and the creation of modern soccer and rugby', *International Journal of the History of Sport*, 18:4 (2001), pp. 73–6.

28 Tony Mason, *Association Football and English Society 1863–1915* (Brighton, 1980), p. 1; Walvin, *The People's Game*, pp. 69–70.

29 Jonathan Wilson, *Inverting the Pyramid: A History of Football Tactics* (London, 2008), pp. 15–24.

30 Wray Vamplew, *Pay Up and Play the Game: Professional Sport in Britain 1875–1914* (Cambridge, 1988), pp. 281–3.

31 *Irish Sportsman and Farmer*, 10 May 1877; Neal Garnham, *Association Football and Society in Pre-partition Ireland* (Belfast, 2004), p. 28 – this is the outstanding work on Irish soccer before 1921, well-written, thoroughly researched and full of original insights and observations.

32 *The Freeman's Journal*, 30 Apr. 1885.

33 *Irish Sportsman*, 26 Oct. 1878.

34 *Sport*, 22 Apr. 1881, 2 Dec. 1882, 27 Oct., 17 Nov. 1883.

35 Garnham, *Association Football*, p. 16.

36 Brodie, *100 Years of Irish Football*, p. 5.

37 Neal Garnham, 'Professionals and professionalism in pre-Great War Irish soccer', *Journal of Sport History*, 29:1 (Spring 2002), pp. 80–1.

38 Barry Flynn, *Political Football: The Life and Death of Belfast Celtic* (Dublin, 2009), p. 38.

39 Padraig Coyle, *Paradise Lost and Found: The Story of Belfast Celtic* (Edinburgh, 1999), pp. 17, 26; Garnham, *Association Football*, pp. 61, 64, 149; Neal Garnham, 'Association football and politics in Belfast: the careers of William Kennedy Gibson', *International Journal of the History of Sport*, 16:1 (1999), pp. 128–9.

40 *Northern Whig*, 13 Mar. 1899 (also *Belfast News Letter*, 13 Mar. 1899 and *Ireland's Saturday Night*, 11 Mar. 1899); IFA Minute Book for 14 Mar. 1899; Garnham, *Association Football*, pp. 121–2.

41 Peter Byrne, *Green is the Colour: The Story of Irish Football* (London, 2012), p. 41.

42 N.L. Jackson, *Association Football* (London, 1900), p. 249; Byrne, *Green is the Colour*, p. 13.

43 Cited in Garnham, *Association Football*, p. 17.

44 *The Freeman's Journal*, 10 Mar. 1894.

45 Patrick J. Flanagan, *Transport in Ireland 1880–1910* (Dublin, 1969), p. 142.

46 David Dickson, *Dublin: The Making of a Capital City* (London, 2014), pp. 386–7.

47 Ulick O'Connor, *Oliver St John Gogarty* (London, 1967), p. 42.

48 *United Ireland*, 18 Apr. 1885; W.P. Mandle, *The Gaelic Athletic Association and Irish*

Nationalist Politics (Dublin, 1987), pp. 26–8, 33.

49   On the codifying of Gaelic football see Mike Cronin, *Sport and Nationalism in Ireland: Gaelic Games, Soccer and Irish Identity Since 1884* (Dublin, 1999), p. 75; Joe Lennon, *Towards a Philosophy for Legislation in Irish Games* (Dublin, 2000), pp. 17–18; and Richard McElligott, *Forging a Kingdom: the GAA in Kerry 1884–1934* (Cork, 2013), p. 63.

50   Donal O'Sullivan, *Sport in Cork: A History* (Dublin, 2012), p. 23.

51   Neal Garnham, 'Accounting for the early success of the Gaelic Athletic Association', *Irish Historical Studies*, 34:133 (May, 2004), p. 65.

52   Mandle, *GAA and Irish Nationalist Politics*, pp. 83–4; Garnham, *Association Football*, p. 31.

53   *Sport*, 24 Mar. 1883.

54   *United Ireland*, 25 Oct. 1884.

55   Neal Garnham, 'Football and national identity in pre-Great War Ireland', *Irish Economic and Social History*, 28 (2001), p. 29.

56   *Sport*, 2 Dec. 1882, 27 Oct. 1883, 17 Nov. 1883.

57   Hamish Stuart, 'The football nations', *Blackwood's Edinburgh Magazine*, vol. clxix, no. mxxvi (Apr. 1901), p. 495.

58   *The Freeman's Journal*, 26 Feb. 1891, 5 Mar. 1894, 20 Feb. 1897, 1 Feb. 1900.

59   Cited in Joe Dodd, 'The first sixty years', in George Briggs & Joe Dodd (eds), *Leinster Football Association: 100 years, the Centenary Handbook* (Dublin, 1992), p. 22.

60   *Sport*, 4 Mar. 1895.

61   *Sport*, 10, 31 Mar. 1888; *The Freeman's Journal*, 26 Jan. 1884.

62   *Sport*, 12 Mar. 1898.

63   *Sport*, 1 Apr. 1899.

64   Cited in Michael Walker, *Green Shoots: Irish Football Histories* (Liverpool, 2017), p. 79; see also Richard Sanders, *Beastly Fury: The Strange Birth of British Football* (London, 2009), p. 153 and Garnham, *Association Football*, p. 32.

65   Garnham, *Association Football*, pp. 112, 114.

66   Alan Lugton, *The Making of Hibernian* (3

vols, Edinburgh, 1995– 8), i, p. 53.

67   Interview in *The Westminster Gazette*, Jan. 1895.

68   *Daily Sketch*, 6 Feb. 1895, cited in Christopher Rowley, *The Shared Origins of Football, Rugby and Soccer* (London, 2015), p. 215.

69   *The Freeman's Journal*, 26 Mar. 1895.

70   Tim Tate, *Girls with Balls: The Secret History of Women's Football* (London, 2013), p. 84; Goldblatt, *The Ball is Round*, p. 78.

2. NORTH AND SOUTH

1   Goldblatt, *The Ball is Round*, pp. 243–4.

2   Matthew Taylor, *The Association Game: A History of British Football* (Harlow, 2007), p. 161; Goldblatt, *The Ball is Round*, pp. 114–16.

3   Goldblatt, *The Ball is Round*, p. 905.

4   Andrew O'Brien and Linde Lunney, 'John H. Kirwan', in James McGuire and James Quinn (eds), *Dictionary of Irish Biography* (Cambridge, 9 volumes, 2009), 5, pp. 233–4; Jim Shanahan, 'Patrick Joseph O'Connell', *Dictionary of Irish Biography*, 7, pp. 219–20; Kristopher McCormack, 'Arthur Johnson: the Irishman who taught Real Madrid how to play football', https://thesefootballtimes. co/2019/02/21/arthur-johnson-the-irishman-who-taught-real-madrid-how-to-play-football/ (accessed 7 Feb. 2020); 'The amazing story of the Tipperary man who helped found Argentina's most famous football club', www.thejournal.ie (accessed 7 Feb. 2020).

5   Barry Landy, *Emerald Exiles: How the Irish Made Their Mark on World Football* (Dublin, 2021), pp. 9–13.

6   On McCarthy see 'The amazing story of the Tipperary man who helped found Argentina's most famous football club', www.thejournal.ie (accessed 7 Feb. 2020).

7   George Briggs and Joe Dodd (eds), *Leinster Football Association: 100 Years, the Centenary Yearbook* (Dublin, 1992), p. 30.

8   Alan Tomlinson, *FIFA (Fédération Internationale de Football Association): The*

Men, the Myths and the Money (Oxford, 2014), p. 14.

9   Walvin, *The People's Game*, p. 104.

10 *The Origins and Development of Football in Ireland being a Reprint of R.M. Peter's Irish Football Annual of 1880 with an Introduction by Neal Garnham* (Belfast, 1999), p. 176; Malcolm Brodie, *The History of Irish Soccer* (Glasgow, 1963), p. 239.

11 *The Freeman's Journal*, 4 Sept. 1912.

12 'Belfast's Victory in Vienna: A Footballing Odyssey', BBC One (NI), 2 May 2022.

13 *The Freeman's Journal*, 30 Jan. 1899.

14 Joe Dodd, 'The first sixty years' in Briggs and Dodd (eds), *Leinster Football Association*, p. 27; N.L. Jackson, *Association Football* (London, 1900), p. 249.

15 Brodie, *100 Years of Irish Football*, p. 9.

16 *The Cork Examiner*, 22 Apr. 1914.

17 Garnham, *Association Football*, pp. 12–13, 29.

18 Hunt, *Sport and Society in Victorian Ireland*, pp. 171, 178.

19 [Anon.], *St Catherine's FC: A Celebration of 100 Years of Soccer in Killybegs* (Killybegs, 1996?), p. 5.

20 Conor Curran, *Sport in Donegal: A History* (Dublin, 2010), pp. 44–6, 53. This work and the others by Conor Curran, cited below, are by far the most detailed and authoritative on the subject.

21 Conor Curran, 'The development of Gaelic football and soccer zones in County Donegal, 1884–1936', *Sport in History*, 32:3 (Sept. 2012), pp. 428–31; Conor Curran, *Irish Soccer Migrants: A Social and Cultural History* (Cork, 2017), p. 63; see also Joseph Murray, Brigade officer Donegal IRA, 1921, NAI, Bureau of Military History (BMH) Witness Statement (WS) 1566, p. 2.

22 Curran, *Sport in Donegal*, pp. 44–74.

23 *Donegal News*, 25 Nov. 1905.

24 Curran, *Sport in Donegal*, pp. 44–6, 73.

25 Conor Curran, 'Networking structures and competitive association football in Ulster, 1880–1914', *Irish Economic and Social History*, 41 (2014), pp. 74–92.

26 *Ireland's Saturday Night*, 24 Dec. 1898.

27 *Sport*, 23 Apr. 1904.

28 Goldblatt, *The Ball is Round*, pp. 62, 71.

29 Garnham, *Association Football*, pp. 115–16.

30 C.S. Andrews, *Dublin Made Me* (Dublin, 1979), pp. 10–12.

31 Garnham, *Association Football*, p. 12.

32 Mary E. Daly, *Dublin: The Deposed Capital: A Social and Economic History* (Cork, 1984), p. 5.

33 *The Leader*, 10 Nov. 1900; Garnham, *Association Football*, pp. 26, 67.

34 Ulick O'Connor, *Oliver St John Gogarty* (London, 1967), pp. 14–15.

35 Eoghan Rice, *We Are Rovers: An Oral History of Shamrock Rovers FC* (Stroud, 2005), p. 38; E.J. O'Mahony, *Bohemian FC Golden Jubilee Souvenir* (Dublin, 1940), p. 13.

36 Tony Reid, *Bohemians AFC: Official Club History, 1890–1976* (Dublin, 1976), p. 17.

37 Christopher Sands, *Shels: A Grand Old Team to Know: A History of Shelbourne FC since 1895* (Dublin, 2016), p. 24.

38 Ibid., pp. 12–14.

39 *The Irish Worker*, 30 Aug. 1913; *The Freeman's Journal*, 30 Aug. 1913; *The Irish Times*, 30 Aug., 5 Oct. 1913, 18 Aug. 2018; Pádraig Yeates, *Lockout: Dublin 1913* (Dublin, 2000), pp. 48–9.

40 Joe Dodd, 'The first sixty years' in George Briggs and Joe Dodd (eds), *Leinster Football Association: 100 Years, the Centenary Handbook* (Dublin, 1992), p. 57.

41 Martin Johnes, *Soccer and Society: South Wales 1900–1939* (Cardiff, 2002), p. 170; Garnham, *Association Football*, p. 50.

42 Goldblatt, *The Ball is Round*, pp. 40, 63.

43 Brendan Power, 'The function of association football in the Boys' Brigade in Ireland 1888–1914' in Leeann Lane and William Murphy (eds), *Leisure and the Irish in the Nineteenth Century* (Liverpool, 2016), pp. 41–58.

44 Dodd, 'The first sixty years' in Briggs and Dodd (eds), *Leinster Football Association*, pp. 43–4; Garnham, *Association Football*, pp. 12, 45; Byrne, *Green is the Colour*, p. 27.

45 Jim Murphy, *The History of Dundalk FC* (Dundalk, 2003), pp. 6–9.

46 Mark Tynan, 'Association football and Irish society during the interwar period, 1918–39' (PhD, NUI Maynooth, 2013), p. 214.

47 Tony Mason, *Association Football and English Society 1863–1915* (Brighton, 1980),

pp. 236–40; Walvin, *The People's Game*, p. 87.

48 Goldblatt, *The Ball is Round*, pp. 52, 61.

49 Liam Kennedy, Lucia Pozzi and Matteo Manfredini, 'Edwardian Belfast: marriage fertility and religion in 1911', in Olwen Purdue (ed.), *Belfast: The Emerging City 1850–1914* (Dublin, 2013), p. 192; Emrys Jones, *A Social Geography of Belfast* (London, 1960), pp. 46–50.

50 David Goldblatt, *The Game of Our Lives: The Meaning and Making of English Football* (London, 2014), p. 102.

51 Arthur Clery, 'Rugby football and the condominium', in *Dublin Essays* (Dublin, 1919), p. 70.

52 Garnham, *Association Football*, p. 108.

53 *The Freeman's Journal*, 17 Mar. 1900.

54 Byrne, *Green is the Colour*, p. 31; Garnham, *Association Football*, pp. 166–7.

55 *The Freeman's Journal*, 7 May 1901; Byrne, *Green is the Colour*, pp. 17–18.

56 *The Freeman's Journal*, 13 May 1901.

57 *The Freeman's Journal*, 25 Mar. 1895.

58 *Sport*, 8 Apr. 1899.

59 (Dublin) *Evening Telegraph*, 30 Apr. 1906.

60 *Sport*, 22 Feb. 1913.

61 *The Freeman's Journal*, 24 Mar. 1902.

62 *The Irish Times*, 19 Mar. 1900.

63 IFA Annual Report, 9 May 1903, in IFA Council minute book, 31 Mar. 1903 to 2 Feb. 1909 (PRONI D/4196/A/2).

64 *The Irish Times*, 17, 22 Feb. 1913.

65 *Sport*, 22 Feb. 1913.

66 *Sport*, 21 Feb. 1914.

67 *Sport*, 28 Mar. 1914; see also *The Irish Times*, 16 Mar. 1914; *Belfast News Letter*, 16 Mar. 1914.

68 Cormac Moore, *The Irish Soccer Split* (Cork, 2015), p. 71.

69 Anthony Clavane, *Does Your Rabbi Know You're Here? The Story of English Football's Forgotten Tribe* (London, 2013), pp. 14–16; T.P. Walsh, *Twenty Years of Irish Soccer 1921–41* (Dublin, 1941), p. 40.

70 Garnham, 'Football and national identity', p. 15.

71 Hamish Stuart, 'The football nations', *Blackwood's Edinburgh Magazine*, vol. clxix, no. mxxvi (April, 1901), p. 494.

72 For the administrative and organisational significance of the ban see especially Paul Rouse, 'The politics of culture and sport in Ireland: a history of the GAA ban on foreign games 1884–1971, part one: 1884–1921', *The International Journal of the History of Sport*, 10:3 (1993), pp. 333–60.

73 J.J. Walsh, *Recollections of a Rebel* (Tralee, 1944), p. 17; Garnham, *Association Football*, p. 29.

74 Douglas Hyde, 'The necessity for de-Anglicising Ireland' in *The Revival of Irish Literature* (London, 1894), p. 119; see also Douglas Hyde, 'Games and nationality' in T.F. O'Sullivan, *The Story of the GAA* (Dublin, 1916), pp. 196–8.

75 *United Irishman*, 29 July 1905; Mandle, *GAA and Irish Nationalist Politics*, p. 133.

76 'An old player', *The Freeman's Journal*, 25 Oct. 1902.

77 *The Leader*, 10 Nov. 1900, 30 Jan. 1904.

78 *United Irishman*, 2 June 1900.

79 Arthur Clery, 'Nationality and amusements', *The Leader*, 23 Jan. 1904.

80 *The Leader*, 5 Mar. 1904.

81 Brodie, *100 Years of Irish Football*, p. 1.

82 IFA Minute Book 1898–1903, 6 May 1899, p. 21, cited in Garnham, *Association Football*, p. 19.

83 *The Freeman's Journal*, 2 Jan. 1899; Garnham, *Association Football*, pp. 18–21.

84 Ulrich Hesse-Lichtenberger, *Tor! The Story of German Football* (London, 2002), p. 25; Goldblatt, *The Ball is Round*, pp. 113, 154, 161.

85 Cited in Mandle, *GAA and Irish Nationalist Politics*, p. 123.

86 *Westmeath Examiner*, 28 Oct. 1899, cited in Hunt, *Sport and Society in Victorian Ireland*, p. 202.

87 *Irish Independent*, 15 Mar. 1913.

88 Byrne, *Green is the Colour*, p. 14.

89 Garnham, *Association Football*, p. 139.

90 *The Northern Whig*, 16 Sept. 1912; *The Freeman's Journal*, 16 Sept. 1912; *The Irish Times*, 21 Sept. 1912.

91 Handbill (20 Sept. 1912) in Irish Football League minute book 1909–13; published in *The Northern Whig*, 28 Sept. 1912.

92 Garnham, *Association Football*, p. 128.

93 Ibid., pp. 144–6.

94 Byrne, *Green is the Colour*, p. 48; Garnham, *Association Football*, p. 150; *The*

Irish Times, 22 Mar. 1913; *The Freeman's Journal*, 2 Apr. 1913.

95 Garnham, 'Football and national identity', pp. 13–31.

3. THINGS FALL APART

1 *The Irish Times*, 7 Nov. 1914.
2 Recruiting bills handed out at football matches in Glasgow, cited in *The Irish Times*, 6 Sept. 1914.
3 *The Freeman's Journal*, 17 Dec. 1914.
4 Garnham, *Association Football*, pp. 169–70.
5 PRONI D4196/U/1, IFA Annual Report, 1914/15.
6 Tynan, 'Association football and Irish society', pp. 19–20.
7 *The Freeman's Journal*, 16 Apr., 3 Dec. 1917.
8 *The Irish Times*, 24 Jan., 16, 26 Nov. 1918.
9 *Belfast Telegraph*, 27 Dec. 1917; Tate, *Girls With Balls*, pp. 138–9.
10 *Irish Independent*, 6 May 1918.
11 *Derry People and Donegal News*, 29 Nov. 1919.
12 *The Freeman's Journal*, 20 Sept. 1917.
13 [Dublin] *Evening Telegraph*, 14 Nov. 1919.
14 *Dundalk Democrat*, 16 Nov. 1922.
15 W.P. Mandle, *The Gaelic Athletic Association and Irish Nationalist Politics* (Dublin, 1987), pp. 166–7.
16 Mandle, *GAA and Irish Nationalist Politics*, p. 188; *Irish Independent*, 9 Nov. 1921.
17 Neal Garnham, 'Accounting for the early success of the Gaelic Athletic Association', *Irish Historical Studies*, 34:133 (May 2004), pp. 65–78; William Murphy, 'The GAA during the Irish Revolution, 1913–23' in Mike Cronin, William Murphy and Paul Rouse (eds), *The Gaelic Athletic Association 1884–2009* (Dublin, 2009), pp. 61–76.
18 Murphy, 'GAA during the Irish Revolution', pp. 62–3, 67.
19 *The Freeman's Journal*, 19 May, 25 Oct. 1917.
20 *The Freeman's Journal*, 8 Oct. 1920.
21 *Irish Independent*, 29 Oct. 1920; *The Freeman's Journal*, 17 Mar. 1921; *Football Sports Weekly*, 26 Mar. 1927.
22 Peadar S. Doyle, Irish Volunteers, Dublin, NAI, BMH WS 155, p. 31; see also Jack Shouldice, Irish Volunteers, Dublin BMH WS 679, p. 17, and Michael Carroll,

Irish Volunteers, Dublin, BMH WS 1210, p. 2.
23 Brian Hanley, 'Oscar Traynor and "the crime of playing soccer"', *History Ireland*, 24:1 (Jan.–Feb. 2016), pp. 48–9.
24 Joe Wickham to Henri Fodor (Hungary), 7 Jan. 1939, FAI Archive, P137/47; Robert Briscoe papers, NLI MS 26,602.
25 C.S. Andrews, *Man of No Property* (Dublin, 1982), p. 41; idem, *Dublin Made Me* (Dublin, 1979), p. 11.
26 *Football Sports Weekly*, 11 Feb. 1928.
27 *The Irish Times*, 19 Oct. 1969.
28 *Irish Independent*, 20 Jan., 9 Mar. 1919.
29 *Irish Independent*, 29 June 1918.
30 Neal Garnham, *The Origins and Development of Football in Ireland being a Reprint of R.M. Peter's Irish Football Annual of 1880* (Belfast, 1999), p. 24.
31 Garnham, *Association Football*, p. 160; Tynan, 'Association football and Irish society', pp. 22–3.
32 Moore, *The Irish Soccer Split*, p. 235 – this is the most detailed and authoritative account of the partition of Irish soccer; see also *Sunday Independent*, 20 Apr. 1919 and *The Freeman's Journal*, 14 Jan. 1920.
33 Moore, *The Irish Soccer Split*, pp. 90–1, 100, 102.
34 Garnham, *Association Football*, p. 176; Tynan, 'Association football and Irish society', p. 37.
35 *Belfast Telegraph*, 18 Mar. 1920.
36 Coyle, *Paradise Lost and Found*, p. 31; *The Cork Examiner*, 18 Mar. 1920.
37 Byrne, *Green is the Colour*, p. 60; Tynan, 'Association football and Irish society', p. 37.
38 Byrne, *Football Association of Ireland*, p. 21.
39 *Irish Independent*, 12 Feb. 1921.
40 *Catholic Bulletin*, xi (1921), p. 246, cited in Garnham, *Association Football*, p. 185.
41 Garnham, *Association Football*, pp. 186–8.
42 *Sport*, 12 Mar. 1921, p. 14.
43 *The Freeman's Journal*, 8 Mar. 1921 and *Sport*, 12 Mar. 1921.
44 *Irish Independent*, 9 June 1921.
45 Moore, *The Irish Soccer Split*, p. 121.
46 Moore, *The Irish Soccer Split*, pp. 120–1.
47 *The Freeman's Journal*, 2 July 1921 and *Irish Independent*, 20 Aug. 1921.
48 *Belfast News Letter*, 8 Feb. 1923.

4. FOOTBALL ON A DIVIDED ISLAND

1 Byrne, *Football Association of Ireland*, p. 23.

2 Tynan, 'Association football and Irish society', pp. 113, 120 – this is the most detailed and comprehensive work on the development of Irish soccer in this period.

3 Tynan, 'Association football and Irish society', pp. 117-18; official confirmation of FAI's provisional admission to FIFA, 10 Aug. 1923 (International minute book of the FAI, FAI Archive, P137/1).

4 Toms, *Soccer in Munster*, pp. 37, 115.

5 Bertie O'Mahony, *Munster Football Association: 75 Years Service to the Beautiful Game 1922-1997* (Cork, 1998), p. 31; Minute Book of the Consultative Committee of the FAI, 25 Oct. 1927, FAI Archive, P137/38.

6 Frank Lynch, *A History of Athlone Town FC: The First 100 Years* (Athlone, 1991), p. 97.

7 David Toms, '"Notwithstanding the discomfort involved": Fordsons' cup win in 1926 and how "the Old Contemptible" were represented in Ireland's public sphere during the 1920s', *Sport in History*, 32:4 (2012), p. 50.

8 *The Cork Examiner*, 18 Mar. 1926.

9 Plunkett Carter, 'Soccer in Cork city' in John Crowley (ed.), *Atlas of Cork City* (Cork, 2005), pp. 322-4.

10 *Football Sports Weekly*, 2 Jan. 1926, p.1, 5 June 1926, p. 1.

11 Minute book of the Finance Committee of the FAI, 1 Dec. 1928, FAI Archive, P137/11.

12 *Irish Independent*, 16 Aug. 1929.

13 Tynan, 'Association football and Irish society', pp. 130, 131, 162, 225.

14 Minute book of the senior council of the FAI, 1932-1937, Annual Report, 18 June 1934, FAI Archive, P137/21.

15 Curran, *Sport in Donegal*, p. 134; Conor Curran, 'Sport and cultural nationalism: the conflict between association and Gaelic football in Donegal, 1905-34', *Éire-Ireland*, 48:1/2 (2013), pp. 79-94.

16 Cited in ibid., p. 89.

17 Eoghan Rice, *We Are Rovers: An Oral History of Shamrock Rovers FC* (Stroud, 2005), pp. 36, 38.

18 *Cork Evening Echo*, 17 Apr. 1936, cited in O'Sullivan, *Sport in Cork*, p. 112.

19 Walsh, *Twenty Years of Irish Soccer*, p. 133.

20 *The Irish Press*, 11 Oct. 1932.

21 *Irish Independent*, 31 Jan. 1929.

22 Walsh, *Twenty Years of Irish Soccer*, p. 118.

23 Tynan, 'Association football and Irish society', p. 212.

24 Murphy, *The History of Dundalk FC*, pp. 4-7.

25 *The Irish Statesman*, 17 Oct. 1925.

26 *The Freeman's Journal*, 25 Apr. 1923, 11 Dec. 1923.

27 *Football Sports Weekly*, 16 Jan.1926, p. 1.

28 Minute book of GAA Central Council (1911– 25), 15 Oct. 1921 (GAA Archive, GAA/CC/01/02, p. 554); also report of meeting of GAA Central Council, *The Freeman's Journal*, 17 Oct. 1921.

29 Toms, *Soccer in Munster*, pp. 87, 92.

30 *The Freeman's Journal*, 27 Apr. 1923.

31 *Gaelic Athlete*, 21 Mar. 1925.

32 *Irish Independent*, 16 Aug. 1924.

33 Mike Cronin, 'Projecting the nation through sport and culture: Ireland, Aonach Tailteann and the Irish Free State 1924-32', *Journal of Contemporary History*, 38:3 (2003), pp. 395-411.

34 *An Phoblacht*, 1 Oct. 1932.

35 Sean Cronin, *Frank Ryan: The Search for the Republic* (Dublin, 1979), p. 69.

36 *The Irish Times*, 30 July 1960.

37 See for example *An Phoblacht*, 5 Feb., 19 June 1926.

38 Cited in Mandle, *GAA and Irish Nationalist Politics*, p. 214; the IRA Volunteer Robert Holland who was also detained at Knutsford recalled the large number of soccer players from the Dublin clubs of Strandville, Distillery and St James's Gate at the camp (NAI, BMH WS 371).

39 'Who are the Shoneens?' in *Football Sports Weekly*, 26 Feb. 1927, p. 16.

40 *Football Sports Weekly*, 9 Apr. 1927, p. 2.

41 Oscar Traynor, 'The crime of playing soccer' in *Football Sports Weekly*, 11 Feb. 1928.

42 Entertainment duty: application to Gaelic games and other sports, May 1932 – June 1932, Extracts from Cabinet Minutes, Cab. 6/29, 23-4 May 1932, item no. 7 (NAI, TSCH/3/S6276).

43 13 July 1932, FAI Archive, P137/21.
44 Ibid.
45 Denis Gorey, Cumann na nGaedheal TD for Carlow-Kilkenny, Dáil Éireann, 7 May 1925; Michael Davis, Cumann na nGaedheal TD for Mayo North, Dáil Éireann, 3 Aug. 1932.
46 Sean Gibbons, Fianna Fáil TD for Carlow-Kilkenny, Dáil Éireann, 7 July 1932, 3 Aug. 1932.
47 Sean McEntee, Fianna Fáil TD for Dublin County, Dáil Éireann, 5 June 1930; Sean Gibbons, Fianna Fáil TD for Carlow-Kilkenny, Dáil Éireann, 7 July 1932.
48 William Davin, Labour Party TD for Laois-Offaly, Dáil Éireann, 3 Aug. 1932.
49 Oliver St John Gogarty, Seanad Éireann, 27 July 1932.
50 Ernest Blythe, Cumann na nGaedheal Minister for Finance, Dáil Éireann, 2 July 1931.
51 Patrick McGilligan, Cumann na nGaedheal TD for the NUI, Dáil Éireann, 3 Aug. 1932.
52 J.J. Byrne, Cumann na nGaedheal TD for Dublin North, Dáil Éireann, 7 July 1932.
53 AGM Record, 29 June 1934, FAI Archive, P137/21; Byrne, Green is the Colour, p. 134.
54 Maurice Gorham, Forty Years of Irish Broadcasting (Dublin, 1967), p. 100.
55 Byrne, Football Association of Ireland, p. 25; Toms, Soccer in Munster, p. 129; Tynan, 'Association football and Irish society', pp. 235–6; for the attitudes of J.J. Walsh, Cumann na nGaedheal Minister for Posts and Telegraphs (1922–7), see Walsh, Recollections of a Rebel, p. 67.
56 Ciara Chambers, Ireland in the Newsreels (Dublin, 2012), pp. 137–9, 248–9.
57 Football Sports Weekly, 9 Apr. 1927, p. 2.
58 'Who are the Shoneens?' in Football Sports Weekly, 26 Feb. 1927, p. 16.
59 Jim Smyth, 'Dancing, depravity and all that jazz: the Public Dance Halls Act of 1935', History Ireland, 1:2 (Summer 1993), pp. 51, 54.
60 James Plunkett, Farewell Companions (London, 1977), p. 30.
61 Football Sports Weekly, 12 Dec. 1925, p. 5.
62 K.S. Isles and Norman Cuthbert, An Economic Survey of Northern Ireland (Belfast, 1957), pp. 566, 577.
63 David Laverty and Neal Garnham, 'Football in inter-war Northern Ireland: Ballymena Football and Athletic Club Limited – religious and political exclusivity or civic inclusivity?', International Journal of the History of Sport, 27:13 (2010), pp. 2212–33.
64 Moore, The Irish Soccer Split, p. 193.
65 Coyle, Paradise Lost and Found, p. 31.
66 Eamonn McCann, 'Belfast Celtic: the day a team died', Sunday Tribune, 20 Dec. 1998.
67 See for example Football Sports Weekly, 28 Aug. 1926.
68 Football Sports Weekly, 12 Mar. 1927, p. 1.
69 Goldblatt, The Ball is Round, p. 698.
70 Gail J. Newsham, In a League of Their Own! The Dick, Kerr Ladies 1917–1965 (London, 1997).
71 Football Sports Weekly, 24 Apr. 1927, p. 6; 28 May 1928, p. 8.
72 The Northern Whig, 28 July 1931.
73 For Seaton's career see the article by Steve Bolton at www.playingpasts.co.uk/articles/football/molly-seaton-irelands-bestmy-tribute-to-the-legendary-irish-woman-footballertalented-pioneer-iconic-figure/ (accessed Apr. 2021)
74 James Quinn, 'Sean Fallon', www.dib.ie
75 Toms, Soccer in Munster, p. 145.
76 Eoghan Rice, We Are Rovers: An Oral History of Shamrock Rovers FC (Stroud, 2005), p. 22; Charlie Willoughby, Come on the Hoops: The Story of Shamrock Rovers (Dublin, 1987), p. 8.

5. LEAGUES OF NATIONS

1 Jack Ryder to the Fédération Française de Football (FFF), 6 Feb. 1922, FAI International Minute Book, FAI Archive, P137/1; H. Delauney (secretary-general of FFF) to Jack Ryder, 10 Mar. 1922, FAI Archive, P137/1.
2 FIFA to the FAI, 19 Feb. 1922, FAI International Minute Book, FAI Archive, P137/1; C.A.W. Hirschman (secretary/treasurer of FIFA) to the FAI, 16 Oct. 1922, FAI International Minute Book, FAI Archive, P137/1.
3 Sunday Independent, 4 Feb. 1923.
4 Jack Ryder's notes from the Shelbourne Hotel conference, 3 Mar. 1923, FAI

International Minute Book, FAI Archive, P137/1.

5   *Irish Independent*, 20 Mar., 31 Mar., 2 Apr. 1923.

6   Jack Ryder to FIFA, 20 July 1923, FAI Archive, P137/1.

7   Osmond Grattan Esmonde to J.F. Harrison, 3 May 1923, FAI International Minute Book, FAI Archive, P137/1.

8   Byrne, *Green is the Colour*, p. 83; M.A. Duchenne (Gallia FC) to R.F. Murphy, 7 Aug. 1923, FAI International Minute Book, FAI Archive, P137/1; Official confirmation of FAIFS's provisional admission to FIFA, 10 Aug. 1923, FAI International Minute Book, FAI Archive, P137/1.

9   24 Nov. 1923, FAI Archive, P137/4; Scottish FA to Jack Ryder, 20 Dec. 1923, FAI International Minute Book, FAI Archive, P137/1; Byrne, *Green is the Colour*, p. 88.

10   Goldblatt, *The Ball is Round*, p. 236.

11   Garnham, *Association Football*, pp. 182 -3; Byrne, *Green is the Colour*, p. 92. This work, along with the same writer's *Football Association of Ireland*, provide excellent surveys of the international game in the twenty-six counties.

12   David Needham, *Ireland's First Real World Cup: The Story of the 1924 Ireland Olympic Football Team* (Dublin, 2012), p. 163; Moore, *The Irish Soccer Split*, p. 169.

13   Tadhg Carey, 'Ireland's footballers at the Paris Olympics, 1924', *History Ireland*, 20:4 (July–Aug. 2012), p. 23.

14   *Irish Independent*, 9 June 1924; Carey, 'Paris Olympics', p. 24.

15   *Sport*, 14 June 1924.

16   Carey, 'Paris Olympics', p. 25; *Sport*, 21 June 1924; Needham, *Ireland's First Real World Cup*, p. 79.

17   *The Irish Times*, 11 June 1924, p. 4.

18   *Irish Independent*, 16 June, p. 8; *The Freeman's Journal*, 16 June 1924.

19   *Football Sports Weekly*, 19 Sept. 1925, p. 3.

20   Byrne, *Green is the Colour*, p. 139.

21   John Foot, *Calcio: The Story of Italian Football* (London, 2007), pp. 389–90.

22   Byrne, *Green is the Colour*, p. 117; *The Irish Times*, 22 Mar. 1926; *Irish Independent*, 22, 25 Mar. 1926.

23   *The Irish Times*, 22, 23 Apr. 1927.

24   *Irish Independent*, 25 Apr. 1927, p. 9.

25   *Sunday Independent*, 24 Apr. 1927; *The Irish Times*, 25 Apr. 1927; *Irish Independent*, 25 Apr. 1927, p. 6.

26   Osmond Grattan Esmonde, Cumann na nGaedheal TD for Wexford, Dáil Éireann debates, 2 July 1931.

27   Byrne, *Football Association of Ireland*, pp. 35–6.

28   *Irish Independent*, 9 Apr. 1934.

29   Diarmaid Ferriter, *Judging Dev: A Reassessment of the Life and Legacy of Éamon de Valera* (Dublin, 2007), p. 222; David McCullagh, *De Valera: Volume 1: Rise 1882–1932* (Dublin, 2017), pp. 35, 41; idem., *De Valera: Volume 2: Rule 1932–75* (Dublin, 2018), p. 375.

30   *Irish Independent*, 9 Dec. 1935.

31   3 Nov. 1935, FAI Archive, P137/45.

32   Trevor White, *Alfie: The Life and Times of Alfie Byrne* (London, 2017), pp. 7, 51.

33   Alfie Byrne, Dáil Éireann debates, 5, 7 July, 3 Aug. 1932.

34   Moore, *The Irish Soccer Split*, p. 191.

35   Tynan, 'Association football and Irish society', pp. 62–3; 20 June 1929, FAI International Minute Book, FAI Archive, P137/3.

36   Brodie, *100 Years of Irish Football*, p. 106.

37   *Belfast News Letter*, 25 Feb. 1929.

38   *Football Sports Weekly*, 4 Feb. 1928, p. 9.

39   *Belfast News Letter*, 22 Oct. 1934.

40   10, 18 Nov. 1930, 3, 10 Feb. 1931, FAI Archive P137/15; *Irish Independent*, 22 Sept. 1931.

41   28 Oct. 193, FAI Archive P137/12.

42   Byrne, *Green is the Colour*, p. 121.

43   Tynan, 'Association football and Irish society', pp. 70–1.

44   Byrne, *Green is the Colour*, p. 146.

45   Walsh, *Twenty Years of Irish Soccer*, p. 28.

46   Correspondence for Sept. 1938 to Apr. 1939, FAI Archive, P137/4.

47   Byrne, *Green is the Colour*, p. 155.

48   10 May 1938, FAI Archive, P137/5.

49   Correspondence between Joe Wickham and J.W. Dulanty, 4 Nov. 1938 to 15 Apr. 1939, FAI Archive, P137/6.

50   Cited in Ged Martin, 'De Valera imagined and observed' in Gabriel Doherty and Dermot Keogh (eds), *De Valera's Irelands* (Cork, 2003), p. 95.

51 'Relations between FAI and IFA', FAI Archive, P137/6, 4 Nov. 1938, 17 Nov. 1938; 15 Apr., 28 Apr., 19 May, 19 July 1939.

52 *Sunday Independent*, 18 Oct. 1936.

53 *The Irish Press*, 8 Nov. 1937.

54 Secretary to the President, Sports fixtures: general procedure, 1938–1946 (NAI, PRES/1/P707); Tynan, 'Association football and Irish society', p. 106.

55 Cormac Moore, *The GAA v Douglas Hyde* (Cork, 2013), p. 88; NAI, PRES 1/P1131, 5 Dec. 1938.

56 *The Irish Times*, 19 Dec. 1938.

57 Moore, *The GAA v Douglas Hyde*, pp. 144–5.

58 'Fanatics out to establish Gaelic State', *Belfast News Letter*, 23 Sept. 1932.

59 *Belfast News Letter*, 13 Mar. 1934.

60 *The Northern Whig*, 21 Dec. 1939.

61 NAI, Office of President, Pres1/ P2888, International soccer matches: attendance of President, 1946–60.

62 Tynan, 'Association football and Irish society', p. 126.

63 *Irish Independent*, 20 Mar. 1939.

64 George Orwell, 'The sporting spirit', *Tribune*, 14 Dec. 1945, in *The Penguin Essays of George Orwell* (London, 1994), pp. 323–4.

65 As late as May 1938 the England team (in keeping with other visiting teams) gave the Nazi salute at a match in Berlin.

66 Donal Cullen, *Freestaters: The Republic of Ireland Soccer Team 1921–1939* (Southend, 2007), pp. 94–5.

67 'Continental tour May 1939', Minute Book of the International Affairs Committee, FAI Archive, P137/39, May 1939.

68 Byrne, *Green is the Colour*, p. 164.

6. NATIONAL SERVICE

1 Owing to the contested nature of the term 'Ireland' in both politics and sport, I refer to the former Free State as 'Éire' between 1937 and 1949. Some dislike its use in the English language, but it was widely used by contemporaries in Ireland as well as abroad, particularly during the war years.

2 J.W. Blake, *Northern Ireland in the Second World War* (Belfast, 1956), pp. 534–5.

3 Brendan Mac Lua, *The Steadfast Rule: A History of the GAA Ban* (Dublin, 1967), p. 85.

4 Sean O'Faolain, 'The stuffed shirts', *The Bell*, 6:3 (June 1943), p. 181.

5 *Belfast Telegraph*, 21 Apr. 1941.

6 Cited in David Birmingham, *A Concise History of Portugal* (Cambridge, 1993), p. 166.

7 *The Irish Press*, 10 May 1946.

8 Byrne, *Green is the Colour*, p. 168.

9 9 Aug. 1946, FAI Archive P137/49.

10 Byrne, *Green is the Colour*, p. 190.

11 2, 24 Sept. 1946, FAI Archive, P137/49.

12 Cited in Byrne, *Football Association of Ireland*, p. 47.

13 *The Irish Press*, 2 Oct. 1946.

14 Cited in Byrne, *Football Association of Ireland*, p. 57.

15 *Daily Herald* (London), 22 Sept. 1949; *The Irish Press*, 22 Sept. 1949.

16 25 May 1950, FAI Archive, P137/39.

17 *The Irish Press*, 24 Sept. 1946; 17 Sept. 1946; IFA Emergency Minutes 1943–1995, D4196/N/2, 17.

18 20 Aug. 1946, FAI Archive, P137/49.

19 1 Nov. 1946, FAI Archive, P137/39; this was confirmed by an assurance by the FAI to the English FA on 13 Aug. 1948, ibid., P137/39.

20 *The Irish Press*, 21 Sept. 1949; see also James Quinn, 'John Joseph Carey', *Dictionary of Irish Biography*, 5, pp. 338–9, and James Quinn, 'Con Martin', www.dib.ie

21 *The Irish Press*, 5 Apr. 1950.

22 Sean Ryan, *The Boys in Green: The FAI International Story* (Edinburgh, 1997), pp. 59–61; *The Guardian*, 25 Aug. 2002.

23 Byrne, *Green is the Colour*, p. 201.

24 Danny Blanchflower, *The Double and Before* (London, 1961), p. 144.

25 Walker, *Green Shoots*, pp. 91–2.

26 Peter Doherty, *Spotlight on Football* (London, 1947), pp. xiii, 80.

27 *The Observer* (London), 19 Apr. 1959.

28 Doherty, *Spotlight on Football*, p. 89.

29 Jimmy McIlroy, *Right Inside Soccer* (London, 1960), p. 11.

30 IFA statement (1954) cited in Byrne, *Green is the Colour*, p. 191.

31 FAI Archive P137/6, July 1952; Robert

Briscoe Papers, 'Summary of FAI–IFA relations, 1921–52', 1 Oct. 1952, NLI MS 26,602, pp. 7–8.

32 See www.britishpathe.com, cited in *Belfast Telegraph*, 28 Apr. 2020.

33 'Minute Book of the International Affairs Committee, 1936–73', FAI Archive, P137/39, 26 June, 1 Sept. 1950, 2 Jan. 1952.

34 J.I. Wickham to Archbishop J.C. McQuaid, 17 Jan. 1952, Dublin Diocesan Archive (DDA), McQuaid Papers, XXII/48/1.

35 John Cooney, *John Charles McQuaid: Ruler of Catholic Ireland* (Dublin, 1999), pp. 172, 310.

36 *The Irish Times*, 17 Oct. 1955; an exchange of letters between the FAI and Archbishop McQuaid is noted in the FAI Minute Book of the International Affairs Committee (FAI Archive P137/39, 24 Oct. 1955), but I have not been able to find the actual correspondence in the FAI Archive.

37 'Proposed visit of Jugoslav [sic] football team, Oct. 1955', 14 Oct. 1955, NAI, DFA/5/305/298.

38 President Seán T. O'Kelly to Oscar Traynor, 17 Oct. 1955, NAI, Office of the President, Pres/1/P2888, 1946–60.

39 Catriona Crowe *et al.* (eds), *Documents on Irish Foreign Policy, Volume X, 1951–1957* (Dublin, 2016), pp. 525, 529–33.

40 Cooney, *John Charles McQuaid*, p. 311.

41 *The Irish Times*, 18 Oct. 1955.

42 *The Sunday Times*, 15 Sept. 1998.

43 20 Oct. 1955, DDA, McQuaid Papers, XXII/48/6.

44 *Irish Independent*, 17 Oct. 1955; Cooney, *John Charles McQuaid*, pp. 310–12; 4 Nov. 1955, DDA, McQuaid Papers, XXII/48/9/1/(1).

45 *Irish Independent*, 18 Oct. 1955.

46 *Belfast News Letter*, 17 Oct. 1955; see also DDA, Press Clipping, XXII/48/3.

47 *The Irish Times*, 17 Oct. 1955.

48 *Irish Independent*, 20 Oct. 1955.

49 Louise Fuller, *Irish Catholicism Since 1950: The Undoing of a Culture* (Dublin, 2002), pp. 26–7.

50 Gerard Madden, 'McCarthyism, Catholicism and Ireland', *History Ireland*, 25:3 (May–June 2017), pp. 47.

51 Cooney, *John Charles McQuaid*, p. 312.

52 17 Oct. 1955, DDA, McQuaid Papers, XL/2/23.

53 21 Feb. 1956, DDA, McQuaid Papers, XXII/48/12/1; Cooney, *John Charles McQuaid*, pp. 315–17.

54 *Irish Catholic*, 10 Oct. 1957.

55 'Football Association Group: Interview with Fr George Finnegan, 13 Oct. 1957', DDA XXII/48/21.

56 'Visit of Roumanian [sic] football team to Ireland', Oct. 1957, NAI, DFA 5/305/345.

7. A COLD HOUSE

1 Cited in Malcolm Brodie, *Glenavon Football Club – 100 Years* (Lurgan, 1989), p. 32.

2 Brodie, *100 Years of Irish Football*, p. 172.

3 Joe Cassidy, *Sunday Tribune*, 20 Dec. 1998.

4 Coyle, *Paradise Lost and Found*, p. 72.

5 Cited in ibid., p. 81.

6 Ibid., p. 82.

7 *The Irish News*, 28 Dec. 1948; *The Northern Whig*, 28 Dec. 1948; *Belfast Telegraph*, 29 Dec. 1948.

8 Barry Flynn, *Political Football: The Life and Death of Belfast Celtic* (Dublin, 2009), pp. 132–3.

9 *Irish Independent*, 29 Dec. 1948.

10 *The Irish News*, 5 Jan. 1949; *The Irish Press*, 5, 12 Jan. 1949; *The Irish Times*, 12 Jan. 1949.

11 Flynn, *Political Football*, p. 141.

12 Coyle, *Paradise Lost and Found*, p. 11.

13 *The Irish News*, 28 Mar. 1949.

14 Ibid., 22 Apr. 1949.

15 *The Northern Whig*, 24 May 1949; *The Irish News*, 24 May 1949.

16 Flynn, *Political Football*, p. 152.

17 *The Irish Times*, 23 Dec. 1988; Coyle, *Paradise Lost and Found*, pp. 108–9.

18 *Irish Independent*, 18 Oct. 1949.

19 Mark Tuohy, *Belfast Celtic* (Belfast, 1978), p. 49.

20 Brodie, *100 Years of Irish Football*, p. 33; Byrne, *Green is the Colour*, p. 168.

21 Jimmy Overend, *The Guardian*, 23 Feb. 2011.

22 Tuohy, *Belfast Celtic*; John Kennedy, *Belfast Celtic* (Belfast, 1989); Coyle, *Paradise Lost and Found*; Flynn, *Political Football*.

23 Terry Conroy, *You Don't Remember Me, Do You? The Autobiography of Terry Conroy* (Durrington, 2015), pp. 60–1.

24 Cited in Daire Whelan, *Who Stole Our Game? The Fall and Fall of Irish Soccer* (Dublin, 2006), p. 114.

25 Benjamin Roberts, *Gunshots & Goalposts: The Story of Northern Irish Football* (Avenue Books, 2017), p. 148.

26 W.H.W. Platt, *A History of Derry City Football and Athletic Club 1929–1972* (Coleraine, 1986), pp. 199–204.

8. RISE AND FALL

1 Secretary's Report to the FAI AGM, 26 May 1943, FAI Archive P137/29.

2 Finbarr Flood, *In Full Flood: A Memoir* (Dublin, 2006), pp. 158–9.

3 Ibid., pp. 158–9.

4 Ibid., pp. 165–7; Eamon Dunphy, *The Rocky Road* (Dublin, 2013), pp. 46, 64–7.

5 *The Irish Worker*, 2 May 1914; Emmet Larkin, *James Larkin: Irish Labour Leader 1876–1947* (London, 1965), p. 148.

6 Michael Milne, 'Soccer and the Dublin working class: Doncaster Rovers in Dublin 1952': Document Study, *Saothar: Journal of the Irish Labour History Society*, 8 (1982), pp. 97–102.

7 *Irish Independent*, 6 Apr. 1953.

8 Gene Kerrigan, *Another Country: Growing Up in '50s Ireland* (Dublin, 1998), p. 36.

9 Dunphy, *Rocky Road*, p. 39.

10 Barry Coldrey, *Faith and Fatherland: The Christian Brothers and the Development of Irish Nationalism, 1828–1921* (Dublin, 1988), pp. 189–94.

11 'John Giles interview', *Hot Press*, 34:24 (12 Jan. 2011); John Giles (with Declan Lynch), *A Football Man: The Autobiography* (Dublin, 2010), p. 42; Colin White, *Dalymount Park: The Home of Irish Football* (Dublin, 2005), p. v.

12 Interview with Mick Meagan (11 Nov. 2013), cited in Curran, *Irish Soccer Migrants*, pp. 82–3; Eoin Hand (with Peter O'Neill), *The Eoin Hand Story* (Dublin, 1986), p. 10.

13 Liam Brady, *So Far So Good … A Decade in Football* (London, 1980), pp. 11–15.

14 *Irish Independent*, 12 Mar. 1965.

15 FAI Archive, P137/65, 5 Oct. 1961.

16 FAI Archive, P137/22, 18 Feb. 1966; P137/16, 19 Apr. 1966.

17 *The Irish Press*, 25 Apr. 1966; *The Irish Times*, 25 Apr. 1966.

18 *Irish Independent*, 12 Mar. 1965.

19 FAI Archive P137/28, 24 Feb. 1938; FAI Archive P137/29, 2 Sept. 1943, 9 Oct. 1943.

20 Brendan Menton, *Home Farm: The Story of a Dublin Football Club 1928–1998* (Dublin, 1999), pp. 6–7; 'Billy Behan's Soccer Story', (Dublin) *Evening Herald*, 9 July 1968.

21 Menton, *Home Farm*, p. 19; Carter, 'Soccer in Cork city', p. 322.

22 Cited in Diarmaid Ferriter, *The Transformation of Ireland 1900–2000* (London, 2005), pp. 606–7.

23 *Dáil Éireann* debates, 25 June 1957.

24 FAI Archive P137/31, 24 June 1952.

25 Bartley Ramsay, *The Finn Harps Story* (Dublin, 2008), pp. 7, 15.

26 Breandán Ó hEithir, *Over the Bar: A Personal Relationship with the GAA* (Dublin, 1984), p. 217.

27 Paul Keane, *Gods vs Mortals: Irish Clubs in Europe* (Kells, 2010), p. 38.

28 *The Cork Examiner*, 29 Dec. 1973, cited in Curran, *Irish Soccer Migrants*, p. 88.

29 Cited in Walker, *Green Shoots*, p. 207.

9. ONE LONG WAR AND THREE WORLD CUPS

1 Peter McParland, *Going for Goal* (London, 1960), p. 26.

2 Gillian McIntosh, *The Force of Culture: Unionist Identities in Twentieth-Century Ireland* (Cork, 1999), pp. 82–3.

3 Ronnie Hanna, *The World at Their Feet: Northern Ireland in Sweden* (Cheltenham, 2008), p. 114.

4 *The Irish Times*, 17 Feb. 1924; Hanna, *The World at Their Feet*, p. 114.

5 McParland, *Going for Goal*, p. 61.

6 McIlroy, *Right Inside Soccer*, p. 28; Hanna, *The World at Their Feet*, p. 121.

7 Hanna, *The World at Their Feet*, p. 116.

8 *The Irish Times*, 5 June 1958.

9 Evan Marshall, *Spirit of '58: The Incredible Untold Story of Northern Ireland's Greatest*

Football Team (Belfast, 2016), p. 131;
McParland, Going for Goal, p. 73.

10   The Irish News, 19 June 1958.

11   The Northern Whig, 9 June 1958.

12   Ireland's Saturday Night, 21 June 1958.

13   The Northern Whig, 18 June 1958.

14   Ibid., 20 June 1958.

15   Cited in Ireland's Saturday Night, 21 June
     1958.

16   The Observer (London), 19 Apr. 1959.

17   Belfast Telegraph, 21 June 1958; The
     Northern Whig, 21 June 1958.

18   See for example The Irish News, 16 June
     1958.

19   NAI, DFA 305/14/162/2 – 'Partition in
     Sport: Soccer Matches', 7, 16 Apr. 1958.

20   The Irish Press, 10 June 1958; Belfast
     Telegraph, 19 June 1958.

21   Belfast Telegraph, 20 June 1958.

22   McIlroy, Right Inside Soccer, p. 27.

23   NAI, DFA 5/305/14/162, 'Partition in
     sport: soccer matches – incident at
     Italian match in Belfast', 7 Dec. 1957.

24   Ireland's Saturday Night, 7 Dec. 1957.

25   The Irish News, 19 June 1958.

26   Derry Journal, 4 July 1958.

27   The Irish Times, 23 Aug. 2002; Brian
     Murphy, 'Charles Patrick Tully',
     Dictionary of Irish Biography, 10, p. 746.

28   Belfast Telegraph, 20 June 1958.

29   McParland, Going for Goal, p. 79.

30   Lawrence William White, 'George Best',
     Dictionary of Irish Biography, 10, pp. 30–6;
     Alan Bairner, 'Simply the (George) Best:
     Ulster Protestantism, conflicted identity
     and "The Belfast Boy(s)"', Canadian
     Journal of Irish Studies, 32:2 (Fall, 2006),
     pp. 34–41.

31   Roberts, Gunshots & Goalposts, p. 160.

32   The Irish Times, 28 June 1982.

33   Ibid.

34   The Irish Times, 25 Apr. 2015.

35   An Phoblacht: Republican News, 1 July
     1982, p. 10.

36   The Irish Times, 29 June 1982.

37   Norman Whiteside (with Rob Bagchi),
     Determined: The Autobiography (London,
     2007), p. 19; Roberts, Gunshots &
     Goalposts, p. 199.

38   Simon Moss, Martin O'Neill: The
     Biography (London, 2010), p. 44.

39   Ibid., p. 44.

40   Teddy Jamieson, Whose Side Are You On?
     Sport, the Troubles and Me (London, 2011),
     p. 115.

41   The Irish Times, 3, 5 July 1982.

42   John Sugden and Alan Bairner, 'Observe
     the sons of Ulster: football and politics
     in Northern Ireland' in Alan Tomlinson
     and Garry Whannel (eds), Off the Ball:
     The Football World Cup (London, 1986),
     p. 155.

43   'When the glory is over', Fortnight, no.
     187 (Jul.–Aug. 1982), p. 3.

44   The Irish Times, 13 June 1986.

45   Ronnie Hanna, Six Glorious Years:
     Following Northern Ireland 1980–86
     (Londonderry, 1994), p. 212.

46   The Irish Times, 6 June 1986.

47   Cited in Paddy Agnew, 'Irish football's
     two contrasting states', Fortnight, no.
     200 (Dec. 1983–Jan. 1984), p. 23.

10. THIRTY YEARS OF HURT

1   The Irish Times, 20, 25 May 1957.

2   Irish Independent, 20 May 1957.

3   The Irish Press, 20 May 1957.

4   The Irish Press, 17 May 1945.

5   The Irish Times, 25 May 1957.

6   Ryan, The Boys in Green, p. 118;
     FAI Archives, P137/22, 6 May 1966;
     Dean Hayes, The Republic of Ireland:
     International Football Facts (Cork, 2008),
     pp. 37–58.

7   'Interview with Arthur Fitzsimons' on
     www.balls.ie (accessed 9 May 2018).

8   Irish Independent, 10 Oct. 1961.

9   James Quinn, 'John Joseph Carey',
     Dictionary of Irish Biography, 5, pp. 338–9.

10   FAI Archives, P137/78, 29 Oct. 1965, 25
     Mar. 1966, 26 June 1967.

11   Goldblatt, The Ball is Round, pp. 334, 398,
     400–3.

12   Christine Geraghty, Philip Simpson
     and Garry Whannel, 'Tunnel Vision:
     Television's World Cup' in Neil Blain,
     Raymond Boyle and Hugh O'Donnell
     (eds), Sport and National Identity in the
     European Media (Leicester, 1993), pp. 20–
     35; Tomlinson and Whannel (eds), Off the
     Ball, p. 21.

13   Magill, June 2002.

14   The Sunday Press, 31 July 1966.

15 Byrne, *Football Association of Ireland*, p. 94.

16 Eoin Hand (with Jared Browne), *First Hand: My Life and Irish Football* (Cork, 2017), p. 35.

17 Conroy, *You Don't Remember Me, Do You?*, p. 174.

18 *Magill*, May 1979, p. 57; see also the quotation from Giles in Paul Rowan, *The Team that Jack Built* (Edinburgh, 1994), p. 37.

19 www.balls.ie (accessed 29 Dec. 2017).

20 *Irish Examiner*, 14 Mar. 2015.

21 Whelan, *Who Stole Our Game?*, p. 40.

22 Seanad Éireann debates, 25 July 1965, 26 Feb. 1964, 17 Feb. 1966; Dáil Éireann debates, 27 Oct. 1966.

23 FAI Archives, FAI P137/16, 9 Jan. 1963, 5 July 1963, 28 May 1965.

24 E.J. O'Mahony, *Bohemian FC: Golden Jubilee Souvenir* (Dublin, 1941?), pp. 21, 23; for Leitch see also Goldblatt, *The Ball is Round*, p. 61.

25 FAI Archives, P137/54, 17 Nov., 18 Dec. 1952.

26 NAI, Department of An Taoiseach, S14650, 'President of Ireland: attendance at football matches', 14 Sept. 1949.

27 Whelan, *Who Stole Our Game?*, p. 26.

28 *Irish Independent*, 14 Oct. 1963.

29 Byrne, *Green is the Colour*, p. 223.

30 Quinn, 'Derek Dougan', *Dictionary of Irish Biography*, 11, pp. 112–13.

31 Derek Dougan, 'The case for an All-Ireland team', *Fortnight*, no. 184 (Dec. 1981–Jan. 1982), p. 19.

32 This was the opinion of Liam Tuohy, cited in Trevor Keane, *Gaffers: 50 Years of Irish Football Managers* (Cork, 2010), p. 110.

33 *Irish Independent*, 4 July 1973; see also Shane Tobin, 'All-Ireland samba: Shamrock Rovers All-Ireland XI 3 – 4 Brazil, Lansdowne Road, Tuesday 3 July 1973', *History Ireland*, 16:4 (2008), pp. 46–7.

34 *The Irish Times*, 4 July 1793; *The Irish Press*, 4 July 1973.

35 Comments of Derek Brookes, secretary of Linfield FC, *The Irish Times*, 31 Dec. 1981.

36 *Irish Independent*, 26 Feb. 1980.

37 Hand, *First Hand*, pp. 43–4.

38 *Evening Press*, 31 Oct. 1974.

39 Eoghan Corry, *Viva! Ireland Goes to Italy* (Dublin, 1990), p. 83.

40 Miguel Delaney, *Stuttgart to Saipan: The Players' Stories* (Dublin, 2010), p. 23.

41 Simon Kuper, *Football Against the Enemy* (London, 1994), p. 36.

42 *The Irish Times*, 21 Sept. 1978; Dave Bowler, *Danny Blanchflower: A Biography of a Visionary* (London, 1997), p. 217.

43 Brady, *So Far So Good*, p. 62; *Magill*, Feb. 1979, p. 56.

44 Hand, *The Eoin Hand Story*, p. 22.

45 FAI Archives P137/51, 6 Apr. 1964.

46 Enda Delaney, *The Irish in Post-war Britain* (Oxford, 2007), p. 17.

47 Hand, *The Eoin Hand Story*, p. 92.

48 17 Apr. 1974, FAI Archives, P137/10.

49 Hand, *First Hand*, p. 95.

50 Ibid., p. 113.

51 Delaney, *Stuttgart to Saipan*, p. 223.

52 Hand, *First Hand*, p. 180.

11. COMING OF AGE

1 *Sunday Independent*, 19 June 1988.

2 *The Irish Press*, 11 Oct. 1989.

3 *The Irish Times*, 20 June 1988.

4 Nuala O'Faolain, 'Soccer and the doctrine of original joy', *The Irish Times*, 20 June 1988.

5 *The Irish Times*, 20 June 1988.

6 Cited in Mary Hunt, *There We Were – Germany '88* (Kilkenny, 1989), p. 7.

7 *Sunday Independent*, 17 June 90.

8 Colin Young, *Jack Charlton: The Authorised Biography* (Dublin, 2016), p. x.

9 *The Irish Times*, 26 June 1990.

10 *The Irish Times*, 2 July 1990.

11 Gianni Melidoni in *Il Messaggero*, cited in *The Irish Times*, 2 July 1990.

12 *The Irish Times*, 30 June 1990.

13 *Belfast News Letter*, 30 June, 2 July 1990.

14 *The Irish Times*, 2 July 1990.

15 *The Irish News*, 16 Nov. 1993; *Belfast Telegraph*, 15 Nov. 1993.

16 *The Irish Times*, 17 Nov. 1993.

17 *The Irish News*, 24 Nov. 1993; *The Irish Times*, 19 Nov. 1993.

18 Scott Harvie, '17 November 1993 – a night to remember?' in Richard English and Graham Walker (eds), *Unionism in Modern*

Ireland: New Perspectives on Politics and Culture (London, 1996), p. 202.

19 Harvie, 'A night to remember?', pp. 201, 211–12.

20 *The Irish Times*, 20 Nov. 1993.

21 Newstalk Radio, *Off the Ball* podcast, 15 Nov. 2014.

22 Harvie, 'A night to remember?', pp. 202, 216.

23 Pete Davies, *All Played Out – The Story of Italia '90* (London, 1990), p. 341; Delaney, *Stuttgart to Saipan*, p. 227.

24 *Sunday Independent*, 10 July 1994.

25 Dermot Bolger, *In High Germany* (Dublin, 1999), pp. 43–4.

26 See Eberhard Bort, '"Come on you Boys in Green": Irish football, Irish theatre and the Irish diaspora' in Eberhard Bort (ed.), *The State of Play: Irish Theatre in the 'Nineties* (Trier, 1996), pp. 88–103.

27 These sentiments are echoed in Doyle's 'Republic is a beautiful word', in Nick Hornby (ed.), *My Favourite Year: A Collection of New Football Writing* (London, 1993) pp. 9–28.

28 *The Irish Times*, 2 July 1990.

29 Delaney, *Stuttgart to Saipan*, p. 224.

30 Walker, *Green Shoots*, p. 129.

31 *The Irish Times*, 9 Oct. 1995.

32 Goldblatt, *The Ball is Round*, pp. 334, 398, 400–3; Neil Blain, Raymond Boyle and Hugh O'Donnell (eds), *Sport and National Identity in the European Media* (Leicester, 1993), pp. 37, 51.

33 Broadcasting (Major Events Television Coverage) Act (1999), p. 5.

34 Brian Glanville, *Story of the World Cup* (London, 2018), p. 337.

35 Pete Davies, *All Played Out – The Story of Italia '90* (London, 1990), p. 229.

36 *Sunday Independent*, 19 June 88, p. 4.

37 Gianni Mura, *La Reppublica*, cited in *The Irish Times*, 30 June 1990; Blain, Boyle and O'Donnell (eds), *Sport and National Identity*, p. 76.

38 Joseph O'Connor, *The Secret World of the Irish Male* (Dublin, 1994), p. 213.

39 Taylor, *The Association Game*, pp. 301, 380; Marcus Free, 'Angels with drunken faces: travelling Republic of Ireland supporters and the construction of Irish migrant identity in England' in Adam Brown (ed.), *Fanatics! Power, Identity and Fandom in Football* (London, 1998), p. 221.

40 Kevin Myers in *The Irish Times*, 30, 27 June 1990.

41 *The Irish Times*, 29 June 1994.

42 Quoted in Hunt, *There We Were*, p. 7.

43 See particularly Free, 'Angels with drunken faces?', pp. 219–32; and Aidan Arrowsmith, 'Plastic paddies vs. master racers: "Soccer" and Irish identity', *International Journal of Cultural Studies*, 7:4 (2004), pp. 460–79.

44 Delaney, *Stuttgart to Saipan*, p. 47.

45 *Radio Times*, 11 June 1988.

46 *Daily Express* cited in *The Irish Press*, 13 June 1988, p. 1.

47 Andy Townsend (with Paul Kimmage), *Andy's Game: The Inside Story of the World Cup* (London, 1994), p. 77.

48 Rowan, *The Team that Jack Built*, p. 61; Delaney, *Stuttgart to Saipan*, p. 57.

49 Hand, *First Hand*, p. 73.

50 Kevin Kilbane (with Andy Merriman), *Killa: The Autobiography of Kevin Kilbane* (London, 2013), pp. 4, 245.

51 *Irish Independent*, 12 Oct. 2018.

52 *Evening Press*, 5 June 1990, p. 20; Townsend, *Andy's Game*, pp. 76–7.

53 Paul Kimmage, *Full Time: The Secret Life of Tony Cascarino* (Dublin, 2000), pp. 16, 179.

54 Rowan, *The Team that Jack Built*, p. 150; Mick McCarthy (with Cathal Dervan), *Ireland's World Cup 2002* (London, 2002), p. 148.

55 Bolger, *In High Germany*, p. 44.

56 Nuala O'Faolain, 'Soccer and the doctrine of original joy', *The Irish Times*, 20 June 1988.

57 *The Irish Times*, 8 July 1994.

58 Packie Bonner (with Gerard McDade), *The Last Line: My Autobiography* (London, 2015), p. 190.

59 Jack Charlton (with Peter Byrne), *Jack Charlton: The Autobiography* (London, 1996), p. 316.

60 Lawrence William White, 'Seán South', *Dictionary of Irish Biography*, 8, p. 1079.

61 Charlton, *Jack Charlton*, p. 286.

62 Goldblatt, *The Ball is Round*, p. 532.

63 Billy Bingham in Rowan, *Team that Jack Built*, p. 168.

64 *The Irish Times*, 20 June 1988.
65 Declan Lynch, *Days of Heaven: Italia '90 and the Charlton Years* (Dublin, 2010), pp. 124–5.
66 Trevor O'Rourke in Young, *Jack Charlton*, p. 171.
67 *The Irish Times*, 30 June 1990.
68 *Sunday Independent*, 1 July 1994.
69 Eoghan Corry, *Viva! Ireland Goes to Italy* (Dublin, 1990), p. 139.
70 *Sunday Independent*, 19 June 1994, p. 14.
71 Ibid., pp. 31, 28.
72 Robbie Best, 'How Irish is the Irish soccer team?', *Bohemian FC Club Programme* (1992) cited in Rowan, *Team that Jack Built*, pp. 180–1.
73 Eamon Dunphy, *The Rocky Road* (Dublin, 2013), p. 373.
74 John Giles in Ryan, *The Boys in Green*, p. 212.
75 Ryan, *The Boys in Green*, p. 165.
76 Eduardo Archetti, 'Argentina and the World Cup, in search of national identity' in John Sugden and Alan Tomlinson (eds), *Hosts and Champions: Soccer Cultures, National Identities and the USA World Cup* (Aldershot, 1994), pp. 37–63; John Humphrey, 'No holding Brazil: football, nationalism and politics' in Tomlinson and Whannel (eds), *Off the Ball*, pp. 128–30.
77 Cited in Kuper, *Football Against the Enemy*, p. 203.
78 Neal Garnham, *Association Football and Society in Pre-Partition Ireland* (Belfast, 2004), pp. 32–4; 'Roughness spoils Irish football', *Football Sports Weekly*, 18 Dec. 1926.
79 *Irish Independent*, 14 Oct. 1963.
80 *The Irish Times*, 9 July 1994.

12. HIBERNIANS AND CELTS

1 T.M. Devine (ed.), *Irish Immigrants and Scottish Society in the Nineteenth and Twentieth Centuries* (Edinburgh, 1991), p. 14; Andy Bielenberg (ed.), *The Irish Diaspora* (London, 2000), p. 39.
2 Alan Lugton, *The Making of Hibernian* (3 vols, Edinburgh, 1995–8), vol. 1, pp. 13, 19 (all subsequent references to volume 1 unless otherwise stated); John R. Mackay,

The Hibees: The Story of Hibernian Football Club (Edinburgh, 1986), p. 1.
3 John Kelly, 'Hibernian Football Club: The forgotten Irish?', *Sport in Society*, 10:3 (2007), p. 518.
4 Lugton, *The Making of Hibernian*, p. 26.
5 John R. Mackay, *Hibernian: The Easter Road Story* (Edinburgh, 1995), pp. 7–8; Lugton, *The Making of Hibernian*, pp. 43, 46, 48, 73, 77.
6 Daniel Burdsey & Robert Chappell, '"And if you know your history...": An examination of the formation of football clubs in Scotland and their role in the construction of social identity', *The Sports Historian*, 21:1 (2001), p. 101.
7 James Handley, *The Celtic Story: A History of the Celtic Football Club* (London, 1960), p. 14.
8 Lugton, *The Making of Hibernian*, pp. 4, 103, 106, 121; Mackay, *The Hibees*, pp. 38–9.
9 Lugton, *The Making of Hibernian*, p. 101.
10 Ibid., pp. 132, 158.
11 David Kennedy & Peter Kennedy, 'Ambiguity, complexity and convergence: The evolution of Liverpool's Irish football clubs', *The International Journal of the History of Sport*, 24:7 (2007), pp. 900–1.
12 Lugton, *The Making of Hibernian*, p. 101.
13 Ibid., p. 111.
14 Willie Maley, *Story of the Celtic* (Glasgow, 1939), pp. 2, 4, 7; Kelly, 'Hibernian Football Club', p. 519; Lugton, *The Making of Hibernian*, p. 140.
15 Alan Lugton, *The Making of Hibernian, 2, 1893–1914: The Brave Years* (Edinburgh, 1997), pp. 82–3.
16 Alan Lugton, *The Making of Hibernian, 3, 1914–1946: The Romantic Years* (Edinburgh, 1998), pp. 179, 218; Kelly, 'Hibernian Football Club', p. 521.
17 Kelly, 'Hibernian Football Club', p. 527.
18 Cited in Joseph M. Bradley, *Celtic Football Club, Irish Identity and the Politics of Difference* (Glasgow, 1995), pp. 21–2.
19 Lugton, *The Making of Hibernian*, p. 23.
20 Kelly, 'Hibernian Football Club', pp. 525–6, 531.
21 John Reid, 'Irish Famine refugees and the emergence of Glasgow Celtic Football

Club' in John Crowley, William J. Smith and Mike Murphy (eds), *Atlas of the Great Irish Famine* (Cork, 2012), pp. 518–19.

22 Lugton, *The Making of Hibernian*, 2, pp. 66–8; *The Irish Post*, 29 July 2016.

23 Joseph M. Bradley, *Ethnic and Religious Identity in Modern Scotland: Culture, Politics and Football* (Aldershot, 1995), p. 47.

24 T.M. Devine, *The Scottish Nation: A History 1700–2000* (London, 2000), p. 379.

25 Lugton, *The Making of Hibernian*, p. 119.

26 Maley, *Story of the Celtic*, pp. 4, 7; Handley, *Celtic Story*, p. 14; Nicholas Allen, 'Andrew Kerins', *Dictionary of Irish Biography*, 5, p. 153.

27 Maley, *Story of the Celtic*, pp. 16–17.

28 Quoted in Bill Murray, *The Old Firm: Sectarianism, Sport and Society in Scotland* (Edinburgh, 1984), p. 27.

29 Handley, *Celtic Story*, p. 168

30 Kevin McCarra, *Celtic: A Biography in Nine Lives* (London, 2012), p. 9.

31 Bradley, *Celtic Football Club*, pp. 4–5; Murray, *Old Firm*, pp. 73, 75.

32 Graham Walker, 'The Protestant Irish in Scotland', in Devine (ed.), *Irish Immigrants and Scottish Society*, pp. 49, 59.

33 *Scottish Referee* (ancillary publication of the *Glasgow Evening News*), 15 Apr. 1904, cited in Murray, *Old Firm*, p. 10.

34 McCarra, *Nine Lives*, p. 158.

35 Handley, *Celtic Story*, p. 62; Bill Murray, *Bhoys, Bears and Bigotry: The Old Firm in the New Age* (Edinburgh, 2003), p. 65.

36 *Daily Express*, 3 Mar. 1931, cited in McCarra, *Nine Lives*, pp. 39–42.

37 Maley, *Story of the Celtic*, p. 29.

38 Walker, 'Protestant Irish in Scotland', pp. 60–2.

39 Devine, *Scottish Nation*, p. 497.

40 McCarra, *Nine Lives*, p. 5.

41 Hansard 272, 24 Nov. 1932, p. 245, cited in Joseph M. Bradley, *Football, Religion and Ethnicity: Irish Identity in Scotland* (London, 1996), p. 13.

42 Andrew Davies, 'Football and sectarianism in Glasgow during the 1920s and 1930s', *Irish Historical Studies*, 35:138 (2006–7), p. 206.

43 Ibid., pp. 205–8.

44 Devine, *Scottish Nation*, pp. 319–20.

45 *Football Sports Weekly*, 29 Oct. 1927, p. 1.

46 Handley, *Celtic Story*, p. 118.

47 *The Irish Press*, 16 Apr. 1952; Brian McGurk, *Celtic FC: The Irish Connection* (Edinburgh, 2009), p. 78.

48 McGurk, *Celtic FC*, p. 79.

49 *The Irish Press*, 18 Oct. 1948.

50 [Glasgow] *News Chronicle*, 26 Feb. 1952, cutting in NAI, DFA 5/301/47/1.

51 Richard Purden, *Celtic: Keeping the Faith* (Glasgow, 2015), pp. 20, 57.

52 T.M. Devine, quoted in *The Irish Post*, 9 Mar. 2020.

53 Murray, *Old Firm*, pp. 212, 235.

54 Bill McArthur in Stephen Walsh, *Voices of the Old Firm* (Edinburgh, 2005), p. 204.

55 *Celtic View*, 9 Mar. 1966, 6 Apr. 1966, 20 July 1966, 19 Apr. 1967, cited in Bradley, *Celtic Football Club*, p. 10.

56 McCarra, *Nine Lives*, p. 130.

57 Walsh, *Voices of the Old Firm*, p. 121.

58 Murray, *Bhoys, Bears and Bigotry*, p. 35.

59 Bradley, *Celtic Football Club*, pp. 16–17.

60 Tom Campbell, *Celtic's Paranoia: All in the Mind?* (Ayr, 2004), p. viii.

61 Steve Bruce *et al.* (eds), *Sectarianism in Scotland* (Edinburgh, 2004), p. 130.

62 Brian Wilson, *Celtic: A Century with Honour* (London, 1988), p. 179.

63 Murray, *Bhoys, Bears and Bigotry*, p. 55.

64 Purden, *Celtic: Keeping the Faith*, p. 158.

65 Campbell, *Celtic's Paranoia*, pp. viii, 56.

66 Bradley, *Celtic Football Club*, pp. 21–3.

67 Paddy Crerand, *Paddy Crerand: Never Turn the Other Cheek* (London, 2014), pp. 14, 345.

68 Walsh, *Voices of the Old Firm*, p. 200.

69 J.M. Bradley, *Celtic-Minded 2* (Argyll, 2006), p. 31.

70 *Sunday Mail* (Glasgow), 23 Oct. 1994.

71 McGurk, *Celtic FC*, p. 97.

72 Purden, *Celtic: Keeping the Faith*, pp. 234, 236.

73 Murray, *Bhoys, Bears and Bigotry*, p. 35.

74 T.M. Devine (ed.), *Scotland's Shame? Bigotry and Sectarianism in Modern Scotland* (Edinburgh, 2000), p. 18.

75 Bradley, *Ethnic and Religious Identity in Modern Scotland*, p. 44.

76 Richard Wilson, *Inside the Divide:*

One City: Two Teams ... the Old Firm
(Edinburgh, 2010), p. 100.

77 Cited in Simon Kuper, *Football against the Enemy*, pp. 212, 214.

78 Bruce, *Sectarianism in Scotland*, p. 150.

79 Murray, *Old Firm*, p. 139 and Tom Gallagher, *Glasgow: The Uneasy Peace: Religious Tension in Modern Scotland 1819–1914* (Manchester, 1987), p. 3.

80 Davies, 'Football and sectarianism in Glasgow', p. 201.

81 David Goldblatt, *The Age of Football: The Global Game in the Twenty-first Century* (Basingstoke, 2019), p. 294.

82 Campbell, *Celtic's Paranoia*, p. 34.

83 *The Guardian*, 31 May 2009.

84 Bradley, *Celtic Football Club*, pp. 23–4.

85 James MacMillan, 'Scotland's Shame' in Devine, *Scotland's Shame?*, p. 19.

86 Steve Bruce *et al.* (eds), *Sectarianism in Scotland* (Edinburgh, 2004), p. 150.

87 McCarra, *Nine Lives*, p. 156.

88 Purden, *Celtic: Keeping the Faith*, pp. 51, 169.

89 Mark Boyle, *Metropolitan Anxieties: On the Meaning of the Irish Catholic Adventure in Scotland* (Farnham, 2011), pp. 56–8.

90 Wilson, *Inside the Divide*, p. 185.

91 Murray, *Bhoys, Bears and Bigotry*, p. 177.

92 'Soccer fans supply strong voice in Scottish independence debate', *The New York Times*, 12 Sept. 2014.

93 Devine, *Scotland's Shame?*, pp. 43, 127, 209, 217.

94 *The New York Times*, 11 Sept. 2014.

95 Wilson, *Inside the Divide*, pp. 230–1; Devine, *Irish Immigrants and Scottish Society*, p. 34.

13. PRIDE AND PREJUDICE

1 David Fitzpatrick, 'The Irish in Britain, 1871–1921' in W.E. Vaughan (ed.), *A New History of Ireland VI: Ireland under the Union 1870–1921* (Oxford, 1996), p. 666.

2 Kennedy and Kennedy, 'Ambiguity, complexity and convergence', p. 902.

3 Ibid., pp. 897–9.

4 Ibid., pp. 902–3.

5 Ibid., pp. 896–7.

6 John Belchem, *Irish, Catholic and Scouse* (Liverpool, 2007), pp. 20, 242; Kennedy and Kennedy, 'Ambiguity, complexity and convergence', p. 906.

7 *The Freeman's Journal*, 17 Apr. 1900, 4 Nov. 1901, 10 Apr. 1903 and 28 Apr. 1906.

8 Garnham, *Association Football*, p. 77.

9 *Football Sports Weekly*, 1 May 1926, p. 5.

10 James Corbett (ed.), *Faith of Our Families: Everton FC, An Oral History 1878–2018* (Liverpool, 2017), pp. 52–9.

11 Mark Metcalf, *Charlie Hurley: The Greatest Centre-Half the World Has Ever Seen* (Cheltenham, 2008), pp. 2, 43.

12 *Irish Independent*, 6 Dec. 1949.

13 'Billy Behan's soccer story', *Evening Herald*, 13 Aug. 1968.

14 Paul Rouse, 'Danny Blanchflower', *Dictionary of Irish Biography*, 1, pp. 594–5.

15 Jim Shanahan, 'Liam Whelan', *Dictionary of Irish Biography*, 9, p. 882.

16 *The Irish Times*, 26 Sept. 1957; Eamon Dunphy, *The Rocky Road* (Dublin, 2013), pp. 64–5.

17 *The Irish Press*, 12 Feb. 1958.

18 *The Irish Times*, 8 Feb. 1958; Dunphy, *Rocky Road*, p. 67.

19 Bertie Ahern (with Richard Aldous), *Bertie Ahern: The Autobiography* (London, 2009), p. 25.

20 *The Observer*, 8 Apr. 2001.

21 Eamon Dunphy, *Sir Matt Busby and Manchester United: A Strange Kind of Glory* (London, 1991), pp. 136, 249.

22 'Billy Behan's soccer story', 9 parts, *Evening Herald*, 18 June to 13 Aug. 1968.

23 Dunphy, *Sir Matt Busby*, pp. 148, 216.

24 Roberts, *Gunshots & Goalposts*, pp. 84, 99.

25 John D.T. White, *Irish Devils: The Official Story of Manchester United and the Irish* (London, 2011), pp. 7, 130; Crerand, *Never Turn the Other Cheek*, p. 150.

26 Bobby Charlton, *My Manchester United Years* (London, 2007), p. 178.

27 Keane, *Gods vs Mortals*, p. 38.

28 Stephen McGarrigle, *Manchester United: The Irish Connection* (Dublin, 1990), p. 7; John Scally, *Simply Red and Green* (Edinburgh, 1998), pp. 90, 101.

29 Stephen McGarrigle, *Green Gunners: Arsenal's Irish* (Edinburgh, 1991), p. 133; Conor Curran, 'Irish-born players in the English Football League, 1945–2010', in

Richard McElligott and David Hassan (eds), *A Social and Cultural History of Sport in Ireland* (Oxford, 2016), p. 90.

30 Eamon Dunphy, *Only a Game?: Diary of a Professional Footballer* (London, 1976).

31 George Best (with Roy Collins), *Blessed: The Autobiography* (London, 2002), p. 326.

32 *The Irish Times*, 10 Sept. 2019.

33 'Survey of Irish Premier League supporters', 10 Sept. 2015, www.the42.ie (accessed 26 Feb. 2020).

34 Crerand, *Never Turn the Other Cheek*, p. 236; Brian Hanley, 'Irish republican attitudes to sport since 1921', in Donal McAnallen, David Hassan and Roddy Hegarty (eds), *The Evolution of the GAA: Ulaidh, Éire agus Eile* (Stair Uladh, 2009), p. 182.

14. STRUGGLE AND SURVIVAL

1 O'Mahony, *Munster Football Association*, pp. 146–52; Michael Russell, *Hibs! A History of Cork Hibernians 1957–1976* (Cork, 2018), pp. 189–93.

2 Whelan, *Who Stole Our Game?*, pp. 108, 124.

3 As both the League of Ireland and Irish League have had numerous sponsors over the years, for the sake of clarity I generally refer to them by their original titles.

4 Whelan, *Who Stole Our Game?*, pp. 106–7.

5 *Irish Independent*, 10 May 1973; *The Irish Press*, 21 Oct. 1975; Curran, *Irish Soccer Migrants*, p. 92.

6 'Interview with John Giles', *Magill*, Dec. 1977, p. 86.

7 Conor Neville, 'How Dublin almost got a Premier League team', 18 Sept. 2014, www.balls.ie (accessed 20 Mar. 2022); Gavin Cooney, 'The Premier League club Ireland might have had: an oral history of the Dublin Dons', 28 Feb. 2021, www.the42.ie (accessed Apr. 2021).

8 Richard Giulianotti, 'Back to the future: an ethnograph of Ireland's football fans at the 1994 World Cup finals in the USA', *International Review for the Sociology of Sport*, 31:3 (1996), pp. 323–47.

9 FAI Archive, P137/9, 24 Jan., 16 Feb. 1973.

10 Robert McAllister, 'The Red Army invades the Brandywell', *Fortnight*, 235 (10–23 Mar. 1986), p. 11.

11 *The Observer*, 8 Apr. 2001.

12 Eddie Mahon, *Eddie Mahon's Derry City* (Derry, 1997), p. 2.

13 Keane, *Gods vs Mortals*, pp. 180, 182–3.

14 Research carried out for the forthcoming *Atlas of Irish Sport*, cited in *The Irish Times*, 29 Feb. 2020.

15 Flood, *In Full Flood*, p. 160.

16 [Football Association of Ireland], 'White Paper on the Strategic Direction of the eircom League', presented by Genesis Strategic Management Consultants, 19 Sept. 2005, pp. 3, 6–7.

17 Macdara Ferris and Karl Reilly, *Tallaght Time: Shamrock Rovers 2009–2012* (Dublin, 2013), pp. 1–15.

18 Roberts, *Gunshots & Goalposts*, pp. 177–8.

19 *The Irish Times*, 15 Mar. 1979.

20 *The Irish Times*, 4 Dec. 1980.

21 David Hassan, 'Sport, identity and nationalism in Northern Ireland' in Alan Bairner (ed.), *Sport and the Irish: Histories, Identities, Issues* (Dublin, 2005), p. 133.

22 P.J. Newland, 'Sick as a parrot', *Fortnight*, 389 (Nov. 2000), p. 9.

23 David Hassan, 'An opportunity for a new beginning: soccer, Irish nationalists and the construction of a new multi-sports stadium for Northern Ireland', *Soccer & Society*, 7:2–3 (2006), p. 345.

24 Alan Bairner, '"Up to their knees?" Football, sectarianism, masculinity and Protestant working-class identity' in Peter Shirlow and Mark McGovern (eds), *Who are 'the People'?: Unionism, Protestantism and Loyalism in Northern Ireland* (London, 1997), p. 98.

25 *Belfast Telegraph*, 17 May 2020; www.the42.ie (accessed Apr. 2021), 21 July 2020.

26 Whelan, *Who Stole Our Game?*, p. 196.

27 *The Irish Times*, 30 Aug. 1979.

28 *Intercultural Football Plan: Many Voices, One Goal* (FAI, 2007), p. 21.

29 See for example the interview with President Higgins in the *Irish Examiner*, 27 Feb. 2016.

30 *Irish Independent*, 22 June 2010; *The Irish Times*, 21 Aug. 2010.

31 Cited in Mark Tighe and Paul Rowan, *Champagne Football: John Delaney and*

the Betrayal of Irish Football: The Inside Story* (Dublin, 2020), pp. 270, 292.

15. ADMINISTRATION AND ITS DISCONTENTS

1   Blanchflower, *The Double and Before*, p. 144; Robert Allen, *Billy: A Biography of Billy Bingham* (London, 1986), p. 73.
2   P.J. Newland, 'Balls up', *Fortnight*, 393 (Mar. 2001), p. 9.
3   David Yallop, *How They Stole the Game* (London, 2011), pp. 134, 139; Mihir Bose, *The Spirit of the Game: How Sport Made the Modern World* (London, 2012), pp. 416–17.
4   James Quinn, 'Harry Cavan', *Dictionary of Irish Biography*, 11, pp. 539–41.
5   FAI Archives P137/13, 4 May 1943, 8 Oct. 1946.
6   Hand, *First Hand*, p. 172.
7   Hand, *The Eoin Hand Story*, pp. 113, 188.
8   Cited by Brian Kerr, *The Irish Times*, 1 Dec. 2020.
9   Hand, *First Hand*, p. 165.
10   Whelan, *Who Stole Our Game?*, p. 89.
11   Brendan Menton, *Beyond the Green Door: Six Years Inside the FAI* (Dublin, 2003), p. 5.
12   Hand, *First Hand*, pp. 108–9, 161.
13   Townsend, *Andy's Game*, p. 146; Kilbane, *Killa*, p. 126; Roy Keane (with Eamon Dunphy), *Keane: The Autobiography* (London, 2002), pp. 35, 244.
14   Byrne, *Football Association of Ireland*, p. 131.
15   *The Irish Times*, 25 June 1988.
16   Cited in Whelan, *Who Stole Our Game?*, p. 173.
17   Cited in Tighe and Rowan, *Champagne Football*, p. 57.
18   Menton, *Beyond the Green Door*, pp. 282–8.
19   *The Irish Press*, 20 June 1988, p. 22.
20   Whelan, *Who Stole Our Game?*, p. 198.
21   Ibid., p. 202.
22   Taoiseach Bertie Ahern TD, Dáil Éireann debates, 11 Apr. 2000.
23   *Irish Independent*, 30 Nov. 2002.
24   Brendan Howlin TD, Dáil Éireann debates, 9 Oct. 2002.
25   Arrowsmith, 'Plastic Paddies', pp. 461, 465.
26   John O'Donoghue TD, Dáil Éireann debates, 26 Feb. 2003; Senator Michael McDowell, Seanad Éireann debates, 9 Dec. 2003.
27   John O'Donoghue TD, Dáil Éireann debates, 3 Nov. 2004.
28   *The Irish Times*, 30 Sept. 2019.
29   Tighe and Rowan, *Champagne Football*, p. 102. The following account of Delaney's tenure as FAI chief executive relies heavily on this work.
30   Tighe and Rowan, *Champagne Football*, p. 121.
31   *The Irish Times*, 15 Apr. 2019.
32   Cited in Tighe and Rowan, *Champagne Football*, p. 127.
33   Ibid., pp. 276–7.
34   *The Irish Times*, 2 Oct. 2019; www.UEFA.com,20 Jan. 2020.
35   Governance Review Group Report, 21 June 2019, www.fai.ie
36   Tighe and Rowan, *Champagne Football*, p. 212.
37   Ibid., pp. 287–8.

16. FOOTBALL FOR ALL?

1   Roberts, *Gunshots & Goalposts*, p. 270.
2   Ibid., p. 242.
3   Ibid., pp. 228–9; Alan Bairner and John Sugden, *Sport, Sectarianism and Society in a Divided Ireland* (Leicester, 1993), pp. 19, 80.
4   Alan Bairner, '"Up to their knees?"', p. 108.
5   Michael Walker, *The Irish Times*, 24 Mar. 2001.
6   Neil Lennon (with Martin Hannan), *Neil Lennon: Man and Bhoy* (London, 2006), pp. 1, 7.
7   Ivan Martin, *Green and White Army: The Northern Ireland Fans* (Belfast, 2008), p. 18.
8   Jamieson, *Whose Side Are You On?*, p. 246.
9   Martin, *Green and White Army*, pp. 72–3; Roberts, *Gunshots & Goalposts*, p. 247.
10   *The Irish Times*, 8 Oct. 2016.
11   William Cherry, *Dare to Dream: Northern Ireland's Euro 2016 Adventure* (Belfast, 2016), p. 114.
12   Roberts, *Gunshots & Goalposts*, p. 266; Goldblatt, *The Age of Football*, p. 196.

13   Kevin McNicholl, Clifford Stevenson and John Garry, 'How the "Northern Irish" identity is understood and used by young people and politicians', *Political Psychology* (2018), pp. 1–19; Census 2021, www.nisra.gov.uk

14   David Hassan, 'A people apart: soccer, identity and Irish nationalists in Northern Ireland', *Soccer & Society*, 3:3 (2002), p. 69; Gareth Fulton, 'Northern Catholic fans of the Republic of Ireland soccer team', in Bairner (ed.), *Sport and the Irish*, p. 156.

15   Survey by N.P. McGivern (BA dissertation, University of Ulster, 1991), cited in Bairner and Sugden, *Sport, Sectarianism and Society in a Divided Ireland*, p. 79.

16   Pat Jennings (with Reg Drury), *Pat Jennings: An Autobiography* (London, 1983), pp. 129, 131–3.

17   Alex Montgomery, *Martin O'Neill: The Biography* (London, 2003), p. 144.

18   *The Irish Times*, 23 Mar. 2001.

19   Darragh McGee and Alan Bairner, 'Transcending the borders of Irish identity? Narratives of northern nationalist footballers in Northern Ireland', *International Review for the Sociology of Sport*, 46:4 (2010), p. 437; *The Irish Times*, 6 Mar. 2018.

20   McGee and Bairner, 'Northern nationalist footballers', pp. 443–4.

21   *The Irish Times*, 4 Aug. 2007.

22   Shane McEleney interview, 29 June 2009, cited in McGee and Bairner, 'Northern nationalist footballers', p. 437.

23   Roberts, *Gunshots & Goalposts*, p. 267.

24   *The Irish Times*, 4 Nov. 2019.

25   McGee and Bairner, 'Northern nationalist footballers', pp. 450–1.

26   *Belfast Telegraph*, 27 May 2011.

27   Keith Gillespie, *How Not To Be a Football Millionaire* (Liverpool, 2013), p. 74.

28   *Belfast Telegraph*, 9 Apr. 2014.

29   Roberts, *Gunshots & Goalposts*, p. 249.

30   Jonathan Magee, 'Football supporters, rivalry and Protestant fragmentation in Northern Ireland' in Bairner (ed.), *Sport and the Irish*, pp. 179, 187.

31   John Sugden and Alan Bairner, 'Observe the sons of Ulster', in Tomlinson and Whannel (eds), *Off the Ball*, p. 153.

32   John Sugden and Alan Tomlinson (eds), *Hosts and Champions: Soccer Cultures, National Identities and the USA World Cup* (Aldershot, 1994), p. 131; Jamieson, *Whose Side Are You On?*, p. 172; *Herald* (Glasgow), 12 Jan. 2012.

33   Alan Bairner and Graham Walker, 'Football and society in Northern Ireland: Linfield Football Club and the case of Gerry Morgan', *Soccer and Society*, 2:1 (Sept. 2010), pp. 81–98.

34   *Belfast Telegraph*, 26 Nov. 2018.

17. ASSOCIATION FOOTBALL IN MODERN IRELAND

1   Curran, *Irish Soccer Migrants*, pp. 56–7, 71.

2   Byrne, *Green is the Colour*, pp. 238, 245; Rowan, *Team That Jack Built*, p. 151.

3   Dave Hannigan, *The Garrison Game: The State of Irish Football* (Edinburgh, 1998), p. 20.

4   *Irish Independent*, 22 Mar. 2018; for representation from individual counties see Dean Hayes, *The Republic of Ireland: International Football Facts* (Cork, 2008), pp. 23–146 and www.balls.ie (accessed 4 Sept. 2020).

5   Plunkett Carter, *A Century of Cork Soccer Memories* (Cork, 1996), p. 222.

6   Tony Fahey, Liam Delaney and Brenda Gannon, *Schoolchildren and Sport in Ireland* (Dublin, ESRI, 2005), pp. 23–4, 45, 55.

7   *The Irish Times*, 23 May 2002; *Sunday Independent*, 26 May 2002.

8   Cited in Conor O'Callaghan, *Red Mist: Roy Keane and the Football Civil War: A Fan's Story* (London, 2004), p. 88.

9   Fintan O'Toole, *The Guardian*, 24 May 2002; Keane, *Keane*, p. 269.

10   *The Irish Times*, 17 June 2002.

11   *The Irish Times*, 17 Jan. 2020.

12   *The Irish Press*, 27, 28, 30 Jan. 1953.

13   Hand, *First Hand*, p. 250.

14   Hannigan, *Garrison Game*, p. 20; Ger McCarthy, *Off Centre Circle* (Cork, 2009), p. 135.

15   Mick McCarthy (with Cathal Dervan), *Ireland's World Cup 2002* (London, 2002), p. 222.

16   John Hynes, *The Irish Kop* (Liverpool, 2009), pp. 106–8, 120, 134.

17 Anon., *The Official History of the FIFA Women's World Cup* (London, 2019), p. 20.

18 *Irish Independent*, 10 May 2020.

19 Anon., *The FIFA Women's World Cup*, pp. 36–7.

20 Barry Landy, *Emerald Exiles: How the Irish Made Their Mark on World Football* (Dublin, 2021), pp. 41–5.

21 'Census of Soccer in the Republic' (1993) by Lansdowne Market Research for the FAI; 'Football FAI: Women's Development Plan Launched', 14 June 2006, www.sportireland.ie

22 Landy, *Emerald Exiles*, pp. 97–102, 129–36, 145–52, 153–7, 189–94.

23 *The Irish Times*, 4 Feb. 2019; 'Lisa Fallon', www.the42.ie (accessed May 2020).

24 *The Irish Times*, 8 Dec. 2019.

25 Ken Early, *The Irish Times*, 13 Nov. 2017.

26 RTÉ news interview with Vera Pauw, 12 Oct. 2022, www.rte.ie

27 *The Irish Times*, 14 Nov. 2016; www.the42.ie (accessed 19 Dec. 2016).

28 *The Irish Times*, 17 Jan. 2020; see also *Annual Reports of the Irish Sports Monitor* at www.sportireland.ie

29 *Football for All Strategy 2017–2020: Promoting Inclusion in Football* (FAI, 2017).

30 Delaney, *Stuttgart to Saipan*, p. 82.

31 *Intercultural Football Plan: Many Voices, One Goal* (FAI, 2007), p. 22.

32 Bríd Ní Chonaill, *Integration Through Football Report* (FAI, 2018), pp. 20–1.

33 *The Irish Times*, 10 June 2021.

Select Bibliography

Primary Sources
Dublin Diocesan Archives (DDA)
John Charles McQuaid papers, 1952–7

National Archives of Ireland (NAI)
Bureau of Military History (BMH)
Witness Statements (WS)

Department of Foreign Affairs
DFA/5/305/298: 'Proposed visit of Jugoslav [sic]
football team, Oct. 1955'
DFA 5/305/345: 'Visit of Roumanian [sic]
football team to Ireland', Oct. 1957
DFA 5/305/14/162: 'Partition in Sport: Soccer
Matches', 1957–8

Department of the Taoiseach
TSCH 3/S6276, Cabinet Minutes, Cab. 6/29,
23–4 May 1932

Office of the President
PRES 1/P1131, Dec. 1938
PRES 1/P707, Secretary to the President,
'Sports fixtures: general procedures, 1938–
1946'
PRES 1/P2888, 'International soccer matches:
attendance of President, 1946–60'

National Library of Ireland (NLI)
NLI MS 26,602, Robert Briscoe Papers

**Public Record Office of Northern Ireland
(PRONI)**
IFA Annual Reports (PRONI D/4196)

University College Dublin Archives
P137/1–97, Archives of the Football Association
of Ireland

Secondary Sources
Books
Anon., *The Official History of the FIFA Women's
World Cup* (London, 2019)
Bairner, Alan, and John Sugden, *Sport,
Sectarianism and Society in a Divided
Ireland* (Leicester, 1993)
Bairner, Alan (ed.), *Sport and the Irish: Histories,
Identities, Issues* (Dublin, 2005)
Bradley, Joseph M., *Celtic Football Club, Irish
Identity and the Politics of Difference*
(Glasgow, 1995)
— *Ethnic and Religious Identity in Modern
Scotland: Culture, Politics and Football*
(Aldershot, 1995)
— *Football, Religion and Ethnicity: Irish Identity
in Scotland* (London, 1996)
Briggs, George, and Joe Dodd (eds), *Leinster
Football Association: 100 Years, the
Centenary Handbook* (Dublin, 1992)
Brodie, Malcolm, *The History of Irish Soccer*
(Glasgow, 1963)
— *100 Years of Irish Football* (Belfast, 1980)
Byrne, Peter, *Football Association of Ireland: 75
Years* (Dublin, 1996)
— *Green is the Colour: The Story of Irish Football*
(London, 2012)
Campbell, Tom, *Celtic's Paranoia: All in the
Mind?* (Ayr, 2004)
Carter, Plunkett, *A Century of Cork Soccer
Memories* (Cork, 1996)
Charlton, Jack (with Peter Byrne), *Jack Charlton:
The Autobiography* (London, 1996)
Cooney, John, *John Charles McQuaid: Ruler of
Catholic Ireland* (Dublin, 1999)
Coyle, Padraig, *Paradise Lost and Found: The
Story of Belfast Celtic* (Edinburgh, 1999)
Crerand, Paddy, *Paddy Crerand: Never Turn the
Other Cheek* (London, 2014)

Cronin, Mike, *Sport and Nationalism in Ireland: Gaelic Games, Soccer and Irish Identity Since 1884* (Dublin, 1999)

Cullen, Donal, *Freestaters: The Republic of Ireland Soccer Team 1921–1939* (Southend, 2007)

Curran, Conor, *Sport in Donegal: A History* (Dublin, 2010)

— *Irish Soccer Migrants: A Social and Cultural History* (Cork, 2017)

Delaney, Miguel, *Stuttgart to Saipan: The Players' Stories* (Dublin, 2010)

Devine, T.M. (ed.), *Scotland's Shame? Bigotry and Sectarianism in Modern Scotland* (Edinburgh, 2000)

Dunphy, Eamon, *Sir Matt Busby and Manchester United: A Strange Kind of Glory* (London, 1991)

— *The Rocky Road* (Dublin, 2013)

Flood, Finbarr, *In Full Flood: A Memoir* (Dublin, 2006)

Flynn, Barry, *Political Football: The Life and Death of Belfast Celtic* (Dublin, 2009)

Garnham, Neal, *Association Football and Society in Pre-partition Ireland* (Belfast, 2004)

Giles, John (with Declan Lynch), *A Football Man: The Autobiography* (Dublin, 2010)

Goldblatt, David, *The Ball is Round: A Global History of Football* (London, 2006)

— *The Game of Our Lives: The Meaning and Making of English Football* (London, 2014)

Hand, Eoin (with Peter O'Neill), *The Eoin Hand Story* (Dublin, 1986)

— (with Jared Browne), *First Hand: My Life and Irish Football* (Cork, 2017)

Handley, James, *The Celtic Story: A History of the Celtic Football Club* (London, 1960)

Hanna, Ronnie, *The World at Their Feet: Northern Ireland in Sweden* (Cheltenham, 2008)

Hannigan, Dave, *The Garrison Game: The State of Irish Football* (Edinburgh, 1998)

Hayes, Dean, *The Republic of Ireland: International Football Facts* (Cork, 2008)

Hunt, Tom, *Sport and Society in Victorian Ireland: The Case of Westmeath* (Dublin, 2007)

Jamieson, Teddy, *Whose Side Are You On? Sport, the Troubles and Me* (London, 2011)

Keane, Paul, *Gods vs Mortals: Irish Clubs in Europe* (Kells, 2010)

Keane, Roy (with Eamon Dunphy), *Keane: The Autobiography* (London, 2002)

Keane, Trevor, *Gaffers: 50 Years of Irish Football Managers* (Cork, 2010)

Landy, Barry, *Emerald Exiles: How the Irish Made Their Mark on World Football* (Dublin, 2021)

Lugton, Alan, *The Making of Hibernian* (3 vols, Edinburgh, 1995–8)

Lynch, Declan, *Days of Heaven: Italia '90 and the Charlton Years* (Dublin, 2010)

Lynch, Frank, *A History of Athlone Town FC: The First 100 Years* (Athlone, 1991)

McCarthy, Mick (with Cathal Dervan), *Ireland's World Cup 2002* (London, 2002)

McGuire, James, and James Quinn (eds), *Dictionary of Irish Biography: From the Earliest Times to the Year 2002* (Cambridge, 9 volumes, 2009); and supplementary volumes 10 and 11: *From 2003 to 2010* (Cambridge, 2018)

McGurk, Brian, *Celtic FC: The Irish Connection* (Edinburgh, 2009)

Mackay, John R., *The Hibees: The Story of Hibernian Football Club* (Edinburgh, 1986)

Maley, Willie, *Story of the Celtic* (Glasgow, 1939)

Mandle, W.P., *The Gaelic Athletic Association and Irish Nationalist Politics* (Dublin, 1987)

Marshall, Evan, *Spirit of '58: The Incredible Untold Story of Northern Ireland's Greatest Football Team* (Belfast, 2016)

Mason, Tony, *Association Football and English Society 1863–1915* (Brighton, 1980)

Menton, Brendan, *Home Farm: The Story of a Dublin Football Club 1928–1998* (Dublin, 1999)

Moore, Cormac, *The GAA v Douglas Hyde* (Cork, 2013)

— *The Irish Soccer Split* (Cork, 2015)

Murphy, Jim, *The History of Dundalk FC* (Dundalk, 2003)

Murray, Bill, *The Old Firm: Sectarianism, Sport and Society in Scotland* (Edinburgh, 1984)

— *Bhoys, Bears and Bigotry: The Old Firm in the New Age* (Edinburgh, 2003)

Needham, David, *Ireland's First Real World Cup: The Story of the 1924 Ireland Olympic Football Team* (Dublin, 2012)

O'Mahony, Bertie, *Munster Football Association: 75 Years Service to the Beautiful Game 1922–1997* (Cork, 1998)

Rice, Eoghan, *We Are Rovers: An Oral History of Shamrock Rovers FC* (Stroud, 2005)

Roberts, Benjamin, *Gunshots & Goalposts: The Story of Northern Irish Football* (Avenue Books, 2017)

Rouse, Paul, *Sport and Ireland: A History* (Oxford, 2015)

Rowan, Paul, *The Team that Jack Built* (Edinburgh, 1994)

Ryan, Sean, *The Boys in Green: The FAI International Story* (Edinburgh, 1997)

Sanders, Richard, *Beastly Fury: The Strange Birth of British Football* (London, 2009)

Tate, Tim, *Girls with Balls: The Secret History of Women's Football* (London, 2013)

Taylor, Matthew, *The Association Game: A History of British Football* (Harlow, 2007)

Tighe, Mark, and Paul Rowan, *Champagne Football: John Delaney and the Betrayal of Irish Football: The Inside Story* (Dublin, 2020)

Tomlinson, Alan, and Garry Whannel (eds), *Off the Ball: The Football World Cup* (London, 1986)

Toms, David, *Soccer in Munster: A Social History 1877-1937* (Cork, 2015)

Walker, Michael, *Green Shoots: Irish Football Histories* (Liverpool, 2017)

Walsh, Stephen, *Voices of the Old Firm* (Edinburgh, 2005)

Walsh, T.P., *Twenty Years of Irish Soccer 1921-41* (Dublin, 1941)

Walvin, James, *The People's Game: The History of Football Revisited* (Edinburgh, 2000)

Whelan, Daire, *Who Stole Our Game? The Fall and Fall of Irish Soccer* (Dublin, 2006)

White, Colin, *Dalymount Park: The Home of Irish Football* (Dublin, 2005)

Wilson, Richard, *Inside the Divide: One City: Two Teams ... the Old Firm* (Edinburgh, 2010)

Young, Colin, *Jack Charlton: The Authorised Biography* (Dublin, 2016)

Articles

Arrowsmith, Aidan, 'Plastic paddies vs. master racers: "Soccer" and Irish identity', *International Journal of Cultural Studies*, 7:4 (2004), pp. 460–79

Bairner, Alan, '"Up to their knees?" Football, sectarianism, masculinity and Protestant working-class identity' in Peter Shirlow and Mark McGovern (eds), *Who are 'the People?': Unionism, Protestantism and Loyalism in Northern Ireland* (London, 1997), pp. 95–113

Carey, Tadhg, 'Ireland's footballers at the Paris Olympics, 1924', *History Ireland*, 20:4 (July–Aug. 2012), pp. 22–5

Carter, Plunkett, 'Soccer in Cork city' in John Crowley (ed.), *Atlas of Cork City* (Cork, 2005), pp. 322–4

Cronin, Mike, 'Projecting the nation through sport and culture: Ireland, Aonach Tailteann and the Irish Free State 1924–32', *Journal of Contemporary History*, 38:3 (2003), pp. 395–411

Curran, Conor, 'The development of Gaelic football and soccer zones in County Donegal, 1884–1936', *Sport in History*, 32:3 (Sept. 2012), pp. 428–31

— 'Sport and cultural nationalism: the conflict between association and Gaelic football in Donegal, 1905–34', *Éire-Ireland*, 48:1/2 (2013), pp. 79–94

— 'Networking structures and competitive association football in Ulster, 1880–1914', *Irish Economic and Social History*, 41 (2014), pp. 74–92

— 'Irish-born players in the English Football League, 1945–2010', in Richard McElligott and David Hassan (eds), *A Social and Cultural History of Sport in Ireland* (Oxford, 2016), pp. 74–94

Davies, Andrew, 'Football and sectarianism in Glasgow during the 1920s and 1930s', *Irish Historical Studies*, 35:138 (2006–7), pp. 200–19

Free, Marcus, 'Angels with drunken faces: travelling Republic of Ireland supporters and the construction of Irish migrant identity in England' in Adam Brown (ed.), *Fanatics! Power, Identity and Fandom in Football* (London, 1998), pp. 219–32

Fulton, Gareth, 'Northern Catholic fans of the Republic of Ireland soccer team', in Alan Bairner (ed.), *Sport and the Irish: Histories, Identities, Issues* (Dublin, 2005), pp. 40–56

Garnham, Neal, 'Football and national identity in pre-Great War Ireland', *Irish Economic and Social History*, 28 (2001), pp. 13–31

— 'Accounting for the early success of the Gaelic Athletic Association', *Irish Historical Studies*, 34:133 (May, 2004), pp. 65–78

Hanley, Brian, 'Oscar Traynor and "the crime

of playing soccer'", *History Ireland*, 24:1 (Jan.-Feb. 2016), pp. 48-9

Harvie, Scott, '17 November 1993 – a night to remember?' in Richard English and Graham Walker (eds), *Unionism in Modern Ireland: New Perspectives on Politics and Culture* (London, 1996), pp. 192-219

Hassan, David, 'A people apart: soccer, identity and Irish nationalists in Northern Ireland', *Soccer & Society*, 3:3 (2002), pp. 65-83

Kelly, John, 'Hibernian Football Club: The forgotten Irish?', *Sport in Society*, 10:3 (2007), pp. 514-36

Kennedy, David, and Peter Kennedy, 'Ambiguity, complexity and convergence: the evolution of Liverpool's Irish football clubs', *The International Journal of the History of Sport*, 24:7 (2007), pp. 894-920

Kerrigan, Colm, 'Ireland's greatest football team?', *History Ireland*, 13:3 (July 2005), pp. 26-30

McGee, Darragh, and Alan Bairner, 'Transcending the borders of Irish identity? Narratives of northern nationalist footballers in Northern Ireland', *International Review for the Sociology of Sport*, 46:4 (2010), pp. 436-55

Milne, Michael, 'Soccer and the Dublin working class: Doncaster Rovers in Dublin 1952': Document Study, *Saothar: Journal of the Irish Labour History Society*, 8 (1982), pp. 97-102

Moore, Martin, 'The origins of association football in Ireland, 1875-1880: a reappraisal', *Sport in History*, 37:4 (2017), pp. 505-28

Murphy, William, 'The GAA during the Irish Revolution, 1913-23' in Mike Cronin, William Murphy and Paul Rouse (eds), *The Gaelic Athletic Association 1884-2009* (Dublin, 2009), pp. 61-76

Tobin, Shane, 'All-Ireland samba: Shamrock Rovers All-Ireland XI 3 – 4 Brazil, Lansdowne Road, Tuesday 3 July 1973', *History Ireland*, 16:4 (2008), pp. 46-7

Toms, David, '"Notwithstanding the discomfort involved": Fordsons' cup win in 1926 and how "the Old Contemptible" were represented in Ireland's public sphere during the 1920s', *Sport in History*, 32:4 (2012), pp. 504-25

Unpublished Thesis

Tynan, Mark, 'Association football and Irish society during the interwar period, 1918-39' (PhD, NUI Maynooth, 2013)

Index